THE LABOUR GOVERNMENTS 1964–70
volume 3

Published in our
centenary year
～ **2004** ～
MANCHESTER
UNIVERSITY
PRESS

THE LABOUR GOVERNMENTS 1964–70

Series editors   Steven Fielding and John W. Young

volume 1   *Labour and cultural change*   Steven Fielding
volume 2   *International policy*   John W. Young
volume 3   *Economic policy*   Jim Tomlinson

THE LABOUR GOVERNMENTS 1964–70
volume 3

Economic policy

Jim Tomlinson

Manchester University Press
Manchester and New York

distributed exclusively in the USA by Palgrave

Published by Manchester University Press
Oxford Road, Manchester M13 9NR, UK
and Room 400, 175 Fifth Avenue, New York, NY 10010, USA
www.manchesteruniversitypress.co.uk

Distributed in the United States exclusively by
Palgrave Macmillan, 175 Fifth Avenue,
New York, NY 10010, USA

Distributed in Canada exclusively by
UBC Press, University of British Columbia, 2029 West Mall,
Vancouver, BC, Canada V6T 1Z2

British Library Cataloguing-in-Publication Data
A catalogue record for this book is available from the British Library

Library of Congress Cataloging-in-Publication Data applied for

ISBN 978 0 7190 8063 0 paperback

First published by Manchester University Press in hardback 2004

This paperback edition first published 2009

Printed by Lightning Source

Contents

Tables

Series foreword

Before the Labour Party entered government in October 1964 its leader, Harold Wilson, raised hopes of creating a 'new Britain', based on furthering the 'white heat' of technological change and aiming to pursue egalitarianism at home and abroad. In June 1970 Labour was ejected from office having lived up to few of these aspirations. Most analysts of the party's period in power consequently characterise it as a miserable failure. The majority focus on the Labour leadership's lack of ambition and reserve much of their censure for Wilson's strategic shortcomings. Present-day 'New' Labour, for which the 1960s are clearly an embarrassment, effectively endorses this glum assessment.

The three volumes in this series tackle different aspects of the 1964–70 Wilson governments' record and assume contrasting approaches to their subjects. Each, however, benefits from access to recently released government files housed in the Public Record Office, as well as other documents lately made available to historians. Together the volumes constitute the most complete record of these governments currently obtainable. While not denying Labour in office was a disappointment when measured against party rhetoric, the authors assume a more nuanced view compared with most previous accounts. In particular, they highlight a wider range of reasons for the governments' relative lack of achievement. If the disposition of Labour's leaders played its part, so did the nature of the party, the delicate state of the economy, the declining place of Britain in the world order and the limited ambitions of the British people themselves.

In testing some well entrenched assumptions about these governments in light of new evidence, the authors dispute their status as the black sheep of Labour history and establish some new perspectives. In this respect, these volumes therefore mark an important stage in the permanent revisionism to which all historians should subject the past. It is hoped they will encourage more research on Labour's period in office and challenge their overly grim reputation among both academics and lay readers alike.

Preface

This is the first book-length study of the economic policies of the Wilson government based on access to public records. Of course, there already exists a vast literature which has bearing on this topic, although surprisingly there is only one book which is both devoted wholly to it and gives comprehensive coverage.[1] There also exists a great deal of relevant material in the published diaries of ministers and key economic advisers.[2] The archives, especially the Public Record Office, have a vast range of material in this area; one could literally spend a lifetime reading everything which could be relevant. In the face of this mountain of secondary and primary material, I have had to be highly selective in what has been used. Broadly speaking, two principles have been deployed in making that selection.

First, while not eschewing judgement on the policies pursued, the primary aim has been to understand the how and why of what was done, rather than to praise or condemn it. This is a deliberate attempt to get away from the overly normative accounts of the Labour governments of 1964–70 (and indeed of others), where the underlying question is 'What went wrong?'[3] As a recent author has rightly said, 'The spleen of Wilson and Callaghan's critics at the time and since is amazing to behold'.[4] While the book is not intended as a 'defence' of the policies of these years, the aim has been to allow distance in time to allow at least some detachment, if not exactly enchantment. Total Olympian detachment is, of course, unachievable, so in the Conclusions I have attempted some tentative judgements on the policies of these years, without, I hope, entering too much into the 'How many marks out of ten?' kind of question, which can so easily distort historical understanding.

While the book covers all the important topics, the second principle employed has been one of emphasising issues underplayed by the existing literature. In particular, while it is well recognised in most accounts that the Wilson government was committed to a programme of 'modernisation', in practice this issue is usually sidelined by discussions of macro-economic policy, especially the endlessly fascinating dramas of the 1967 devaluation. This book tries to restore some balance by giving the prominence to 'modernisation' that its historical importance justifies. In doing so, I have tried 'plumbing new depths' of at least some of the archives, rather than wholly succumbing to the sometimes misleading allure of records of Cabinet discussions and Prime Minister's papers.[5]

Finally, this book is essentially about the trials and tribulations of *national* economic management. This level of analysis has meant that, sadly, but inevitably, I have had to neglect the stories of individual industries, where there are already extremely good published accounts which cover this period in detail, but also great archival riches to be exploited by future scholars.[6]

Notes

The place of publication is London unless otherwise specified.

1 W. Beckerman (ed.), *The Labour Government's Economic Record 1964–1970* (1972). Other books which have a great deal on this period include: F. Blackaby (ed.), *British Economic Policy 1960–74* (Cambridge, 1978); A. Cairncross, *Managing the British Economy in the 1960s: A Treasury Perspective* (1996); M. Stewart, *Politics and Economic Policy in the UK Since 1964: The Jekyll and Hyde Years* (1978); C. Cohen, *British Economic Policy 1960–69* (1971); S. Brittan, *Steering the Economy: The Role of the Treasury* (1971); R. Caves (ed.), *Britain's Economic Prospects* (Washington, DC, 1968); A. Cairncross (ed.), *Britain's Economic Prospects Reconsidered* (1971).

2 T. Benn, *Out of the Wilderness. Diaries 1963–67* (1987), and *Office Without Power. Diaries 1968–72* (1988); B. Castle, *The Castle Diaries, 1964–70* (1984); R. H. S. Crossman, *The Diaries of a Cabinet Minister*, 3 vols (1975–7); A. Cairncross, *The Wilson Years: A Treasury Diary, 1964–1969* (1997).

3 For an antidote, see D. Tanner, P. Thane and N. Tiratsoo (eds), *Labour's First Century* (Cambridge, 2000).

4 L. Baston, 'The age of Wilson', in B. Brivati and L. Heffernan (eds), *The Labour Party: A Centenary History* (2000), pp. 87–8.

5 R. Lowe, 'Plumbing new depths: contemporary historians and the Public Record Office', *Twentieth Century British History*, 8 (1997), pp. 239–65.

6 For example, W. Ashworth, *The History of the British Coal Industry. Vol. 5, 1946–1982: The Nationalised Industry* (Oxford, 1986); T. Gourvish, *British Railways 1948–73* (Cambridge, 1986); L. Johnman and H. Murphy, *British Shipbuilding and the State Since 1918* (Exeter, 2002).

Acknowledgements

I am grateful to a large number of people who have commented upon draft chapters of this book or discussed aspects of the Wilson government with me. These include Andrew Blick, Martin Chick, David Edgerton, Steve Fielding, Rodney Lowe, Roger Middleton, Glenn O'Hara, Helen Parr, Hugh Pemberton, Neil Rollings, Raj Roy, Catherine Schenk, Peter Scott, Richard Toye, Richard Whiting and John Young.

I gratefully acknowledge financial support from the British Academy that enabled me to visit archives in the USA. Archivists at the Public Record Office, the Bank of England, the Labour Party Archives (Manchester) and the Modern Records Centre (University of Warwick) have also been extremely helpful.

Significant individuals

Ministers

Tony Benn: Paymaster-General, 1964–66; Minister for Technology, 1966–70

George Brown: Deputy Leader of Labour Party, 1960–70; First Secretary of State and Minister for Economic Affairs, 1964–66; Foreign Secretary, 1966–68

Jim Callaghan: Chancellor of the Exchequer, 1964–67; Home Secretary, 1967–70

Barbara Castle: Minister for Overseas Development, 1964–65; Minister for Transport, 1965–68; First Secretary of State and Secretary of State for Employment and Productivity, 1968–70

Frank Cousins: Minister for Technology, 1964–66

Tony Crosland: Minister of State at the Department of Economic Affairs, 1964–65; Minister for Education, 1965–67; President of the Board of Trade, 1967–70

Richard Crossman: Minister for Housing and Local Government, 1964–66; Lord President, 1966–68; Secretary of State for Social Security, 1968–70

Denis Healey: Secretary of State for Defence, 1964–70

Douglas Jay: President of the Board of Trade, 1964–67

Roy Jenkins: Minister for Aviation, 1965–67; Chancellor of the Exchequer, 1967–70

Michael Stewart: Minister for Education, 1964–65; Foreign Secretary, 1965–66, 1968–70; First Secretary of State, 1966–68; Minister for Economic Affairs, 1966–67

Advisers and civil servants

Thomas Balogh: Economic Adviser to the Cabinet, 1964–67

Wilfred Beckerman: Economic Consultant to the Department of Economic Affairs, 1964–65; Economic Adviser to the Board of Trade, 1967–69

Kenneth Berrill: Special Adviser to the Treasury, 1967–69

Alec Cairncross, Head of the Government Economic Service, 1964–69

Fred Catherwood: Chief Industrial Adviser to the Department of Economic Affairs, 1964–66; Director General of the National Economic Development Council, 1966–70

Richard 'Otto' Clarke: Second Permanent Secretary to the Treasury, 1964–66; Permanent Secretary, Ministry of Aviation, 1966; Permanent Secretary, Ministry of Technology, 1966–70

Andrew Graham: Economic Assistant at the Department of Economic Affairs, 1964–66; Economic Assistant, Cabinet Office, 1966–67; Economic Adviser in the Prime Minister's Office, 1968–69

Nicholas Kaldor: Special Adviser to the Chancellor, 1964–68

Robert Neild: Economic Adviser to the Treasury, 1964–67

Michael Posner: Director of Economics in the Ministry of Power, 1966–67; Economic Adviser to the Treasury, 1967–70

Eric Roll: Permanent Under-Secretary of State to the Department of Economic Affairs, 1964–66

Robert Shone: Director General of the National Economic Development Council, 1962–66

Michael Stewart: Economic Assistant, Cabinet Office, 1964–67

Burke Trend: Cabinet Secretary, 1964–70

Abbreviations

BPC	British Productivity Council
CAP	Common Agricultural Policy (of the EEC)
CBA	cost–benefit analysis
CBI	Confederation of British Industry
CET	Common External Tariff (of the EEC)
CSA	Commonwealth Sugar Agreement
DCE	domestic credit expansion
DCF	discounted cash flow
DEA	Department of Economic Affairs
DEP	Department of Employment and Productivity
DSIR	Department of Scientific and Industrial Research
EDCs	economic development councils ('Little Neddies')
EEC	European Economic Community
EFTA	European Free Trade Association
GATT	General Agreement on Tariffs and Trade
GDP	gross domestic product
GNP	gross national product
IMF	International Monetary Fund
IPOS	*In Place of Strife*
IRC	Industrial Reorganisation Corporation
ITBs	industrial training boards
LPA	Labour Party Archives
LPACR	*Labour Party Annual Conference Report*
LRC	Labour Representation Committee
MinTech	Ministry of Technology
MRC	Modern Records Centre
NBPI	National Board for Prices and Incomes
NEDC	National Economic Development Council (Neddy)
NEDO	National Economic Development Office
NRDC	National Research and Development Corporation
OECD	Organisation for Economic Co-operation and Development
PRO	Public Record Office

REP	regional employment premium
RoSLA	raising of the school-leaving age
RPA	Redundancy Payments Act
RPI	retail price index
SET	selective employment tax
TDR	test discount rate
TUC	Trades Union Congress
UNCTAD	United Nations Commission on Trade and Development
VAT	value added tax

1

Labour, modernisation and the external constraint

What have been the key aims of the Labour Party in its 100 or so years of existence? One simple answer has come from New Labour, which has sought to define and defend its novelty by constructing its own version of the history of the party. In the field of economic policy, New Labour has contrasted its central commitment to faster economic growth with Old Labour's alleged focus on redistribution. For example, at the beginning of the 1999 budget statement, Chancellor of the Exchequer Gordon Brown made a characteristic New Labour assertion that governments of the left (clearly intended to include 'Old Labour') have 'too often undervalued wealth creation and enterprise' in their excessive desire for redistribution. Other New Labour ideologues have deployed a similar dichotomy.[1]

Such a tendentious and dichotomous account of Labour's history is plainly an attempt to make a political point. Yet its suggestion that 'economic modernisation' is a new concern for Labour chimes with much that is commonly written and said about the Labour Party. But what relation does this bear to the evidence of Labour's history?

Labour has always been a very 'broad church'. It is therefore extraordinarily difficult to pin down beliefs, let alone policies, that all strands of the party have consistently supported. Most histories of the party have recognised this and so have commonly split their analysis of the party into divergent strands of thinking. That divergence is multi-dimensional and, most notably, attempts to present it as spread across a clear and single left–right spectrum are always unsatisfactory.[2]

An important component of this variety of belief has always been what may be called 'golden ageism' – a belief that, at some time in the past, a better, fairer and more equal society existed on this sceptred isle, and that Labour should seek to restore this past. Yet few have combined such rhetorical attitudes with the serious suggestion of seeking the re-creation of past forms of economic and social organisation. The only major exception was William Morris's and John Ruskin's ideas of a return to a medieval golden age of independent artisans, which found

1

important support in guild socialism around the time of the First World War. But even in that case, converts, such as G. D. H. Cole, soon gave their advocacy of the guilds a decidedly 'modernist' terminology.[3] In fact, many, probably most, appeals to a golden age have been by those in Labour's ranks who wanted to argue that the substance of such happy days could be regained only by embracing the technologies and institutions of 'the modern', a trope of such diverse figures as Tony Benn and Tony Blair.[4]

One consistent theme of Labour's politics has been a commitment to economic reform; in the economic field at least, it has not been a party of conservatism in the literal sense. This commitment to improving the economy has, in turn, been driven by notions of social justice; and for most of its history Labour has believed that social justice will arise in large part from state action involving the redistribution of resources. But the great bulk of Labour's ideologues and policy-makers have believed that redistribution should be accompanied by (or, in other versions, should only follow *after*) improved economic performance.[5]

Another feature of Labour's thinking which has predisposed it to economic modernisation has been enthusiasm for science and technology. At least down to the 1970s, the belief that 'progressives' should embrace the rationality of science, and apply both the products and methods of science to society at large, were staple parts of Labour thinking. It is important to emphasise this as a contrast to left thinking in the last three decades, which has become much more sceptical about both the products of scientific endeavour and its supposed 'rationality'.[6]

Drawing on recent historiography, the first part of this chapter argues that, for all its diverse strands, Labour almost from its foundation has had a strong commitment to economic modernisation, and that this forms an important context for understanding the Wilson governments' ideas and policies. What is offered below is a brief narrative of the party's history which seeks to make industrial modernisation a central part of that history (without seeking to suggest it is the *whole* of that history). The second part then looks at the specifics of what modernisation meant by the 1960s, and then finally the chapter looks at what was and is usually seen as the major obstacle to such modernisation: the external constraint.

Labour, the party of industrial modernisation

The Labour Party before 1918 was not a programmatic party. Its central aim was to represent the working class in Parliament, largely by propaganda and agitation. While a socialist objective was adopted in 1908, this was combined with an explicit rejection of a programme of common ownership. The prevalent attitude to programmes was put by a union leader at the 1903 conference of the Labour Representation Committee (LRC): 'wherever parties trusted to programmes they were very hard up. Programmes wrecked parties. Let this conference stick to principles'.[7] But even If a programme had been formulated at this time, it is unlikely to have been much concerned with industrial modernisation. While the rise of US and German competition caused some questioning of the strength of British capitalism, the assumptions about industry prevalent in the party at this time were mainly evolutionist. Grounded in both Marxist and Fabian ideas, most Labour thinkers based their arguments on the belief that British capitalism was moving inevitably towards a largely efficient but inegalitarian future, in which the primary socialist aim would not be the reorganisation of production, but instead the seizure by the state of the existing means of production, in order to subject them to control other than by 'parasitic' capitalists.[8] Insofar as industrial inefficiency was an issue within this framework, it was seen as a consequence of monopoly control, which could be prevented by state ownership. But most socialists took a benign view of monopoly; Sidney and Beatrice Webb, for example, argued in 1902 that the arrival of a monopoly (known then as a trust) 'almost necessarily implies an improvement in industrial organisation, measured that is to say by a diminution of the efforts and sacrifices involved in production'.[9] This belief seems to have been challenged only by the coming of the First World War. The remaking of the party in 1918 involved not only the new constitution, but also an elaboration of the underpinnings of that constitution in *Labour and the New Social Order.* This document spelt out the case for the new Clause 4 commitment to public ownership, on grounds that seemed to be new:

> And the Labour Party refuses absolutely to believe that the British people will permanently tolerate any reconstruction or perpetuation of the disorganisation, waste and inefficiency involved in the abandonment of British industry to a jostling around of separate private employers…. What the nation needs is undoubtedly a great bound onwards in its aggregate productivity. But this cannot be secured merely by pressing the manual workers to more strenuous toil, or even by encouraging the Captains of Industry to a less wasteful organisation of their several enterprises on a profit-making basis. What the Labour Party looks to is a genuinely scientific re-organisation of the nation's industry no longer deflected by individual profiteering on the basis of the Common Ownership of the Means of Production.[10]

This rhetoric was backed up in the specific nationalisation proposals, such as for electricity, where existing production was denounced as being on 'a contemptibly small scale', whereas what was needed was 'a score of gigantic "superpower stations" which could generate, at incredibly cheap rates, enough electricity for the use of every industrial establishment and every private household in Great Britain'.[11]

While historians are rightly cautious of allocating too precise dates to changes in something as amorphous as ideology, the link between the war and this shifting assessment of the efficiency of British industry does seem strong. As the Webbs reflected: 'it was one of the unexpected discoveries of government during the Great War that the system of capitalist profit-making, as a method of producing commodities and services, habitually fell so enormously short of the maximum efficiency of which it was capable'.[12] This shift in perception was, as hinted by the Webbs, by no means theirs alone. Governments did conduct an 'audit of war' for the years 1914–18 in Britain, and this led to a range of damning indictments of much of Britain's industry from right-wing as well as left-wing opinion. Following this trend, the left saw the need to put forward policies to improve efficiency, and again such ideas were not voiced just by the Webbs. For example, at the 1918 Labour Party conference Ramsay MacDonald proposed a resolution asserting 'the need for increased production', aided by a 'productivity commission', as a key post-war objective. In 1921 R. H. Tawney, in his bible of ethical socialism, *The Acquisitive Society*, while, of course, generally downplaying the importance of high output and consumption, in fact bases a surprising proportion of his argument on the assertion that modern capitalism is inefficient as well as degraded because it has detached property ownership from economic 'function'.[13]

In part, such views were undoubtedly just a short-term response to wartime conditions, but they were not only that. From the early 1920s onwards, wartime failings of the economy could be seen as continuing, manifested in the mass unemployment arising from depression in the staple industries. While most people on the left as well as the right initially hung on to the idea that these industries could eventually be revived by a reconstruction of the international economy, as the 1920s wore on such views became less plausible and less widely held.[14] Increasingly, Labour ideologues came to doubt that, at least in Britain, socialism could be built on a pre-existing and technically efficient capitalism. Evidence of this trend of opinion can be found in *Labour and the Nation* of 1928. Here the party displayed its interest in what had come to be called industrial 'rationalisation', which in Britain at least was mainly associated with policies to amalgamate firms in order to slim down capacity and achieve economies of scale. The attractions of rationalisation were that it 'seemed to offer a way of making the staple industries more competitive without the need for wage cuts, and, like socialism, it denied the validity of the "free market", hence providing some common ideological ground'.[15]

As was to be true on subsequent occasions, Labour's enthusiasm for industrial modernisation in the form of 'rationalisation' was to face substantial obstacles. Most obviously, initial trade union support for this policy faded as unemployment mounted after 1929; the obvious short-term jobs cuts associated with such a policy were no longer regarded as bearable.[16] The history of the 1929–31 Labour government is not one of major achievement in industrial modernisation. Some limited legislative steps were taken, for example in coalmine reorganisation, but only after a gruelling passage through Parliament which left the party unwilling to follow such a strategy in any other industry.[17] But if, as usual, policy achievement fell short of political ambition, for the current argument it is the strength of the continuing ambition which is of note. One of the most interesting examples of Labour's attitude to industry at this time is a memo by the junior minister (and future leader) Clement Attlee, which decried 'short-termism' in past industrial policy and emphasised the need for 'conscious direction of industrial development' to displace control by private owners, because, 'if any lesson is to be learnt from the experience of the past ten years, it would seem that those responsible for British industry have proved incapable of so managing their affairs as to promote the economic welfare of the community'.[18] The resultant proposals for a Ministry of Industry to oversee rationalisation made no progress, but Attlee's approach to the economy was increasingly to become standard in Labour circles.[19]

In the 1930s the party's enthusiasm for policies aimed at enhancing industrial efficiency is most evident in the discussion of public ownership. It had long been characteristic of advocacy of such ownership that the aims were presented as multiple, combining practical industrial concerns with broader political ambitions. The 1930s saw the same breadth (or ambiguity) of aims embedded in the more detailed programmes, most noticeably in *For Socialism and Peace*, the key policy document of the decade. Central to this document's case for public ownership was the need for 'the phenomenal increase in modern productive capacity' to be released, which might be achieved by 'enforcing reorganisation' of recalcitrant firms in the private sector, but which ultimately could be guaranteed only by public ownership. Increased efficiency was not the only aim of public ownership, but in the 1930s it was the most prominent.[20] Stephen Brooke's view that, in these years, Labour's 'ethical concerns seemed left behind in the desire for an efficient, largely corporate economy' may be a little overstated, but only a little.[21]

Another sign of this commitment to industrial modernisation was the enthusiasm of Labour thinkers for holding down consumption in order to provide resources for investment. When, in 1930, the Soviet ambassador extolled the virtues of the Soviet working class, and their willingness to accept 'low wages and a relatively hard life in order to

save money for capital improvements', Philip Snowden replied 'That's
sound', and said he sometimes despaired of the British working class
because of their claims for higher wages when Britain 'ought to be saving
in order to bring our old-fashioned plant up to date'. In the same vein
ten years later, Evan Durbin's key text in early British socialist revisionism was making it central to future strategy that 'ameliorative measures',
meaning welfare provision, had to be held back to free savings from
taxation in order to finance a higher level of investment.[22]

This desire for modernisation was strongly reinforced by depreda-
tions of Britain's industrial base in the Second World War, and well
before it came to power in 1945 Labour was searching for policies to
improve industrial efficiency, as a foundation for the full employment
and welfare provision it wanted to deliver. The nationalisation programme
of the Attlee period, while having no single motive, was underpinned
by powerful notions (held well beyond the Labour Party) that only large-
scale, national control could 'rationalise' and revive many of the
industries taken over by the state. Similarly, the government attempted
to persuade leaders of the private sector to invest more, reorganise their
industries, improve their management and employ the latest technology to improve their productivity.[23] This 'modernising' attitude of
Labour seems so well established in the literature that the interesting
questions now are not whether the Attlee government saw industrial
efficiency as a key goal, but whether its policies in that area were appropriate to the problem, and the constraints the government faced in
pursuing its efficiency agenda.[24]

The eight or so years after the demise of the Attlee government in
1951 appear exceptional in the lack of interest evident in Labour circles
in industrial modernisation. On one side of the party, the revisionists
displayed what in retrospect appears an insouciant faith in the capacity
of the British economy to deliver efficiency and growth; they desired
economic efficiency, but did not believe new policies were needed to
achieve it. On the other side, on the left, the Bevanites' enthusiasm for
public ownership appears wholly ideological; they showed few signs of
a detailed interest in any aspect of industrial policy, barring a few
mavericks.[25] This brief interval in the main trajectory of Labour policy
may be compared to the years before 1914, when key figures in the
party believed that British capitalism was, literally, 'delivering the goods',
and that questions of efficiency and modernisation were not priorities.[26]

This interregnum ended in the late 1950s with Labour's growing
belief that the Conservatives were vulnerable to claims that they had
failed in the growth stakes, as well as the more positive notion that
'industrial modernisation' would provide a unifying slogan around which
disparate Labour factions could unite.[27] This was the beginning of the
shift towards the modernisation agenda that Labour was to take into

government in 1964. As is argued in some detail below, this agenda was by no means distinctively Labour's own: it drew a great deal on arguments and assumptions with wide circulation under the Conservatives from the late 1950s onwards. In other words, Labour's modernisation 'project', while drawing on both themes from the party's past and its contemporary internal dynamics, was also part of a cross-party (partial) consensus. While so far this chapter has stressed Labour's own trajectory in relation to modernisation, it is therefore also important to sketch where this cross-party agreement stemmed from.

In his account of the left across Europe, Donald Sassoon has argued that it is characteristic of social democracy that it does not have a distinctive economic programme to call its own.[28] Certainly, in the British case it is indeed doubtful whether there has been a clear dividing line between Labour and other 'progressive' forces in the assumptions embodied in much economic policy. In particular, Labour's attitude to efficiency and growth has been close to the terms of the broader national debate.

Since the rise of German and US economic power in the 1880s, and after a considerable fillip from the First World War, fears of economic weakness have been a staple of British political discourse. In the late nineteenth century, debates about Britain's economic strength were initiated by conservative protectionists, who were more concerned to preserve existing industry than actively to 'modernise', but from 1914 onwards the assumption that 'something must be done' to improve industrial endeavour was accepted by almost everyone, a feeling greatly reinforced by inter-war unemployment.[29] Labour's enthusiasm for 'rationalisation' of the staple industries in the 1920s was part of a general partiality for that beguiling term across the political spectrum. In similar fashion, the widespread belief in planning in the 1930s reflected a consensus that the private sector had failed to reform itself and that, even if at some remove, the state should step in to do the job of industrial 'modernisation'.[30] In the 1940s the 'audit of war' revealed the fragility of some parts of British industry, and the common presumption of policy debate in the war years and immediately after was that economic modernisation was the only sound foundation for welfare improvement. The conduct of the Attlee government in office showed that it accepted that priority, despite Conservative claims of excessive concern with creating a 'New Jerusalem'.[31]

On the back of the worldwide boom, fast-growing investment, favourable terms of trade and cutbacks in military expenditure after the Korean War, Britain for much of the 1950s enjoyed unprecedented prosperity. Inflation and unemployment were both low, and growth rapid and sustained by historic standards. In public especially, the Conservatives tended, understandably, to emphasise the successes of economic performance. They proclaimed the coming of affluence, and talked of the unprecedented possibilities of doubling the standard of living within twenty-five years.[32] We can say, therefore, that, until the late 1950s, general political concern with economic performance was significant but episodic, and there was no clear sense of a systemic, persistent 'decline' in the economy. But from the late 1950s 'declinist' accounts of Britain increasingly dominated public discussion. Declinism was invented on the centre-left of politics, but quickly spread to embrace almost all parts of the political spectrum.[33]

The embracing of modernising themes by the Conservatives in the early 1960s was in substantial part a response to being thrown on the defensive by Labour's claims that the Conservative government was failing because of its lack of strategy for faster growth.[34] Politically, it was plainly difficult for the Conservatives to accept that the economy was suffering from the kind of fundamental problems the Labour Party alleged; after all, the Tories had been in office since 1951 and it was difficult to avoid the conclusion that, if there were major faults in economic policy, those responsible were the Conservatives. However, by the beginning of the 1960s the Conservatives accepted major economic reform was necessary. In 1962 the Prime Minister, Harold Macmillan, could write: 'We have now reached a stage in our post-war history where some more radical attack must be made upon the weakness of our economy, both productive and structural'.[35]

The modernisation agenda of the 1960s

The modernisation agenda that emerged in the early 1960s was built up from the diagnosis of a very wide range of perceived weaknesses in the economy, and though their combination into a general discourse of economic decline and modernisation occurred only in the specific circumstances of those years, perception of these individual weaknesses often went back well into the previous decade.

Perhaps the most commonly identified of these weaknesses was that of 'stop–go'. This term was used to describe the frequent changes in macro-economic policy used to try to 'fine tune' the economy. Policy was deflationary when the balance of payments got into difficulties, but reverted to expansionary measures when the level of unemployment threatened to become politically unacceptable. There is no doubt that macro-economic policy in the 1950s was extremely active, with frequent changes of direction. Whether these changes had that much impact on economic performance has been doubted by many subsequent commentators, but there is no doubt that allegations of 'short-termism' in policy damaging Britain's economic growth prospects were widely believed at the time.[36]

At its most general, stop–go was seen to register a conflict between domestic policy goals of growth and employment, and external goals of maintaining the international status of the pound and of Britain more generally. This argument came sharply into focus in a highly influential book by Andrew Shonfield, first published in 1958.[37] But the idea that Britain was trying to do too much with too few resources had been a persistent concern in political and official circles since the war. The Attlee government was in part characterised by a slow and reluctant recognition that economic weakness required a lessening of world ambitions, until in 1950 the start of the Korean War gave occasion for a reckless reversal of the trend towards economy in military spending.[38] Under the Conservatives there was a political reluctance to accept waning economic strength as a reason for lessening the world role. The Treasury from the mid-1950s was pointing out to ministers that the country was trying to do too much with too little, but the response was mainly to look for ways to strengthen the economy by cutting public spending and civilian consumption, to allow for expanding investment and exports. While after Korea military spending was cut as a share of gross domestic product (GDP) in order to make tax cuts possible, *overseas* military and political spending was not. The 1956 Suez crisis, despite what might be expected, did not immediately lead to a fundamental reappraisal of Britain's overseas commitments, although it did encourage ways of trying to deliver these more cheaply.[39]

While the Conservatives did not want to give up military commitments, they were sensitive to arguments that these commitments used large quantities of scarce scientific and technological resources, especially in terms of the labour force, to the detriment of the civilian sector. Thus Anthony Eden in 1956 expressed views on this issue which bear a very close resemblance to what Harold Wilson was to be famous for expressing several years later. The move to a nuclear strategy heralded in the defence White Paper of 1957 was partly driven by the belief that this would be a way of economising on scarce labour resources, including in science and technology, although this seems to have been an illusion.[40]

Stop–go was commonly criticised for the disincentive it was supposed to offer to potential investors, by leading to fluctuating markets and therefore uncertain profits. This argument was made with particular force because in the 1950s it was almost universally accepted that investment was the key to better economic performance. Through the early and mid-1950s, Conservative Chancellors emphasised the need for higher investment. They continued with the Attlee government's policies of giving depreciation allowances to encourage manufacturing investment, and in 1954 these were added to by investment allowances. However, these allowances were themselves cut in the two big 'stops' under the Conservatives, in 1956–8 and 1961–3.[41] The Conservatives also cut taxes on profits, including eventually abolishing the discrimination against distributed profits in 1958, but these changes were broadly offset by the fall in pre-tax profits in these years.[42] Nevertheless, investment did rise in the 1950s, though probably more as a reflection of new technological opportunities and the world trade boom than because of domestic policy measures.

While Eden and others recognised the opportunity cost of so much of Britain's research and development effort being used by the military sector, the direct use of government money to supplement these resources was quite limited. Government expenditure on civilian 'non-strategic' research and development rose from £20.7 million in 1950/51 to £96.9 million in 1963/64, but this was quite small compared with the total spending of over £400 million. Even these sums led to considerable dispute and Conservative policy in this area remained confused until they lost office in 1964.[43]

The Conservative Party and government were mainly hostile to trade unions in these years, as ever, but after 1951 this was initially tempered by a sense of electoral vulnerability and perceptions of union strength. After a second and more decisive election victory in 1955, policy started to shift. A portion of this hostility followed from the Conservatives' concern with inflation, and their common belief that this was to a large extent caused by the unions. They made various attempts to address this problem, with little success. Unions were also blamed for 'restrictive practices' and this allegation received more prominence as declinist ideas gathered momentum. In 1956 the Ministry of Labour sought to establish evidence of these practices as a prelude to action, but in the event found the evidence of a problem on the scale believed was simply not available.[44]

In the early 1960s the Conservatives adopted rather different stances, and tried to gain union agreement to reforms, both of pay bargaining and of the labour market more generally. One reason for their embrace of the rhetoric of planning and of 'Neddy' (the National Economic Development Council, NEDC) was the hope that this would facilitate agreement on an incomes policy (see below). More broadly, the government sought policies to increase labour mobility as a way of increasing efficiency. It recognised that such mobility often imposed formidable costs on workers, and moved towards redundancy payments and higher short-term unemployment benefit to tackle this issue, but neither impetus was strong enough to produce legislation before 1964. However, one piece of reform was enacted just before the general election, the introduction of industrial training boards and of levies on industry to support workplace-based training.[45]

The Attlee government had focused a great deal of attention on the 'productivity problem', but the Conservatives put much less emphasis on this issue. Partly this was due to the association of 'productivity initiatives' with what they saw as the dirigiste meddling of their Labour predecessor. Partly it was because a focus on the broader term 'competitiveness' suited the Conservatives better. It was a word ideologically more congenial to laissez-faire attitudes, but also served to emphasise the importance of costs, especially labour costs, in economic performance and thus could be linked to anti-union feelings.[46]

While the rhetoric of competitiveness was important to the Conservatives, their policies on competition were much more ambiguous than such pronouncements might suggest. Domestically, the 1956 Restrictive Practices Act was undoubtedly an important piece of pro-competition legislation; on monopolies, however, the Conservatives not only resisted pressures to strengthen the 1948 Monopolies Act but also discussed abolition of the Monopolies Commission. The abolition of resale price maintenance in 1964 was also an important step, though one which was the cause of much dispute in Conservative ranks.[47]

Externally, protectionism only slowly gave way to liberalisation. In the early 1950s enthusiasm for imperial preference was clearly evident at Conservative conferences, but the leadership won the argument that Britain's long-term interests lay in the liberalising agenda of the General Agreement on Tariffs and Trade (GATT). But both tariff and non-tariff barriers remained significant into the early 1960s. However, there was a growing element within the party which saw a more liberal attitude to imports as likely to bring an invigorating 'cold shower' of stimulus to Britain's allegedly complacent industries. This was a significant aspect of the application to join the European Economic Community (EEC) in 1961.[48]

Apparently at ideological odds with this emphasis on competition was the revival of interest in 'planning', most evident in the creation of the NEDC in 1961. This ideological tension can be overstated; 'planning' under the Conservatives meant little more than tripartite consultation with unions and employers, and the discussion of possible future economic scenarios and their implications for specific sectors. There was little dirigisme involved, certainly much less that in contemporary French indicative planning, which was supposed to have inspired the British version.[49]

Enthusiasm for 'planning' was in part just political rhetoric – a response to allegations of short-termism, and a desire to be seen as purposive and forward-thinking. But it also chimed with more substantive concerns. One of these was to use tripartism to try to broker an incomes policy with the trade unions. However, the unions showed little inclination to give up their commitment to free collective bargaining for what they regarded as the uncertain promises of a Conservative government.[50] Planning was also linked to the desire to reform the control of public

spending, most evident in the Plowden report. A key element in the
background to Plowden was the argument that a focus on short-term
economic management led to a lack of proper control of public spending, and that there needed to be a longer-term approach to that control.
Concern with the medium-term performance of the public sector also
embraced the nationalised industries, and a 1961 White Paper tried to
set down some principles for their conduct. An important point to emphasise here is that, in an age when investment was regarded as central
to overall economic performance, the public sector was responsible for
around two-thirds of all fixed capital, with the nationalised industries
controlling around 40 per cent of the national total, and housing,
hospitals, roads and schools another 25 per cent.[51] The public sector
therefore had to be a large part of any 'modernising' agenda.

For all Labour's attempts to portray the Conservatives in the early
1960s as Neanderthal anti-modernisers, the sketch above shows how
far, in fact, the Tories had embraced this concern. By 1964 much of
Labour's modernisation agenda had already become the common sense
of much of Westminster and Whitehall. On the other hand, little of that
agenda had been implemented. Partly this was because of opposition
from important interest groups, such as the British Employers' Confederation, to reforms of the labour market. Partly it was because of
divisions in Conservative ranks: not all Conservatives believed economic
modernisation should be a top priority, while others worried about the
dirigiste rhetoric which seemed to accompany it.[52]

In substantial part Labour's need in the years after 1964 was not to
impose a new policy agenda, but to try to overcome obstacles to a largely
existing set of objectives. But what were these obstacles? As we have
seen in the introduction, many accounts of the Wilson government tell
a tale of modernising ambitions thwarted by an external constraint, the
constraint of a weak balance of payments, for which there was a remedy
in the form of devaluation, but a remedy Labour misguidedly rejected.
Chapter 10 returns to the issue of how far the modernising agenda was
indeed thwarted. But here we need to look at the crucial notion of an
'external constraint' and what this meant in the 1960s.

The external constraint

Most historians and other commentators take it for granted that Britain
suffered from serious balance of payments problems for several decades
after 1945. There would be no problem in citing in support of this view
the speeches of contemporary politicians. The phrase 'export or die',
coined in the 1940s, would be paraphrased by almost every senior poli-
tician for thirty years. In public pronouncements, at least, the nature of

this problem was straightforward: as Harold Wilson pithily put it in 1964, 'it is time exporters got off their backsides and worked for Britain'. Three years later the Chancellor of the Exchequer made the same point in more measured tones: 'I am not seeking to ascribe any responsibility to anybody for failing to try to export. I am merely pointing out the fact that it is industry which does the exporting, and industry which imports, and if the two do not balance, eventually we get into a disequilibrium.'[53]

The implication of such statements seems clear: Britain is failing to export enough to pay for its imports and is living beyond its means. Yet a glance at Table 1.1 shows that the picture is by no means so straightforward.[54] As the first column records, throughout the 1960s (and 1970 was a wholly exceptional year), Britain was in deficit on visible account, that is, trade in goods. But this was nothing new; indeed, it had been the normal state of affairs at least as far back as the mid-nineteenth century, and reflected the impact of free trade in making Britain reliant on imports for a large proportion of its food and raw materials. (Manufactures were a tiny, if growing, proportion of total imports in the 1960s; see Chapter 2.) Britain had traditionally paid for this excess of visible goods by a surplus on total invisibles (shipping, financial services, profits on overseas investment plus government payments), and this, as the second column shows, continued through the 1960s. The fourth column tells us that if we look purely at commercial transactions (excluding the

Table 1.1 British balance of payments in the 1960s (£millions)

Year	Visible balance	Invisible balance	Official balance[a]	Private invisible balance[b]	Long-term capital net outflow[c]
1960	−406	+151	−282	+433	−175
1961	−152	+158	−332	+490	−134
1962	−102	+224	−360	+584	−130
1963	−80	+204	−382	+586	−145
1964	−519	+143	−432	+575	−159
1965	−237	+185	−447	+632	−170
1966	−73	+156	−470	+626	−139
1967	−552	+254	−463	+717	−197
1968	−643	+355	−466	+821	−327
1969	−141	+581	−467	+1,048	−351
1970	+3	+576	−486	+1,062	−257

[a] Government services and transfers (net).
[b] Invisible balance minus government services and transfers.
[c] Private investment overseas minus overseas investment in the UK public and private sectors.
Source: *UK Balance of Payments* ('Pink Book') *1971*, Tables 1, 2, 5.

government's activities) the surplus was very much larger. In other words, the commercial sector of the economy was comfortably paying its way; Britain was successfully paying for current consumption of imports by current production of exports.

What drove the current account into deficit was the increasing size of government net spending overseas (the third column); this figure, it should be noted, included foreign aid as well as military spending overseas. In addition, as shown in the final column, the overall balance of payments was driven into further difficulties by the scale of long-term investment overseas. While relative to GDP these outflows were much smaller than before 1914, they were still sufficient to make Britain the second biggest foreign investor in the world, after the USA.

To emphasise the story from the figures, we can take the example of 1964, the year Labour came to power to face a 'desperate' balance of payments problem. First, note that on no measure did the deficit reach the £800 million commonly quoted at the time as the scale of the problem. Though this figure was derived from contemporary official calculations, it was quickly reduced, so that by the end of the decade the official figures are as shown in the table. The table shows a deficit in visible goods for 1964 of £519 million, only partly offset by a balance in invisibles of £143 million, leaving a substantial current account deficit. But the government balance for that year was a deficit of £432 million, and there was a net outflow of long-term capital of £159 million; plainly, there was a balance of payments problem in 1964, but the roots of that problem lay some way from a simple failure of Britain to 'pay its way'.

If we are to get a sense of the nature of the external constraint in the 1960s, we need to step back from the political rhetoric and look with some historical perspective on the construction of the post-war balance of payments 'problem'.

At the end of the Second World War, Britain did have a serious and compelling current account problem, due to the allocation of resources away from export industries during the war coupled to loss of markets disrupted by war. Imports had been cut, but much less than exports, so there was an immediate need to expand exports while holding imports in check. Under the Attlee government, and despite frequent crises, this readjustment was essentially achieved, though the Korean War again disrupted the position from 1951.[55] After the end of that war, the position improved markedly as import prices fell and world trade expanded fast. In the 1950s only 1955 saw a current account deficit and that, significantly, was an election year for which a boom had been engineered.

In many ways the British balance of payments performed remarkably well in the 1950s. The loss of profits on overseas assets sold to pay for the Second World War was offset in part by the expansion of visible earnings, and in part by rebuilding the stock of assets by further very large capital exports. One of the curious features of the Attlee period was the huge capital outflow at a time when the government was seeking to persuade the public that 'England's bread hangs by Lancashire's thread'. In those years, and in the following Conservative era, controls were in place on foreign investment, but only if it was going outside the sterling area.[56]

Despite this apparent health, worries about the foreign balance mounted in the 1950s. Partly this was due to evidence of Britain's shrinking share of world trade in manufactured goods, which fell from 25 per cent in 1950 to 16 per cent in 1960, though it could well be argued that this was bound to happen as other countries grew, and was in itself not evidence of a problem. Another source of concern was the idea that inflation was making British goods uncompetitive. But apart from the lack of evidence in the trade balance that Britain was uncompetitive, it is important to note that Britain's inflation in this period was no faster than that of its major competitors, so that relative inflation could not have been a real problem.[57]

The problem really lay elsewhere. Four features of British policy underlay the balance of payments 'problem' in the 1950s and into the 1960s. First was the rising trend in overseas government expenditure, which meant a growing surplus on commercial balances was required to offset it. Second was the continued high level of foreign investment. Of course, this outflow eventually generated inflows of profits, but in the short run it, too, worsened the payments position. Third was the government's commitment to a fixed exchange rate, which was entwined with the fourth element, the support for the continuation of the sterling area. This area, which had been formalised and expanded in the 1930s and 1940s, comprised those, mainly Commonwealth, countries that fixed their exchange rate to the pound and held most of their reserves in sterling. These two features together meant that British governments in the 1950s and early 1960s regularly ran into a 'confidence' problem. This arose because the sterling area meant that Britain had huge liabilities in sterling, but much more limited foreign currency assets, and a low level of reserves. Because of this unfavourable asset–liability ratio, holders of sterling always worried that their holdings could not be realised, and that devaluation might occur.

It is important here to stress that this sense of the vulnerability of Britain to a rundown of sterling balances, while a constant preoccupation of policy-makers, was not matched by a rundown in practice. Indeed, in retrospect, the remarkable feature of the sterling balances in the 1950s (and most of the 1960s) was their buoyancy and stability.[58] But what matters for policy is, of course, contemporary perceptions, not retrospective analysis. And for policy-makers the perceived need was to respond to this 'weakness'.

The response was to try to build up a current account surplus in order to finance foreign investment and improve the reserve position, while sustaining the exchange rate. The Treasury's evidence to the Radcliffe Committee in the late 1950s talked of a target of a current account surplus of £300–350 million, later raised to £450 million.[59] How to achieve this aim was a matter of growing controversy between those who believed that a lower level of domestic demand would slow price rises and thereby increase competitiveness, and those who sought some form of incomes policy to allow high levels of demand to continue but with a reduced inflationary consequence. But these endeavours were never very successful, so that, in its own terms, balance of payments policy was clearly seen to be failing by the early 1960s.

In the new decade the debate on the payments problem was given a whole new twist by the rise of declinism. Indeed, this process had begun at least as early as Shonfield's key book of 1958, which, as noted above, linked the overburdening of the balance of payments by government spending, foreign investment and the defence of the pound to 'stop–go', and stop–go in turn to the 'decline' of the British economy. This was to become a standard argument of the 1960s, establishing itself with varying levels of sophistication as the common sense of the left and centre-left.[60] What this debate clearly established is the point that the balance of payments 'problem' is always politically defined. Thus, for example, Strange argued that the key element was Britain's un-willingness to give up the aim of a global role for sterling:

> This is not the conventional and familiar wisdom about the British balance of payments which, year after year, has blamed the British predicament on the failing productivity of British industry and the inadequate performance of British exports in world markets. My con-tention is that the *main* cause of this predicament has not been the British economy but rather the decline of sterling and the failure of British policy to adapt to that decline.[61]

The argument that the external constraint was a product of a very wide range of policy ambitions, and cannot be understood in terms of the simple rhetoric of competitive failure, is vital to any adequate under-standing of the 1960s. In that regard the work of authors such as Shonfield, Hirsch and Strange is a crucial starting point for the analysis of policy in that decade. But the argument that this external orientation of policy greatly damaged British economic performance does not logically follow from their account. As already noted, the mechanism usually suggested for linking the complex of global ambitions to domestic 'decline' is stop–go, yet that process seems much exaggerated in its effects. If that link is substantially discounted, it is by no means clear that these global ambitions were the key to Britain's growth performance. That, however, is a topic best returned to in the concluding chapter.

Notes

The place of publication is London unless otherwise specified.

1 *Hansard* (Commons), vol. 327, 9 March 1999, col. 173; S. Byers, speech at the Mansion House, 2 February 1999. The *Guardian* reported this speech as 'burying the central tenets of the Labour movement'.
2 N. Ellison, *Egalitarian Thought and Labour Politics: Retreating Visions* (1994); N. Thompson, *Political Economy and the Labour Party* (1996).
3 Thompson, *Political Economy*, chs 1, 3; A. Wright, *G. D. H. Cole and Socialist Democracy* (Oxford, 1979), ch. 5.
4 A. Benn, *Arguments for Socialism* (1979). On Blair, see A. Finlayson, 'Tony Blair and the jargon of modernisation', *Soundings*, 10 (1998), pp. 11–27.
5 For social justice and economic efficiency under Attlee, see J. Tomlinson, *Democratic Socialism and Economic Policy: The Attlee Years 1945–51* (Cambridge, 1997), ch. 12.
6 P. Werskey, *The Visible College* (1979); B. Luckin, *Questions of Power* (Manchester, 1990).
7 Labour Party Archives (LPA), *Labour Party Annual Conference Report* (*LPACR*) 1908, pp. 57–9, 64, 76–7; LPA, Third Conference of the Labour Representation Committee, February 1903, p. 36. For the context of such remarks, see D. Tanner, 'Ideological debate in Edwardian Labour politics: radicalism, revisionism and socialism', in E. F. Biagini and A. Reid (eds), *Currents of Radicalism. Popular Radicalism, Organised Labour and Party Politics in Britain, 1850–1914* (Cambridge, 1991), pp. 271–93. This aversion to programmes was coupled to an aversion to economics: 'For the majority of pre-war socialists ... socialism was a matter of ethics, not economics'. A. Booth, 'The Labour Party and economics between the wars', *Bulletin of the Society for the Study of Labour History*, 47 (1983), p. 36.
8 S. Webb and B. Webb, *Problems of Modern Industry* (1902). Tanner, 'Ideological debate', pp. 278–9, and *idem*, 'The development of British socialism, 1900–1918', in E. H. H. Green (ed.), *An Age of Transition: British Politics 1880–1914* (Edinburgh, 1997), pp. 48–66. On Marxist and Fabian influences, see M. Bevir, 'The Marxism of George Bernard Shaw', *History of Political Theory*, 13 (1992), pp. 299–318, and *idem*, 'Fabianism and the theory of rent', *History of Political Theory*, 10 (1989), pp. 313–27.
9 Webb and Webb, *Problems*, pp. xxi–xxvii.
10 Labour Party, *Labour and the New Social Order* (1918), pp. 11–12.
11 *Ibid.*, p. 15.
12 S. Webb and B. Webb, *Constitution for a Socialist Commonwealth of Great Britain* (Cambridge, 1920), p. 324.
13 J. Tomlinson, *Government and the Enterprise Since 1900: The Changing Problem of Efficiency* (Oxford, 1994), ch. 3; *LPACR*, 1918, pp. 44–6; R. H. Tawney, *The Acquisitive Society* (1921), ch. 9, 'The new condition of efficiency'. Another key Labour ideologue whose views moved in the same way to emphasise efficiency was G. D. H. Cole; see M. Freeden, *Liberalism Divided* (Oxford, 1996), pp. 323–4.

14 R. Boyce, *British Capitalism at the Crossroads 1919–32* (Cambridge, 1987);
    W. R. Garside, *British Unemployment 1919–39* (Cambridge, 1990), part III.
    In this light, it is noteworthy that when Philip Snowden famously sought to
    condemn capitalism by parliamentary motion, the words of that motion
    emphasised the inefficiencies of capitalism: 'in view of the failure of the
    capitalist system to adequately utilise and organise natural resources and
    productive power, or to provide the necessary standard of life for vast
    numbers of the population'. *Hansard* (Commons), vol. 161, 20 March 1923,
    col. 2472.

15 Labour Party, *Labour and the Nation* (1928); A. Thorpe, 'The industrial mean-
    ing of "gradualism": the Labour Party and industry, 1918–1931', *Journal of
    British Studies*, 35 (1996), p. 104.

16 Thorpe, 'Industrial meaning', p. 109.

17 M. W. Kirby, *The British Coalmining Industry 1870–1946* (1977), ch. 7.

18 Public Record Office (PRO), CAB 24/214, 'The problem of British industry',
    29 July 1930.

19 Attlee's memo was not taken up by the Cabinet. See Thorpe, 'Industrial
    meaning', p. 108.

20 Labour Party, *For Socialism and Peace* (1934), p. 304; for a critical account of
    this document, see A. Booth and M. Pack, *Employment, Capital and Economic
    Policy: Great Britain 1918–1939* (Oxford, 1985), pp. 125–33, and A. Oldfield,
    'The Labour Party and planning – 1934 or 1918?', *Bulletin of the Society for
    the Study of Labour History*, 25 (1972), pp. 41–55.

21 S. Brooke, *Labour's War* (Oxford, 1992), p. 21; for the continuing import-
    ance of ethics and ideology, see M. Francis, *Ideas and Policies Under Labour
    1945–1951: Building a New Britain* (Manchester, 1997), pp. 72–4.

22 N. MacKenzie and J. MacKenzie (eds), *Diaries of Beatrice Webb. Vol. 4, 1923–
    1943* (1985), p. 225; E. Durbin, *The Politics of Democratic Socialism* (1940),
    pp. 298–300.

23 Labour Party, *Let Us Face the Future* (1945), p. 6; L. Johnman, 'The Labour
    Party and industrial policy, 1940–45', in N. Tiratsoo (ed.), *The Attlee Years*
    (1991), pp. 29–53; N. Tiratsoo and J. Tomlinson, *Industrial Efficiency and
    State Intervention: Labour 1939–51* (1994).

24 The view that Britain pursued a 'New Jerusalem' of welfare without regard
    to economic needs, most recently and vehemently expressed by C. Barnett,
    The Lost Victory (1995), must be regarded as discredited. See J. Harris, 'Enter-
    prise and the welfare state: a comparative perspective', in A. O'Day and
    T. Gourvish (eds), *Britain Since 1945* (1992), pp. 39–58; and J. Tomlinson,
    Democratic Socialism, ch. 11; S. Broadberry and N. Crafts, 'British economic
    policy and industrial performance in the early post-war period', *Business
    History*, 38 (1996), pp. 65–91; M. Chick, *Industrial Policy in Britain 1945–
    1951* (Cambridge, 1997).

25 A. Crosland, *The Future of Socialism* (1956); *idem*, 'On economic growth',
    Encounter, 91 (1961), pp. 65–8; A. Thorpe, *A History of the British Labour
    Party* (1997), p. 237; A. Bevan, *In Place of Fear* (1952); on the lack of policy
    focus among Bevanites, see J. Campbell, *Nye Bevan: A Biography* (1994),
    chs 20, 25; among the mavericks were A. Albu, 'The organisation of industry',
    in R. H. S. Crossman (ed.), *New Fabian Essays* (1952), pp. 121–42.

26 I owe this illuminating comparison to Andrew Thorpe.

27 J. Tomlinson, 'Inventing "decline": the falling behind of the British econ-
    omy in the post-war years', *Economic History Review*, 49 (1996), pp. 731–57.

28 D. Sassoon, *One Hundred Years of Socialism: The West European Left in the
    Twentieth Century* (1996).

29 A. Friedberg, *The Weary Titan: Britain and the Experience of Relative Decline 1895–1905* (Princeton, 1988). Given the proposals of Chamberlain and his allies, we must be sceptical of those accounts of British history which see him as an unsuccessful advocate of 'modernisation'. See, for example, A. Gamble, *Britain in Decline* (4th edn) (1994), pp. 53–8; C. Newton and D. Porter, *Modernization Frustrated* (1988), ch. 1.

30 D. Ritschel, *The Politics of Planning* (Oxford, 1997); as Booth, 'Labour Party', p. 38, acerbically notes of this period, 'Labour intellectuals, freed from the tyrannies of liberal orthodoxy, were also smitten by planning'.

31 H. Jones, 'The Cold War and the Santa Claus syndrome: dilemmas in Conservative social policy-making, 1945–1957', in M. Francis and I. Zweiniger-Bargielowska (eds), *The Conservatives and British Society, 1880–1990* (Cardiff, 1996), pp. 240–54.

32 For Conservative policy-making in the 1950s, see A. Booth, 'Inflation, expectations, and the political economy of Conservative Britain, 1951–1964', *Historical Journal*, 43 (2000), pp. 827–47.

33 Tomlinson, 'Inventing "decline"'. The two key popular texts of early declinism – A. Shonfield, *British Economic Policy Since the War* (Harmondsworth, 1958) and M. Shanks, *The Stagnant Society* (Harmondsworth, 1961) – were written from slightly different centre-left perspectives.

34 J. Tomlinson, 'Conservative modernisation, 1960–64: too little, too late?', *Contemporary British History*, 11 (1997), pp. 18–38.

35 PRO, CAB 129/111, H. Macmillan, 'Modernisation of Britain', 3 December 1962.

36 A. Cairncross, *The British Economy Since 1945* (1992), pp. 141–2.

37 Shonfield, *British Economic Policy*.

38 A. Cairncross, *Years of Recovery: British Economic Policy 1945–51* (1985), ch. 8.

39 G. Peden, *The Treasury and British Public Policy 1906–1959* (Oxford, 2000), pp. 445–8.

40 Eden's 'Preface' to the White Paper *Technical Education*, Cmd 9703, BPP 1955/56, vol. 34; *Defence: Outline of a Future Policy*, Cmnd 124, BPP 1956/57, vol. 23.

41 Organisation for European Economic Co-operation, *4th Report on Europe: The Way Ahead* (Paris, 1952), p. 340; B. Mellis and P. Richardson, 'Value of incentives for manufacturing industry 1946 to 1974', in A. Whiting (ed.), *The Economics of Industrial Subsidies* (1976), pp. 23–43.

42 M. King, 'The profits crisis: myth or reality?', *Economic Journal*, 85 (1975), pp. 33–54.

43 P. Gummett, *Scientists in Whitehall* (Manchester, 1980), pp. 39–40; D. Edgerton, *Science, Technology and the British Industrial 'Decline' 1870–1970* (Cambridge, 1996), p. 39; PRO, DSIR 17/385 and 386, 'Evidence submitted to the Trend Committee, 1962–3'.

44 Booth, 'Inflation'; N. Tiratsoo and J. Tomlinson, *The Conservatives and Industrial Efficiency, 1951–64: Thirteen Wasted Years?* (1998).

45 PRO, CAB 134/1702, Ministry of Labour, 'Provision for redundancy', 29 July 1963; CAB 134/1695, Ministry of Education, 'Industrial training', 7 May 1962; CAB 134/1701, Ministry of Labour, 'Industrial Training Bill', 5 July 1963.

46 Tiratsoo and Tomlinson, *The Conservatives*, pp. 19, 98–9; Booth, 'Inflation'.

47 H. Mercer, *Constructing a Competitive Order: The Hidden History of British Antitrust Policies* (Cambridge, 1995).

48 G. Brennan and A. Milward, *Britain's Place in the World: A Historical Enquiry into Import Controls 1945–60* (1996); PRO, CAB 134/1852–4, Economic Steering

(Europe) Committee, 'Minutes and memoranda' 1960–63; D. Howell, 'Expanding prosperity', in L. Beaton (ed.), *Principles into Practice* (1961), p. 25.

49 G. O'Hara, 'British economic and social planning, 1959–70' (unpublished PhD dissertation, University of London, 2002), ch. 2.

50 R. Jones, *Wages and Employment Policy 1936–1985* (1986), pp. 56–65.

51 R. Lowe, 'Millstone or milestone? The 1961 Plowden Committee and its impact on British welfare policy', *Historical Journal*, 40 (1997), pp. 463–93; White Paper, *The Financial and Economic Obligations of the Nationalised Industries*, Cmnd 1337, BPP 1960/61, vol. 27; investment figures from *National Income and Expenditure of the UK* ('Blue Book') (1965).

52 Tomlinson, 'Conservative modernisation'; R. Shepherd, *Iain Macleod* (1994), pp. 282–4; Conservative Party Archives, Bodleian Library, CRD 2/5/3, Policy Committee on Science and Industry, 1961/62.

53 Callaghan, cited in A. Manser, *Britain in Balance: The Myth of Failure* (1971), p. 1. Of course, as always, politicians' rhetoric was adjusted to audience and purpose. Formal statements of policy such as *The National Plan*, Cmnd 2764, BPP 1964/65, vol. 30, pp. 17–18, 69–83, gave a much more complex picture of balance of payments problems and the policies to address them. For a recent insightful discussion of the balance of payments in this period, see R. Middleton, 'Struggling with the impossible: sterling, the balance of payments and British economic policy, 1949–72', in W. Young and A. Arnon (eds), *The Open Economy Macro Model: Past, Present and Future* (Amsterdam, 2002), pp. 202–31.

54 It is important to note that in the 1960s economic data, especially balance of payments statistics, were subject to constant and substantial revision, so that policy was often guided by figures which might soon be regarded as significantly in error. On this, see P. Mosley, *The Making of Economic Policy: Theory and Evidence from Britain and the US Since 1945* (Brighton, 1985), appendix V; R. Middleton, *Charlatans or Saviours? Economists and the British Economy from Marshall to Meade* (Cheltenham, 1998), pp. 257–61.

55 Cairncross, *Years of Recovery*, ch. 4.

56 Tomlinson, *Democratic Socialism*, pp. 58–64.

57 Manser, *Britain*, p. 111.

58 C. Schenk, *Britain and the Sterling Area: From Devaluation to Convertibility in the 1950s* (1994), ch. 2.

59 Committee on the Working of the Monetary System (Radcliffe), *Report*, Cmnd 827, BPP 1958/59, vol. 17, para. 62.

60 F. Hirsch, *The Pound Sterling: A Polemic* (1965); S. Strange, *Sterling and British Policy* (Oxford, 1971).

61 Strange, *Sterling*, p. 300. Original emphasis.

2

Labour and the international economy from Attlee to Wilson

Much of the day-to-day economic policy-making of the 1964–70 period was dominated by international issues. Almost continuous balance of payments worries, fears about the value of sterling, questions about Britain's international economic status as the anchor of the sterling area, and as a potential member of the EEC, often crowded out purely domestic concerns. These immediate problems of managing Britain's economy, as well as the associated international issues, are discussed at length in Chapter 3. Nonetheless, the approach Labour took to these concerns was conditioned not only by immediate circumstances, but also by long-developed ideas and arguments in Labour ranks about Britain's international economic policies. This chapter outlines and discusses how these arguments developed, from the highly formative years of government under Attlee (1945–51), the long years in opposition, and through the new period in government after 1964.

The three circles

Britain since the late nineteenth century had been the most inter-nationalised of the world's large economies, and the scale and complexity of those international linkages, let alone possible policy options in this area, defy simple summation. But a useful way of approaching the development of Labour's ideas and policies is to start with the Attlee government's sense of Britain's place in the world as being at the centre of 'three circles', consisting of the Commonwealth, the connection with the USA, and Western Europe.[1] Relationships within these three broad zones can be seen as embracing most of the economic as well as political issues facing policy-makers in the post-war years.

If the Labour Party had always been the party of anti-colonialism, after 1945 it also liked to see itself as the party of the Commonwealth, enthusiastic for the idea of an alliance of independent or soon-to-be-independent countries, united around progressive principles of economic and social advance and parliamentary democracy. In addition to such ideals was the pragmatic recognition that if Britain's claim to be a world power (and most Labour leaders wanted it to be such a power) was to be sustained, it would only be as leader of a worldwide Commonwealth. As Attlee put it in 1943: 'I take it to be a fundamental assumption that … it will be our aim to maintain the British Commonwealth as an international entity, recognised as such by foreign countries…. If we are to carry our full weight in the post-war world with the US and USSR it can only be as a united British Commonwealth.'[2]

In the 1940s, the economic significance of the Commonwealth to Britain seemed to underpin such grand designs. Stimulated first by the Ottawa agreements on imperial preference in 1932, and even more by the desperate need to economise on dollar goods through the 1940s, the Commonwealth was at the peak of its trading significance for Britain by 1951. As is normal with governments, the Attlee government made a virtue of this necessity of closer trading links with the Commonwealth, seeing it as part of a desirable and sustainable long-term structure, rather than a highly contingent result of passing circumstances. Around the time Labour lost office in 1951, the tide turned and the Commonwealth began its long decline in significance as a trading zone. By 1965, 30 per cent of British imports came from the sterling area and 37 per cent of exports went there.[3]

In the long years in opposition Labour did work to strengthen Commonwealth links. In 1958 the Commonwealth Advisory Committee of the party's National Executive Committee became a full 'Commonwealth Department', energetically led by John Hatch. It organised meetings of Commonwealth socialist leaders; although the practical results of these are difficult to see, they did provide a channel for articulating Labour's allegiance to the Commonwealth, and in the early 1960s for attacking the Conservatives' 'betrayal' of the Commonwealth by their starting negotiations for Britain's membership of the EEC. Some voices were raised against this posture; for example, Roy Jenkins in 1962 dismissed the idea of the Commonwealth as a feasible 'tight economic unit'.[4] But in the years running up to the 1964 election, the main thrust of Labour policy was to present the weakening economic link with the Commonwealth as an undesirable and reversible consequence of Conservative policy. This stance flowed from a number of factors. Doctrinally, the Commonwealth (along with the sterling area) could be made to fit with long-held notions of 'planned trade' and the rejection of Tory 'laissez-faire' and liberalisation. Such views were still strong in Labour circles into the 1960s, articulated most forcefully by Thomas Balogh, a key economic adviser and long-term critic of post-war mutilateralism.[5] Particularly on the left of the party, such views were often allied to a growing concern with aiding the development of the poor countries of the Commonwealth, which were seen as potential gainers from greater exchanges of their exports of commodities for Britain's manufactures. The establishment of an Overseas Development Ministry under Labour signalled the seriousness of this concern with development, but how far such concerns were compatible with an emphasis on encouraging Commonwealth trade links was to prove a thorny issue for Labour in power. Another economic aspect of the Commonwealth link was the access it gave Britain to the cheap temperate food products of the developed Commonwealth countries (grain from Canada, butter and cheese from New Zealand, meat from Australia), which could be seen as significant contributors to the standard of life of the British worker. This was a key concern of a figure such as Douglas Jay on the right of the party.[6]

Of course, these seeming economic attractions of the Commonwealth were combined with political and electoral calculation. The Conservative attempt to secure British entry into the EEC in 1961–3 (and the hostility this approach aroused in the Commonwealth) provided an opportunity for Labour to present itself as the champion of the Commonwealth, a theme of Hugh Gaitskell's famous anti-EEC speech of 1962. Gaitskell's successor, Harold Wilson, had been Trade Minister in the 1940s, when the Commonwealth economic link was reaching its peak, and combined this potent memory with an only partly sentimental view that the Commonwealth was a key to Britain's status as a world power. It was characteristic, therefore, that in a House of Commons debate in 1961 on the EEC application he had acted as a defender of the Commonwealth: 'We are not entitled to sell our friends and kinsmen down the river for a problematical and marginal advantage in selling washing machines in Dusseldorf'. But Wilson and Labour's concern with the Commonwealth was not just opportunistic politics and high-flown words. In the pre-election years a detailed programme aimed at reinvigorating the economic links with the Commonwealth was developed, and this was central to Labour's approach to the economy in 1964, a fact obscured in most of the accounts of the period by the subsequent turn away from the Commonwealth and application for EEC entry.[7]

In a debate in the Commons in 1964, Wilson cited the figures on the weakening of the Commonwealth trade link and attacked Tory 'defeatism' on the issue. 'This doctrine of the inevitability of Commonwealth decline has become part of the tribal mythology of the party opposite.' In that speech, Wilson put forward a ten-point plan to encourage Commonwealth trade. This included a proposal for 'preferences in the way of capital contracts' in publicly financed projects, guaranteed markets for Commonwealth products in Britain, development of industries in Britain to supply Commonwealth investment needs, worldwide commodity agreements to stabilise the prices of primary products, and the expansion of world liquidity especially to favour underdeveloped countries. Most of these proposals found their way into a prominent position in Labour's election manifesto, which asserted that 'the Labour Party is convinced that the first responsibility of a British Government is still to the Commonwealth'.[8] These were the main elements in a programme which was to be at the centre of Labour's economic discussions about the Commonwealth in the years after 1964, but which was ultimately to prove largely unworkable.

The failure to find a plausible 'Commonwealth alternative' in the early years of the Wilson government was one important element in Labour's decision to apply for EEC membership, as analysed further below. But was this immense change of direction simply a giving up of a sentimental illusion in the face of the realism of policy-making in office, or was the Commonwealth option ditched too easily for the sake of what was, in some respects, an equally problematical and emotional attachment to 'Europe'?

Governmental discussions of Labour's programme for strengthening Commonwealth links were largely organised around preparations for major formal Commonwealth meetings. The first of these after the election of 1964 was of Commonwealth Prime Ministers, in June 1965. The agenda of this meeting was dominated by the contentious issue of Rhodesia, which was preparing to make a unilateral declaration of independence (in November 1965), but it provided a platform for Wilson to push the key items of his 'plan', which was focused on: gaining an agreement to have a Commonwealth Trade Minister's conference to encourage trade links; holding a meeting to develop the idea of co-ordinating Commonwealth countries' plans as a basis for preference in public procurement; and, much more specifically, reviving previous Commonwealth discussions of aircraft development, which Britain hoped would lead to more orders for its aircraft industry.[9] The meeting of Trade Ministers was a key event in exposing doubts about the other elements of this 'plan', as the meeting itself as well as the preparatory gathering of officials showed the difficulties of reversing the trend away from close Commonwealth economic ties.

Much of the internal governmental discussion on Commonwealth economic issues came together in the Official Committee on Commercial Policy. A key initial paper was put to a meeting of this committee in spring 1965 by the Board of Trade, at which its 'disappointing conclusions' were endorsed by other departments.[10] In this paper scepticism was expressed about the prospects of realising the government's ambitions, on grounds that were to be largely echoed in all discussions over the next few years. These grounds, though overlapping and inter-related, may be summarised as fourfold: how far the Commonwealth was the key arena in which Britain should pursue its trade policies; whether Britain could expect to gain from any trade concessions it might make to other

Commonwealth countries; whether there could be closer links between British provision of finance to Commonwealth countries and their trading decisions; and whether there was any realistic scope for co-ordination of 'plans' leading to Commonwealth preference in public procurement.

On the first point, the core aim of Labour's international trade policy, following that of the Conservatives, was to support liberalisation through the GATT process, which meant at this time pushing for tariff and quota reductions in the Kennedy Round, which began in 1962 but was not concluded until 1967, with implementation beginning in 1968.[11] This strategy reflected worries that the world was developing a growing number of trading blocs, which threatened to restrict British trade opportunities. Such fears had, of course, informed the Conservative approach to the EEC at a time when that body was seen as likely to develop its forbidding Common External Tariff (CET), and that therefore Britain would be better off inside than out.[12] As the Board of Trade spelt out in frank terms, this focus clearly meant the Commonwealth had second place in British policy: 'our main concern in the Kennedy Round is to negotiate concessions with the major non-Commonwealth developed countries (and we would not wish to jeopardise an advantageous settlement with them *merely* in deference to Commonwealth interests)'.[13] Officials at the preparatory meeting in November 1965 endorsed this view, spelling out the implications that: 'The world-wide reduction of tariffs and other barriers to trade was likely to be the most successful and rapid method of developing trade both within and between the Commonwealth and the rest of the world' and 'Commonwealth trade has to be considered in the context of world trade and a closed Commonwealth trading system would be neither feasible nor desirable'.[14]

The practical implication of this perspective was that the primary arenas in which Britain and the other Commonwealth countries should pursue trade policy aims were global bodies like the GATT and the United Nations Commission on Trade and Development (UNCTAD), not the Commonwealth. Thus when, for example, Ceylon suggested a revival of the Commonwealth Shipping Committee, the view of the Committee on Commercial Policy was clear: 'the Commonwealth was not an economic unit nor a shipping unit', and the issue should be pursued through UNCTAD. This meant that, at best, Commonwealth trade discussions would be about co-ordinating approaches to GATT and UNCTAD meetings. But even this much reduced aim was reliant on a belief in a commonality of interest within the Commonwealth, which became an increasingly difficult view to sustain. The result was that Commonwealth meetings became more of a framework for bilateral bargaining than a basis for general discussion and agreement.[15]

This leads on to the second problem enumerated above, the degree of likely reciprocal concessions between Britain and its Commonwealth partners. As far as the underdeveloped countries of the Commonwealth (the majority by the early 1960s) were concerned, any belief in commonality of interest which might have once existed was undermined by the deterioration in their terms of trade from their Korean War peak, especially when this was widely seen as a secular trend rather than a cyclical phenomenon. This pessimistic view was most ably articulated by Raúl Prebisch, who became the first Secretary-General of UNCTAD in 1962, that body in turn becoming unambiguously a mouthpiece for the poor countries of the world in their search for more favourable market conditions. Because of the concern to be seen as supporting the aims of the poor countries, Britain and other rich countries accepted, at least in principle, the view articulated at UNCTAD that they should grant trade concessions to underdeveloped countries without seeking reciprocity.[16]

Because it had adopted this role as advocate for the poor, UNCTAD had obvious attractions to underdeveloped Commonwealth countries superior to those of a body which contained both the rich and the poor. Increased consciousness and articulation of the division between rich and poor were unlikely to aid the coherence of the Commonwealth. More practically, a concern with raising global prices for primary products, central to the politics of underdevelopment in this period, was bound to leave the Commonwealth largely on the sidelines, as its main markets for such products (within which Britain overwhelmingly predominated) were simply not large enough to be able much to affect the world price – tea being the one and only major exception to this generalisation.[17]

While the Labour government's concern with the conditions of the world's poor was genuine, it clearly had its limits. Trade concessions which aided (mainly) poor countries, such as the Commonwealth Sugar Agreement (CSA), were under scrutiny in Britain because of the perception of their radical impact on import prices. The CSA, begun in 1951, was until 1967 annually 'rolled over' for a further period of six years. The stated reason for ceasing to do so was the impending discussions with the EEC, but there seems to have been a determination to restrict its scope irrespective of the EEC.[18]

Poor countries were keen to expand their exports of manufactured goods as well as to get better prices for primary products. Here again, the Commonwealth proved to be of limited benefit to them. While Britain was more generous in allowing access to a key product market like textiles than other rich countries, for balance of payments and employment reasons the trend in this period was towards a tightening, not loosening, of import controls.[19]

Third, Britain under Wilson was, of course, seriously concerned with the balance of payments and public expenditure, and this was bound to lead to questioning of the amount of aid given to poor countries. The establishment of a Ministry of Overseas Development signalled Labour's recognition of the new agenda of world poverty, but the level of aid channelled through it was constrained by these macro-economic problems. This aid (most of which went to Commonwealth countries) rose sharply in the early years of the Wilson government, but then, after sharp disputes within government, fell back.[20] Conversely, the view of poor members of the Commonwealth in this period was increasingly that the purpose of belonging to that body and attending its meetings was to increase economic aid, rather than to bargain over mutual benefits. This circle might have been squared by more aid tied to purchases of British exports, but the results of investigations of this possibility were uniformly negative. It was pointed out: that Britain was not and could not be a big enough aid giver to affect trade volumes greatly; that, in any event, tied aid was generally unpopular with its recipients; and that tying might even worsen the situation, because currently Britain did well in competing for orders from untied aid in countries like India, whereas if more were tied the country might end up with a smaller share of the market.[21]

Reciprocal trading agreements with the rich Commonwealth countries faced obstacles well known since the time of Joseph Chamberlain. Australia, Canada and New Zealand, while happy with any concessions granted in the British market, were developing their own manufacturing industries, and wanted protection against British manufactures. They were not willing to play the role of simply suppliers of cheap food and raw materials to Britain, and recognised that to develop their manufacturing exports they had to look beyond Britain and the Commonwealth. This was well recognised in Britain. The Board of Trade noted that: 'they wish to build up their new industries and would not wish to impair their relations with their other trading partners who now do twice as much business with the Commonwealth as we do, and offer more scope for increase'. In addition, while some British ministers emphasised the benefits to the consumer and to industrial costs of cheap food and raw materials, the National Plan of 1965 had called for further reinforcement of the trend towards an expansion of temperate food output in Britain to aid the balance of payments, a policy which threatened the scale of Australia's and New Zealand's primary product sales to Britain.[22]

Fourth, the Wilsonian enthusiasm for domestic economic planning had its reflection in debates about the Commonwealth. Wilson's idea was that discussion of each other's plans would enable market opportunities to be identified, especially in capital goods, and governments would then encourage Commonwealth preference in those areas where the state had procurement responsibilities. Such a policy faced clear obstacles. First, planning was not in vogue in all of the Commonwealth, especially Australia and Canada, so there was often little to co-ordinate.

On the other hand, India, with much more planning than Britain, had to be reminded that in a capitalist economy the amount of control exercised by government was strictly limited.[23] Second, all governments were wary of buying other than on the basis of cost-effectiveness. Somewhat embarrassingly, the British government itself made little use of procurement as a domestic policy instrument, the only example where this was done in the early years of the Labour government being computers. Finally, even if the political will existed, key countries such as Australia and Canada had federal constitutions, where central government did not control the activities of state or provincial governments. This meant the proposal was at best plausible only in areas, such as defence, where national governments were always the responsible bodies. But here Commonwealth governments had often developed strong ties to US armaments suppliers, which would be hard for Britain to break. In sum, while pious declarations on this issue, such as the one already secured at the Commonwealth meeting in Montreal in 1958, might be endorsed, the idea of international planning remained largely empty words.[24]

All of the lines of argument outlined above tell a story of unrealistic hopes being entertained by Labour, at the time it entered office, about the prospect of developing closer economic ties with the Commonwealth. Overwhelmingly the advice from within the official machine was that such expectations were unrealisable. But was this a case of civil servants articulating a 'Whitehall view' and blocking policies that might otherwise have been pursued by a more radical Labour government?

Three arguments tell against such a view. First, powerful ministerial advocates of closer Commonwealth ties, most notably Douglas Jay at the Board of Trade, were unable to find any arguments against those put forward by the civil servants. He was reduced to making proposals – notably for Commonwealth free trade areas – that he himself stated to be unrealistic and purely gestural. This rather pathetic posturing was clearly a recognition that there were no other serious proposals that could be put forward, and that all Britain could offer was gestures.[25]

Second, lack of enthusiasm was not just a feature of Whitehall in the face of Wilson's Commonwealth ideas. Governments in other Commonwealth countries reacted extremely cautiously to invitations to discuss Britain's initiatives; they were willing to discuss British proposals, but they found little to engage their enthusiasm. Many were more concerned with pursuing their own trade agendas, such as Nigeria's search for a trade link with the EEC, which was causing much annoyance in Whitehall at this time.[26]

Third, the most persistent advocate of the Commonwealth idea was Balogh and, apart from the general distrust he aroused, there was the clear problem that he unashamedly saw the Commonwealth as a protective bloc, which put him at odds with the general Labour as well as

Whitehall perception that such blocs were a danger to Britain. A key reason for Labour support for the Kennedy Round was the belief that it offered a defence against the perceived threat of the growth of trade blocs; in this way, Labour had for pragmatic reasons become noticeably more pro free trade than in the 1950s. Balogh seems to have under-estimated the strength of this tide of opinion among Labour's leaders, and this led him to focus too much attention on official attitudes as the obstruction to his proposals. He was also out of kilter with the in-creasingly consensual 'common sense' view that British industry needed more competition rather than protected markets in order to become more efficient.[27]

The failure of Labour's ambitions for closer economic links with the Commonwealth was evident within little more than nine months of Labour taking office. After the Commonwealth Trade Ministers' confer-ence of 1965, it was clear to all who looked that, as Wilson later put it, 'there was virtually no willingness to improve intra-Commonwealth trading arrangements'. The following year he told the Commonwealth Secretary-General of a more general disillusion: 'The Commonwealth showed little disposition to help Britain or to play a constructive part, for example, at the UN'.[28] Part of the problem was the souring of rela-tions by political issues, most importantly Rhodesia. But the economic obstacles were also immense. As noted above, intra-Commonwealth trade had been declining from its post-war peak since the early 1950s. This was not largely the result of what Wilson called 'Conservative neglect', except in the sense that it followed from the general Con-servative encouragement of trade liberalisation. This dismantling of the discriminatory trade rules of the 1930s and 1940s allowed market forces to exert themselves, and the resulting trade pattern reflected the new dynamics of international trade emerging in the 1950s and 1960s. Britain's historic nineteenth-century role as overwhelmingly an importer of food and raw materials was shifting as manufactured goods became increas-ingly dominant in imports as well as exports, aided by support for domestic agriculture (Table 2.1). This was a key part of the 'golden age' of capitalism, as the major Western European and North American economies increasingly swapped manufactures for manufactures as the staple of their trade. In this process, the Commonwealth, outside Britain, consisting largely of rich but small or large but poor countries, was increasingly marginal to Britain, and they themselves were also enthusi-astically developing trade links with non-Commonwealth countries.

Most Labour policy-makers were reluctant to accept this trend. In part this related to a hostility to trade liberalisation, which was seen as allowing a 'fragmentation' of the Commonwealth. Such views were most consistently aired by Balogh, long an advocate of retaining discrimin-atory rules to encourage Commonwealth trade.[29] But even those with

Table 2.1 Composition of British imports, 1946–49 to 1960–69 (percentages)

	Manufactures	*Primary products*
1946–49	17	83
1950–59	23	77
1960–69	41	59

Source: R. Rowthorn and J. Wells, *De-industrialization and Foreign Trade* (Cambridge, 1987), p. 173.

more liberal economic views tended to believe that it was Tory 'mismanagement' between 1951 and 1964 which was weakening Commonwealth trading links, rather than this reflecting new patterns of trade growth. A more sophisticated view recognised the growth of intra-industry (and, by extension, largely non-Commonwealth) trade, but argued this was less advantageous than the Commonwealth pattern of swapping manufactures for food and raw materials. In this view, swapping Renault Dauphines for Morris Minors was less beneficial than swapping cars for raw materials.[30] But even if one ignored the rising appetite of British consumers for sophisticated imported manufactures made by other rich countries, the obvious problem of the Commonwealth was that it contained too few of the rich of the world to form a major expanding market for the products of the poor. The degree of commonality of interest was limited and declining.

The pro-Commonwealth attitudes of Labour around 1964 were in part a reflection of Labour's accurate perception that the Attlee government had effectively encouraged Commonwealth trade, and that this had been to Britain's immediate advantage. Disillusion swiftly followed from Labour 'bringing a 1951 approach to bear on a situation which fourteen years had radically changed'.[31] But, more specifically, the pro-Commonwealth attitude was reinforced by Labour's hostility to the first Conservative application to join the EEC in 1961. The likely implications of this policy for links with the Commonwealth provided an easily wielded stick for Labour to beat the Tories with during the latter's last years in government.[32] Labour presented itself as the defender of Commonwealth interests against Tory betrayal. Yet such a stance became less politically attractive as relations with much of the Commonwealth cooled after 1964, and simultaneously Commonwealth countries became less vociferous in their concerns about Britain's possible entry.[33] Whereas the Commonwealth had been portrayed as a key obstacle to membership of the EEC in 1961, by 1966/67 Labour was willing to treat the question as one of a limited number of negotiable problems (New Zealand dairy products, tropical produce).[34]

The sterling area

Officially, the sterling area was quite distinct from the Commonwealth, the former being an economic entity that excluded Canada but that included some Middle East non-members of the latter. But politically the two were often treated as a common issue: 'Britain's leadership of the economic grouping helped to reinforce its traditional leadership of the political grouping'.[35] The area was a bloc of countries which held the bulk of their international exchange reserves in pounds, and which tied the value of their currency to sterling. As with Commonwealth trade, this sterling system had been immensely advantageous in most respects for Britain in the 1940s. In wartime it had facilitated Britain's extraordinary devotion of resources to the war effort by financing a large proportion of imports by the creation of sterling balances in favour of such countries as India and Egypt; this was, in effect, Britain paying for imports by future promises to pay. In the Attlee years it had aided the settlement of British dollar deficits, by Britain squeezing positive dollar trade balances out of dependent Commonwealth countries such as Malaya and the Gold Coast at a time of acute shortages of that currency. (Though it should be said that, in turn, much of this deficit arose from the payments position of other sterling countries, such as Australia.)[36]

The sterling area was not only closely linked to the idea of the Commonwealth as the key underpinning of Britain's world status, but it also, in most people's eyes, underlay the role of London as a key financial centre. Certainly in the 1940s and 1950s, most of the City's invisible business (trade finance, insurance, banking) was tied to sterling's place as the world's second most important currency after the dollar. The pound was a 'top' currency, whose status seemed assured.[37] Thus the value of sterling seemed to be linked to the sustaining of both the area itself and the success of an important part of Britain's trading economy.

Some questions about the benefits of the sterling area to Britain had been asked under the Attlee government, especially the way in which, because British investment in the area was unregulated, it facilitated the huge outflow of capital in the late 1940s. But the predominant assumption in Labour circles then and for a good few years after was that the area was a symbol of the continuing economic importance of Britain, and part of the cement of the Commonwealth. Tony Crosland, for example, in his book about the balance of payments published in 1953, while recognising the problem of its encouragement of very high capital outflows from Britain, overall clearly saw the area as a 'good thing'. He assumed that, in a world of continuing US export surplus and consequent dollar shortage, a discriminatory Commonwealth/sterling area bloc was vital for Britain, his main concern being to get the Dominion countries (Australia, New Zealand and South Africa) to accept more of the costs of running the area.[38]

In the early 1950s a more sceptical attitude became apparent in some academic literature, but it was not really until the area's role was linked to the nascent declinism of the late 1950s that criticism gained force and was taken up by some in Labour circles. A key text in declinism generally, but particularly in linking 'decline' to the sterling area, was Andrew Shonfield's *British Economic Policy Since the War*, first published in 1958. Shonfield presented a wide-ranging indictment of the area, which was to be a foundation for most future critiques. The area, he argued, starved British industry of capital by allowing free movement of funds to the Commonwealth (most of which went not to poor dependencies but the rich white Dominions). The area underpinned the 'obsession' with the international value of sterling. Its encouragement of the use of sterling made the pound inescapably vulnerable to speculative 'flurries', which then had to be fought off by deflationary domestic policies, reducing investment and retarding growth. He also suggested that much of the City of London's activity was *not* dependent on the strength of sterling, and therefore the direct economic benefits were almost vanishingly small.[39]

Such arguments, coming broadly from the centre-left, were taken seriously by Labour. In December 1957 the party set up a Working Group on the Sterling Area, within which the issues were debated. For this group, chaired by Roy Jenkins, and including Harold Wilson, Douglas Jay, Patrick Gordon Walker and Thomas Balogh, the problem of the area was intimately linked to the viability of the Commonwealth as an economic zone. On one hand was the view expressed by Robert Neild and Alan Day, and similar to that of Shonfield, that the key aim was to reduce Britain's overseas commitments, cut back on capital exports, and that broadly the sterling area was a burden on Britain rather than an advantage.[40] On the other hand was the Balogh view, that the key issue was to reverse the movement towards trade and exchange liberalisation in order to rebuild a sustainable Commonwealth/sterling bloc as the key to the improvement of Britain's payments position. The report of the Working Group did not come out clearly in favour of either of these views, but recommended further exchange control within the area, the encouragement of bulk purchasing agreements within the Commonwealth, agreements with the holders on an orderly rundown of sterling balances, the end of official support for transferable sterling, and greater co-operation within the area on the use of the area's exchange reserves. It concluded by noting the broader issue of international liquidity within which the sterling issue was embedded.[41] These discussions showed the continuing strength of pro-Commonwealth views in the party, the continuing attachment to trade controls, a growth in scepticism about the benefits of the sterling area, but an unwillingness to accept the full logic of the declinist case for effectively abolishing the area and ceasing to regard safeguarding the pound's international role as a significant policy goal.

Roy Jenkins, in a book written to coincide with the 1959 general election, *The Labour Case*, accepted Shonfield's argument that the benefits of sterling's role in terms of aiding the prosperity of the City of London was greatly overstated, and in general regarded sterling's status as a problem, but did not spell out how this problem was to be dealt with.[12] As with the issue of Commonwealth trade, the early 1960s seem to have witnessed a more positive attitude towards the sterling area, as something to be defended against emergent Tory 'Europeanism'.

During the course of the government's life after 1964, we can crudely summarise the policy position on the sterling area as evolving from one of defending its value to Britain (and the Commonwealth) to one of acceptance that it imposed burdens which were no longer outweighed by its benefits. To some extent this was part of the bigger story of disillusion with the Commonwealth and a growing enthusiasm for Europe, where the area was at best irrelevant, and at worst positively harmful to Britain's chance of entry into the Common Market – it became a significant problem for the second British application, in 1967.[13] But this evolution was never straightforward, and came only after some painful re-evaluations.

Labour's broad position in the face of the balance of payments deficit it faced on coming to office was famously that, while it could be solved by avoiding either devaluation or deflation, it would better be solved by pursuing a 'third way' of modernisation of the economy and greater efficiency. In this perspective, balance of payments difficulties were largely a problem of Britain's lack of competitiveness. This stance was used to argue that the vulnerability of Britain to sterling crises arose neither from the currency's overvaluation nor from the existence of the sterling area. If holders of sterling withdrew their holdings, this was because of their perception of the weakness of the British balance of payments; once this was corrected, the vulnerability to sterling flight would disappear.

In a post-mortem on the problems of sterling in 1964/65, this emphasis on the competitiveness issue was sustained by Treasury advisers. They argued that while the imbalance of sterling assets and liabilities was linked to the role of the pound as a key currency, the underlying issue was Britain's payments weakness.[14] But they also recognised that this broad stance did not rule out action to correct the asset–liability ratio, though they had no specific suggestions on how to do this. This kind of focus on domestic matters was, of course, music to the ears of conservative forces such as the Bank of England, and the advisers' report was for the Bank a useful weapon to use in its urging of cuts in public spending and other deflationary policies. But it would be wrong to suggest that criticism of the sterling area was not heard in ministerial circles at this time. The covering summary of the Treasury experts' report to the Prime Minister rightly suggested the existence of 'a general feeling that the Sterling Area has become in some respects one-sided', though it also noted a lack of 'radical proposals to dismantle it'.[45]

These doubts about the area were partly due to the recognition of Britain's problems on the *capital* as well as current account of the balance of payments, and the way in which the sterling area encouraged such flows. But any proposal to regulate British investment elsewhere in the area would undermine the main reason for those countries being members, and therefore bring the whole edifice into question.[46]

Another problem of the area that was subject to increasing concern in the mid-1960s was the diversification of reserves out of pounds by member states. Generally the problem was not one of an absolute fall in sterling holdings, but rather that the volume was stagnating as countries increased total reserves and holdings of dollars and marks.[47] Such patterns tended to reinforce doubts about the extent to which the area could be seen as reinforcing Commonwealth links, especially when the countries involved included Australia and India. Like the weakening of Commonwealth trade links, a large part of this reserve diversification reflected long-term 'structural' patterns rather than short-term policy options, though enthusiasm for holding sterling was hardly encouraged by the persistent exchange rate pressure of 1964–67. This pressure led Commonwealth countries like Australia, as well as oil producers like Kuwait, to seek dollar guarantees for their sterling reserves, another sign of the weakness of Commonwealth solidarity. London's view was that this risk of a fall in the value of sterling holdings should be offset against the favourable access sterling area countries had to the London capital market, although 'voluntary' restraint operated on these out-flows from 1966.[48]

One other underlying change of importance in shifting opinion against the area was the growing recognition that the role of the City of London would not be hard hit by any diminution in the role of sterling – that the City was an 'offshore' entity which could happily operate in other currencies, especially dollars. An important change here was that in the mid-1960s this argument was being made by City supporters as well as critics, most notably William Clarke. He cut across the traditional declinist doctrine that commitment to the pound had favoured the City at the expense of industry by arguing that: 'It is the City's usefulness both to Britain and to the world that attracts pounds to London, not the prestige surrounding a reserve currency'. By late 1966 this view was readily accepted in the Treasury.[49]

All these growing doubts about the area could have little direct effect on policy while devaluation remained 'unmentionable'. But after the government was forced to devalue the pound in November 1967, events moved swiftly towards an effective dismantling of the area, the Basle agreements of 1968 offering a guarantee for sterling holdings in dollars. Formal control over investment in the sterling area followed in 1972.[50] While sterling was long to continue as a 'vehicle' currency, its future was dependent on straightforward financial calculation by holders, and was no longer part of any grand design.

There is a sense in which the demise of the sterling area was inevitable in the 1960s, as its raison d'être evaporated, and the crisis of the global monetary system meant international help was available to help manage the process.[51] When the French used its existence as an excuse to veto Britain's Common Market application in 1967, they were looking backwards rather than forwards. The very fact of that application signalled that Britain had radically re-evaluated the Commonwealth–sterling area link, and decided the future lay elsewhere. After devaluation this became evident to all. As Chancellor after 1967, Jenkins unsuccessfully sought the help of Australia in stemming the flow of capital out of Britain. 'Not much kith and kin about that', he remarked.[52] That may stand as an epitaph on both the Commonwealth and sterling area by the end of the 1960s.

The US connection

Under the Attlee government, a range of competing attitudes were at work in shaping policy towards the USA. In grand political terms, there was acceptance that, in the short run, Britain could revive its world status only in co-operation with the USA, and on most foreign policy issues co-operation was indeed notable, despite occasional signs of resentment at the Americans' clear ability to dominate in the West.[53] Economically, too, despite doubts and even anger at US 'high-handedness' and unwillingness to treat Britain as necessarily 'special', it was generally recognised in Labour circles that the 1945 loan and Marshall aid were crucial to Britain's economic and political position. Mindful of the scale of Britain's dependence on international trade, most Labour policy-makers in the late 1940s were willing to go along with the US view that, *in the long run*, Britain's prosperity would be best served by a liberal international trade regime. However, across the spectrum of Labour opinion was the view that such liberalisation would be a very slow process, not only because of the scale of the post-war dollar shortage, but also because the USA itself might well be a major source of instability in the international economy, and defences would need to be maintained against such an eventuality. Thus, for all the vaunted liberalisation of economic policy in the last phase of the Attlee government, ministers and advisers were still strongly committed to controls over international transactions, as Neil Rollings has emphasised. This meant, in particular, a belief that discrimination against the dollar by the imposition of limits on US imports would have to be sustained for a very long period into the future.[54]

Because of such views, Labour was critical of the Conservatives after 1951 as they slowly liberalised trade and payments. Imperial preference remained notionally intact in the 1950s, but was rapidly eroded by the changing composition of trade and the effects of inflation on specific duties. The Conservative leadership, while not explicitly repudiating the importance of Commonwealth trade, allowed the link to fade. Similarly, they pursued sterling convertibility, which inescapably reduced the significance of the sterling area to the fortunes of the pound, and the de facto convertibility of sterling from 1954. These were not explicitly 'pro-American' policies, but they did link British policy to the US liberalisation agenda.[55] The Labour leadership in these opposition years remained committed to the political and military alliance with the USA, but became increasingly critical of the scale of overseas military spending, though the Conservatives were also starting to worry about this in the second half of the 1950s.[56] Other aspects of the US alliance also came to be questioned, especially in the light of declinist allegations about the seriousness of Britain's economic position. For example, Labour even under Attlee had been keen to maximise trade with the Soviet bloc, and a similar attitude was taken in support of the Conservative government's desire to trade with Cuba in the early 1960s. But such economic issues, or even big political issues like the recognition of Communist China, were pinpricks in the overall close relations between post-war British and US governments, and nothing in Labour's approach before 1964 heralded a sharp break. There was no ambition to reverse the general trend towards trade liberalisation; even the inveterate anti-free-trader Balogh accepted by 1961 that, however regrettable, the trend to liberalisation was largely irreversible.[57] Similarly, especially in the light of the easing of the dollar shortage, Labour did not seek to reverse the trend towards the pound's convertibility.

Under Wilson, relations with the USA were to be characterised by frequent and highly publicised summits between the Prime Minister and President Johnson. The frequency of these meetings (usually initiated by the British side) partly reflected Wilson's desire to be seen as a world statesman, able to talk 'man to man' with the American leader. Critics of the Wilson government have linked this anxiety to be heard in Washington to a subordination to US policy, not least on the Vietnam issue. Yet one of the features of these visits was that while the President wanted to speak mainly (and eventually almost exclusively) about Vietnam, the British by and large wanted to talk about economic matters.[58] For the British, to make an obvious point, Vietnam was not a very important issue in its own right, whereas for Johnson it became almost an obsession.

Anglo-American economic relations in the 1960s have to be set firmly in the broader 'crisis' of the Bretton Woods financial system.[59] In brief, this crisis resulted from the conjunction of two major problems – liquidity and balance of payments adjustment. The Bretton Woods system was essentially a dollar system, in which most countries built up dollar reserves at the (relative) expense of gold and pounds. But these accumulations were possible only as long as the US ran payments deficits and non-Americans felt confident about the value of the dollar. In the 1960s there were growing concerns about the capacity of this arrangement to finance rapidly growing world trade, not least because of US worries about the deficits (as well as attacks, especially by France, on the power this arrangement gave to the USA). In response to such fears, new sources of liquidity were sought, resulting in the General Agreement to Borrow among the G10 countries in 1962, and the creation of special drawing rights in the International Monetary Fund (IMF) from 1968.[60]

Parallel worries arose from the issue of exchange rate adjustment. Bretton Woods established a system of stable but not irrevocably fixed rates, but these became invested with enormous political significance, so adjustment either up (e.g. West Germany) or down (e.g. Britain) became a source of great trauma. Linked to this growth of rigidity was the question of 'surveillance'. If countries were to borrow to defend the existing exchange rate, what degree of oversight would be acceptable from the IMF and other lenders? Given the political sensitivity of national economic management, this issue again raised concerns going far beyond the technicalities of international finance.[61]

In this context, while Britain was undeniably the weaker economic partner in the Anglo-American relationship, this weakness, paradoxically, could strengthen its bargaining power.[62] Britain was a supplicant in Washington, seeking support for the pound, but the US response to these supplications was strongly influenced by the feeling that if the pound were to 'go', the dollar would follow. Help to Britain therefore became a first line of defence for the dollar, at a time when, because of the USA's own balance of payments deficit, the value and role of that currency were coming under question. This was linked to the broader agreement between Britain and America on the need for an expansion of world liquidity, not dependent upon the supply of pounds, dollars or gold. This was eventually to lead to the creation of special drawing rights at the IMF.[63] But broadly similar views about the desirable shape of the international monetary system did not necessarily lead to convergence on an appropriate British strategy to defend the pound. There were sharp divisions of opinion in Washington about how Britain should be advised to proceed. On the one hand, Robert McNamara, the US

Defense Secretary, wanted Britain to share the burden of defence spending, especially in Asia, and not to allow the USA to become 'the world's only policeman'. When, from 1965, British ministers talked in public about the need for defence cuts east of Suez, this received a distinctly cool response in Washington. Wilson's pointing out to the Americans that Britain spent a larger proportion of its GDP on overseas military expenditure than the USA was a further part of this argument. In recognition, the USA did negotiate hard with Germany to help Britain offset the costs of the British Army of the Rhine, which were a prominent part of this overseas military spending.[64]

On the other hand, there was the presidential adviser George Ball, who broadly accepted the 'declinist' account of Britain, and believed it had to cut the coat of its global ambition to the reduced cloth available. This negatively meant an acceptance that its role east of Suez would have to be curtailed, but more positively reinforced the long-standing US view that Britain should join the Common Market.[65] (This argument also tied in with the US view that Britain should be realistic about its status and resources and not attempt to be an independent nuclear power.)

While resistance to devaluation from 1964 to 1967 was reinforced by US support, the reasons why Labour followed this course were fundamentally matters of domestic politics. The government believed that devaluation would be a fatal condemnation of Labour's capacity for economic management, would lead to a cut in real wages, and that 'modernisation' provided a way of avoiding such a policy without recourse to a damaging deflation.[66] In this endeavour ministers were able to rely on US support for all measures to defend the pound. There were no American protests over the import surcharge of 1964, though this could clearly be seen as a blow to the multilateral trade system.[67] The deflationary measures which followed were also welcomed in Washington, as was the attempt to pursue an incomes policy.

The records of the meetings in this period show how keen the Americans were to secure British support for US policy in Vietnam, and there was considerable fury in the Johnson administration when Wilson equivocated in this. Generally, his line was to offer overall support but also to question American tactics. This caused much disquiet in the Labour Party, and much condemnation from subsequent historians. Two points may be made about this issue. At the most general level, it is worth noting that, whatever the merits of the matter, the British stance was not important to US decision-making; it was a comfort to have British general support, and an annoyance when Wilson equivocated, but basically US policy on Vietnam was decided by the course of the war and its effects on American public opinion. Whatever Britain did or might have done would have made little practical difference. On the specific economic issue of how far US financial support was dependent on Labour's stance on Vietnam, no conclusive answer can be provided, but, given the weight of other reasons for the USA helping in the defence of the pound, again it seems reasonable to conclude that the importance of the Vietnam issue can be overstated.[68]

After devaluation in 1967, the sterling crisis continued, and both Washington and London were concerned about a second devaluation. The USA was upset by the cancellation of the F-111 fighter aircraft in 1968, but generally co-operation continued to be close, and was helped by the ending of the sterling area, which many Americans had seen as a hindrance to the defence of the pound.[69]

The third circle: Europe

The Attlee government was not as uniformly hostile to ideas of European unity as later proponents of the 'Britain missed the bus' thesis would suggest. Most strikingly, Ernest Bevin as Foreign Secretary showed considerable sympathy for such ideas, his main objection being to what he saw as the lack of pragmatism shown in the hurried pursuit of this idea. Ultimately, while Labour policy-makers were not unaware of the attractions of closer European integration, the counter-pulls of Commonwealth trade and the desire to appease the US desire for multilateral trade outweighed such attractions, especially as the European Coal and Steel Community and later the EEC were seen as likely to involve the creation of a highly protected trading bloc. Also important was the opposition to any diminution of sovereignty, and this was another theme which was long to have an echo in Labour's discussions of Europe.[70]

The issue of European integration did not figure much in Labour discussions in the 1950s; the Commonwealth and the USA were much more important. Labour broadly supported the Conservatives' refusal to participate in the founding of the EEC, and backed the counter-proposal for what became the European Free Trade Association (EFTA). EEC membership was not a straightforward left versus right issue, and this complicated the debate, especially as for some on the revisionist right pro-Europeanism was *the* article of faith.[71] But the issue had little prominence in the party until the Conservatives' approach to an application for membership in 1961 was accompanied by a very wide-ranging debate in Labour circles about the costs and benefits of membership. Much of this debate focused on political issues, but the economic differences were also intensive as well as divisive.

In early 1961, a sub-committee of the party's Finance and Economic Policy Committee produced a draft statement on the issue that played down the likely economic impact of British entry, arguing that the greater economic dynamism of the Six was due to their national policies, not the EEC. The report accepted that increased competition within a free trade area might stimulate British competitive efficiency, but played down the significance of this. In this way, the report dismissed the two main economic arguments which were being put forward in favour of Britain's entry, to the annoyance of both Euro enthusiasts, like Jenkins, and those wholly hostile, like Jay. Balogh, while recording his continuing preference for a Commonwealth bloc, was willing to accept that membership might be 'the sole means by which British industry can be jolted into a new dynamic mould', but he regarded this as a last resort 'if all else fails'. However, the following year he was arguing in the 'Common Market Alternatives' group that the 'co-ordination and fiscal incentives for investment planning' he believed were needed in Britain would be impossible under EEC rules, although also, bizarrely, that what Britain needed was the policies which had produced the French and Italian economic 'miracles'.[72]

In the light of such confusion, it is not surprising that Labour's position appeared unclear until Gaitskell made his famous '1000 years of British history' speech in September 1962, which, like much of the Labour Party debate, relied primarily on political assertion rather than economic calculation. This partly reflected Gaitskell's clear perception that the economic case was very well balanced, a view common among economists at the time. This speech set down five conditions for Britain's entry, covering Commonwealth trade, Britain's EFTA partners, home agriculture, the freedom to plan the economy, and the freedom to pursue an independent foreign policy. These five conditions were to be incorporated in the policy statement *Labour and the Common Market* (1962) and retained by Labour as the official stance down to the 'reassessment' of 1965/66.[73] Gaitskell's speech seriously divided the Labour right, its stress on the Commonwealth link being, in Jenkins' view, based on a 'false premise' that 'the Commonwealth is capable of offering Britain the same advantages, from an alternative source, as Europe offers. What Europe offers us economically is the stimulus of becoming part of a very large, unified, dynamic, and highly competitive market.' But for the time being Gaitskell's posture seemed to settle the debate on Labour's policy, unifying the party against the Conservatives in the run-up to the 1964 election.[74] But when Harold Wilson emerged as leader the following year, the way was open for a 'pragmatic' adjustment of Labour's policy in the years of government.

Labour's decision to seek entry into the EEC (culminating in Charles de Gaulle's veto in 1967, but renewed in 1970 after his departure) was fundamentally strategic and political or, as Wilson put it, aimed at achieving Britain's 'politico-military objectives'. This political motivation is dealt with in depth in John Young's companion volume on international policy, and here it is necessary only to summarise the always subordinate economic debate, a debate which in any event had few immediate policy consequences, given de Gaulle's veto of Britain's application.[75]

The pro-EEC political and economic arguments had a common starting point in their assumption that it was only as part of a bigger bloc of countries that Britain could prosper, either as a world power or economically. As a senior official argued in 1966: 'On her own Britain is an outsider looking in on the other three power complexes, and whether in the political or in the economic context, the lot of the outsider in these circumstances is an unenviable one'.[76] Advocacy of EEC entry on economic grounds therefore fitted with Labour beliefs that 'big is beautiful'. This was expressed in three main ways. The first two were the 'cold douche' of competition and economies of scale already gone over in the early 1960s. A third, very Wilsonian argument was the technological: that only within the framework of the EEC would the full benefits of advanced technology be realised.[77] In 1966 Wilson summarised his view on the first two of these points: 'the arguments based on the advantages of scale to be derived from membership of a much larger market, were of greater weight than those related to the "cold douche" of competition to be expected in these circumstances'. As well as expressing an ideological preference, this line may also have been affected by the enthusiasm of the Confederation of British Industry (CBI) for the EEC, and the government's belief that, because of the economies of scale argument, entry would stimulate employers to invest more, always a key government ambition, and particularly important after Labour's increasingly deflationary policies.[78]

The technological argument was highly vulnerable to the riposte that Britain was already, without being a member, co-operating with EEC members on such projects as Concorde, the Channel Tunnel and the European Launcher Development Organisation. Advocates of entry argued that such bilateral deals are 'cumbersome and are limited in scope and they offer no real alternatives to the close technical involvement and the tariff-free exchanges over a wide field which can only be obtained from membership of a wider group'.[79]

The obvious problem with these arguments was their vagueness. The competition/economies of scale points were in principle perfectly respectable economic arguments, but supported by little in the way of evidence. Pointing to the recent faster growth in EEC members than in Britain was hardly convincing evidence of the effects of the EEC, given the more plausible argument, made especially clearly by Nicholas Kaldor, the Chancellor's adviser, that rapid Continental expansion was a consequence of the rundown of agricultural employment. The technological argument was, as Broad suggests, 'a bargaining chip and a rhetorical device' rather than a serious economic position.[80]

While the postulated economic benefits were highly speculative, the costs, although not easily calculable, could be stated with greater precision. Exclusion of food at world prices would increase both the price of imports and the cost of living; a shift to the Common Agricultural Policy (CAP) would raise domestic food prices and lead to substantial net payments to Brussels. Numbers could be attached to these effects, within broad ranges. Not surprisingly, EEC enthusiasts did not like these numbers, and tried to suggest they were unduly 'pessimistic', and that they ignored the unattractiveness of non-membership. Indeed, this latter point was a common refrain of enthusiasts – for them, there was no other big unit available as a viable alternative. Of course, such arguments assumed rather than demonstrated the premise that in the future only big units would work.[81] The emphasis on the EEC as the only appropriate arena for scale economies assumed that, outside the EEC, Britain's trade with members would be significantly constrained by the CET on manufactures. Yet Britain's trade with the EEC had been increasing by leaps and bounds, fuelled by the same switch to trade in manufactures which was reducing the importance of the Commonwealth. In any event, the CET was being reduced in the 1960s, and would become almost trivial by the end of the Kennedy Round.[82]

It is clear that the available economic arguments and calculations could not be used to make a strong case for Britain's EEC membership, but the search for entry went on regardless. For a time, in 1965 and 1966, the extent to which membership would inhibit the use of policy instruments like investment and regional subsidies and foreign exchange controls do seem to have figured significantly in the debate. Such worries were articulated at a time when the strategy of the National Plan still seemed broadly intact, and when faith in the capacity of national governments to control their economies was strong. But after the deflationary measures of July 1966 there was a clear loss of such faith; to an important degree EEC entry offered a replacement 'grand design' to the now discredited Plan.[83] By October 1966, while still concerned with the issue of controls over foreign investment, Wilson was arguing that 'experience suggests that our international financial obligations placed greater constraint on our economic and political independence than would the Treaty of Rome'.[84] In the context of economic modernisation, the realisation expressed by Wilson may have been the most important immediate consequence of the EEC debate – it suggested how difficult *any* programme of national improvement would be, given the tightness of external constraints.

Conclusions

Labour in its wilderness years after 1951 was slow to recognise the contingent nature of the strengthening of the Commonwealth and sterling
area in the 1930s and 1940s. While different policies under the Conservatives could have produced a different outcome, the dynamic of trade
growth in Europe, and the political and economic pressure for economic
liberalisation, meant that the rundown of these discriminatory zones
was inescapable. To a degree, the party's ideologues lurched too readily
from a striking complacency about these two issues in the early 1950s
to an excessively 'declinist' account of their effects in the late 1950s.
The evidence suggests that neither was that important in Britain's economic performance. Imperial trade did link Britain to a slow-growing
market, but it was a market that absorbed rapidly growing amounts
of fast-growing exports of metal and engineering goods. Equally, the
sterling area seems not to have been the key concern in accounting for
policy-makers' attachment to the value of sterling; it was not a significant cause of external instability; and, while it might have facilitated
foreign investment, this was *not* a major cause of domestic economic
shortcomings. In government after 1964, the romanticism about the
Commonwealth remained powerful in Labour circles, but attachment
to the sterling area proved less robust, and the area was effectively ter-
minated after devaluation.

Labour's attitudes to the USA were ambivalent. The Cold War reinforced a knee-jerk anti-Americanism on the left of the party while
simultaneously encouraging an unquestioning attitude of support on
the right. These attitudes came to matter to economic policy after 1964,
when the need for US support in defence of the pound ran up against
well grounded hostility to American intervention in Vietnam. The
(actually rather limited) attempt by the USA to use its financial leverage
to influence British foreign policy was much more overt than anything
attempted when Attlee had been in office, and turned economic policy
into a source of great bitterness in Labour ranks. Here, Labour's discussions in opposition proved of little value, though the experience of
the Suez crisis should have shown the party how ruthless the USA could
be in using its financial strength to pursue foreign policy objectives.

Labour was slow to recognise the dynamics of Europe's post-war growth,
though the extent to which this was dependent upon EEC membership
was exaggerated by Euro-enthusiasts like Jenkins. A greater understanding in this area would, at a minimum, have reduced the nostalgic yearning
after the Commonwealth as an economic unit, and at best would have
facilitated earlier entry into the Community, which, while probably not
transforming Britain's economic fortunes (nor giving 'the leadership'
of Europe to Britain),[85] would have necessarily been accompanied by a

more realistic understanding of Britain's economic and political status.
It would also have avoided that 'unexploded time bomb'[86] of European
policy from so disrupting Labour's next term of office, in the 1970s.

Notes

The place of publication is London unless otherwise specified.

1 A. Bullock, *Ernest Bevin, Foreign Secretary* (Oxford, 1985), part I. Gaitskell
   explicitly used this framework in his account of Britain's place in the world:
   see P. Williams, *Hugh Gaitskell* (Oxford, 1982), p. 390.
2 P. S. Gupta, *Imperialism and the British Labour Movement 1914–1964* (1975);
   Bullock, *Bevin*, p. 65.
3 A. R. Prest and C. Coppock, *The UK Economy: A Manual of Applied Economics*
   (1972), p. 119.
4 LPA, Conferences with Commonwealth Labour and Socialist leaders, June
   1957 and September 1962; Roy Jenkins, in D. Jay and R. Jenkins, *The
   Common Market Debate* (1962), p. 11.
5 T. Balogh, *Unequal Partners. Vol. 2* (Oxford, 1963).
6 For a critical account, see D. Seers and P. Streeten, 'Overseas development
   policies', in W. Beckerman (ed.), *The Labour Government's Economic Record
   1964–1970* (1972), pp. 118–56; D. Jay, *Change and Fortune: A Political Record*
   (1980), ch. 13.
7 Williams, *Gaitskell*, pp. 406–8; P. Ziegler, *Wilson: The Authorised Life* (1993),
   p. 131, also pp. 64, 66, 219; B. Pimlott, *Harold Wilson* (1992), pp. 433–4;
   J. B. D. Miller, *Survey of Commonwealth Affairs* (Oxford, 1974), p. 291.
8 *Hansard* (Commons), vol. 688, 6 February 1964, cols 1367–82, reprinted in
   H. Wilson, *The New Britain: Selected Speeches 1964* (1964), ch. 8; Labour
   Party, *Let's Go with Labour for the New Britain* (1964), pp. 13–14.
9 H. Wilson, *The Labour Government 1964–70: A Personal Record* (1974), p. 161.
10 PRO, CAB 134/1470, Chairman's note, 'Britain's trade with the Commonwealth', 29 March 1965, covering Board of Trade, 'Britain's trade with the
   Commonwealth', 1 March 1965.
11 D. Lee, *Middle Powers and Commercial Diplomacy: British Influences at the Kennedy
   Trade Round* (New York, 1999); E. H. Preeg, *Traders and Diplomats: An Analysis
   of the Kennedy Round Under the GATT* (New York, 1970).
12 The most detailed account of Labour and the EEC remains L. J. Robins,
   Labour and the European Community (Ormskirk, 1979), but see also U. Kitzinger,
   The Second Try: Labour and the EEC (Oxford, 1968).
13 PRO, CAB 134/1472, Board of Trade, 'Commonwealth preference and the
   Kennedy Round', 13 May 1965. Emphasis added.
14 PRO, CAB 134/1475, R. Powell, Board of Trade, 'Meeting of Commonwealth trade officials Nov. 1965', 15 December 1965; also PRO, DO 215/
   135, Note by Chairman of Economic Development (Official) Committee,
   'Commonwealth PM's Conference June 1965', 7 April 1965.
15 PRO, CAB 134/2626, Official Committee on Commercial Policy, 'Minutes',
   2 May 1966; CAB 134/1475, 'Meeting of officials'; PRO, CAB 134/1473,
   Board of Trade, 'UK objectives at meeting of Commonwealth trade officials',
   6 September 1965.
16 S. Dell, 'The origins of UNCTAD', in M. Z. Cutajor (ed.), *UNCTAD and the
   South North Dialogue* (Oxford, 1985), pp. 10–32; PRO, CAB 134/1472,
   'Britain's trade with the Commonwealth'.

17 PRO, CAB 134/1474, Board of Trade, 'Commodities', 22 November 1965.
18 Prices under the CSA were commonly asserted to be twice world prices, but world prices had very little meaning in such a restricted market. See Miller, *Survey*, p. 289; CAB 134/3036, 'Extension of Commonwealth Sugar Agreement', 9 November 1967, and 'Extension of Commonwealth Sugar Agreement', 29 October 1968. Australia also benefited from the CSA.
19 A. D. Morgan, 'Commercial policy', in F. T. Blackaby (ed.), *British Economic Policy 1960–74* (Cambridge, 1978), p. 527.
20 Seers and Streeten, 'Overseas development policies'; compare B. Tew, 'Policies aimed at improving the balance of payments', in Blackaby, *British*, pp. 319–20.
21 Wilson, *Labour Government*, p. 161; PRO, CAB 134/2628, Treasury, 'Procurement by public authorities', 2 May 1966; PRO, T 312/1113, Treasury, 'Financial advantages of Commonwealth membership', 16 March 1965, points out that the Franc Zone was not a relevant model for Commonweath relations, as it consisted of a small group of poor countries and one overwhelmingly dominant 'mother country'. On this see also PRO, DO 215/135, 'Commonwealth PM's Conference'.
22 PRO, CAB 134/1472, Board of Trade, 'Britain's trade with the Commonwealth', 1 March 1965, and Board of Trade, 'UK objectives at meeting of Commonwealth trade officials', 6 September 1965; CAB 134/3038, Board of Trade, 'Imports of butter', 24 January 1969.
23 PRO, CAB 134/2626, Official Committee on Commercial Policy, 'Meeting', 2 May 1966; CAB 134/2627, 'Three Indian papers for discussion by Commonwealth trade officials', 20 March 1966.
24 PRO, CAB 134/2628, Treasury, 'Procurement by public authorities', 2 May 1966; CAB 134/1472, Board of Trade, 'Britain's trade with the Commonwealth', 1 March 1965; PRO, CAB 134/1473, Board of Trade, 'Proposals for meetings on Commonwealth trade agreements', 22 July 1965.
25 PRO, PREM 13/183, D. Jay to H. Wilson, 3 June 1965.
26 PRO, CAB 134/1746, 'Meeting of Commonwealth trade officials', 29 November 1965; PRO, DO 162/37, Michael Stewart to Harold Wilson, 3 March 1965; CAB 134/1475, Official Committee on Commercial Policy, 'Meeting', 23 March 1965.
27 PRO, PREM 13/182, 'Commonwealth trade and aid', 1 April 1967.
28 Wilson, *Labour Government*, p. 117; Miller, *Survey*, pp. 293, 300; PRO, PREM 13/1367, Note of meeting, PM with Secretary-General of Commonwealth, 5 April 1967.
29 PRO, PREM 13/183, T. Balogh to G. Brown, 17 July 1965; PREM 13/773, T. Balogh, 'UK objectives at the meeting of Commonwealth trade officials', 22 September 1965; Jay, *Change and Fortune*, p. 349.
30 P. Streeten and H. Corbet (eds), *Commonwealth Policy in a Global Context* (1973).
31 Miller, *Survey*, p. 293.
32 For Tory attempts to revive Commonwealth links after the failure of the application for Common Market entry in 1963, see PRO, T 312/706, 'A. Douglas-Home to Commonwealth Secretary-General', 31 January 1964; T 312/1114, 'Proposals for strengthening economic, commercial and cultural links with the Commonwealth', February 1964.
33 PRO, FCO 20/24, J. Callaghan to H. Wilson, 22 September 1967; FCO 20/38, Brief for Secretary of State, 'Commonwealth aspects of application to join EEC', 28 September 1967; PRO, T 312/1113, M. Widdup, 'Dr. Balogh on Commonwealth trade and aid', 2 April 1965.

34 P. Alexander, 'The Labour government, Commonwealth policy and the second application to join the EEC, 1964–67', in A. May (ed.), *Britain, the Commonwealth and Europe. The Commonwealth and Britain's Application to Join the European Communities* (2001), pp. 132–55.
35 Miller, *Survey*, p. 271.
36 A. Cairncross, *Years of Recovery: British Economic Policy 1945–1951* (1985), pp. 117–20; J. Tomlinson, *Democratic Socialism and Economic Policy: The Attlee Years 1945–51* (Cambridge, 1997), pp. 58–64.
37 S. Strange, *Sterling and British Policy* (Oxford, 1971).
38 A. Crosland, *Britain's Economic Problem* (1953), ch. 7.
39 A. Shonfield, *British Economic Policy Since the War* (Harmondsworth, 1958), especially ch. 6.
40 LPA, Finance and Economic Policy Sub-committee, Working Group on the Sterling Area, Minutes and papers 1957–59; R. Neild, 'Capital movements and the problem of sterling', *District Bank Review*, 124 (1957), pp. 3–20; A. C. L. Day, *The Future of Sterling* (Oxford, 1954); idem, 'What price the sterling area?', *Listener*, 21 November 1957.
41 LPA, Re 254, Balogh, 'Thoughts on the sterling area' (1957); LPA, Re 299, 'The Labour Party and the future of sterling' (1958).
42 R. Jenkins, *The Labour Case* (1959), ch. 5.
43 C. Schenk, 'Sterling, international monetary reform and Britain's application to join the European Economic Community in the 1960s', *Contemporary European History*, 11 (2002), pp. 345–69.
44 PRO, T 312/1484, R. Kahn *et al.*, 'Report of the enquiry into the position of sterling 1964–5', 1 June 1966.
45 PRO, PREM 13/853, 'Meeting of Governor of Bank of England with PM and Chancellor', 15 July 1966; PRO, T 312/1706, 'Sterling balances: ways to improve asset:liability ratio', June 1967; PREM 13/852, 'Report of enquiry into the position of sterling 1964–5'.
46 PRO, PREM 13/250, T. Balogh to W. Armstrong, 'Overseas investment', 11 February 1965.
47 PRO, T 312/1700, Bank of England, 'The problem of the sterling balances', 1 November 1965, and Treasury, 'Diversification of sterling area reserves' (n.d.).
48 PRO, T 312/1487, 'Policy on exchange guarantees 1961–66'; T 312/1701, Bank of England, 'Treasury paper on OSA diversification', 1 November 1967; T 312/1487, D. Hubback, 'Dr. Coombs', 20 July 1965; Tew, 'Policies', pp. 335–6.
49 W. Clarke, *The City in the World Economy* (Harmondsworth, 1967), p. 245; PRO, T 312/1949, W. Clarke, 'How far does the City depend on sterling?', 21 November 1966.
50 Tew, 'Policies', pp. 336–7.
51 C. Schenk, 'The sterling area and British policy alternatives in the 1950s', *Contemporary Record*, 6 (1992), pp. 271–4.
52 Cited in Miller, *Survey*, p. 295.
53 J. Kent, *British Imperial Strategy and the Origins of the Cold War* (Leicester, 1993), ch. 1. For an insightful assessment of the tensions within Labour's international economic policy, see R. Toye, 'The Labour Party's external economic policy in the 1940s', *Historical Journal*, 43 (2000), pp. 189–215.
54 J. Tomlinson, 'Marshall aid and the "shortage economy" in Britain in the 1940s', *Contemporary European History*, 9 (2000), pp. 137–55; N. Rollings, '"The Reichstag method of governing"? The Attlee government and permanent economic controls', in H. Mercer, N. Rollings and J. Tomlinson (eds), *Labour Governments and Private Industry: The Experience of 1945–51* (Edinburgh,

1992), pp. 15–36; H. Wilson, *In Place of Dollars* (1952); Crosland, *Britain's Economic Problem.*

55 C. Schenk, *Britain and the Sterling Area: From Devaluation to Convertibility in the 1950s* (1994), p. 61; N. Tiratsoo and J. Tomlinson, *The Conservatives and Industrial Efficiency, 1951–64: Thirteen Wasted Years?* (1998), pp. 104–8.

56 Tiratsoo and Tomlinson, *Conservatives*, pp. 159–62.

57 Miller, *Survey*, p. 352; LPA, RD 146, T. Balogh, 'Britain's relations to the Common Market' (1961).

58 C. Ponting, *Breach of Promise. Labour in Power 1964–1970* (1989); PRO, PREM 13/1906, '1967 US visit', record of conversation L. B. Johnson and H. Wilson, 2 June 1967.

59 For an excellent discussion, see R. Roy, 'The battle of the pound: the political economy of Anglo-American relations 1964–1968' (unpublished PhD dissertation, University of London, 2001). Key points from this thesis are addressed in R. Roy, 'The battle for Bretton Woods: America, Britain and the international financial crisis of October 1967–November 1968', *Cold War History*, 2 (2002), pp. 33–60.

60 H. James, *International Monetary Co-operation Since Bretton Woods* (Washington, DC, 1996), ch. 6.

61 *Ibid.*, ch. 7.

62 S. Strange, *The Sterling Problem and the Six* (1967), p. 39.

63 Lyndon Baines Johnson Library, NSF, NSC History Box 53, 'Gold crisis Nov. 1967–Mar. 1968'; PRO, T 312/1704, 'Measures to protect sterling 1964–66'; T 312/1207, R. Neild to J. Rickett, 7 December 1965; T 312/1768, Treasury, 'International liquidity and monetary reform', 22 May 1967.

64 PRO, T 312/1206, 'Chancellor of the Exchequer meeting with McNamara', 30 June 1965; PRO, CAB 148/72, Defence and Overseas Policy (Official) Committee, 'British defence contribution to NATO', 18 January 1966; J. Dumbrell, 'The Johnson administration and the British Labour government: Vietnam, the pound and east of Suez', *Journal of American Studies*, 30 (1996), pp. 211–31.

65 G. Ball, *The Past Has Another Pattern* (New York, 1982), p. 210; Lyndon Baines Johnson Library, NSF, Files Box 209, 'UK Vol. 3', Ball to President, 22 July 1967; Lyndon Baines Johnson Library, Country File UK, Box 216, W. Rostow to President, 29 July 1966; PRO, PREM 13/2450, Meeting, PM, Chancellor of the Exchequer and G. Ball, 9 September 1965.

66 T. Bale, 'Dynamics of a non-decision: the "failure" to devalue the pound, 1964–7', *Twentieth Century British History*, 10 (1997), pp. 192–217; R. Stones, 'Government–finance relations in Britain 1964–7: a tale of three cities', *Economy and Society*, 19 (1990), pp. 32–55.

67 Lyndon Baines Johnson Library, NSF Country File UK, Box 206, PM Wilson visit briefing book, Rostow to President, 29 July 1966; J. Young, 'Britain and LBJ's war 1964–68', *Cold War History*, 2 (2002), pp. 63–92.

68 PRO, T 312/1470, Treasury, 'Brief for Chancellor of the Exchequer visit to Washington', 25 January 1966.

69 PRO, PREM 13/2454, 'USA 1968', February 1968; T 312/2271/2/3, 'Visit of Chancellor of the Exchequer to USA April 1969', March–June 1969; T 312/2454, 'Dean to Foreign Office', 5 February 1968, 12 February 1968. On this period see also Chapter 3.

70 J. Young, *Britain, France and the Unity of Europe* (Leicester, 1984), introduction, pp. 38–9, 151, 153.

71 M. Camps, *Britain and the European Community 1955–1963* (1964), p. 109; S. Haseler, *The Gaitskellites: Revisionism in the Labour Party* (1969), pp. 227–36.

72 LPA, RD 126, 'Britain and Europe: a draft statement' (1961); LPA, RD 146, 'Britain's relations'; LPA, RD 360, 'The alternative to the Common Market' (1962).

73 Williams, *Gaitskell*, ch. 23; Haseler, *Gaitskellites*, p. 230; Labour Party, *Labour and the Common Market* (1962).

74 R. Jenkins, *Essays and Speeches* (1967), p. 119 (first published in *Encounter*, August 1961); Haseler, *Gaitskellites*, pp. 227–36.

75 PRO, CAB 134/2705, 'Ministerial Committee on Europe', 9 May 1966; Wilson in *Hansard* (Commons), vol. 746, 2 May 1967, cols 310–14. The EEC application, despite being unsuccessful, affected policy discussions in such areas as value added tax, monopolies and decimal currency.

76 PRO, CAB 134/2705, 'Future dealings with Europe', 4 May 1966. On the policy dynamics of the time, see H. Parr, '"Gone native": the Foreign Office and the second application', in O. Daddow (ed.), *Wilson and Europe 1964–67* (2002), pp. 89–120.

77 PRO, T 312/1567, 'Broad outlines of the case for membership', April 1966; H. Parr, 'Harold Wilson, Whitehall and Britain's policy towards the EEC, 1964–1967' (unpublished PhD dissertation, University of London, 2002), pp. 152–3.

78 PRO, CAB 128/41, 'Cabinet conclusions, Wilson's report on Exchequer discussions of 22 October', 1 November 1966; PRO, PREM 13/1474, 'Membership of EU–CBI/TUC consultations 1966/7'. For CBI views, see N. Rollings, 'British industry and European integration, 1961–1973', *Business and Economic History*, 27 (1998), pp. 444–54.

79 PRO, BT 241/1360, D. Jay, 'Balance of advantage to UK trade of membership of EEC', 20 May 1965.

80 N. Kaldor, *Causes of the Slow Rate of Growth of the United Kingdom* (Cambridge, 1966); R. Broad, *Labour's European Dilemma: From Bevin to Blair* (2001), p. 63.

81 PRO, CAB 134/2757, 2758, 'Official Committee on Europe: Sub-committee on economic implications of UK membership of European Community', 1966; PRO, CAB 134/1771, 'Official External Economic Policy Committee', 9 April 1965; PRO, T 312/1776, 'Note by Chairman of Official Committee on Europe', September 1966.

82 Organisation for Economic Co-operation and Development, *Policy Perspectives for International Trade and Economic Relations* (Paris, 1972), pp. 53–4, shows that by the end of the Kennedy Round the EEC had lower industrial tariffs than the USA, Japan or the UK.

83 Parr, 'Harold Wilson', pp. 102–8, 150–1.

84 PRO, CAB 134/2705, 'Economic implications of UK membership of European Communities', 14 October 1966; PRO, CAB 128/41, 'Cabinet conclusions', 1 November 1966. On the government's strategy on EEC entry, see CAB 134/2803–6, 'Ministerial Committee on the Approach to Europe', 1967/68.

85 R. Denman, *Missed Chances: Britain and Europe in the Twentieth Century* (1996); E. Dell, *The Schuman Plan and the British Abdication of Leadership in Europe* (Oxford, 1995).

86 S. George, *Britain and European Integration* (1991), p. 75.

3

From crisis to crisis:
a narrative of policy

First term in office, 1964–66

Almost the whole period from 1964 to 1970 saw the government lurching from crisis to crisis as it grappled with short-term macro-economic
problems, mostly arising from external problems. The period began, as
it was to continue, with a foreign exchange crisis in the days surrounding the election in October 1964. As soon as they came into office, the
three senior ministers who dominated policy in the early days – Harold
Wilson, Chancellor of the Exchequer James Callaghan, and First Secretary
of State and effectively Deputy Prime Minister George Brown – were
faced with responding to the evidence of a much larger balance of payments deficit than anticipated by either them or the Treasury, which
was leading to a loss of confidence and consequent outflow of funds
that necessitated immediate action.[1]

The triumvirate resolutely ruled out devaluation, for predominantly
political reasons. Wilson summarised these as threefold: the consequent
loss of credibility by the government in its role as an economic manager,
especially given Labour's 1949 devaluation; the fear that competitive de-
valuations might follow, bringing down the whole international financial
system; and the belief that, to be successful, devaluation would necessitate
sharp deflationary policies. Deflationary policies would be insufferable
because, as Callaghan put it, they would involve 'a reduction in the
standard of living of the people'. This rejection of devaluation may also
be linked to the Labour Party's and its leader's scepticism about the
effectiveness of the price mechanism as an economic instrument, changing relative prices being, of course, the essence of devaluation.[2]

The Treasury briefing for the new government strongly urged against
devaluation, which it described as 'an act of desperation that would have
far-reaching consequences extending well beyond the immediate impact
on the economy'. These consequences were seen as disruption of the
international economy and the sterling system, as well as inflationary
pressure at home; in addition, there was no belief that the policy would

make possible a long-term increase in the growth rate.[3] Economic advisers to the government were divided on the issue, but this was probably not that important in the decision to defend the value of the pound; politics was in command.[4] The Prime Minister wanted devaluation ruled 'unmentionable' and certainly did his best to suppress public and ministerial discussion, but in the Treasury and Bank of England contingency planning went on throughout the next three years, until in fact the government was forced to take this step.[5]

The government was also committed by its whole posture in opposition to ruling out deflation as a response; the Treasury did not urge this response because of its (erroneous) belief that the expansion of demand and the consequent increased demand for imports was already decelerating.[6] The 'third way' of industrial modernisation was plainly no solution to the immediate crisis. The economic statement issued by the government on 26 October followed plans already prepared in the Treasury for a surcharge on imports to begin in November, coupled to a limited system of export rebates. The broad impact of these measures in macro-economic terms was neutral, neither adding to nor subtracting significantly from demand, but aimed to improve the balance of trade.[7]

The announcement of these measures sought, in Callaghan's words, 'to demonstrate to public opinion both in this country and overseas that we did not intend to rely either on borrowing or on deflationary policies to help us overcome our current difficulties'. This attempt at reassurance also embodied a promise of a 'stern review' of public spending, so that, from the beginning of its tenure in office, the tension between the desire to maintain 'confidence' and pressures for increased public spending was at the heart of Labour's policy debate. The import surcharge was a radical measure, in breach of international trade agreements, and one resented by many trading partners, especially in the EFTA, within which Britain was by far the biggest importer. While it did succeed in reducing imports below what they would otherwise have been, its announcement failed to restore 'confidence'.[8]

The budget of November worsened the situation, with the pre-announcement of a package of tax and spending increases to come into effect in the spring of 1965; the 'stern review' of spending was offset by Labour's commitment to increased social security spending. The tax increases included a rise in capital gains tax and the introduction of corporation tax, measures ill-designed to curry favour with financial markets. Speculation against the pound worsened in the wake of the budget, and only after major clashes between Wilson and Lord Cromer, the Governor of the Bank of England, was the bank base interest rate raised. As well as showing undisguised hostility to the government, the Governor made the perceptive – if unhelpful – comment that 'it was the government's misfortune to come to power at an awkward moment in the cycle'.[9] International financial support was obtained from a group of central banks (led by the USA) and the Bank for International Settlements. These measures stabilised the pound for the time being, albeit at the cost of Britain acquiring new international debts of around £1,200 million.

The flight from sterling when policies were already in place to improve the private current account underlined the common view in Labour circles that much of the external problem lay on the governmental and capital side of the accounts, with excessive overseas military spending and foreign investment as particular targets of criticism. On the first of these, the 1965 budget drew attention to the rapid growth since 1959, with an increase from about £175 million in 1959 to over £300 million in 1964, and the need to cut back on this spending for balance of payments reasons was reiterated in successive defence White Papers from February 1965.[10]

On the second point, despite opposition from the Bank of England, the same budget announced that 25 per cent of the proceeds of sales of foreign securities would have to be sold on the official exchange market, yielding significant amounts of foreign currency, though no measures were taken to restrict investment in the sterling area until 1966. The introduction of corporation tax was also expected to reduce the incentive to invest overseas, by reducing the tax advantages. In general, overseas investment was one of those issues almost obsessively discussed in policy-making circles, but where policy action was limited and not very effective.[11]

The broad thrust of the 1965 budget was mildly deflationary, and this occasioned serious dispute in ministerial circles. Brown in particular saw the whole approach as one of conjuring up increased taxation to 'restore foreign confidence' and 'make sterling strong', and he denounced it as a 'very old-fashioned way of running our affairs'. However, he had no alternative to offer, and most other members of the government and their advisers could see no alternative. Foreign borrowing necessarily gave an influence to the lender, though in 1965 the IMF's role was a limited one. Pierre-Paul Schweitzer, the Managing Director of the IMF, stressed to Callaghan and Wilson that he did not support the central bankers' deflationary orthodoxies, but nevertheless, following a negative evaluation by an IMF team in February, gave a message in which, as Brown commented, 'an iron hand frequently showed through splits in his velvet glove'.[12] However, the logic of the government's position made some deflation of domestic demand inescapable, whatever the IMF might say. It was clearly recognised that in a fully employed economy *any* measure to raise exports would require an accompanying switch of resources from domestically oriented activities. Thus, the Chancellor minuted that: 'the main object of the budget should be the shifting of resources from production for the domestic market to production for the export market'.[13]

While demand management dominated economic policy-making in the first period of the new government, this was more because of force of circumstance than choice. The government's aim to end 'stop–go' led to policy activity on three broad fronts. First, there was what may be generically entitled 'industrial modernisation policy', which led to a whole range of important but relatively low-profile actions, and which are discussed at length in the core of this book. Second, there was the attempt to implement an incomes policy (discussed in Chapter 6). This was the responsibility of the Department of Economic Affairs (DEA) and George Brown, who, in December 1964, announced the signing of a *Joint Statement of Intent* (see Chapter 8) with the Federation of British Industries (which became the CBI in 1965) and the Trades Union Congress (TUC). This provided for scrutiny of wage claims by new joint machinery, and possible reference of settlements to the newly established National Board for Prices and Incomes (NBPI), but essentially relied for its effectiveness on 'persuasion and the pressure of public opinion'. Third, there was the National Plan, unveiled by Brown in September 1965. The central point of this was to explore the implications and conditions for an acceleration of the British growth rate, and it focused attention on a 25 per cent increase in GDP between 1964 and 1970, a growth rate of 3.8 per cent. The Treasury regarded this projected rate of growth as 'dangerously unreal', and it was well above the 2.5 per cent rate envisaged in the 1965 budget, but, by the time the Plan appeared in September 1965, even that projection had been overtaken by events.[14]

The 1965 budget only temporarily allayed the loss of confidence in sterling. In July a new foreign exchange crisis blew up, following a deterioration in the current account and continuing pessimism in foreign exchange markets over Britain's ability to sustain the value of the pound. The crisis was (eventually) fought off by a combination of further foreign financial support and domestic deflationary measures. The foreign support had been secured at the time of Callaghan's visit to Washington in June, the first of many that he, his successor Roy Jenkins, and Wilson were to make. As was to become the pattern, US aid was accompanied by pressure for more British support in Vietnam and criticism of Britain's cuts in overseas military spending. But ultimately the US perception of the defence of the pound as the first line of defence for the dollar ensured that a deal was done.[15]

The domestic deflationary policies focused on restrictions on hire purchase, cuts in public investment, and the reintroduction of building licences in the private sector. Alec Cairncross (Head of the Government Economic Service at that time) plays down the effects of these measures, stressing the boom in most forms of investment both before and after their introduction.[16] As yet, the government was unwilling to give up its hostility to tough deflationary measures. Through 1965 and 1966 investment and public expenditure rose rapidly and, as the incomes policy seemed to have little impact on wages, consumption soon recovered from its slowdown in 1964/65. These conditions meant that, in the preparations for the 1966 budget, the government's advisers were urging the need for tougher measures to slow the growth of demand in the face of continuing prospective balance of payments deficits. While discussion of the scale of capital outflows continued, most policy attention focused on the need to correct the current account by reducing the demand for imports. Responding to Brown's paper on 'An economic strategy for Britain' in February 1966, Robert Neild, an economic adviser to the Treasury, doubted whether it offered a long-run solution to Britain's problems, but in any case stressed that what were needed were 'short-run measures which will correct the deficit immediately in prospect'. But while the advisers were saying that action had to be taken urgently, the prospect of a general election made this implausible politically. Instead, with an election in March, the budget was delayed to May, with a statement by the Chancellor at the beginning of March leaving the options open. Between this statement and the election, strong downward pressure on the pound led to another bitter clash between the Prime Minister and Cromer (with support from Callaghan), the Governor calling for the bank rate to be raised to respond to pressure on the pound, but Wilson asserting the right of the elected government to determine policy, and carried this line in Cabinet.[17]

From the 1966 general election to devaluation

The May budget that followed Labour's election victory included the introduction of the selective employment tax (SET), one of the most innovative but controversial of Labour's 'modernisation' policies. This was said by the Chancellor to be 'adducing mainly the value of showing that the government was capable of applying new ideas to control the economy'.[18] The fiscal effects of the SET were relatively small, and did not come into effect until September, but did contribute to the (limited) overall deflationary effect of the budget. However, the budget was quickly followed by a further sterling crisis, in part stimulated by a strike by the National Union of Seamen, and, despite quite healthy current account figures, the government was driven into further drastic action: the 'July measures', often seen as a turning point for the government, both economically and politically.[19] A tightening of controls on bank lending was announced on 11 July 1966, and the following day the bank rate was raised. A week later, and following significant ministerial debate of the devaluation option, a major fiscal tightening was announced, along with a further tightening of hire purchase terms.[20] Politically most significant was the accompanying announcement of a standstill or 'freeze' on increases in prices and incomes, to be followed by six months of 'severe restraint'. Up to this time, the government had adhered entirely to 'voluntarism' in its relationship with the trade unions, but from July 1966 there was a fundamental shift away from such 'laissez-faire' attitudes. The TUC reluctantly went along with the policy at its September congress, but after the policy was challenged by the white-collar union ASSET, the government activated the compulsory elements in October.

Brown was one of the minority of ministers who voted for devaluation in July, believing that it would provide a way to avoid the deflation which he had long opposed, as the key figure charged with using the National Plan to bring about an acceleration of Britain's growth rate. The Plan, in its grand form, was now plainly dead, and Brown was soon shifted to the Foreign Office, with the DEA effectively downgraded. The pre-eminence of 'getting the balance of payments right' as a policy goal was now clear, and with it the pre-eminence of the Treasury in policy-making was reasserted. But alongside was clear evidence of a shift in focus towards productivity. At a Cabinet meeting in July it was strongly asserted that increasing productivity was 'the only long-term answer' to Britain's problems, and preparations began for a national productivity conference.[21]

When Wilson visited the USA in late July, the crisis was still far from over, and the discussions reflected the sense of Britain's continuing economic weakness. The Americans on this occasion seem to have been particularly keen to press the benefits of Britain joining the Common Market.[22] The briefing papers for the Prime Minister suggested the strength of the case for reducing the international role of sterling as a way of reducing the frequency of exchange crises, but it was decided that it was not a good time to press this argument on the Americans. Another paper emphasised that, measured as a percentage of gross national product (GNP), Britain was easily the biggest military spender in the West, far outstripping the USA as well as European countries. This was no doubt intended as a riposte to the perennial US protests at Britain's reductions of its military spending overseas, though that issue seems not to have figured largely in the July discussions.[23] But, as Pimlott suggests, by 1966 the tide was clearly turning against the role 'east of Suez', which had been more or less taken for granted by Labour when it first came into government. The severity of the July crisis reinforced that trend, and cuts in military spending were an important component of the measures taken. In April 1967 the decision was taken to withdraw from Singapore and Malaysia by 1974/75.[24]

In the autumn of 1966 the July measures, coupled with the postponement of imports until the abolition of the import surcharge in

November, seemed to have halted the crisis of the pound. Both official and public forecasts indicated a balance of payments surplus in 1967. For a while, other matters took more attention, most notably the decision once again to seek entry into the Common Market, which was effectively decided in October 1966. This led to a series of European visits by the Prime Minister and new Foreign Secretary in the spring of 1967, and the application was formally endorsed by the Cabinet in April.[25]

Mild monetary relaxation was pursued in the winter, and the budget in April 1967 was neutral, with a 'steady as she goes' theme. Behind the scenes, the Treasury was increasingly worried about the level of government borrowing, an issue of increasing concern in official circles in the mid-1960s and a sign not only of the growing scale of this borrowing, but also of increasing worries about the consequences of fiscal policy for inflation and the balance of payments.[26] For the moment, however, nothing was done on this front, and as late as August 1967 there were more mild reflationary measures, as unemployment, at over 2 per cent, remained high by contemporary standards. On the wages front, the legally backed 'standstill' and 'severe restraint' were replaced in the summer of 1967 by a wholly voluntary agreement, with guidelines but no sanctions provided by the NBPI.

But from May the balance of payments position and forecasts started to deteriorate, and the pound to weaken. The latter may have partly been stimulated by the announcement of Britain's Common Market application, which many saw as likely to require a devaluation.[27] The situation deteriorated sharply in September, exacerbated by a worsening of the trade balance clearly evident in that month's figures. Cairncross's insider account suggests a marked shift in opinion towards belief in the inevitability of devaluation in September/October 1967.[28] But the Prime Minister and Chancellor remained opposed, and the search continued for a financial package that could support the pound. The Americans were very anxious to help because of the belief that a fall in the value of sterling could threaten the whole international financial system. But by early November, the almost unanimous advice from Treasury advisers and the Bank of England was persuading these two key people that devaluation was unavoidable. Wilson, as he puts it in his account of this government, would no longer impose a 'political veto' on devaluation. A ministerial meeting endorsed this willingness to contemplate letting the pound go, and a final decision to devalue was taken on 13 November. Devaluation was a clear defeat for the government, though this was to a degree self-inflicted: making the pound a symbol of 'national strength' was a deliberate strategy of Labour. Yet it is notable that public (as opposed to elite) opinion seems to have regarded the subsequent rise in the cost of living and deflation of demand more adversely than devaluation per se.[29]

Much of the debate at the time (and quite a lot since) assumed that devaluation was an alternative to deflation. But this was not the case, as indeed Wilson had always pointed out to his colleagues.[30] Devaluation, like any measure which significantly increased the demand for exports, would have to be accompanied by measures which ensured there would be resources in the export industries to supply this demand. In a full-employment economy, this must mean reduced resources elsewhere. In November 1967 the trauma of devaluation was soon followed by the trauma of recognition that, if the lower value of the pound were to work as a measure to restore the balance of payments, it would require a domestic deflation of substantial scale. In that sense devaluation did *not* mark a major watershed in economic policy: it was followed by 'more of the same', in the form of deflation, a policy which had been pursued, albeit with some relaxation in the summer of 1967, since the 'July measures' of the previous year.

The failure of many outside the Cabinet to grasp the basic economics of devaluation is demonstrated by the outrage of many on the Labour side over the measures which accompanied devaluation, which included a £400 million cut in planned public expenditure. Yet the weight of official advice was that this level of cutback in demand was inadequate. Leslie O'Brien, Cromer's successor as Governor of the Bank of England, thought the measures little more than half what was needed, though Callaghan defended the view that it was appropriate to follow a 'two-step' process, allowing time for the measures to come through.[31]

From devaluation to electoral defeat

Callaghan was replaced at the end of November by Roy Jenkins, but only after he had provided a 'letter of intent' to the IMF as required in return for the credits provided by the Fund to accompany devaluation. The drafting of such a letter, setting out Britain's policy proposals over the medium term, underlines again that devaluation was in no sense an escape from policy constraints. Money had to be borrowed to ensure that the devaluation did not encourage further speculation against the pound, a worry that was by no means unrealistic in the manic atmosphere that then, as so often, shrouded foreign exchange markets.

However, the letter's importance was perhaps more symbolic than actually very constraining on policy options. All the domestic advice supported the IMF view about the scale of deflation required. The major disquiet about the terms of the letter arose from its enthusiasm for a target for 'domestic credit expansion' (DCE), a measure of monetary expansion which was distrusted in Britain because of the belief that it was not a reliable index of monetary pressure. But the debate in Cabinet

about the letter was emphatically not about the IMF forcing on Britain
a package seriously out of line with what the domestic experts thought
necessary.[32]

The new Chancellor seems to have had few inhibitions about embracing the deflationary aspect of devaluation. Cairncross, usually critical
of the unwillingness of politicians to face unpalatable facts, found himself suggesting that Jenkins was taking too pessimistic a view of the
balance of payments prospects, and was therefore in danger of suggesting a 'too violent' increase in taxation. The new Chancellor from the
beginning was also much more overtly sensitive to the alleged disincentive effects of direct taxation, so that the stage was set for massive increases
in indirect taxation, which were realised over the next eighteen months.[33]

The precise size required of the package of tax increases was much
debated in the early weeks of 1968 because of fears that if exports did
not rise quickly, the resources 'freed' by deflation would run into unemployment. As the Chancellor put it in the House of Commons on 5
December, 'We do not want to dig a hole and leave it empty. We want it
to be there only when the export demand is ready to fill it.' Generally,
however, Treasury advice was that too weak a package ran the risk of
provoking further pressure on the pound. In the event, a package of
tax increases amounting to around £500 million was agreed.[34]

The other part of the package was a sharp cut in planned public
sending. Public spending had long had a 'symbolic' as well as substantive
role in Labour's thinking about the economy. It was almost universally
believed in Labour circles that public expenditure was a good thing,
the main issue between right and left usually being how much of it could
be afforded. The cuts in 1968 were therefore especially painful, marking, as they did, a real break in the trend of fast expansion which had
begun under the previous Conservative government. Politically this was
bound to be controversial, but doubly so when one of the measures
involved the imposition of prescription charges on patients within the
National Health Service, a measure which cut to the quick of Labour's
self-image as a party of the welfare state. Prescription charges had, of
course, occupied pride of place among Labour's 'sacred cows' since
Aneurin Bevan's resignation over the issue under the Attlee government, and had been removed by Labour in 1964.[35]

The battle over spending cuts occupied the Cabinet for many hours
in the first days of 1968. The Chancellor reinforced the symbolic
importance of the prescription charges, by arguing that 'the reintroduction of prescription charges had, rightly or wrongly, come to be
regarded – at home and abroad – as a sign of the Government's determination to take all the measures necessary to restore the economy and
would therefore be crucial for confidence'. The Cabinet eventually agreed
to this measure along with other politically painful proposals, such as

the postponement of the raising of the school-leaving age, the tying of benefit levels to prices instead of wages, and a cash ceiling on overseas aid. Expenditure on industrial modernisation was, however, to be increased by £165 million. At the height of the devaluation crisis, the Cabinet decided to go ahead with the Industrial Expansion Bill.[36]

Alongside these domestic cuts Jenkins proposed further economies on overseas military expenditure. The supporting argument, whose terms became something of a mantra in the following months, was that: 'Our standing in the world depends on the soundness of our economy not on a world wide military presence.' In consequence, the government needed to make 'radical and credible' cuts. Surprisingly, perhaps, for a future leader of the Social Democratic Party, for whom Britain's bomb was inviolate, he also suggested that Britain should consider abandoning its nuclear capability, including Polaris.[37] Sadly, this was one area where even the traumas of devaluation could not sufficiently shatter old shibboleths, and resources continued to be poured down this particular drain.

Jenkins' proposals led to a heated debate, especially because of US opposition to the stated aim of accelerating the withdrawal of British forces from both the Far East and the Persian Gulf to March 1971, and the linked decision not to go ahead with purchase of the American F-111 fighter aircraft. The Foreign Secretary (Brown) reported that his US opposite number, Dean Rusk, was 'shocked and dismayed' by the decision, and implored 'For God's sake act like Britain'. The resulting discussion showed a wide range of views of the USA: while some stressed that Britain 'could not afford to disregard the views of the US Government', others asserted that 'the time had come for a decisive break with our previous policies. We should no longer adopt policies merely because the US wished us to adopt them and out of fear of the economic consequences if we did not do so.' In the event, a decision on the withdrawal date was postponed and, after a report on the unhappiness of Australia, New Zealand, Singapore and Malaysia with the acceleration proposal, a compromise date of the end of 1971 was agreed. The F-111 cancellation went ahead, though this was used to justify the retention of the nuclear capability.[38]

Devaluation proved a decisive moment in changes in Britain's world role. The withdrawal from east of Suez was reaffirmed and accelerated. The role of sterling as a reserve currency was effectively ended by the Basle agreements of 1968, which gave sterling holders a dollar guarantee. Surprisingly, perhaps, capital was still allowed to flow without formal control to the sterling area, though voluntary controls were continued.[39] Jenkins, a pioneer critic of the costs of the sterling area in senior Labour circles, was able to preside over the running down of this perceived anachronistic incubus. This, of course, also fitted with his pro-Common

Market stance, which continued despite the rejection of Labour's approach, de Gaulle's veto coming in the same month as devaluation.

Despite all the political problems, both domestic and international, the package of cuts proposed by the Chancellor to make the devaluation effective went through largely intact. But this proved to be only the beginning of the transition to an improved balance of payments, which was not to become clearly evident until 1969.[10] In the meantime, 1968 turned out to be another year of crisis.

Part of the problem was the inevitable lag in response to devaluation. Assuming that import prices rose and export prices fell as a result of the change in the value of sterling, the immediate effect would be to reduce export receipts and increase expenditure on imports, creating the 'j-curve' effect, where devaluation worsens the balance of payments before improving it. Only as demand altered in response to the change in prices would the improvement come through. Such an analysis helps us to understand the delay that occurred after 1967, and it seems clear that, eventually, devaluation did work as expected.[11] But this approach is a simplified, textbook story, which, of necessity, neglects all sorts of complicating factors. It assumes, for example, that exporters operate in competitive markets and do not offset the fall in the foreign price of their goods brought about by devaluation by raising sterling prices. Such rational behaviour undoubtedly did occur, and there was considerable agonising in official and ministerial circles about the potential conflict between private and national interest in this respect.[12] Again, the retrospective evidence suggests that this offsetting process was not typical, and export prices did fall, but uncertainty on this issue underpinned some part of the crisis atmosphere of 1968.

Another problem with gauging the effects of devaluation is that changes in the growth of world trade may overwhelm any effects of changes in the price of exports. In 1968 world trade growth was slowing, whereas part of the improvement in export performance in 1969 was due to a faster growth in that trade. But in 1968 a larger part of the problem was the behaviour of imports. Against forecasts of a slight slowing in the growth of imports as higher prices worked their way through, they actually rose in volume by 10 per cent in 1968. To a degree, this reflected the partially successful attempt by trade unions to obtain compensation (i.e. higher increases in wages) for the real wage cut that results from devaluation. This in turn fuelled consumption, including of imports.[43] This process, coupled to the impetus devaluation gave to the 'wage–price spiral', helps to explain why in the period after devaluation fiscal policy aimed at checking consumption was combined with a growing government concern with wage bargaining, which was to come to a head in 1969 with the battle over the proposals to reform industrial relations set out in *In Place of Strife*, discussed in Chapter 6.

Finally, the direct effects of devaluation work to change the *current* account by altering the relative price of exports and imports. But, as already emphasised, many of Britain's foreign exchange problems of the 1960s had little directly to do with the current account, but related to shifts in capital flows, which were extraordinarily difficult to predict, and often hard to understand, even in retrospect. One of the reasons for opposition to devaluation in Britain, and the USA especially, was a fear that it would precipitate widespread instability in the international monetary system. In the event, the worst fears on this front were not realised, but the post-devaluation period saw increased uncertainty about the viability of the Bretton Woods system, and this tended to encourage flows between currencies, from all currencies into gold, and especially out of those perceived to be weak.

The first crisis of 1968 was in March, when downward pressure on the pound reflected in particular the flight into gold that accompanied uncertainty about future international financial policy, and about the fate of the dollar. The problem was at least temporarily resolved by the creation of a two-tier gold price, with a higher price available in the private market than to those who wished to convert their dollars into precious metal. But the sense of crisis in London was perhaps the greater because the recent traumas of devaluation did not seem to have resulted in a more stable situation for the pound. Cairncross records his sense that: 'The situation ... was more frightening than in the run-up to devaluation, perhaps more than in any crisis in the last twenty years'. All sorts of radical contingency plans were drawn up for use if the new exchange rate proved unsustainable. Many of these assumed that any future movement would have to be, at least for a time, to a floating rate combined with blocking the exchange of sterling balances for other currencies, backed up by further tough deflationary measures, compulsory incomes policy, a 'siege economy' to control imports, and perhaps compulsory liquidation of privately held dollar assets to supplement Britain's dollar reserves.[44] The blocking of the sterling balances (code-named 'Operation Brutus') would have been a particularly radical step. Wilson saw such a proposal not only as contingency planning but also 'as some means of blackmail with the Americans so that we could point out to them the horror of the alternatives before us'.[45] In the event, none of the more extreme measures was required, but the existence of such plans emphasises how fragile the situation remained for many months after devaluation.

The March episode also precipitated the resignation of Brown as Foreign Secretary, who, in angry exchanges, accused the Prime Minister and Chancellor of 'arrogance' in excluding him (as he saw it) from decisions over the policy response to the crisis.[46] This opened the way to a reorganisation of ministerial responsibilities, with responsibility for prices and incomes moving from the DEA to the Ministry of Labour (soon to be the Department of Employment and Productivity). This reflected not only a further downgrading in the importance of the DEA, but also the attempt to tie wage bargaining more effectively to productivity.

Incomes policy was moving up the agenda. In March the government published its proposals for the period to December 1969, which involved no norm, but a ceiling of 3.5 per cent, except for circumstances where genuine productivity gains were made. The government also made it clear that it would renew its existing statutory delaying powers, first introduced in 1966, when they expired in August 1968. However, both the TUC and Labour Party at their conferences that year rejected any statutory policy. Despite a growing tide of resentment at government 'interference' in free collective bargaining, wages did not accelerate notably in 1968/69, no doubt in part because of the relatively depressed labour market conditions that accompanied the post-devaluation deflation.[17]

The budget of 1968 inaugurated what the Chancellor expected to be 'two years' hard slog'. It was the most deflationary budget since the war, aimed above all at curbing private consumption. (And the first to be accompanied by the publication of the economic forecasts on which it was based.) It tried to cut private spending by putting most emphasis on indirect taxes, though with a special levy on investment income, while offsetting the regressive effects of this on the income distribution by raising family and other allowances. The SET was also increased, though this was delayed until September to allow for the phased effects of devaluation.[18]

Minor crises occurred through the middle months of 1968. Estimates of the current account balance worsened, and the actual trade figures fell short of what had been expected in the spring. There was widespread discussion in both public and official circles of the imposition of import controls to stem their growing volume without recourse to further devaluation or deflation.[19] The target surplus for the second half of the year, notified to the IMF at the end 1967, was £100 million, but by the summer this was clearly impossible. Alongside trade problems, the political crisis in France surrounding student and worker unrest further destabilised foreign exchange markets from April onwards. Things temporarily improved in the early summer, but this proved a brief respite. There was a minor crisis in July, and then in November an expected devaluation of the franc and revaluation of the Mark inaugurated a new bout of serious instability in foreign exchange markets. Coupled with evidence of continuing weakness in the trade accounts, this pressure led to a new deflationary package in November, plus a 50 per cent import deposit scheme, which required importers to deposit half the value of their purchases for six months. But pressure on the pound continued in December, so that, more than a year after devaluation, there was little sign that underlying improvement was taking place.

In January 1969 the government issued its White Paper *In Place of Strife*. In economic terms this may be seen as an ambitious attempt to offset the inflationary effects of devaluation (and its effects on real wages) by holding down nominal wages so that some at least of the competitive benefits of the change in the value of sterling were sustained. In political terms it ignited the most serious ever breakdown in relations between the trade unions and the Labour Party. From a union point of view, the government was attempting to infringe on what unions regarded as a fundamental right to bargain freely – at a time when real wages were being eroded by faster inflation and public expenditure cuts were seen as reneging on past government promises.[50] Led by Callaghan, the opposition within the Labour Party successfully fought the proposals set out in the White Paper, the government having to be satisfied with a 'solemn and binding' agreement with the TUC about future scrutiny of wage claims and attempts to reduce the number of strikes.

The defeat of the government on this issue did not prevent a further White Paper on incomes policy in December 1969, which called for a 'guiding light' for pay increases of 2.5 to 4.5 per cent. But this was unrealistic in the light of the economic and political conditions of the time, and in fact average annual wage settlements accelerated from around 10 per cent in 1969 to 14 per cent in 1970. The White Paper also announced plans to merge the NBPI with the Monopolies Commission to form a Commission on Industry and Manpower. Legislation to set up this body was introduced early in 1970 but fell because of the election. Its main significance was in triggering a wide-ranging debate in Labour circles about the scope and nature of government intervention in company affairs.[51]

On the figures available at the time, the trade balance appeared to be seriously in deficit in the early months of 1969, though revised figures show a clear movement into surplus. The budget in April was thus produced before it was clear that the tide had turned. Right up to March, Nicholas Kaldor (now a part-time adviser) was suggesting that there was no reason to suppose things would ever come right at the current exchange rate, and reiterated his call for floating the pound.[52] The result was a further deflationary budget, with £340 million extra in taxation, mainly from indirect taxes, including large sums from an increase in the SET, but also a rise in corporation tax. The budget also projected an overall budget surplus for the first time since Stafford Cripps had been Chancellor in the late 1940s.[53]

The concern with the overall budget financing position had been growing in the mid-1960s and had been stressed by the IMF in the negotiations surrounding the 1967 'letter of intent'. Soon after the budget,

in May 1969, the death of General de Gaulle stimulated another exchange crisis, and Britain, seeking further borrowing to repay its as yet
unpaid borrowings of December 1965, was once more subject to
detailed IMF scrutiny. This scrutiny led to the IMF requesting another
letter of intent, but this time a new twist was a requirement for targets
for DCE. This requirement was strongly resisted in Britain. The view in
official and ministerial circles was that the DCE concept did not fit with
British circumstances, and that the requirement to provide targets for
this variable might lead to pressure for changes of policy when these
targets were breached, even though they were misleading. In part this
was a technical matter, relating to the effectiveness of monetary targets
as a policy instrument, a debate which was beginning in earnest in the
late 1960s.[54] As Jenkins emphasised, opposition to the targets was not
opposition to tight monetary policy. Jenkins seems to have taken this
threat to Britain's ability to conduct policy in its own way very seriously,
and talked at one stage as if a break with the IMF was a bearable price
to pay for such autonomy.[55] But in the event the Fund was adamant,
and the targets were incorporated in the letter. However, the Bank of
England had no trouble in reaching the DCE targets in 1969/70, though
they were again exceeded in 1970/71.[56]

By June 1969 it was clear that the balance of payments position was
radically improving. In addition to a sharply narrowing deficit recorded
in May, it was discovered that there had been systematic under-recording
of exports, which altered the picture significantly. By August, a £40 million
surplus on the visible trade account was recorded, and from then on
the trend was unambiguously one of improvement. This turn-around
did not, however, initially stop speculation against the pound. Indeed,
in August itself the devaluation of the franc led to a fresh bout of selling
of sterling. But after the revaluation of the Mark in September the situation stabilised, and for the last nine months of its tenure the Labour
government was to be favoured by stability in the international financial
system and an absence of downward pressure on the pound.

Elected to end stop–go, the government had in the end imposed an
unprecedented stop. It proved reluctant to change tack, regardless of
the radical improvement in the balance of payments and the impending
general election. The import deposit scheme was relaxed slightly in
October 1969 and the irritating limit on foreign travel expenditure was
withdrawn in January but, despite evidence of the severity of the squeeze,
ministers proved reluctant to expand demand. The 1970 budget made
about £200 million of tax cuts, mainly in direct taxes. The nature of the
political calculations governing economic policy is shown in an exchange
between Jenkins and the Prime Minister in February 1970. Wilson
emphasised the need to avoid confrontation over wages in the run-up
to the election, as this could provoke a foreign exchange crisis which

would necessitate further deflationary measures. Jenkins emphasised the need to come down hard on public sector wage claims. He further stated that:

> it could be argued to be better for the Labour Party that they should lose the next general election but should leave behind them a record of sound management of the economy than that they should put that record at risk in order to achieve an election victory which might be no more that marginal.[57]

Sadly, in a cruel world, Labour's 'responsible' economic policies, as in 1951, proved to be a route into opposition.

Notes

The place of publication is London unless otherwise specified.

1 PRO, T 171/758, Treasury, 'Immediate problems of reserve movements and financing the deficit', 15 October 1964; K. Morgan, *Callaghan: A Life* (Oxford, 1997), p. 203.

2 H. Wilson, *The Labour Government 1964–70: A Personal Record* (1974), p. 6; J. Callaghan, *Time and Chance* (1987), p. 160. On the politics of not devaluing, see T. Bale, 'Dynamics of a non-decision: the "failure" to devalue the pound, 1964–7', *Twentieth Century British History*, 10 (1999), pp. 192–217; M. Stewart, *Politics and Economic Policy in the UK Since 1964: The Jekyll and Hyde Years* (1978), p. 28; R. Middleton, *Charlatans or Saviours? Economists and the British Economy from Marshall to Meade* (Cheltenham, 1998), pp. 254–7.

3 PRO, T 171/758, Treasury, 'Devaluation', 15 October 1964. Neild later suggested that this paper was 'disgraceful' for its moralistic tone. R. Neild, in S. Brittan (ed.), 'Symposium: 1967 devaluation', *Contemporary Record*, 1 (1988), p. 46. There was also a hostile Treasury paper on floating: T 171/758, 'Floating exchange rates', 15 October 1964.

4 D. MacDougall, *Don and Mandarin: Memoirs of an Economist* (1987), p. 152; A. Cairncross and B. Eichengreen, *Sterling in Decline* (1983), p. 199. Cairncross's view at the time was that, while in principle in favour of devaluation, he 'saw no point in devaluing in an overheated economy without the support of stringent deflationary measures which there was no likelihood that the Labour government would adopt'. *The Wilson Years: A Treasury Diary, 1964–66* (1997), p. 1.

5 The records of the 'FU' committee that drew up these contingency plans are in PRO, T 312/1398–1401, 1636–7, 1827, 'Contingency planning for sterling devaluation', 1964–67. It is noteworthy that the size of the eventual devaluation (from $2.80 to $2.40) was anticipated almost from the beginning of these discussions.

6 PRO, T 267/22, R. Bretherton, Treasury historical memorandum, 'The control of demand 1964–1970', January 1975, pp. 9–11.

7 PRO, CAB 128/39, 'Cabinet conclusions', 19 October 1964: A. Cairncross, *Managing the British Economy in the 1960s: A Treasury Perspective* (1996), pp. 91–5; A. Graham and W. Beckerman, 'Introduction: economic performance

and the foreign balance', in W. Beckerman (ed.), *The Labour Government's Economic Record 1964–70* (1972), pp. 19–20.

8 PRO, CAB 129/39, 'Cabinet conclusions', 19 October 1964; for estimates of the effects of the surcharge, see Cairncross, *Managing*, pp. 115–16.

9 PRO, PREM 13/261, 'Meetings of Chancellor, Prime Minister and Governor', 24 November 1964. Wilson threatened to call another election to get a mandate for devaluation, to stop the policy being 'dictated' by foreign bankers. Cromer said this would 'mean putting Party before country'.

10 B. Tew, 'Policies aimed at improving the balance of payments', in F. Blackaby (ed.), *British Economic Policy 1960–74* (Cambridge, 1978), p. 321; PRO, T 171/801, Budget papers, 4 January–31 March 1965.

11 Cairncross, *Managing*, p. 111; PRO, T 171/801, T. Balogh, 'The advantages of foreign investment', 11 March 1965; T 171/809, Drafts of 1965 budget speech.

12 PRO, T 171/801, G. Brown to H. Wilson, 19 March 1965, and 'Note of Schweitzer's meeting with PM', 3 February 1965.

13 PRO, T 171/803, 'Budget Committee meeting', 26 February 1965.

14 PRO, T 267/22, Bretherton, 'Control of demand', p. 20. The Plan is discussed in detail in Chapter 4.

15 R. Roy, 'The battle of the pound: the political economy of Anglo-American relations 1964–1968' (unpublished PhD dissertation, University of London, 2001); Morgan, *Callaghan*, pp. 224–7; PRO, T 312/1204–6, 'Chancellor's visit to Canada and the USA June 1965'.

16 Cairncross, *Managing*, pp. 131, 134–7.

17 PRO, T 171/811, R. Neild, 'First Secretary's paper on "An economic strategy for Britain"', 3 February 1966; T 171/812, Lord Cromer to J. Callaghan, 22 December 1965; PRO, PREM 13/851, 'Meeting of PM, Chancellor and Governor of the Bank of England', 9 March 1966; PRO, CAB 128/41, 'Cabinet conclusions', 10 March 1966 and 19 July 1966; CAB 128/46, Confidential annexe to 'Cabinet conclusions', 19 July 1966.

18 PRO, T 267/22, Bretherton, 'Control of demand', p. 28. The SET is also discussed in Chapter 6.

19 R. Crossman, *The Diaries of a Cabinet Minister. Vol. 1, Minister of Housing 1964–1966* (1975), pp. 567–90; B. Pimlott, *Harold Wilson* (1992), pp. 408–37; Callaghan, *Time and Chance*, pp. 193–205; E. Dell, *The Chancellors* (1997), pp. 334–9.

20 As Pimlott, *Wilson*, pp. 411–13, points out, the rejection of devaluation continued to be on the political grounds clearly articulated in 1964.

21 R. Jenkins, *A Life at the Centre* (1991), p. 195; PRO, CAB 128/41, 'Cabinet conclusions', 12 July 1966. On the productivity issue, see Chapter 8.

22 Morgan, *Callaghan*, p. 253.

23 PRO, T 312/471, 'Visit of the PM to Washington July 1966'.

24 Pimlott, *Wilson*, p. 388; PRO, CAB 128/42, 'Cabinet conclusions', 4 April 1967; M. Jones, 'A decision delayed: Britain's withdrawal from S.E. Asia reassessed, 1961–68', *English Historical Review*, 117 (2002), pp. 569–95.

25 PRO, CAB 128/42, 'Cabinet conclusions', 30 April 1967.

26 PRO, T 171/820, 'The financing prospect', 24 January 1967; F. Blackaby, 'Narrative', in F. Blackaby (ed.), *Economic Policy 1960–74* (Cambridge, 1978), pp. 39–40.

27 Cairncross, *Managing*, pp. 180–1; Stewart, *Politics*, p. 81; S. Brittan, *Steering the Economy: The Role of the Treasury* (1971), p. 171. At the same time, entry to the EEC was seen as ruling out floating the exchange rate, which many regarded as the best alternative to defending an exchange rate value of the

pound of $2.80. PRO, T 312/1827, F. Atkinson and C. McMahon, 'A fixed or floating rate?', 24 May 1967.

28 Cairncross, *Managing*, pp. 180–91.

29 Wilson, *Labour Government*, p. 570; Morgan, *Callaghan*, pp. 268–72. The most detailed discussion of the economics of devaluation is in A. Cairncross and B. Eichengreen, *Sterling in Decline* (Oxford, 1983), ch. 5. On public opinion, see D. Blaazer, '"Devalued and dejected Britons": the pound in public discourse in the mid-1960s', *History Workshop Journal*, 47 (1999), pp. 121–40.

30 Wilson, *Labour Government*; PRO, CAB 128/46, Confidential annexe to 'Cabinet conclusions', 19 July 1966, where the Prime Minister pointed out to advocates of devaluation that: 'even if sterling were devalued, it would remain no less essential to free resources for exports and for import substitution'.

31 *Hansard* (Commons), vol. 754, 20 November 1967, cols 939–5, 21 November, cols 1140–274, and 22 November, cols 1314–44; PRO, T 171/829, L. O'Brien to J. Callaghan, 17 November 1967.

32 Cairncross, *Managing*, p. 191. Monetary policy under the Labour government focused on credit rationing, mainly by bank lending ceilings and hire purchase rules. Control of credit allowed the government, at least in principle, to discriminate in favour of some borrowers, for example exporters. PRO, T 267/22, 'Control of demand', pp. 91–2.

33 PRO, T 171/829, A. Cairncross to P. Baldwin, 18 January 1968, and 'Meeting with W. Armstrong', 18 January 1968.

34 Cited in Blackaby, 'Narrative', p. 44; PRO, T 171/829, W. Armstrong, 'Budget', 13 February 1968.

35 T. Bale, *Sacred Cows and Commonsense: The Symbolic Statecraft and Political Culture of the British Labour Party* (Aldershot, 1999).

36 PRO, CAB 128/43, 'Cabinet conclusions', 5 January 1968; CAB 128/42, 'Cabinet conclusions', 20 December 1967; CAB 129/134, 'Industrial Expansion Bill; draft White Paper', 15 December 1967. On the importance of this Bill, see Chapter 5.

37 PRO, CAB 129/135, Chancellor of the Exchequer, 'Public expenditure: post devaluation measures', 3 January 1968. Jenkins does not mention this in his memoirs, *Life at the Centre*, pp. 227–8. His defeat on this issue is discussed in T. Benn, *Office Without Power: Diaries 1968–72* (1988), pp. 5–6.

38 PRO, CAB 128/43, 'Cabinet conclusions', 12 January 1968, 15 January 1968.

39 On the Basle agreements, see Tew, 'Balance of payments', pp. 351–2.

40 Devaluation exposed in an extreme form the difficulties of economic forecasting in the 1960s. PRO, T 267/22, 'Control of demand', pp. 69–72.

41 Cairncross and Eichengreen, *Sterling*, pp. 197–213.

42 PRO, PREM 13/2421, 'Speech by A. Crosland to American Chamber of Commerce in London', 10 January 1968; PRO, T 230/1052, 'Economic consequences following devaluation', November 1967–January 1969.

43 C. Cohen, *British Economic Policy, 1960–69* (1971), pp. 220–3.

44 Cairncross, *Managing*, p. 209; the discussions of contingency plans are in PRO, T 312/2130–1, 2137–9, 2544–9, 2552, 'Sterling contingency planning', 1968–69. See also A. Blick, 'The origins and history of the government adviser with special reference to the 1964–70 Wilson administrations' (unpublished PhD dissertation, University of London, 2002), pp. 194–201.

45 PRO, PREM 13/2051, 'Conversation PM with Chancellor', 17 March 1968; P. Hennessy, *The Prime Ministers: The Office and its Holders Since 1945* (2000), pp. 316–19. Various versions of Brutus can be found in PRO, CAB 130/ 497–8, 'Ministerial Group on International Monetary Problems', 1968/69.

46 PRO, CAB 128/46, Confidential annexe to 'Cabinet conclusions', 15 March 1968; see also Pimlott, *Wilson*, pp. 493–503. Brown had, a short time previously, been at the centre of major row about Britain's sale of arms to South Africa; see T. Bale, 'South African arms and the statecraft of British social democracy', *Labour History Review*, 62 (1997), pp. 22–40.

47 *Productivity, Prices and Incomes Policy in 1968 and 1969*, Cmnd 3590, BPP 1967/68, vol. 39; PRO, PREM 13/2057, 'Meeting of PM, Castle and President of CBI', 10 April 1968; R. Jones, *Wages and Employment Policy 1936–1985* (1987), pp. 76–7.

48 PRO, T 171/829, J. Nicholson, 'The redistributive effects of the budget', 15 March 1968; T 171/839, W. Pattinson, 'Penal taxation and incentives', 8 April 1969, and F. Butler, 'Effect of budget on income distribution', 10 April 1969. For further discussion, see Chapter 9. The SET issue is discussed in Chapter 6.

49 PRO, PREM 13/2068, 'T. Balogh to PM' (n.d. but June 1968); 'The economic situation and the home economy', *National Institute Economic Review*, 45 (1968), pp. 10–11.

50 PRO, T 171/848, 'Chancellor's meeting with the TUC', 16 December 1968, also suggests considerable resentment by union leaders at the emphasis on indirect taxes in the Chancellor's budgets.

51 *Productivity, Prices and Incomes After 1969*, Cmnd 4237, BPP 1969/70, vol. 9; PRO, PREM 13/3233, 3234, 'Commission on Industry and Manpower', 1970. For the significance of the Commission, see Chapter 5.

52 Blackaby, 'Narrative'; PRO, T 171/841, 'Implications of the forecast for the budget', 7 February 1969; T 171/869, D. Allen to D. Dowler, 20 March 1969. Floating had been Kaldor's favoured option *before* November 1967, and had been seriously discussed by the contingency committee: see PRO, T 312/1398, 'Fixed or floating rates', 26 April 1964 and 12 July 1965.

53 It is important to note, however, that budget current account surpluses had been the norm throughout the post-war period.

54 PRO, PREM 13/8151, A. Graham, 'Monetary policy and the IMF', 30 April 1969, emphasises the ignorance of how monetary policy works. British policy still followed the focus on the growth of credit of the Radcliffe report, Cmnd 827, BPP 1958/59, vol. 17, but this was coming under challenge: D. Croome and H. Johnson (eds), *Money in Britain 1959–69* (1970).

55 PRO, PREM 13/8151, Jenkins to PM, 29 April 1969; PRO, T 171/845, D. Dowler to E. Figgures, 8 April 1969.

56 Cairncross, *Managing*, pp. 252–3.

57 PRO, CAB 128/46, Confidential annexe to 'Cabinet conclusions', 12 February 1970.

4

Planning

Labour's traditional and deeply ingrained hostility to both the ethical and economic costs of capitalism's reliance on market forces had its logical counterpoint in a persistent attachment to ideas of economic planning.[1] The 1945 election manifesto followed on from the party's position established in 1931 and made that word central to Labour's lexicon. The failure of inter-war capitalism was to be corrected by a combination of public ownership and planning, the former in large part justified by its role as the foundation stone of 'the planned economy'.

The retreat from planning

Yet the heartfelt desire for planning in this period did not lead to any long-term sustainable strategies and, crudely put, the high ambitions of 1945 quickly degenerated into a pragmatically guided set of controls (many inherited from wartime), which the Attlee government eased as economic and political circumstances allowed. Part of the problem was that Labour had no clear doctrine of planning to inform policy, the term being used to cover advocacy of everything from Keynesian-style control of the major macro-economic aggregates through to full-blown Soviet-style micro-economic allocation of resources.[2] Actual policy centred on the use of physical controls to allocate scarce resources, combined with a growing if always qualified use of Keynesian methods. As scarcity diminished, the attractions of controls, especially of consumer goods, sharply declined and by 1951, while many domestic controls remained, the trend was towards close control of external transactions combined with a reliance on broad, macro-economic regulators. Labour remained committed to controls, but on a much narrower front than in 1945.[3]

The retreat from planning was a serious ideological and political defeat for Labour's ideas as widely understood in 1945, but one that did not lead to the high-profile, agonising reappraisals associated with public ownership. This was not because the revisionists failed to turn their fire on this part of Labour's heritage. Indeed, as Nicholas Ellison points out, they were earlier and more vigorously into the fray on planning than on public ownership.[4] Tony Crosland, in *The Future of Socialism*, directly confronted the issue by arguing that 'at present levels of material welfare' there was little divergence between production for profit and production for use, traditionally a central ground for socialist advocacy of planning. Hence, apart from being used to ensure that a proper share of the national income went on investment, planning should be limited to cases where, in capital-intensive 'basic industries', the private sector could not provide rapid expansion of capacity, and in clear cases of externalities, where public and private costs and benefits emerged.[5] Despite his and others' willingness to assert such heterodox views, Crosland rightly claimed that planning was 'a diminishing area of controversy' in British politics. This reflected the fact that Labour recognised the Conservatives' success in the late 1940s and early 1950s in associating planning with rationing and austerity, and therefore turning the term and its connotations into a powerful anti-Labour weapon.[6] Thus, while the word never disappeared entirely from Labour's lexicon, it lost the central role in Labour argument it had occupied in the 1930s and 1940s.

This is not, however, the whole story of Labour's thinking on planning in the 1950s. In 1950 Harold Wilson had, as President of the Board of Trade in the Attlee government, reflected on that experience in office in a widely discussed – if ultimately rejected – paper on economic policy entitled 'The state and private industry'. A central concern of this paper was to assess the impact of the regime of controls with which Wilson had been closely involved. He explicitly attacked those on the left of the party associated with the pamphlet *Keeping Left*,[7] who saw those controls as 'the most effective and subtle means of imposing selective pressure on industry'. In Wilson's view, 'nothing could be wider of the mark', because controls were a blunt instrument, particularly ineffectual in changing the behaviour of individual firms. The alternative policy tentatively advocated by Wilson was one of identifying the 'key firms' which dominated each sector's industrial output, getting information from them about their production and investment intentions, and then 'the possibility of taking powers to issue directions to these firms on the lines of those included in the nationalised sector should be examined'. Here may be seen the beginnings of a distinctive notion of 'planning' associated with Wilson and those who gathered around him, whom Ellison has usefully named the 'left technocrats'.[8] While careful not to renounce public ownership, this strand of thinking emphasised the need for the state to find new mechanisms to influence and to some degree control the large enterprises that dominated the industrial economy, above all in the name of greater efficiency.

In the early 1950s such views were far from prominent in Labour's debates. Wilson's own writings reflected the difficulties of advocating planning in those years, and his 'Plan for Britain', while suggesting a seeming desire for a measure of Crippsian-style austerity, nevertheless makes clear that planning relates primarily to the foreign trade and investment sector, and that consumption, politically the most sensitive sector, is to be regulated by subsidies rather than controls.[9]

The revival of planning

The context for economic argument changed with the long stagnation of the economy that followed the Conservatives' 1955 election victory. In 1957 Wilson published a Fabian pamphlet entitled *Post-war Economic Policies in Britain*, which presaged many of the themes of Labour's economic ideas of the 1960s, emphasising the need for 'purposeful direction' of the economy, a term synonymous with 'planning' in the sense in which Wilson usually deployed it. Labour's policy review following the 1955 defeat yielded, among many other documents, a *Plan for Progress*, published in 1958 (and produced by a committee chaired by Wilson). Like most contemporary Labour discussions, this document was careful to distance itself from the post-war controls, which were presented as necessitated by the war's legacy of economic crisis. By contrast, in today's circumstances, 'day-to-day decisions can be left to industry and the customer', though an ambiguous rider was added – 'so long as they do not conflict with the nation's vital needs'.[10]

Planning was presented as necessary both to maintain macro-economic balance and to increase the production of goods essential to the national interest. It was made clear that the purpose of planning would be to facilitate expansion and that investment was the key to this process. This high-investment policy was to be secured by ending 'stop–go', tax incentives, and the encouragement of profit plough-back. Priorities in investment would be pursued by requiring large firms to submit investment plans to the Board of Trade, and building licensing would be used to control the direction of industrial investment. Also advocated was that hardy perennial a National Investment Board, though it was made very clear that its role would be purely advisory.[11]

It is instructive to contrast *Plan for Progress* with the much better-known product of the 1950s policy review, *Industry and Society* (1957). The latter was the document which attempted to grasp the nettle of Labour's attitude to public ownership, and which provoked a huge row when it was presented at the 1957 Labour conference. It eschewed the use of the word 'planning', but did talk about the need for 'control' of the economy and the role of the public sector in achieving that control.

That role was clearly modest – partly because control could be exercised without ownership, but also because the amount of control envisaged was so limited, being largely limited to capital issues and building licensing.[12] The contrast between this low-key position and the more assertive tone of *Plan for Progress* can perhaps be accounted for by the growing belief that 'declinism' offered an opportunity to change the connotations of planning from negative to positive. If planning was about growth and modernisation, it self-evidently could not be about restriction and austerity – or this at least was the ideological shift that Labour was slowly engineering.

Another important ingredient of the revival of enthusiasm for planning came from the perceived economic successes (symbolised by technological 'marvels' like Sputnik) of the Soviet-style planned economies. Because of the importance of anti-Communism in Labour circles in the 1950s, it is easy to understate the extent to which hostility to Soviet political ambitions was coupled with enthusiasm for their planning system. This attitude was far from confined to the left of the party. For example, at the 1958 Labour conference the right-wing Labour MP Desmond Donnelly asserted: 'we have a great deal to learn about economic expansion from the Communist countries'. The following year Roy Jenkins, in writing *The Labour Case* for the general election, numbered the Soviet Union among 'the most dynamic economies'. Michael Shanks, also on the right of the party, and author of the archetypal declinist text, *The Stagnant Society*, recounted in the introduction to that book how it had been inspired by a visit to Bulgaria and the purposefulness he found there, sadly contrasted with the stagnation of Britain. For Wilson, these kind of comparisons were commonplace; for example, in 1959 he told the House of Commons that 'the challenge we are facing as a nation is the growth of industrial production, of investment, and the vast technological and educational advance in the USSR and China'.[13]

But if planning was, by the end of the 1950s, being rehabilitated, the important question is, what sort of planning? First, as already suggested, the weight of discussion of planning focused on foreign trade and investment. Any kind of direct regulation of consumption was much more difficult to present in a positive light. This arose from the 1940s experience of consumer rationing and austerity. Yet Labour was also reluctant simply to go to the other extreme and embrace the virtues of consumerism. Labour had very serious ideological problems with the affluent consumer, and these were deeply rooted in Labour's anti-hedonistic thinking, which was especially strong on the left of the party.[14] But even those on the right had to qualify their enthusiasm for what Wilson was famously to denounce as the 'candy floss society'. Jenkins, for example, while arguing that the Attlee government had tilted the balance 'too much towards the austerity of fair shares, and too little

towards the incentives of free consumer choice', was careful to go along
with the idea of investment priorities for the 'basic' industries: 'I am
not one of those who is instinctively censorious of "frivolous" investment.
Milk bars, petrol stations, soft drink factories, and even greyhound
stadiums are not amongst our most basic economic activities, but as we
want them, it is on the whole better that they are efficient and well-
designed'. But, he noted, even 'the Soviet Union, which is now con-
siderably expanding her secondary industries, did not do so until she
had devoted many years to a powerful heavy industry base'.[15]

Expanded investment, above all in the 'basic' industries, was for the
Labour Party a key purpose of planning. In emphasising an increase in
investment as the key to 'planned expansion', Labour clearly recognised
the implication that consumption would have to be held back, but saw
the solution to this in a combination of incomes policy and exhortation,
plus perhaps hire purchase and credit ceilings, rather than austerity
and consumption controls. Equally, notions of 'wage planning', which
had surfaced in the 1940s (and which implied a government role in
changing differentials), were wholly absent from Labour's debate on
'planned growth of incomes' in this period.[16]

Another important theme in Labour's advocacy of planning was its
links with the idea of automation. Like almost every generation since
the industrial revolution, people in Britain in the 1950s saw themselves
as living through unprecedented technological change, and this belief
was closely associated with the idea that automation offered immense
possibilities for changing industry. Hence the characteristic Wilson
theme of the need for a planned economy, in order to cope with the
consequences of this automation, helped to link planning to one of the
key concerns of the era.[17]

These themes of higher investment and coping with rapid technological change were brought together in the party document *Signposts
for the Sixties* in 1961. This argued that to reverse decline what was
needed was 'a plan for expansion ... a national plan, with targets for
individual industries'. The key body would be the National Industrial
Planning Board, integrated with the government's own planning
machinery and 'in close touch with both sides of industry'. Its central
purpose would be 'speedy and purposive industrial investment'. Alongside and of equal importance to this expansion in directed investment
would be the 'application of science to our industries'.[18]

In 1961 Wilson produced a 'A four-year plan for Britain', which
envisaged a 50 per cent rise in investment between 1961 and 1966,
focused on 'the industries which strengthen our industrial base and
provide the means to further production, particularly of the goods we
can best hope to sell in the markets of the world'. In the light of subsequent events, Wilson's discussion of the phasing of the plan is piquant:

The essential decisions will be taken in the first year, particularly the spectacular leap in industrial investment. By the third year many of the new investment projects will be yielding their dividend, and by the fourth year it will be possible to harvest the fruits in economic and social terms.

The mechanisms to achieve this growth were a National Investment Board, to work out the rate of expansion needed in each industry, and then the use of government-guaranteed orders, selective investment allowances and building licences, to hold back inessential projects. Public ownership would be used 'where a firm or industry refuses to meet the demand placed upon it by the national programme'. This way of approaching the issue of public ownership was underlined in the conclusion: Labour's approach should be 'to relate our proposals for extended public ownership to the fulfilment of a plan designed to restore Britain's place in the world'.[19]

Wilson's approach to planning drew a great deal on the work of the economist Thomas Balogh, the two having worked together through most of the 1950s. Balogh was a strong critic of the 'liberal socialism' of economists like James Meade, who questioned the efficacy of detailed planning (as well as supporting a liberal international trade regime).[20] He argued that the concentration of economic power, increased levels of risk and increased externalities all undermined the efficacy of the price system and therefore made the case for planning. But while Balogh is much more explicit than Wilson about the economic arguments underlying the 'left technocrat' case for planning, he is little more specific on the mechanisms. Like Wilson, he invokes a combination of physical and financial policies to be used in a discriminatory fashion to generate rapid expansion of investment in favoured sectors, but how such measures might be guaranteed to work (and therefore, perhaps, properly deserve the name 'planning') is left vague.[21]

By 1961 such arguments had captured the high ground of Labour Party policy-making. A key document here was *Signposts for the Sixties*, endorsed by conference in that year. This publication included a chapter on 'Planning for expansion', in which the Wilson/Balogh themes were reiterated, and a call was made for the creation of what was now called 'a National Industrial Planning Board', whose 'central directive would be to ensure speedy and purposive industrial investment', and which would operate alongside a revamped National Research and Development Corporation to develop and apply the benefits of the 'scientific revolution' to British industry. By 1964 the Labour manifesto was dominated by a large section entitled 'Planning the new Britain', which not only proposed the formulation of a National Plan by a new Ministry of Economic Affairs but also talked of 'A plan for industry', 'A plan for the regions', 'A plan for transport', 'A plan for stable prices' and 'A plan for tax reform'. The language of the manifesto makes it clear that, for Labour, 'planning' was both a specific proposal (the National Plan and a new ministry to draw it up) and a much wider term designed to suggest a more purposive, medium-term approach to the economy, which would embrace every area of policy.[22]

The first of these meanings for 'planning' was given sharper focus by the decision to create a 'Department of Economic Affairs' with a clear remit to challenge the alleged short-termism and financial focus of the Treasury, in the name of the interests of industry and economic growth. Like the idea of planning, this notion of a new economic ministry had complex roots, but also drew on common themes of the late 1950s about the short-sightedness of the Treasury and senior civil servants, the need for government to draw on more economic expertise, and the need for much closer government–industry links. The DEA also allowed a prominent economic policy role for the Deputy Leader of the Labour Party, George Brown, who, while a right-winger in most party debates, was strongly committed to the idea of planning as the route to faster growth.[23]

As in the 1930s and 1940s, the resurgence of enthusiasm for planning in Labour's ranks was part of a broader shift of opinion in Britain. In the last years of the Conservative government the Tories, too, were willing to use the term. This shift was, in part, a consequence of Labour's attacks, which put the Conservatives on the defensive about their economic management and made them more willing to embrace a more directive approach to the economy. This impetus became all the stronger with the Federation of British Industry joining in the attacks and suggesting the need for an end to 'stop–go' and a more planned approach to increasing economic growth. In 1961 the government proposed the establishment of the NEDC and the supporting National Economic Development Office (NEDO) as tripartite bodies (i.e. with representation for government, employers and employees) that would look for ways of raising the growth rate. The politics of the NEDC were complex, and it was by no means commonly seen in the government or in Whitehall as a powerful independent source of economic policy-making. But it did produce documents of some importance, such as *Growth of the British Economy to 1966* in 1963, and later the same year *Conditions Favourable to Faster Growth*. These publications endorsed the priority to be accorded to the aim of faster economic growth. Employers and unions were brought together to discuss the issues set out in the documents, but they failed to arrive at an agreed set of ways in which the 'conditions' were to be attained and, unsurprisingly with a Conservative government in power, the NEDC did not push the notion of 'planning' as far as Labour desired.[24]

The creation of the NEDC was a shift of policy broadly in line with Labour's planning ideas. But both Wilson and Balogh argued that, as an independent body, not integrated with an (unreformed) government machine, it might be able to produce useful 'paper plans', but these would not be implemented without a much broader shift in both government machinery and policy. For Wilson, 'A Planning organization needs to acquire its authority from the Cabinet and the economic departments if it is to be able to call, in the national interest, for the co-operation that will be required'. For Labour, the NEDC could not be the apex of the planning machinery; for that, a new ministry with a senior minister in charge would be necessary.[25]

The National Plan

In September 1965, the DEA produced the National Plan, designed 'to achieve a 25 per cent increase in national output between 1964 and 1970'.[26] This plan unambiguously failed: GDP actually rose by 21 per cent.[27] Yet despite this failure, the Plan is central to the story of the Wilson government's economic policies. As Pimlott suggests, the under-lying approach of the Plan 'amounted to the Labour Government's raison d'être: that it was possible to improve economic performance and boost growth, over a period of years, by the national co-ordination of resources and investment. If Wilson and his Government in the 1960s were for something distinctive, it was for this'.[28] George Brown in his foreword to the Plan proclaimed that 'it covered all aspects of the country's economic development for the next five years', and this was literally true: the Plan did cover everything from the balance of pay-ments, investment, pay, regional policy, through to detailed projections of output in individual industries. This conspectus was itemised as a thirty-nine-point checklist that summarised Labour's overall 'modernis-ation agenda' in a manner unlike any other government document.[29]

The DEA was created primarily to draw up the Plan, but because of the ambition of the new Department to be the overall co-ordinator of economic policy, the creation of the Plan was by no means its only concern. The DEA had five divisions, which in addition to that for economic planning covered industrial policy, regional policy, 'economic co-ordination home', and 'economic co-ordination overseas'.[30] The DEA was thus in part an attempt at a major reform of the machinery of government, and considerable attention has been given to this aspect of its existence.[31] On issues of overseas economic policy, especially the imposition of import controls, and on aspects of regional policy, the DEA came into conflict with the Board of Trade.[32] Much more import-ant was the relationship with the Treasury, which, as noted above, had been identified by many Labour sympathisers as a key obstacle to faster growth, and the body to which the DEA was seen as a necessary counter-weight if Labour's ambitions were to be realised.

The archives certainly show a great deal of tension between the Treasury and the DEA in the drawing up of the Plan, but it is important to try to understand the basis of this conflict.[33] In his memoirs, George Brown suggested that 'the DEA and the Treasury were running two diametrically opposed policies. We were vigorously stirring things up to try to get the whole economy running ahead; the Treasury was con-tinuously damping things down'. In one sense this was true: in the face of balance of payments problems and pressure on the exchange rate, the Treasury was the key department in designing the deflationary responses that punctuated the period, beginning as early as October 1964.[34] In the short run, the DEA had few alternative strategies to pro-pose to these measures to protect the balance of payments, and in any case Brown did not support even these. He was party to the decision right at the beginning of the government's period in office to defend the value of the pound, and when he changed his mind in the summer of 1966 he seems to have had little desire to press for devaluation. Equally, the DEA did not support Douglas Jay's proposals to use import quotas on a long-term basis to defend the balance of payments.[35]

There is little evidence of Treasury hostility to planning on the basis of traditional left/right arguments about the costs and benefits of markets. While there was a broader ideological debate on planning in this vein in the 1960s, discussion inside the government machine rarely reflected this debate. Partly this was because, for all the dirigiste rhetoric of people like Balogh and others in Labour circles, the National Plan was largely 'indicative' (or, more accurately, subjunctive): it consisted of asking industries how they would respond *if* GDP growth were 25 per cent over the Plan period, given also that the balance of payments would have to be in surplus and that labour force growth would be slow.[36] The responses of industry to these enquiries were then collated and, after limited iteration, reconciled within an input–output framework derived from the Cambridge Social Accounting Matrix (more detail is given on this below).[37] The capacity of government then to ensure that these industry-level projections were delivered was extremely limited and involved very little in the way of physical controls (except in the area of building licensing and industrial development certificates); instead it remained reliant on financial incentives. While the British planners, encouraged by Balogh, talked to Soviet Gosplanners, any interchange of methods was purely at the technical/methodological level; as a Soviet trade union delegation was told: 'planning in the UK does not involve the central allocation of resources but aims to set out the general pattern of growth'.[38]

From a Treasury perspective, just setting out 'the general pattern of growth' posed serious problems for economic management. The starting point for discussion in formulating the Plan was a 4 per cent per annum growth rate, which had been used in previous NEDC work. This figure was ultimately political; the Conservatives had talked of a 4 per cent rate and, as Brown told ministerial colleagues, 'from the point of view of public presentation it would be difficult to set a lower figure'. At that same meeting Brown had suggested making the Plan's figure of 25 per cent growth relate to the years 1965–70, whereas the final Plan was less optimistic, with its target of 25 per cent for 1964–70, an average of 3.8 per cent but, because of a lower rate was set for 1964 and 1965, it still required a 4 per cent annual rate to be achieved 'well before 1970'.[39] Apart from the need to make the Plan embody a clear message that the government intended a significant acceleration of growth, Brown was also in the winter of 1964 concentrating a great deal of attention on negotiating his 'Declaration of Intent' on productivity, prices and incomes, and this task would have been much harder with more pessimistic projections of the 'planned growth of incomes' Brown was promising to the TUC.[40]

Behind this decision lay months of arithmetical wrangling, in which the Treasury expressed strong worries about the high-profile publication of optimistic projected growth rates; it favoured instead the setting of a range of possible rates, from 22.5 to 25 per cent.[41] A central concern was the impact of such rates on public expenditure. In preparation for Labour's accession to power, the Treasury had prepared briefings for the new government that spelt out the scale of public expenditure expansion launched by the Conservatives. Projections in September 1964 suggested that that expansion, without any additions from Labour's promises, would show increases of 4.4 per cent per annum up to 1968/69. Thus Labour would be faced with 'a very serious and difficult' fiscal problem, because 'even with a rate of increase of GNP, only a remarkable further growth of savings would prevent a continuing need to increase taxation'.[42]

The Treasury recognised that some components of public expenditure such as investment in electricity and roads would need to grow rapidly if an acceleration of growth were to be feasible. On the other hand, it believed that Labour would be under tremendous pressure to increase public spending in general and that a high projected national growth rate would make resistance to such pressure very much harder. One suggestion was to have a different figure for growth-inducing expenditure – one higher than that for the generality of public spending. Another was to have a lower projected growth rate for public spending purposes than that to be announced in the Plan.[43] In the event, these discussions in the context of formulating the Plan were overtaken by the separate decision in January 1965 to announce that public spending would be allowed to rise at 'only' 4.25 per cent per annum.[44]

The Treasury was not here acting only in its traditional role as guardian of the public purse. The difficulty about a high projected growth rate was not just its impact on public spending, but on the whole balance of the economy. If this fast growth projection encouraged both a rapid growth in public expenditure and a very substantial switch of resources into exports, as well as a sharp rise in investment to make the growth possible, as assumed at the time, there would be a very serious squeeze on the resources available for private consumption. The Treasury doubted the viability of such a squeeze even if growth did reach 4 per cent; how much more difficult it would be if investment and public spending grew at 'optimistic' rates but GDP (perhaps because of slow growth of exports) failed to do so.[45]

Not surprisingly, therefore, it seems to have been in the area of public spending that the 'Concordat' setting out the respective responsibilities of the DEA and Treasury was most problematic. The distinction between the Treasury's responsibility for 'functional' blocks of expenditure and the DEA's for the 'resource' implications of such spending made little sense in the light of the issues about the overall balance of the economy noted above.[46] If departmental (i.e. functional) expenditure rose rapidly, this would have to draw resources from either investment or private consumption, with huge implications for the overall development of the economy, especially in a context where reasonably rapid growth of private consumption looked like a precondition for an effective incomes policy.

The most problematic aspect of the Plan was its treatment of the balance of payments. The approach embodied in the Plan was to work back from the 25 per cent growth target to the prospective level of imports, then calculate what increase in exports would be required to finance those imports. (There were also some strong assumptions about the behaviour of other parts of the balance of payments – see below.) The simple answer to such arithmetic was a 5.5 per cent annual increase in exports; when the planners approached industry in the industrial enquiry, this figure was quoted as that compatible with the growth target. Such figuring was not at all to the Treasury's taste. It believed that the Plan should have as a central focus not growth but the correction of the balance of payments. As a senior adviser urged in relation to the Plan: 'I would like the DEA [to be] told to concentrate their economic planning on the export drive'.[47] This was partly an argument about being realistic in relation to the constraints facing the British economy. But it also reflected scepticism about the attainment of a 5.5 per cent increase in exports. This figure had been supported by industries consulted in the enquiry, and the DEA deployed this fact in aid of its successful effort to get such a figure included in the published Plan. But, as was widely recognised, the industry figure was hardly a reliable, independent estimate. As the DEA itself noted, 'in many cases there was little evidence in the replies that the industries had made a careful assessment of export markets for their products, which would indeed have been difficult to complete in the short time available'.[18]

From a Treasury point of view this insouciant optimism about exports went along with an even worse fault: an absence of recognition that the expansion of exports would directly compete with domestic investment in its demands for engineering goods. For the Treasury, this highlighted the dangers of the planners' beguilement by the 'investment mystique', which gave excessive weight to the ability of a rise in the volume of investment to generate faster growth, and in doing so unwittingly made projections of export growth even more unrealistic.[49] Finally on this aspect, the Treasury stressed how much the export projections relied on policies to hold down British costs, and for the DEA that meant especially a prices and incomes policy. While the Treasury certainly supported such a policy, it was sceptical about the scale of its effects, especially if, as the DEA envisaged, the economy was being run at a very high level of demand and therefore very low level of unemployment, which would make it much more difficult to hold down wage costs.[50]

The other area of quantification where the Treasury was sceptical of the approach of the DEA was productivity. The 3.8 per cent growth rate could easily be decomposed into the sum of the rate of growth of the labour force (which was reasonably foreseeable over the near future) and a rate of growth of (labour) productivity. The former was slowing down in the mid-1960s, but the DEA saw regional policy as a way of allowing a more rapid increase, by redistributing employment and so making possible a lower average rate of unemployment. This focus on labour supply in substantial part explains why regional policy had so much emphasis in the DEA and in the Plan (see 'Regional planning and policy', below).

Even with the addition of the regional factor to projected labour supply, the productivity figure had to be optimistic to make the numbers add up. There was evidence of some acceleration in productivity from the 1950s into the early 1960s; a widely cited article of 1964 suggested that the figure had gone from 1.8 per cent in 1952 to 2.7 per cent in 1964.[51] But to achieve the 3.8 per cent average annual increase in output required by the 25 per cent target would require a further increase in productivity expansion to 3.4 per cent, even with an optimistic projection of labour supply.[52]

The disagreements between the Treasury and the DEA in the preparation of the Plan were therefore multiple. In part this followed from a different perception of what a Plan should be about and should try to achieve. For the Treasury, the argument for planning was that it would yield evidence of bottlenecks and so aid better policy-making. Thus the Treasury was, in principle, quite keen on the industrial enquiry if its purpose was to inform government about specific production bottle-necks and inefficiencies, and identify where government might be able to help. This approach fitted in with a scepticism about putting too much emphasis on increasing the quantity of investment, as opposed to using existing equipment and labour supply more effectively.[53]

On the other hand, the Treasury was sceptical of quantified 'targets', especially when they related to a year in the future without the path to that year being spelt out. This approach derived from the Treasury's understanding of the policy process. Thus, for example, the Treasury was not opposed, in principle, to the policies of cutting back overseas government expenditure and foreign investment to aid the balance of payments. But it was opposed to writing into a published plan quanti-fied targets for such policies, because it foresaw great difficulty in getting the decisions that would deliver these outcomes through the political process. Publishing implausible figures on the international accounts would give hostages to fortune and might actively damage international confidence if they were seen as implausible. Implausible projections for growth would also be damaging in that they would make it possible to ignore the hard choices that would have to be made on, for example, public expenditure and private consumption.[54]

Doubts about the wisdom of publishing the Plan continued through the summer of 1965. Robert Neild, economic adviser to the Chancellor, after noting that the section on the balance of payments 'was not credible', went on to spell out the politics of the question of publication: 'Politically, the answer depends on how one balances the risk of con-firming the views of people abroad that our long-term policies are not credible against the possible political gains at home from publishing a plan full of long-term priorities'.[55] The National Plan was in fact pub-lished in September 1965, after last-minute insertions were made to reflect the deflationary measures of July and the centrality of the balance of payments issue.

At the Cabinet meeting which decided on publication, Brown con-ceded that the July measures (see Chapter 3) meant 'it might prove to be impossible to ensure sufficient acceleration in later years to achieve the full objective of 25 per cent' but, he argued, 'a period of relatively slow growth would not necessarily be an inappropriate time at which to publish a plan designed to encourage industry to take the necessary measures to achieve a faster rate'. Wilson, too, spoke up in support of maintaining the 25 per cent target 'on the grounds that the Plan could not be simply an extrapolation of past economic trends but must be designed to encourage industry to aim at a higher level of output'. Doubts were expressed by some ministers about the credibility of the export figures, and more generally about whether the Plan was strong enough on the means of implementation and sufficiently clear on 'the extent to which the Government would take deliberate action to ensure that it would be fulfilled'.[56] In one sense, the answer to the last query was already evident by the time the Plan was published: the deflationary measures of November 1964 and July 1965 showed the government was using its most powerful instruments of policy (fiscal and monetary) to ensure that the Plan could *not* be achieved.

The decision to publish the Plan – despite the decisions already taken which rendered the achievement of its targets highly implausible – was politically inescapable. The whole build-up in Labour's thinking on planning outlined above made it impossible not to produce a plan of some sort, and early on in the lifetime of the government. In fact, Brown had hoped to publish an outline plan much earlier, but the draft met opposition from his own DEA as well as the Treasury and was given a rough time at the NEDC meeting which considered it.[57] This may in part have reflected the sidelining of the NEDC in the preparation process for the Plan, and the general dislike on the part of the CBI and TUC for the NEDC losing its autonomy. Both the CBI and the TUC also believed that the outline of the Plan was too general in tone to be of much practical use. In fact, the scepticism on the employers' side was sustained right up to the last minute, and they agreed to endorse the final version of the Plan only after considerable arm-twisting by the Secretary of State.[58]

The delay in the spring and summer of 1965 allowed the completion of the industrial enquiry. In this, the DEA set out certain macro-economic parameters on GDP growth, the overall allocation of resources, the balance of payments and public spending, and then asked industries for estimates of output and exports for 1967 and 1970. The questionnaire asked for these forecasts to be based on 'present plans and expectations', and asked that these be linked to forecasts of demand (including exports), investment and labour requirements.[59]

Given the speed with which this enquiry was conducted (approximately two months), the results were patchy. The answers on demand in 1970 and labour and investment requirements were reasonable, but those on output, investment, exports and employment in the intervening period were 'of doubtful value'.[60] This, of course, replicated a problem of the overall Plan – it laid down objectives for the relatively distant future (1970) but had no story about how the economy was to get to that happy state.

Most of the questionnaires, sent out via the NEDO and the economic development councils (EDCs – the 'Little Neddies'), were filled in by trade associations. Samuel Brittan's critique of the planning process used this fact to deride the Plan's emphasis on 'industry' as an entity, saying that this gave undue encouragement to 'grey' committees rather than individual firms, where real change was initiated.[61] Inside the DEA, the same point was made, but with a rather different gloss. There was much discussion of how effective planning and especially its implementation required more contact between government and individual firms, the real decision-makers in industry. While links with individual firms already existed, if unevenly, across government, contrary to Brittan's views the planning process did initiate more intensive contacts, and fed into the idea that the structure of firms in Britain was itself a problem that needed to be addressed, and hence on to the policy of creating the Industrial Reorganisation Corporation (IRC).[62]

In the period between the publication of the Plan (September 1965) and the following July, intensive work continued on trying to turn policies announced there into reality. Despite the deflation in the summer of 1965, the Plan could still be regarded as having some plausibility, and certainly in the DEA the impetus of the search for faster growth was sustained. However, industry was already very sceptical about the Plan. Follow-up enquiries after its publication found a very mixed picture of performance compared with Plan forecasts, but most tellingly that, when asked if they wanted to revise their 1970 forecasts, 'few were willing to undertake complex new calculations on the basis of an overall growth rate now regarded as unrealistic'.[63]

In the Treasury, increasingly gloomy estimates were being made of growth prospects. By January 1966 the Treasury forecast for the 1965–70 period was down to 16 per cent, based on the rate of expansion that would be allowed by aiming to achieve a balance of payments surplus by 1970.[64] But this was before the balance of payments crisis which blew up in the summer of 1966, which in July provoked a package of sharply deflationary policies, along with a wage freeze (see Chapter 2). After these there could be no doubt that the Plan as a realistic assessment of how fast the economy might grow was dead, and after seeing through his prices and incomes measure Brown moved from the DEA to become Foreign Secretary. The DEA itself continued in existence until 1969, first under Michael Stewart, and then from September 1967 under Wilson himself.[65]

As well as causing a major crisis within the government, the July measures compromised the fragile consensus around planning that had previously existed. The CBI regarded the government's measures as a major blow to the expansion of output and investment, and sought reassurances about the future pattern of demand management. At the second productivity conference, in 1967, the CBI successfully pressed for a discussion on planning as a way of putting pressure on the government to provide such reassurances.[66] On the TUC side there was also much disillusion with the planning process, though the implication drawn was very different from that of the CBI. For the TUC, the need was for a much more dirigiste approach to industry, with binding plans on output and investment.[67] The government accepted the need for a debate on planning at the productivity conference, but successfully steered discussion away from the public attack on the government some in the CBI hoped for.[68] No concessions were made to the TUC's version of planning, which was at odds both with the 'indicative' character of the original Plan, but even more with the government's keen desire to rebuild confidence in the private sector to encourage investment.

If the drama of the summer of 1966 made the public relations of 'the social partners' much more fraught, it also encouraged a re-focusing of that classic tripartite body, the NEDC. In July Fred Catherwood replaced Robert Shone as the Director General of the NEDC, and had to deal with the diverging views of the CBI, TUC and the government about the future of economic policy. One response was to focus much more of the attention of the NEDC and the 'Little Neddies' on highly specific issues of industrial efficiency and away from grand strategies at the aggregate level. This approach, soon labelled 'Catherwoodery', found considerable favour in Whitehall, including in the Treasury, which had always seen such micro-activity as the most effective aspect of 'planning'.[69] Such an approach was linked to the striking growth in concern with the productivity issue evident from the summer of 1966 (see Chapter 8). At the time of the July crisis, Wilson stressed in Cabinet that 'it was essential that both public opinion and industry at all levels should be more conscious of the importance of the increase of productivity' and went on to emphasise the importance of the forthcoming productivity conferences and 'the educational opportunity provided by the spare television time which would be available until a University of the Air could be introduced'. At a time when industrial investment was expected to be hard hit by deflation, increased productivity by greater effort appeared an attractive 'alternative': at the same meeting, another Cabinet member urged the need to foster 'a conviction that improvement of productivity should be achieved not only by better machines and better methods but also greater individual effort arising from a sense of social purpose'.[70]

Planning after the Plan

The National Plan included the sentence: 'The Plan will be kept under regular review in the light of developments and periodic re-assessments will be made so that Government and industry can base their plans on the latest information available'.[71] But after July 1966 this 'review' process looked highly problematic. The failure of the 1965 Plan had discredited planning in the eyes of many. But in their very different ways the CBI and TUC, acting through the NEDC, wanted to keep some kind of planning process going, as of course did the DEA. In 1967 a summary of the attitudes to planning of these three groups spelt out their differences. 'The TUC wanted to identify obstacles and understood the plan as a map of the way to overcome them ... the CBI wanted independent forecasts, which [had been] discussed with Trade Associations and EDCs, with [the] CBI identifying the policy implications ... the DEA wanted two numerical projections of growth, followed by an industrial inquiry'.[72]

After July 1966 the government remained committed to the publication of some further planning document, but the DEA was now understandably wary. In January 1967 the Chancellor suggested that a new plan would be useful for the discussion of future public expenditure, but Stewart argued that 'his primary concern was to avoid a repetition of the fate of the last Plan' as it would be 'highly undesirable to put before the country a facile and optimistic programme'. Shortly after, he noted the argument that setting a target in excess of past performance would lead everyone to plan for faster growth, but 'Whatever the general merits of this argument, it does not appear relevant to our present situation. Business will have confidence in more rapid expansion only if there is a credible strategy for attaining it'.[73]

Divisions about the meaning of planning within the NEDC, the DEA's concern to avoid another still-born plan, plus uncertainties about the Common Market meant nothing was published before devaluation, which then altered the whole context of discussion, although a draft document had been discussed at the NEDC earlier in 1967.[74] Early in 1968 the NEDC discussion of a draft 'Economic assessment to 1972' showed considerable disagreement between the CBI, TUC and the government and doubts about whether any statement could represent the views of all three.[75] There was a promise of a 'more substantial planning document' in the autumn, but any such document raised serious problems about the future pattern of resource allocation, especially public spending and, of course, the balance of payments. In July it was decided to postpone any publication until the path of the balance of payments was clear, Wilson commenting that: 'a weakness of the National Plan had been its basis upon an assumed rate of growth rather than a realistic assumption about the development of the balance of payments'.[76]

By 1969 the cuts in public expenditure had gone through and the balance of payments was at last coming right, allowing the publication by the DEA of *The Task Ahead*. This followed the idea of 'alternative scenarios' of slow (just under 3 per cent), basic (3.75 per cent) and faster

(4 per cent) growth paths down to 1972.[77] The balance of payments was now at the centre of the projections, with the acceptance that a continuing big shift of resources into exports was essential, though the projection for the growth of personal consumption was, arguably, still optimistic.[78] *The Task Ahead* was intended as a guide for extensive consultation with industry, what was now called 'the dialogue'; it was a 'planning document not a plan'.[79] Just over a year later, in May 1970, and after the demise of the DEA, Labour's final planning document was published, entitled *Economic Prospects to 1972: A Revised Assessment*, following the completion of 'the dialogue' but postponed until after the budget of that year – a sign of the secondary and subordinate nature of 'planning' by this stage of the government.[80] By now, government thinking had moved away from planning to a focus on more direct and selective mechanisms of intervention (Chapter 5) and productivity (Chapter 8).

Regional planning and policy

Even before the National Plan had been published, the government announced the setting-up of new regional planning councils and boards, the former with a representative role, the latter bringing together local officials of central government departments. Such bodies reflected the new 'regional consciousness' which had developed over the preceding decade.[81] The National Plan (after pointing out that much new regionally based statistical material was being generated) placed these new bodies in a national context: 'The Central government, together with these regional economic planning Councils and Boards that have been set up, will now use all this material, together with detailed local knowledge, as a basis for planning in the regions consistent with the National Plan as a whole'.[82]

In the Plan, the key role of regional policy was located in the context of labour force policy; fuller use of workers in high-unemployment areas would allow a higher level of demand nationally without excessive cost inflation. The resulting 'balanced growth' would involve self-sustaining expansion in the regions, while relieving congestion in the South East and Midlands.[83]

In practice, the Labour government strongly pursued regional *policy*, while doing little that deserves the name regional *planning*. Policy for the regions was largely under the control of the Board of Trade until 1969, and the policies pursued were those the Board had initiated in the 1940s – essentially subsidies and grants to take work to the workers, with some negative control over new building in the prosperous regions. The policies were driven by the desire to narrow the gap in unemployment rates between areas dominated by the old staples (coal, steel, shipbuilding) and the national average. With this aim, there were major extensions of policy. In 1964 control of industrial development in London and the South East was extended to offices. In 1966 larger 'development areas' were substituted for existing 'development districts', regionally enhanced investment grants were brought in instead of allowances, and the new SET included a regional component. In 1967 the regional employment premium (REP) was introduced, which gave a substantial subsidy (amounting to about 7 per cent of labour costs) in the affected areas (see below).[84] Also in 1967 'special development areas' were introduced to give greater help to regions hit by the accelerated pit closure programme. Finally, in 1969, reduced-rate subsidies were extended to intermediate or 'grey' areas, mainly in Yorkshire, Humberside and East Lancashire.

Policy changes were driven mainly by unemployment considerations, which were especially important when the national rate turned upwards after 1966. This was despite the argument made in the 1966 White Paper on regional policy, which promised a move away from an exclusive focus on unemployment to 'wider regional policies', in which 'account will be taken of such factors as population change, including migration, and employment trends as well as the level of unemployment'.[85] But this was, of course, before deflationary pressures made unemployment rather than labour shortage a compelling issue. The political significance of unemployment is evident in Wilson's questioning of the effectiveness of Board of Trade's policy in this regard.[86] Beneath the focus on unemployment was an implicit (and sometimes explicit) rejection of the alternative 'growth pole', ideas which had been increasing in influence since the 1950s, and which had had some effects on Conservative policy in the late 1950s. In this account, regional policy should focus on stimulating areas of regional expansion, rather than applying what was disparagingly called 'first aid' to troubled areas. There was much debate on this issue in the Wilson years, but despite support from some officials scepticism was much more common, and unemployment remained the key issue for regional policy, as illustrated by the introduction of the REP.[87]

The economic advice which lay behind the REP stressed the high costs of investment subsidies and the logic of subsidising the use of the under-used factor, labour. Arguments that such policies encouraged wasteful use of labour were deemed largely irrelevant while unemployment persisted. Despite criticism, notably from the CBI, the REP went ahead just before devaluation. In effect, it was like a regional devaluation, but argued for in terms of offsetting the bias to capital intensity resulting from investment allowances.[88] The scale of these new subsidies evoked pressure from those in intermediate areas, where unemployment exceeded the national average but was too low to lead to development area status. As a result, an enquiry was set up, which produced the Hunt report. This proposed a major extension of the areas in receipt of subsidies, albeit at a lower rate, but also a shift towards infrastructure projects and away from direct employment support. This followed the ideas of the industrialists on the Hunt committee.[89] These proposals met with considerable hostility in the ministries, because of their cost, the political problems of giving lower priority to the development areas, and their emphasis on infrastructure. This last point was deemed both expensive and lacking short-term and readily calculable effects. The eventual policy offered only a watered down version of Hunt's proposals.[90]

Discussions around the Hunt report showed fundamental uncertainties about the aims and means of regional policy. Spending had shot up under Labour, and some success could be seen in decreasing unemployment disparities, despite a rising national trend.[91] But the contribution to national policy goals, especially that of growth, remained obscure. Hunt had argued that policy should be aimed 'primarily at modernisation rather than the provision of employment' but this would not be an accurate description of the policy that was actually formed.[92]

Regional policy under Labour saw a reinforcement of existing approaches rather than a new departure into regional economic planning. The regional planning boards and councils drew up plans, but their main role was in physical planning, and they never became economic planning bodies in the sense of having significant autonomous power over actions in their regions. Their limited role, and confinement largely to town and country planning issues, is suggested by the fact that when the DEA was abolished in 1969 responsibility for them was transferred to the Ministry of Housing and Local Government, at the same time as responsibility for regional economic policy was shifted from the Board of Trade to the Ministry of Technology (MinTech). While in existence, the DEA had shown some interest in regional economic planning, aided by the growing 'regional' consciousness evident in Wales and Scotland, but the Board of Trade (in alliance with the Treasury) remained in control of the policy instruments. After Crosland replaced Jay at the Board of Trade in 1967, the emphasis on reducing unemployment by nationally determined measures remained the centre of regional policy. As W. A. Parsons argues, in this area the division between the DEA and the Board of Trade reflected a distinction between those who (to an untested extent) were willing to allow some regional policy devolution as a basis for meaningful regional planning, and those who regarded unemployment reduction by the most tried and tested instruments as the highest priority.[93]

Conclusions

There is a bathetic air to Labour's National Plan. Reflecting a political imperative to be seen to aim at breaking out of Tory stop–go, and aiming to generate the resources upon which Labour could deliver its improvements, it was already out of date by the time of publication, having been undermined by successive deflationary measures designed to defend the balance of payments. The 1966 'July measures' gave it the *coup de grâce*. In many respects the use of the word 'planning' mis-states what was involved in Labour's approach as embodied in the National Plan. It involved no significant new deviations from the scale of state activity that existed under the Conservatives. Some new ideas that might enhance the government's role were discussed (for example, greater use of government purchasing to shape industry), but by and large the Plan was never even intended to involve anything beyond a more co-ordinated and effective deployment of public resources com-bined with a similarly co-ordinated use of existing or marginally reshaped sticks and carrots in the private sector. It ran into problems not because it tried to tell the private sector what to do in an econom-ically or politically unsustainable fashion, but essentially because it simultaneously fudged the macro-economic arithmetic and exaggerated how far such fudging could be offset by micro-economic improvement over the relatively short run.

The Plan embodied a set of views about the sources of economic growth, and in particular the role of investment, which actually made it harder for the macro-economic numbers to add up. At the same time, it enumerated an agenda of micro-economic reforms which in principle it is hard to fault, even if their likely scale of effects was exaggerated. DEA and NEDC insiders naturally rejected the view that the July measures rendered the whole National Plan irrelevant. They rightly pointed out that many of the items in the 'checklist' could be pursued irrespective of the state of demand and many of them indeed were followed through in the late 1960s.[94] In that sense the Plan set a generally sound agenda for industrial reform and shifts in government policy which informed subsequent action. The problem with this 'defence' of Labour's Plan is that, as Opie pointed out, 'All the so-called "Actions" in the Action list [checklist] made sense and *would have made sense without any Plan*'.[95] In other words, the use of the word 'plan' for what was in-tended by Labour was, in terms of economic mechanisms, not logically required and was indeed confusing. However, this is to miss the point that 'planning' in the 1960s usually connoted not so much a set of economic devices as a commitment to 'purposive action', designed to contrast with alleged Conservative 'drift'. This use of the term is evident not only across a range of the Labour government's policies (not just economic) but also provided the terms of debate for critics. For example, much of the criticism of its social policy was couched in terms of the *absence* of planning, despite the rhetoric.[96]

Planning as a term had deep resonances for Labour, but it should not be seen primarily as concerned with economists' debates about the role of markets, or about the role of competition versus the state's interventionist role. Those kinds of arguments were much less evident in the 1960s than the 1940s. In part this reflected the very limited dirigisme of Labour's Plan, in turn rooted in Labour's profound ambivalence towards markets and competition. Many important figures in Labour circles, such as Jenkins, Jay and Crosland, had long been advocates of competition as a central part of the mixed economy. Furthermore, the planning experiment of the 1940s had been most successful where it was now most disregarded – in the international area. While Labour in the 1960s used import controls as an emergency measure, the general thrust of its policy was towards freer international trade. In an open economy, state intervention is necessarily constrained (though not of course prevented) by international pressures, especially in a country anxious to improve its international competitiveness. But even at the purely domestic level, Labour was ambivalent in its attitudes to 'market forces'. Thus the strengthening of monopolies legislation in 1965 was, as suggested in Chapter 5, complicated by the concurrent enthusiasm for mergers, but nevertheless represented a genuine attempt to extend competition across much of the private economy. Thus we should not allow the undoubted importance of the word 'planning' in the 1960s to blind us to the fact that competition (both international and domestic) was also an important facet of Labour's drive for 'modernisation'.

Notes

The place of publication is London unless otherwise specified.

1 See D. Ritschel, *The Politics of Planning* (Oxford, 1997), for the inter-war debates on planning.
2 J. Tomlinson, *Democratic Socialism and Economic Policy: The Attlee Years 1945–51* (Cambridge, 1997), ch. 6; R. Toye, 'Gosplanners versus thermostatters: Whitehall planning debates and their political consequences, 1945–49', *Contemporary British History*, 14 (2000), pp. 81–106.
3 N. Rollings, '"The Reichstag method of governing"? The Attlee government and permanent economic controls', in H. Mercer, N. Rollings and J. Tomlinson (eds), *Labour Governments and Private Industry: The Experience of 1945–51* (Edinburgh, 1992), pp. 15–36.
4 N. Ellison, *Egalitarian Thought and Labour Politics: Retreating Visions* (1994), p. 80.
5 A. Crosland, *The Future of Socialism* (1956), pp. 504–5, 508–11.
6 I. Zweiniger-Bargielowska, *Austerity in Britain: Rationing Controls, and Consumption 1939–1955* (Oxford, 2000).

7   R. Acland, *et al.*, *Keeping Left* (1950).
8   PRO, PREM 8/1183, 'The state and private industry', 4 May 1950; Ellison, *Egalitarian Thought*; I. Favretto, '"Wilsonism" reconsidered: Labour Party revisionism, 1952–64', *Contemporary British History*, 14 (2000), pp. 54–80.
9   H. Wilson, *In Place of Dollars* (1953), p. 15.
10 H. Wilson, *Post-war Economic Policies in Britain*, Fabian Tract 309 (1957); Favretto, 'Wilsonism', pp. 55–6; Labour Party, *Plan for Progress* (1958), p. 9.
11 *Plan for Progress*, pp. 11–17.
12 *LPACR* 1957, pp. 128–35; Labour Party, *Industry and Society* (1957), pp. 42–5.
13 *LPACR* 1958, p. 165; R. Jenkins, *The Labour Case* (1959), p. 52; M. Shanks, *The Stagnant Society* (Harmondsworth, 1961).
14 N. Tiratsoo, *Reconstruction, Affluence and Labour Party Politics: Coventry 1945–60* (1990); Crosland, *Future of Socialism*, ch. 13.
15 Wilson, *LPACR* 1963, pp. 133–40; Jenkins, *Labour Case*, p. 83.
16 T. Balogh, *Planning for Progress*, Fabian Tract 346 (1963), pp. 14–19, sets out the case for incomes policy very clearly, but micro-economic wage planning is not mentioned.
17 Favretto, 'Wilsonism', pp. 64–7. On automation, see LPA, Research Department correspondence, 'Automation', 1956.
18 Labour Party, *Signposts for the Sixties* (1961), p. 13.
19 H. Wilson, 'A four-year plan for Britain', *New Statesman*, 24 March 1961, pp. 462–3, 464, 468.
20 Generally on Balogh, see P. Streeten (ed.), *Unfashionable Economics: Essays in Honour of Lord Balogh* (1970); Balogh, *Planning*, pp. 4, 25; also T. Balogh, 'The drift towards economic planning', in R. Blackburn and P. Anderson (eds), *Towards Socialism* (1965), pp. 53–76.
21 Balogh, *Planning*, pp. 13–14.
22 *Signposts*, pp. 13–15; Labour Party, *Let's Go with Labour for the New Britain* (1964), pp. 46–51.
23 M. Shanks, 'The "irregular" in Whitehall', in Streeten, *Unfashionable Economics*, pp. 244–62. There were, of course, in all this echoes of the short-lived experiment with Stafford Cripps as Minister for Economic Affairs outside the Treasury of 1947; G. Brown, *In My Way* (1971), ch. 5.
24 NEDC, *Growth of the British Economy to 1966* (1963); *idem*, *Conditions Favourable to Faster Growth* (1963). A. Ringe, 'Background to Neddy: economic planning in the 1960s', *Contemporary British History*, 12 (1998), pp. 82–98; N. Rollings and A. Ringe, 'Responding to relative decline: the creation of the NEDC', *Economic History Review*, 53 (2000), pp. 331–53. For general accounts of planning, see J. Leruez, *Economic Planning and Politics in Britain* (1975), chs 6–14; A. Budd, *The Politics of Economic Planning* (1978), ch. 6; S. Brittan, *Steering the Economy: The Role of the Treasury* (1971), ch. 8.
25 H. Wilson, 'Planning in a vacuum', *New Statesman*, 26 October 1962, p. 558; T. Balogh, 'The weakness of Neddy', *New Statesman*, 11 May 1962, pp. 670–1. To emphasise the implications of the new arrangements, the Chancellor was excluded from the NEDC 'on the grounds that it would be concerned with questions of physical rather than financial planning': PRO, CAB 134/1736, 'Ministerial Committee on Economic Development', 2 November 1964.
26 *The National Plan*, Cmnd 2764, BPP 1964/65, vol. 30, pp. 1–2. A popular version of the plan, entitled *Working for Prosperity*, was published simultaneously.
27 F. Blackaby (ed.), *British Economic Policy 1960–74* (Cambridge, 1978), p. 416; M. Surrey, 'The National Plan in retrospect', *Bulletin of the Oxford University*

Institute of Economics and Statistics, 34 (1972), pp. 249–68, has the most detailed comparison of the Plan's targets against outcomes.

28 B. Pimlott, *Harold Wilson* (1992), p. 361.

29 *National Plan*, pp. 17–21; *Working for Prosperity* had an abbreviated list of eight items.

30 C. Clifford, 'The rise and fall of the DEA 1964–69; British government and indicative planning', *Contemporary British History*, 11 (1997), pp. 94–116.

31 *Ibid.*; Ringe, 'Background to Neddy'; G. O'Hara, 'British economic and social planning, 1959–1970' (unpublished PhD dissertation, University of London, 2002), pp. 100–6.

32 D. Jay, *Change and Fortune: A Political Record* (1980), pp. 297–300.

33 O'Hara, 'British', pp. 106–11.

34 Brown, *In My Way*, p. 113.

35 PRO, CAB 128/46, confidential annexe to 'Cabinet conclusions', 19 July 1966, where Brown said he was unconvinced that 'an immediate devaluation might not be the wiser course' than the deflationary policy being pursued. However, he is not recorded as responding when, at the next Cabinet meeting (4 August), Callaghan said that ministers 'should dismiss devaluation from consideration'.

36 For insider comments on Samuel Brittan's *Inquest on Planning* (1967), see PRO, T 230/846, 'Comment on PEP pamphlet by Brittan', 2 February 1967, where Cairncross notes a 'splendid job of criticism' but in turn criticises Brittan's emphasis on the power of demand management and the centrality of industrial investment to economic performance.

37 Estimates Committee, *Government Statistical Services* (4th report), appendix A, DEA, Preparation of the National Plan, HCP 246, BPP 1966/67, vol. 12, pp. 290–316. Also, 'UK: use of an input–output model in the preparation of the National Plan', in United Nations, *Macro-economic Models for Planning and Policy-Making* (Geneva, 1967), pp. 85–90. For criticisms of this approach, see PRO, EW 24/93, C. Goodhart, 'The strategy of planning', 6 September 1965. For British interest in French planning, see PRO, LAB 10/1757, W. Hopkins, 'French planning', 25 and 29 February 1961.

38 PRO, EW 24/211, Conversations with Gosplan, 1966/7; EW 24/153, 'Brief for speech to Soviet TU delegation', 27 September 1967.

39 PRO, CAB 134/1737, 'Ministerial Committee on Economic Development', 28 January 1965; *National Plan*, p. 1. As Callaghan noted in his memoirs: 'An incoming Labour Government after thirteen years in opposition could aim no lower than that'. *Time and Chance* (1987), p. 164.

40 PRO, EW 8/1, 'Incomes policy: brief for First Secretary's meeting with TUC', 9 November 1964, and 'First Secretary's meeting with TUC Economic Committee', 23 November 1964.

41 PRO, EW 24/7, 'National Plan papers', 12 November and 31 December 1964; EW 24/8, 'National Plan papers', 1 January 1965–31 May 1965; PRO, T 230/845, 'The plan for development of the national economy by 1970', October 1964–May 1965.

42 PRO, T 320/293, 'PESC: preparation of revised report', 28 September 1964.

43 PRO, CAB 129/120, Treasury, 'Public expenditure', 26 January 1965; PRO, T 230/845, L. Petch to R. Clarke, 'Expansion and the Plan', 6 January 1965.

44 For the public spending decision of January 1965, see Chapter 9.

45 PRO, T 230/845, A. Cairncross to W. Armstrong, 'A plan for economic development', 20 November 1964; also PRO, EW 24/11, 'Draft papers for Plan Co-ordination Working Party', 12 October 1965; T 230/584, R. Clarke to L. Petch, 5 January 1965.

46 PRO, CAB 129/119, B. Trend, 'Co-operation between the DEA and the Treasury', 16 December 1964. One of Brown's formulations of this division of labour made clear its arbitrary nature: 'proposals of industrial departments would have to be related to the total prospects of demand and activity formulated by the DEA and the prospects for public expenditure proposed by the Treasury'. PRO, CAB 134/1736, 'Minutes of Economic Strategy Committee', 23 November 1964.

47 PRO, T 230/845, 24 March 1965; T 230/847, W. Hopkins to A. Cairncross, 26 November 1964.

48 *National Plan*, pp. 80–2; Estimates Committee, 'Preparation', p. 296.

49 PRO, T 230/847, W. Hopkins to A. Cairncross, 26 November 1964.

50 PRO, T 230/740, D. McKean to R. Clarke, 'The National Plan', 20 July 1965.

51 W. Godley and J. Shepherd, 'Long-term growth and short-term policy', *National Institute Economic Review*, 29 (1964), pp. 26–38.

52 *National Plan*, p. 2; A. C. L. Day, 'The myth of four per cent growth', *Westminster Bank Review*, November 1964, pp. 2–13.

53 PRO, T 230/845, W. Hopkin to F. Atkinson, 'The Plan', 24 March 1965, which suggests that the DEA was wasting its time on 'model building' rather than focusing on supply bottlenecks.

54 PRO, T 230/740, P. Vinter to R. Clarke, 'The National Plan', 2 August 1965.

55 *Ibid.*, R. Neild to I. Bancroft, 20 July 1965.

56 PRO, CAB 128/39, 'Cabinet conclusions', 3 August 1965.

57 PRO, EW 24/48, 'NEDC meeting', 3 March 1965; PRO, CAB 128/39, 'Cabinet conclusions', 1 April 1965. See also O'Hara, 'British', p. 106.

58 Brown, *In My Way*, p. 105; F. Catherwood, 'Witness seminar: the NEDC 1962–67', *Contemporary British History*, 12 (1998), pp. 99–130.

59 PRO, EW 24/48, 'The preparation of the Plan', 20 December 1965 (a copy of the questionnaire is in *National Plan*, appendix C).

60 *Ibid.* Unsurprisingly, perhaps, the export figures especially were treated with great scepticism by the Treasury, an official describing them as 'pretty worthless'. PRO, T 230/740, D. Hubback, 'The Plan', 28 May 1965.

61 Brittan, *Inquest*, pp. 16–17; PRO, EW 24/71, 'The Plan and the firm', 1965–67; Brown, *In My Way*, pp. 101–2. The IRC is discussed in Chapter 5.

62 PRO, EW 24/93, 'National Plan', July 1965–December 1966; EW 24/96, 'National Plan: 1966 review'.

63 PRO, EW 24/71, 'Private industry in the first year of the National Plan', 27 June 1966.

64 PRO, T 230/846, P. Vinter to R. Clarke, 17 January 1966.

65 Clifford, 'Rise and fall', p. 101.

66 PRO, EW 24/90, 'National conference on productivity', 1967.

67 PRO, EW 24/131, 'NEDC meeting to consider TUC "Planning"', June 1967.

68 PRO, EW 24/90, 'Note for CBI meeting on planning', 3 March 1967.

69 PRO, EW 24/8, J. Grieve-Smith to D. MacDougall, 'The budget and the Plan', 23 April 1965.

70 PRO, CAB 129/41, 'Cabinet conclusions', 12 July 1966. The University of the Air was later renamed the Open University.

71 *National Plan*, p. 21.

72 PRO, CAB 134/2744, CBI, 'Industry's views on planning', 25 April 1967; PRO, EW 24/131, A. Stevens to D. Kirkness, 24 August 1967.

73 PRO, EW 24/131, 'Future planning work', 31 January 1967; PRO, CAB 134/3198, M. Stewart, 'Future planning work', 16 March 1967.

74 PRO, FG 2/681, 'Papers on planning for NEDC 1967', 2 August 1967; *Times*, 10 October 1967.

75 PRO, FG 1/18, 'NEDC minutes', 14 January 1968, 5 February 1969.

76 PRO, CAB 134/3201, 'Economic Strategy Committee', 4 March 1968, 30 July 1968.

77 DEA, *The Task Ahead* (1969).

78 T. Barker and J. Lecomber, *Economic Planning for 1972: An Appraisal of 'The Task Ahead'* (1969), pp. 784–5.

79 F. Catherwood, 'The dialogue', *National Westminster Bank Quarterly Review*, May 1969, pp. 2–9.

80 PRO, T 338/32, 'Review of the economic assessment to 1972', 1969/70.

81 W. A. Parsons, *The Political Economy of British Regional Policy* (1986), ch. 7.

82 *National Plan*, p. 12.

83 *Ibid.*, pp. 11, 12; PRO, CAB 134/2442, DEA, 'Economic growth and regional development – benefits and costs', 30 June 1965.

84 J. Hardie, 'Regional policy', in W. Beckerman (ed.), *The Labour Government's Economic Record* (1972), pp. 218–46.

85 *Investment Incentives*, Cmnd 2874, BPP 1965/66, vol. 13, para. 45; PRO, BT 177/2454, DEA, 'Reconsideration of regional policy in relation to development areas', 11 December 1967.

86 PRO, BT 177/2702, H. Wilson to D. Jay, 9 April 1967.

87 PRO, BT 177/2454, 'Reconsideration of regional policy development areas (draft)', 5 October 1967.

88 PRO, BT 177/2700, 'A regional employment subsidy: proposal for extra premium in the development areas', 1 February 1967; PRO, CAB 129/130, 'Regional employment premium', 24 May 1967.

89 *Report of Hunt Committee on Intermediate Areas*, Cmnd 3998, BPP 1968/69, vol. 35; PRO, T 224/1952, 'Treasury working group on fiscal/economic aspects of regional policy', 7 March 1969, p. 8.

90 PRO, T 224/1952, 'Treasury working group on fiscal/economic aspects of regional policy'; PRO, BT 177/2455, 'President's meeting with officials: the Hunt Committee', 28 November 1968.

91 Hardie, 'Regional policy', p. 241; PRO, T 277/2084, DEA, 'Regional incentives', 17 December 1968.

92 PRO, T 224/1952, 'Treasury working group on fiscal/economic aspects of regional policy', 7 March 1969.

93 Parsons, *Political Economy*, pp. 224–6.

94 Catherwood, 'Dialogue', p. 4; D. MacDougall, *Don and Mandarin: Memoirs of an Economist* (1987), p. 169, says the checklist 'was largely independent of the figuring'.

95 R. Opie, 'Economic growth and planning', in Beckerman, *Labour Government's Economic Record*, p. 177. Emphasis added.

96 P. Townsend, 'Social planning and the control of priorities', in P. Townsend and R. Bosanquet (eds), *Labour and Inequality* (1972), pp. 274–300.

5

Investment, technology and the firm

The National Plan set out a very wide range of policies required to achieve its growth target, but, it asserted, 'Investment lies at the heart of the Plan'.[1] The aim in particular was to increase manufacturing fixed investment at a rate of 7 per cent per annum, with total investment rising at 5.5 per cent. This overall rate of increase was slower than that given in the Plan for the 1960–64 period (6.6 per cent), but the aim was to tilt the increase away from distribution, roads, housing and public services towards manufacturing plus construction. It was anticipated that the share of investment in GNP would increase, but this was implicitly accepted as tolerable as, with a projected higher growth rate, consumption would still grow faster in absolute terms than in the previous (Conservative) period.[2]

The Plan also argued that, in order to promote greater efficiency in industry, the government had an important role to play in 'stimulating technological innovation'. This heading covered a range of activities, especially the activities of MinTech, in such areas as expanding the role of the National Research and Development Corporation (NRDC), diverting research and development resources from military to civilian use, spreading the use of advanced machine tools and computers, and encouraging automation.[3] The diversion of labour supply from military to civilian use is taken up in Chapter 6, but in other respects the activities of MinTech and other bodies seeking to speed up technological change are sensibly considered alongside the investment issue.

A third, related issue in the Plan was that of the scale of industry. Under the heading of 'Rationalisation' it suggested Britain faced problems because of 'the small size of many of its production units compared with those in the US and some other competing countries'. While recognising the need to prevent restrictive practices and monopolies, the government signalled its enthusiasm for mergers which promoted greater efficiency, and concluded that, 'Where the government can assist in the promotion of these desirable developments they are ready to do so and in some instances they may wish to take the initiative in helping to bring them about'.[4] At this stage there was no clear intent, but eventually such considerations were to lead to a major institutional innovation in the form of the IRC, which is discussed under its own heading, below.

Against the grain of its enthusiasm for scale and mergers, the government also passed the 1965 Monopolies and Mergers Act. In policy terms this was unimportant, but competition policy did raise difficult doctrinal and analytical issues for Labour in the 1960s, and these are surveyed before the concluding section of the chapter.

Investment

The focus on manufacturing investment meant a focus on private industry, given that Britain's pattern of public ownership left almost all manufacturing in private hands. The government was, of course, concerned with the pattern of public investment in both nationalised industries and the public sector generally, not least because this accounted for over half of total fixed investment. But because of the centrality of manufacturing investment to Labour's agenda, it is focused on here, while public sector investment is dealt with in Chapter 7.

The belief that physical investment is at the heart of economic growth has a long pedigree in Labour thinking. Most broadly we may say that this derives from a Fabian idea that efficiency comes from large-scale, capital-intensive and technologically sophisticated production units.[5] The Attlee government had certainly been of this view, and had encouraged a sharp rise in investment, concentrated in manufacturing. It had introduced the first investment subsidies, though these were general in nature rather than discriminatory, the discrimination in favour of manufacturing deriving from extensive physical controls.[6] As in other areas, there was an erosion of the scope of such controls in the later years of the Attlee government, and this led to much debate on how the encouragement of private investment could be combined with Labour's other policy goals. In particular, there was the attempt to uncouple profit as a source of personal income from its role in paying for investment, by taxing distributed profits more heavily than those retained within the company. This was especially important as the government was pursuing an incomes policy and believed that to do this successfully, it needed to demonstrate that the control of personal income encompassed profits and dividends as well as wages and salaries.[7] These concerns were to have important parallels in the Wilson period.

Labour's general attitude to the centrality of investment to growth had changed little in the period in opposition. Among academic economists, the precise link between investment and growth was much debated, but the dominant view remained that expanding physical productive capacity was the key issue for the expansion of GDP, and most of the 'declinist' literature of the early 1960s regarded raising Britain's investment rate as central to reversing 'decline'. The Conservatives in their propounding of 'modernisation' regarded higher investment as crucial, and it was central to the Neddy ideas of 1963–64.[8]

In opposition, much of Labour's attitude to raising investment was shaped by the popular idea that the Conservatives' stop–go policies were a major hindrance to investment because of the uncertainty they created. This, of course, lay very much behind the idea of the National Plan, with its assumption that increasing industry's confidence about the future path of the economy would create a much more favourable investment climate. Although Labour had also investigated in some detail the issue of how to encourage investment more directly, this discussion had failed to come to a conclusion. As the National Plan in 1965 stated, 'the Government are examining the effectiveness of the present system of investment allowances to see whether any changes are necessary'.[9] These examinations, completed late in 1965, led to a White Paper in January 1966. This announced that the government would introduce an investment grant scheme to largely replace the investment allowances which the Conservatives had expanded on following Labour's 1945 initiative. These would be paid only for plant and machinery investment in manufacturing and extractive industries, with a higher rate paid (40 per cent rather than 20 per cent) in development areas.[10]

These new grants were designed to be highly discriminatory in comparison with investment allowances. In part this flowed from a broad doctrinal belief that the expansion of the production of goods rather than services was the measure of a 'socialist' economy.[11] More specifically, this focus was based on the belief that manufacturing was the key area in which rapid productivity gains were available. This idea was especially associated with the work of the economist Nicholas Kaldor, a government adviser, who suggested that Britain's slow growth was due to its inability to raise output in manufacturing fast enough to gain the productivity benefits available. But while Kaldor undoubtedly influenced the general climate of discussion of investment incentives, the most direct policy idea flowing from his ideas was a tax to discriminate in favour of manufacturing *employment*, the SET, which is discussed in Chapter 6. Discrimination in favour of manufacturing also derived from the argument that it provided the bulk of exports, with extractive industries providing inputs to help that provision. The emphasis on plant and machinery as opposed to buildings seems to have been linked with the idea that this part of investment most directly embodied new technology. This concern with new technology led to special treatment of computers, which were eligible for a flat rate 20 per cent grant irrespective of location or the sector in which they were to be employed.

For similar reasons, plant and machinery for use for scientific research were eligible.[12]

This radical shift in policy was the product of months of tough debate in government circles. A new committee was established by the incoming government to look at the use of taxation 'as an instrument of long-term economic and social policy'.[13] This discussed a wide range of proposals, but focused on the use of taxes to help exports, including the ideas that eventually evolved into the SET. Scepticism about the effectiveness of investment allowances in government circles was almost universal by this time, based on the Richardson report on turnover tax, evidence from the NEDC, and work by one of the government's new advisers, Robert Neild. The emergent consensus was that, in making investment decisions, firms were largely concerned with calculations of expected pre-tax profits.[14] But finding an acceptable replacement was much easier than criticising the existing allowance system. Partly this was because of the diversity of aims – export promotion, acceleration of technical change and the promotion of regional growth were all at issue. Also important was the hostility of the CBI.

The employers' organisation was attached to allowances precisely because they were not discriminatory, but also because they did not show up as government expenditure, and therefore did not appear to be a 'dole' to industry.[15] Discussion with the CBI was complicated by the government's introduction of corporation tax and long-term capital gains tax in the 1965 budget. Corporation tax was in part intended to encourage profit retention (and hence investment) by more heavily taxing distributed profits, as Labour had done in the 1940s. The measure was extremely complicated, and disliked by the CBI, which also objected to such a large swathe of tax reform in such a short period.[16] In addition, the introduction of corporation tax, because it was combined with a reduction in tax on retained profits, paradoxically reduced the value of investment allowances, and the CBI was worried that investment grants would further reduce government assistance.[17]

Initially the DEA and the Treasury seem to have been in agreement about the investment grant system, though the Treasury pushed to limit the expenditure commitment. This meant, for example, trying to narrow exemptions like the payments for the purchase of computers. More importantly, it led to arguments over the rate of grant. The DEA, mindful of the CBI's hostility, was insistent that the rate must be demonstrably more favourable to industry than the allowance system, and this led to the 20 per cent figure.[18] But as the cost of the scheme, as well as the hostility of much opinion outside the government, became apparent, the Treasury tried to back off the whole idea of grants. Even after the principle was accepted by ministers in October 1965, the Chancellor wrote to the Prime Minster that he had 'now come to the view that the plan as it has evolved does not contain enough economic and political advantages to us to justify going on with it in its present form'.[19] But no alternative method of encouraging investment was available, and the hostility to allowances, plus the enthusiasm of the DEA, produced the 1966 White Paper, though the comment made by Eric Roll, Permanent Under-Secretary of State to the DEA, on the 20 per cent rate – that 'it would appear to be right though it could not be demonstrated rationally' – suggests how much the new system was an act of faith.[20]

The new system was greeted with a great deal of criticism, especially because of its attempt to privilege manufacturing investment.[21] But the government had an extra incentive to try to boost 'productive' investment when the July measures of 1966 exposed the government to criticism that it was reintroducing stop–go, and thereby hitting at investment. Sensitive to this point, and to criticism on the issue at the September productivity conference, Wilson in October 1966 was calling for more aid to investment to demonstrate that the government 'would not allow the resources released to stagnate into idleness'; at the same time, he suggested that they should 'covertly put back a little of the cuts in public productive investment' (introduced by the July measures), though he added, 'I don't mean roads or social investment'.[22]

Despite the strength of the CBI's complaints, investment held up well in late 1966 and into 1967. As a sceptical Alec Cairncross pointed out in June: 'Ever since 1964 the prophets have been forecasting a large, if not calamitous, fall in industrial investment. So far it has not happened.' Despite this, the rate was increased for 1967 and 1968 to 45 and 25 per cent (the DEA had wanted 60 and 30 per cent).[23] Even with this further subsidy, by the summer of 1967, and in the wake of further deflationary measures, there was some evidence of slackening in investment, and Wilson called for a 'crash programme for capital investment and re-equipment'.[24] By this time, however, Treasury concerns about the cost of the scheme were growing.

Estimates made in August 1967 put its total cost at £300 million per annum, and this was in a context where total subsidies and grants to industry were running at about £800 million, and when total manufac-turing investment was £1,200 million per annum.[25] These worries led to Treasury resistance to any further spending in this area, and proposals by a working group on industrial investment to speed up the payment of grants were successfully resisted by the Treasury.[26] After devaluation in November, Treasury scepticism increased, partly because it had regarded investment grants as a substitute, to some degree, for devaluation in trying to improve competitiveness, and partly because it saw a need for a tough stand on public expenditure to accompany devaluation.[27]

The post-devaluation story is, then, one of growing disenchantment on the part of the Treasury about both the scale and effects of investment grants (and other industrial subsidies), in opposition to the DEA and others, who continued to argue that stimulation of investment was crucial to industrial efficiency and competitiveness, and that this should override public spending considerations.

On the effectiveness of grants, a number of lines of criticism emerged. One was that the focus on plant and machinery was questionable, because it hindered industrial mobility – instead it encouraged putting new machines in old factories. This specific criticism was accompanied by a broader question about the aims of government investment policy, given that evidence from the Organisation for Economic Co-operation and Development (OECD) suggested that 'machinery and equipment' investment in Britain was the one element of total capital spending that was not below that of other West European countries. Data distributed at the time showed this figure running at 8.3 per cent of GNP for the 1960–67 period, similar, for example, to that in France (8.8 per cent) and Italy (8.9 per cent). While the message from this was far from straightforward, as, for example, much of this machinery was in electricity generation and telecommunications and not in manufacturing, it suggested grounds for doubt about whether Britain's position was so out of line with other countries as was often assumed at this time. Also worrying to advocates of investment grants was the suggestion that they biased investment towards short-term projects with a quick pay-off, because (in contrast to the allowance system) they did not rely on benefits accruing over the long term.[28] This scepticism threw into relief the growing expenditure in this area. As a senior Treasury official put the point in 1969:

> The case against investment grants must not be that investment is a bad thing to encourage, but that the very large (absolute and proportional) increase in this area of public expenditure in the last decade has signally failed to show any discernible results commensurate with its cost, but has contributed materially to increased public expenditure.[29]

It was this fiscal pressure that, after devaluation, proved so important to the policy debate on support for investment. The new Chancellor pursued an extremely tough review of public spending to try to ensure that resources went into exports, while at the same time trying to ensure that consumption was not squeezed to a politically unacceptable extent.[30] Thus in early 1969, faced with calls from the NEDC for greater assistance in terms of investment, the Treasury line was clear: they would be resisted because, in the short run, 'our pre-occupations at present are more with how to cut back the escalation of this expenditure' and, in the long run, 'it is desirable to repudiate over-simplified propositions about the correlation between investment incentives and the level of investment'. This latter point referred to work which seemed to show that stable profit expectations were the key to investment, as indeed the anti-stop–go argument had always suggested.[31]

By 1968 the government's economic advisers were divided over the future of investment grants. Some, such as Alec Cairncross and Wilfred Beckerman, 'were doubtful about the wisdom of maintaining the present rate of grant', but others liked the focus on manufacturing, with its balance of payments connotations. But if the balance of payments was the key issue, then, plainly, there were anomalies in aiding only manufacturing – as was recognised by the giving of special help to hotels because of their ability to attract tourist dollars.[32]

One response to this scepticism was to try to accentuate the discriminatory nature of government support for industry. This, perhaps unsurprisingly, was an idea supported by MinTech. In 1969 it argued that: innovation is the prime cause of growth; innovation causes investment, but investment grants also encourage replacement investment; and if more innovation was wanted, investment grants should be redirected towards stimulating new rather than replacement investment. Such views were also expressed by Michael Posner, economic adviser to the Treasury, who suggested a cut in investment grants coupled to redeployment of the money saved to more selective projects.[33]

This theme of scepticism about general support for investment was allied, at least in some quarters, to increased questioning of the efficacy of expensive 'doles' for industry as a way of generating improvement in industrial performance. While this did not lead to cuts in the grant before Labour left office, it did lead to the setting up of an enquiry into their effects.[34] More broadly, it can be seen as feeding the selective emphasis of Labour's 1968 Industrial Expansion Bill, which is returned to in the next section.

While Labour focused a great deal of attention on trying to stimulate private manufacturing investment, policy also recognised that a large proportion of investment was by the public sector. But the argument here was that fiscal incentives were inappropriate because government directly controlled that investment.[35] However, the mechanisms of control were extremely problematic, and were linked to the broader problems of government regulation of nationalised industries and the extent to which control over public spending should include nationalised industries. These issues are addressed in Chapter 7.

The 1966 White Paper announcing the new system of investment grants had been published on the same day as that announcing the setting up of the IRC.[36] This was no coincidence because, in part, the IRC grew from a recognition that investment grants, while they could embody broad selectivity between sectors, could not be used to discriminate between firms or to change their structure or behaviour in any detail. Thus, during the discussion of the grants legislation, Brown asked for the development of proposals for a specialised agency which would favour firms playing a particularly large role in exports or those installing 'particularly advanced types of machinery'.[37]

This discussion emphasises the overlapping concerns of Labour's policies with investment, technology and firm structures, and these are dealt with in the remainder of this chapter.

Technology

Labour's approach towards issues of technology, like that towards investment, was embedded in a long history of doctrinal assumptions and policy debates. From the 1930s to the 1960s, most discussion on the left took it for granted that scientific and technological advance was desirable, but slowed down by capitalism. In many discussions in this era there was an implicit, if not explicit, use of Marxist notions about the development of the 'forces of production' being slowed down by capitalist 'relations of production'. The solution was for the state to plan and co-ordinate both scientific and technological research and its application to industry. Thus enthusiasm for science and technology was part of a general approach that distrusted markets and held that only planned state action could bring rational progress to society.[38]

Under the Attlee government such attitudes were reinforced by the perception that the war had been won by state-led innovation. More pragmatically, the government, as part of its policy to raise productivity, launched the NRDC as a state-funded body designed to get into commercial use inventions made in the public sector. The government raised its expenditure on civil research and development about fivefold, but this was dwarfed by its commitment of resources to military areas (including nuclear power, which was largely driven by military considerations).[39] The Wilson government was to share the Attlee period's enthusiasm for state support of science and technology, but regarded the dominance of state-funded research and development by military concerns as a major problem.

In the years of opposition, Labour's ideological commitment to progress via the application of technology was reinforced by the seeming pace of technological advance, especially the achievements of both superpowers. On the Soviet side, the impact of Sputnik was very considerable in reinforcing the idea that a planned economy could secure more rapid change than market economies. But the enormous concern with automation, which is such a feature of the late 1950s, was also very much affected by the US 'model', which, like the Soviet, was influential in Labour's thinking. Here the ideology was complex, but one approach was to argue that the US experience showed both the possibilities of technology but also its dangers in an unplanned society, such as high unemployment – a common trope of the 1950s and 1960s.[40]

The policies of a future Labour government in this area were a major source of discussion in Labour circles from the late 1950s.[41] Wilson's famous speech of 1963 on the need to harness the 'white heat' of the technological revolution was then not a tactical rhetorical flourish (though it served tactical purposes) but grounded in both a long tradition of Labour thinking as well as much shorter-term policy debate. By 1961, in *Signposts for the Sixties*, the rhetoric was firmly in place and the problem identified: 'the reluctance of British businessmen to invest in research and development and the refusal of the government to make good this deficiency'. This was to be addressed by a reconstructed and enlarged NRDC, which would use development contracts (as used in defence procurement) for civil research and development, would create subsidiary or jointly owned companies to develop new products, and would 'help in revitalising and modernising existing industries which are declining or backward'.[42] Two years later, in 'Labour and the scientific revolution', the policy had evolved, and great emphasis was now put on increasing the supply of scientists and technologists to economically productive areas: by reform of the education system; by diversion of resources from military to civilian research and development; and by a major expansion of state spending on research and development. Also important was the argument that 'any boy or girl who enters industry during the 1960s may well find his or her skill rendered obsolete more than once in the course of working life', which would require a big expansion of training capacity, as well as a cushioning of the fall in income which might be felt while transition from one job to another was pursued.[43]

The 1964 election manifesto reiterated many of these themes, but also spoke of Labour's ambition to create a 'Ministry of Technology to guide and stimulate a major national effort to bring advanced technology and new processes into industry'.[44] This Ministry was created alongside the DEA as Labour's most important ministerial innovation in pursuit of modernisation. While important technology-related issues were also pursued elsewhere (most importantly, in the workforce field, the Ministry of Labour – see Chapter 6), MinTech, as it came to be known, should be placed at the centre of any account of Labour's policies on technology and industrial policy more widely.

The great importance that should be accorded to MinTech in this respect has been persuasively argued by David Edgerton and Richard Coopey. Edgerton places the policies of the 1960s in a broader framework, arguing that Britain in the twentieth century was a 'militant and technological nation', in which the state consistently spent large sums on science and technology, largely in pursuit of strategic rather than economic objectives.[15] From this perspective, one of the most important features of Labour's policies in the 1960s was the attempt to shift resources from military to civilian uses and to challenge the 'military–industrial complex' that had grown up in the 1940s and 1950s. This was certainly a key issue for Labour, which recognised that Britain was the biggest spender on research and development in Europe but, initially at least, believed that this was not generating appropriate levels of economic growth because too much was going on unproductive military projects. The assumption was that there was a close link between growth and *the right sort* of research and development but that government would have both to redirect its own efforts and to prevail upon the private sector to expand its spending in order to get more of this right, productive sort.

In retrospect, Labour's policies seem to have been based on mis-apprehensions both about the volume of private sector research and development (which was *high* by European standards) and about the directness of the link between such spending and growth.[16] But the ambition both to expand research and development spending and to redeploy it from military uses was one underpinning for the expanding role of MinTech during Labour's period in office. The other was the growing recognition that a purely quantitative approach, which emphasised increasing the volume of commercially oriented research and development, was inadequate and that, for technology policy to be effective, it had to broaden out to embrace not only workforce issues, but investment, firm structure and behaviour, and industrial management. This recognition meant, as Coopey argues, that after 1964 MinTech 'underwent a series of phased expansions until it emerged in the late 1960s as one of the first "superministries" with control over virtually the whole of the administration's industrial policy'.[17]

MinTech went through three major phases, which can be summarised in crude administrative terms. In it first form, headed by Frank Cousins, it took responsibility for the NRDC, most of the Department of Scientific and Industrial Research (DSIR) and the Atomic Energy Authority (which spent a large part of the government's research and development budget). Its industrial focus was on the 'high-technology' sectors of computers, electronics and telecommunications, plus machine tools, long a Labour concern, where it was believed that much automation would be stimulated. The second phase, with Tony Benn in charge from July 1966, involved the merger with the Ministry of Aviation in 1967, and responsibility for military procurement. Finally, in 1969 came the absorption of the Ministry of Power, the takeover of most of the Board of Trade's functions (except foreign trade and industrial regulation) and responsibility for the IRC after the demise of the DEA.

In the first phase of MinTech's existence there were administrative rearrangements that broadly followed the recommendations of the Trend

report of 1963 concerning the organisation of government support for
civil science.[48] The Science and Technology Act of 1965 made MinTech
the sponsor for computers, machine tools, electronics and telecommunications, and allowed the Atomic Energy Authority to work in non-nuclear
areas. More money was given to the NRDC.

Cousins articulated the governmental rhetoric of the time when he
talked of the computer as 'the hottest invention of recent times'.[49] A
Computer Advisory Service was established to co-ordinate government
purchasing, and a National Computing Centre was set up in July 1966
to standardise and simplify the programming of computers and advise
on training. While providing money for such activity was relatively
straightforward (though the Treasury was keen to put such services on
as commercial a basis as possible),[50] like other areas of technology policy
it soon opened up wider debates. Co-ordination of government purchasing of computers led straight into the issue of how far British
companies would gain preference. As MinTech argued: 'If the Government adopted a policy of invariably accepting the lowest tender, US
interests would gradually establish a monopoly of UK orders and there
would be no prospect of creating an economic UK industry'.[51] But, as
the Board of Trade pointed out, preferences in favour of UK-owned
companies would breach international trade obligations and harm regions
(especially Scotland) where US computer companies were already providing substantial employment. In addition, it was not at all clear that
the small-scale British industry could produce computers to compete
with IBM and Honeywell, even with a substantial preference.[52] The
compromise was to give an unpublicised preference of 25 per cent to
computers produced in Britain, while also looking for ways of 'ration-
alising' the industry. It was recognised that government support for
individual companies' research and development efforts might actually
discourage merger, but the government rejected the option of with-
drawing money (or the threat of nationalisation) as a way of forcing the
companies to come together.[53]

The design of effective action in the machine tools industry was even
more complex. The industry had long been regarded as a problem case,
as it had a poor export record and used relatively old technology. Labour
had seen the industry as ripe for a stiff dose of science and technology.[54]
Dealing with this industry was complicated by the sharp cycles in demand
for its product. In January 1965, Cousins said that he aimed to 'pick up
the industry and shake it', but the eventual policy package, announced
in June of that year, amounted to rather less.[55] Simple ideas of getting
production ministries like Aviation and Defence to buy more advanced
machine tools ran up against the problem of who was to pay: if the
machines were economic, they would be bought anyway; if not, then
would MinTech pick up the tab?[56] As with computers, the question of

the structure of machine tool producers loomed large. A MinTech document summarised the current doctrine on this issue:

> One obstacle to progress is the structure of the machine tool industry,
> which consists of a large number of small companies and only a few
> larger ones. Small firms cannot always support design and development
> teams adequate to modern needs and too many make inefficient use
> of skilled workers who could be employed to better effect by the
> efficient companies.[57]

Apart from simply channelling more money into research and development in this area, the main government initiative was the pre-production
order scheme, whereby MinTech brought advanced models and freely
lent them for trial by potential purchasers. This scheme had the advantage that it could be used counter-cyclically, as in April 1967.[58]

Expenditure on civil research and development rose sharply after
Labour came to office, though this was a trend that had been established under the Conservatives. By 1966 the speed of this expansion
was worrying the Treasury, and a Ministerial Committee on Science and
Technology was set up to co-ordinate the area.[59] But the really big money
was being spent outside the control of MinTech. In May 1965, the Minister
for Power announced the government's commitment to the advanced
gas-cooled nuclear reactor with the words: 'We have made the greatest
breakthrough of all time … we have hit the jackpot this time'.[60] Sadly,
this technological hubris was misplaced, and the reactor was to take its
place alongside Concorde as an expensive 'white elephant' in Labour's
high-technology programmes.[61] The crucial decision on Concorde had
been taken by the Conservatives in 1962 and it was quickly recognised
by the Labour government that it was unlikely ever to be a commercial
proposition. But the costs of cancellation, plus French enthusiasm for
the project at a time when Britain was keen to conciliate Paris to aid
EEC entry, prevented abandonment of the project.[62] Cousins had argued
against one major cut which did take place in this period, in the development of the TSR-2 fighter plane. Cousins had based his opposition on
employment grounds, but the government was committed to a 'swords
into ploughshares' policy, of which this was the first major fruit.[63]

Cousins resigned over prices and incomes policy in the summer of
1966 and was replaced by Tony Benn. Expansion of MinTech's scope
had already begun with its takeover of responsibility for the whole of
engineering in February 1966 and for merchant shipbuilding in November
1967. This expansion reflected the view, as stated by the Permanent
Secretary, that 'the Ministry could not make a wide enough impact or
rapid progress with its remit so long as it operated from such a limited
industrial base'.[64] Most important, however, was the amalgamation with
the Ministry of Aviation in February 1967, which brought together almost

all the government's research and development and large parts of its industrial procurement. Following the report of a Treasury committee, Wilson insisted on this amalgamation, against Ministry of Defence pressure to put all military-related sectors under its control. Wilson linked the decision to 'our policy of building up the Ministry of Technology as the instrument of progress in the engineering field. These two industries (aircraft and electronics) are so much in the forefront of technical progress that the Ministry of Technology would hardly be a viable project if they were assigned elsewhere.' MinTech was subsequently divided into three main groups: engineering, aviation and research.[65]

Engineering encompassed a huge range of industries. Government policy in this area had to cover, for example, the decidedly 'old tech' of shipbuilding, where the government was attempting to 'rationalise' the industry through a Shipbuilding Industry Board, the expensive problem of Concorde, the continuing concerns with machine tools, and the search for a viable British computer industry.[66] In much of engineering, issues of industrial structure were central to the government's ambitions for change, so that MinTech's agenda became increasingly entwined with that of the IRC (see next section).

Benn faced the problem that, under the Ministry of Aviation, as the Treasury saw it, 'anything that could in theory fly received the unquestioning support of the Ministry'.[67] While reluctant to have Labour seen as the 'party of cancellers', Benn was increasingly aware how resources were sucked into the industry without much commercial pay-off. Though he retained lingering hopes for Concorde, in other areas, as he told the manufacturers, it would no longer be like 'pinching pennies off an old man's drum'.[68] Devaluation produced a much tougher attitude to spending on expensive aircraft; though Concorde survived, the F-111 fighter was cancelled with Benn's support. Benn regarded the extension of public ownership as one way of tackling the structural problems of industry. He floated this idea for both shipbuilding and airframes, but in neither case found much political support.[69]

In the area of research, MinTech's attitude was in part guided by the argument that a great deal of government spending was misdirected towards military projects, and that much of this should be diverted to commercially oriented civilian projects. This was a major theme on the Ministerial Committee on Science and Technology.[70] Of course, civil projects were not necessarily commercial, as Concorde and nuclear energy demonstrated. Nevertheless, this diagnosis was important to MinTech's agenda. In January 1968, Benn told the Cabinet that his agenda for research was 'a shift from defence to civil projects; second, from aerospace and nuclear to other engineering; third from intra-mural to extra-mural research; and fourth, a shift from research itself, wherever it was done, to development and production technology'.[71]

This strategy was pursued in a much tougher fiscal climate after devaluation. A general questioning of the links between research and development and growth was allied to more specific pressure both to cut total government spending on research and development and to hasten its redeployment. The latter process was complicated by questions about the role of MinTech-sponsored bodies like the Atomic Energy Authority. From 1965, that Authority's resources were being partly diverted away from nuclear research, but this very possibility led to the argument that such 'big science' bodies should continue in being on this redeployment path rather than be run down, despite doubts about their costs. A similar argument was deployed by Air Force research establishments.[72] Unsurprisingly, the Ministry of Defence fought against the rundown of military-oriented research and development. Even after devaluation and the decision to withdraw from east of Suez, the Ministry argued that this should not lead to significant cuts in research and development because 'few weapons had an exclusively East of Suez role'. Such arguments led to agreement to only limited cuts (around £15 million), though defence research and development was still absorbing half of all government research spending in 1968/69.[73]

Emerging out of all these diverse concerns by the end of 1967 was a MinTech desire for legislation to allow greater *selective* powers to intervene in industry. What became the Industrial Expansion Act of 1968 contained two parts. One was concerned to clarify the Ministry's powers to provide money for a variety of existing projects, such as Concorde and for the Cunard Company to build the liner *Queen Elizabeth II*. The other was to give enabling powers so that any future project would be fundable without further legislation.

Benn saw the measure as a logical development of the switch in MinTech's focus from 'the limited approach to growth implicit in the support of R and D to a more direct recognition that production technology – production itself and marketing – are at least as essential to industrial strength'. He went on to argue that 'the object of industrial policy is to pick winners and not to run an undiscriminating "meals-on-wheels" service for British firms whether they are efficient or inefficient'.[74]

The Act was very much disliked by both the CBI and the Treasury. The CBI objected to its discriminatory and open-ended character, and in particular the possibility of industrial boards being created, like that in shipbuilding, which it saw as a major extension of government intervention. The Treasury's opposition was partly motivated by the CBI's hostility; for example, it got agreement to an advisory board to represent outside interests being written into the Act, partly to conciliate the CBI. This desire for conciliation was particularly acute because the Bill came to Cabinet just before devaluation, after which relations with the CBI slipped to what was described as 'an all time low'.[75] The Treasury's opposition was also in part conjunctural: devaluation was supposed to lead to a tough public spending regime, yet here was legislation which suggested a big increase of spending on industrial support. But more generally it was part of a growing questioning of the spending on industry, and the seeming lack of control over this, worsened by the Expansion Act's discretionary powers for MinTech, plus the threat that the new industrial boards would spend as much public money as that in shipbuilding.[76]

The legislation was delayed but eventually passed into law in the summer of 1968. Its political importance was substantial. It symbolised the government's (and especially MinTech's) sense that the initial enthusiasm for science and technology had been, to a degree, naïve and that much more direct intervention in the structure and conduct of firms might be required to change British industry radically. At the same time, the Act worsened relations with the private sector and thereby added to the sense that a fresh look was needed at Labour's whole approach to that sector.[77] Economically, the new Act was much less significant. While it provided a framework for spending on such projects as Concorde, it did not unleash a new expansion of industrial spending, and no new industrial boards were ever established.

The final phase in MinTech's expansion came with the abolition of the Ministry of Power and then the DEA in 1969. This led to responsibility for the steel and fuel industries and the IRC. In addition, MinTech took over responsibility for investment grants and regional policy from the Board of Trade. All this meant that MinTech had a degree of control or responsibility for most manufacturing and energy industries and controlled most of the defence procurement budget (over £400 million per annum). It also ran seventeen government research establishments, with a combined staff of over 22,000 qualified scientists and engineers. As a Ministry publication put it: 'An articulated chain of Government activity has now been forged, linking together scientific and technological research and innovation, the problem of industrial structure, and the role of public procurement'.[78]

While the growth of MinTech can be seen as following an internal logic, a 'learning by doing', that logic was, in part, one of discovery about the *weaknesses* of government and the limitations of the instruments at its disposal. Much money could be spent, but could industry be changed? Benn's published diaries for the period are entitled *Office Without Power* and, making all the necessary allowances for both hindsight and ideological perspective, it is not unreasonable to think that that title had a good deal of truth about the position of MinTech. While the 1970 general election supervened before the new expanded ministry had time to do much, it may be doubted whether, even if it had continued for some years, it would have been able to effect the transformation it aspired to.

The Industrial Reorganisation Corporation

The creation of the IRC was announced in a White Paper in January 1966, published simultaneously with the new scheme for investment grants. The case for this new body was 'the need for more concentration and rationalisation'. The reason for pursuing this was explained as follows:

> many of the production units in this country are small by comparison with the most successful companies in international trade, whose operations are often based on a much larger market. In some sectors the typical company is too small to achieve the long production runs; to take advantage of economies of scale; to undertake effective research and development; to support specialist departments for design and marketing; to install the most modern equipment or to attract the best qualified management.[79]

There was a long delay (partly because of the March general election) before the IRC came formally into being, in December 1966, though it met informally from the summer of 1966.[80] It was empowered to draw up to £150 million from the Exchequer, and over the period until April 1971, when it was wound up, £120 million was spent, in support of mergers, rationalisations and other interventions.[81] The IRC has been extensively analysed, and this account focuses not on the details of its activities but on the political and policy-making context within which it was set up and operated.[82]

The DEA was immediately behind the creation of the IRC. The impetus for the 1966 White Paper emerged from the discussion of investment grants and the recognition that they could not be used in a highly discriminatory way to favour firms with, for example, good export records or 'for the installation of particularly advanced types of machinery'. Thus, from a DEA point of view, the new Corporation (initially called the Industrial Reorganisation *Finance* Corporation) was in part a complement to grants in providing more discriminatory funding.[83]

Within MinTech there was a parallel idea about the problems caused by British industry's fragmented industrial structure, which, as noted at the beginning of this chapter, was reflected in the formulations of the National Plan in terms of rationalisation. This argument was powerfully articulated by the industrialist B. Cant, who became a MinTech adviser in 1964. Before entering the Ministry he had written a paper entitled 'Attrition or breakthrough? Some notes on Britain's industrial future', which brought him to MinTech's attention.[84] This was subsequently rewritten and circulated within the government as 'The influence of industrial structure upon national economic viability', which provided a comparative economic history of Britain and sought to explain the development of an excessively 'diversified' economic structure. According to Cant, what made Britain stand out, especially in the capital goods and engineering sector, was the dominance of conglomerate companies producing ranges of unrelated products, each within units too small to compete internationally. While he recognised that a merger movement was under way, he stressed the 'urgent need' for a state agency to press forward with this process of rationalisation.[85] These ideas chimed in well with MinTech's growing concern with the capacity of many British firms to take advantage of the new technologies it was promoting.

In the run-up to the publication of the White Paper, there was much discussion of the scope of the Corporation's activities. Cant's arguments implied a clear focus on mergers and rationalisation (which might include 'de-mergers' of some conglomerates). Others saw a more ambitious role for it. MinTech, as we have seen, was groping its way towards a broader and more ambitious interventionist agenda, though the shape of the IRC was largely settled before Benn arrived at MinTech and this agenda really took off. Balogh offered strong support to the IRC, which he put in the context of his hostility to 'the pure dogma of perfect competition, which is completely irrelevant', and saw the new body as an agency for implementing 'plans worked out by little Neddies and DEA in conjunction with the Ministry of Technology'.[86]

Balogh's arguments bring out the point that the creation of the IRC was caught up in a wider ideological debate about the role of the state in industry. At its broadest, this debate was linked to the traditional arguments about the desirability of state ownership of industry, and whether a body like the IRC would be seen as a means of expansion of such ownership. D. C. Hague and G. Wilkinson rather misleadingly suggest that, alongside Balogh, such ideas were articulated only by the 'even more left-wing' theorists Michael Posner and R. Pryke in their 1965 Fabian pamphlet *New Public Enterprise*, with its advocacy of a state holding company as an alternative to traditional forms of nationalisation.[87] In fact, the idea of such a form of state ownership was at that time still mainly a preserve of the right or 'revisionist' wing of the Labour Party (to which Posner and Pryke belonged), and whose origins lay with the writings of Douglas Jay as far back as the 1940s. Jay, as President of the Board of Trade, argued the case for such a state holding company and a broad agenda of intervention when the IRC proposal came to Cabinet.[88] Far from the Board of Trade's doubts about the IRC being based on the Board's attachment to laissez-faire, as the press at the time alleged, it was based on a long-standing argument in Labour circles about *how* to pursue an extended state role, not whether such a role was desirable.[89]

In many respects this broader version of the role of the IRC was defeated by the political circumstances of 1966. The government was under attack from industry following the deflationary measures of July, and the CBI made clear that it would fight strongly against any idea of a state holding company, representing it as amounting to 'backdoor nationalisation'.[90] While the official report that lay behind the IRC combined ideas of a primary focus on the encouragement of mergers with the possibility of a broader interventionist role, the emphasis was on the former and there was no suggestion of the creation of a state holding company.[91] The government responded to the CBI by emphasising the narrow version of the IRC's role and by seeking people to staff the Corporation who would inspire employers' trust. In the latter they were successful, recruiting Frank Kearton from Courtaulds as chairman and Ronald Grierson as his deputy and managing director from the merchant bank Warburg.[92]

This arrangement did not mean that the government had a very clear and fixed vision of the IRC and its role. For example, in the preparatory stage the DEA unsuccessfully pushed for a merger of the NRDC with the new body.[93] Kearton raised the possibility that the Corporation might be the channel for selective allocation of investment grants.[94] The legislation itself combined an explicit remit to pursue mergers and rationalisation with a much broader clause that allowed it to do anything to promote 'industrial efficiency and profitability' or assist 'the economy of the UK or any part of the United Kingdom'.[95] The focus on mergers was always paramount in the IRC's activities, but this broader role came into greater prominence in 1969 as the problems of focusing just on organisational merger became apparent. Weaknesses of management were particularly stressed in the IRC's report for 1969/70.[96]

The very success of IRC in maintaining good relations with employers and the City also led the government to see it as a more free-ranging agency for the pursuit of a selective industrial policy and, for example, used it to investigate Rolls-Royce and rescue the shipbuilders Cammell Laird.[97] To a degree, then, the IRC came full circle. Having had its agenda narrowly focused in 1966/67 for reasons of short-term political viability, its role expanded in 1969/70 as the government sought for an effective selective mechanism of intervention across a wide range of issues. Of course, this raised complex issues about the relationship between the IRC and government ministries and their policies.

Until 1969, the IRC came under the sponsorship of the DEA. This mainly reflected the political importance of George Brown at the time when it was created, and the initial idea that the IRC's activities would be strongly guided by the National Plan and the work of the EDCs. Reports from the EDCs as well as other bodies were indeed fed to the IRC at its inauguration, but the idea of the Corporation pursuing a clear 'plan' of intervention were unrealistic, partly because of the limits on its resources and partly because of its desire, where at all possible, to proceed with consent. While most of the early mergers supported by the IRC were therefore 'opportunistic' rather than driven by a clear strategy, the majority of them were in the broad area of engineering and electronics, sectors that, by 1967, were the remit of MinTech.[98] The expanding MinTech did aspire to incorporate the IRC in its strategy, with Benn as early as January 1967 implying that the IRC was an agency for his ministry's policy for the motor industry.[99] One reason for MinTech's enthusiasm for the Industrial Expansion Act was a belief that the constraint on the IRC only to invest in potentially profitable activities was too limiting, but once the Act became law the IRC was drawn into a role on the Advisory Board established under the Act. Kearton welcomed this link with MinTech, seeing the Act's purpose as fitting with the IRC's mission to 'adopt more positive measures to find and promote projects designed to stimulate industrial investment'.[100] So, despite some tensions between the IRC and Benn (for example over the role of foreign companies in Britain), there was a policy logic to the movement of the IRC to MinTech when the DEA was abolished in 1969.[101]

The IRC's main role was to encourage mergers, but in doing so it was to some extent pushing at an open door, as the 1960s was a decade of 'merger mania', with an average of over 600 firms a year disappearing through merger under Labour, with a peak (measured by value) in 1969.[102] The IRC may have brought about mergers in a few cases which would not otherwise have occurred, such as that of Ransome Hoffmann Pollard in ball bearings and Kent–Cambridge in scientific instruments, or speeded up others, such as the creation of British Leyland.[103] But in the context of the concurrent mania, its contribution, given its resources, was bound to be limited. Does that mania suggest that the market and the IRC were both securing a solution to the problems of scale that lay behind the IRC's creation? The evidence for this is necessarily imperfect, but it can be argued that the private merger boom was driven largely by financial considerations rather than the 'productionist' logic, and that its impact on efficiency was, at best, marginal. Post-merger profits were often not enhanced, and Prais's work suggested that mergers did little to create larger *plants* as opposed to larger conglomerates, which Cant had identified as part of the problem rather than the solution. The IRC's growing concern with management capacity in the firms in which it intervened can be seen as another side of that coin: large, multi-plant companies posed huge managerial difficulties, which belied any simple story of mergers generating economies of scale.[104]

Monopolies and mergers policy

Labour's enthusiasm for planning in general and mergers and rationalisation in particular should have left little space for competition policy.

Table 5.1 Mergers referred to the Monopolies and Mergers
Commission in the 1960s

	Qualifying mergers *(assets over £5 million)*	*Number referred*	*Percentage*
1965	48	2	4.2
1966	63	4	6.3
1967	96	1	1.0
1968	133	2	1.5
1969	126	3	2.4
1970	80	2	2.5

Source: S. Wilks, *In the Public Interest: Competition Policy and the Monopolies and Mergers Commission* (Manchester, 1999), p. 225.

Yet, as always in the party, there was great ambiguity of approach in this area, an ambiguity nicely summarised by Wilks with reference to the political spectrum more broadly: 'Preserving competition is a right-wing principle, but attacking monopoly is a key principle of the Left'.[105] This ambiguity partly lay behind Labour's passing of the first Monopolies Act in 1948, while at the same time pursuing planning and sectoral nationalisation. In the 1950s revisionists like Crosland had explicitly argued that competition had 'greater advantages than pre-war socialists realised'.[106] When Labour came to power in 1964, pro-competition views were little in evidence, and throughout the next six years other issues were centre stage in industrial policy.[107] Nevertheless, Labour did pass the 1965 Act. In part this was because a draft White Paper was inherited from the Conservatives, and in part because of fears about the impact of the on-going wave of mergers on industrial efficiency. The 1965 Act strengthened the Monopolies Commission, but most significantly extended its remit to mergers. However, the practical impact of this was extremely marginal: a tiny proportion of mergers were referred to the Commission, and, of those that were, very few were prevented (Table 5.1).

The conflict between those who believed that the key need was for industrial rationalisation and merger and those who worried about the effects of monopoly and restrictive practices was not straightforward. At one extreme (as usual) was Balogh. Commenting on the (unusually) critical comments by the Commission on the Courtaulds merger, he wrote:

> the basis of this document is a static analysis of the immediate effects
> on the consumer of short-term price and production policies of
> Courtaulds. What would have been needed is historical-dynamic

analysis of the long-term effects for the British consumers and the
strength of the industry in international relations.[108]

Few in the government were inspired by the laissez-faire principles that
Balogh demonised, but some ministers did worry about the impact of
mergers that they were generally so enthusiastic about. On the one hand
was the worry not about predatory monopolies exploiting the consumer,
but rather the 'lethargic industrial giant'. Crosland, the minister responsible for merger policy during 1967–69, argued that:

> the threat from these giant concerns is not usually that they will be
> too ruthless or too little public-spirited; rather for psychological and
> sociological reasons which I explained in *The Conservative Enemy* this
> is most unlikely. It is rather that they will become complacent, un-
> dynamic and unenterprising with the passage of time (like, for
> example, ICI).[109]

Another perspective was articulated by Wilson, who was concerned that
mergers, and government support for them, were creating powerful
bodies to which Labour had no coherent attitude and about which the
public were increasingly concerned.[110]

Worries such as those of Crosland and Wilson about the impact of
mergers were sufficient to get the 1965 Act on to the statute book, despite
the opposition of Balogh.[111] But there ensued a tussle about the relationship between competition policy and industrial policy that lasted until
the end of the government. Not all of this concerned mergers. The
DEA was concerned about the impact of restrictive practices law (out-
lawing collusion between firms) on efforts by the EDCs to encourage
co-operation and rationalisation between firms. Jay, as President of the
Board of Trade (1964–67), resisted pressure for change in this area, but
eventually made concessions in exchange for an extension of the scope
of restrictive practices law to cover information agreements between
firms.[112]

Another tussle was over who should determine referrals to the
Monopolies and Mergers Commission, traditionally the role of the Board
of Trade. The Board conceded the right of the DEA to be consulted,
which helps to account for the very low level of referrals. Conversely,
despite agreements to the contrary, the Commission often had little or
no notice of mergers sponsored by the IRC.[113] The propensity of the
Commission to find little wrong with the few mergers referred to it was
explained by its chairman as being partly the result of the understanding of government pro-merger views and partly as a result of the
Commission's enquiries being dominated by pro-industry views and the
search for consensus.[114] The Board of Trade did try to keep the Commission active, but its suggestions of new cases to be referred could be

met by the following kind of response from the DEA: 'We feel that these submissions on new cases are like saying to the police "we haven't had any decent trials recently; go out and arrest some people and let them prove they haven't done anything wrong"'.[115]

In the light of such tensions it is unsurprising that, by 1969, the whole future of the Commission was in doubt. After a battle by the Board of Trade to maintain the identity of the Commission was lost, it was agreed to create a 'Commission on Industry and Manpower' through a merger of the Monopolies and Mergers Commission and the NBPI. Crosland argued that such a body with wide powers was 'too great an uncertainty to impose on so large a section of British industry'. But the project was pushed particularly hard by Barbara Castle, whose Department of Employment and Productivity (DEP) was scheduled to take responsibility for the new body.[116]

This new body was never created because of the result of the 1970 election. The case for it reflected Labour's continuing ambiguity about competition: this new body was designed to avoid any pre-supposition that competition was a good thing, while giving extensive powers of investigation and control in cases where there were fears of the illegitimate exercise of monopoly power. Such fears had grown substantially in the late 1960s, as the merger wave seemed to be creating industrial giants without evidently delivering the increases in efficiency that Labour had hoped. As Wilson had recognised, the legitimacy of these giants was coming into question, perhaps among the public at large, but certainly in Labour Party circles.

Conclusions: filling the vacuum?

In 1950 Harold Wilson, reflecting on his period as President of the Board of Trade under the Attlee government, described government relations with the private sector as 'a vacuum in socialist thought'.[117] How far had that vacuum been filled by the time his government lost office in 1970? During the period in opposition, while much passion had gone into the debates over public ownership, there had also been attempts to understand the evolution of the private sector and the policies that might be needed to change its behaviour. *Industry and Society* of 1957 was a landmark document in suggesting that most large firms 'served the nation well' and in focusing attention on policies that did not fundamentally challenge the structures or behaviour of private industry. But the benign stance of the late 1950s was altered by the rise of declinism, part of which suggested that the private sector suffered as much as the Conservative government from domination by effete, myopic gentlemen whose conservatism was holding back British industry. Thus, by 1964, Labour had developed a large reformist agenda, and this chapter has outlined how that worked out in practice after 1964.

Crudely put, Labour in office initially put forward a predominantly 'quantitative' agenda, in which the performance of industry would be transformed by greater inputs of investment, research and development and skilled labour. The DEA and the National Plan would provide the framework of stability to encourage investment, which would also be heavily subsidised; government would pay for much more research and development and switch much of it from military and 'big science' projects to commercially related ones; similarly, more labour would be trained and more of it diverted into productive industry. Total government spending on industry, particularly manufacturing, rose very sharply, from 0.4 to 9.0 per cent of net output in that sector between 1964 and 1967.[118]

While none of these ambitions can be counted a complete failure, in each case their pursuit threw up problems which, in summary terms, amounted to a recognition that increasing efficiency was as much a problem of how resources were used as the quantity available. Of course, from the beginning, Labour had recognised weaknesses in British industrial organisation, but again these were seen as largely 'quantitative' – a problem of size. But that proved too crude a measure of the problem, as the IRC discovered when it looked for the management capable of handling the newly enlarged enterprises it sought to create or encourage.

Practical problems of policy implementation (plus their mounting cost in a period of fiscal stringency after devaluation) led in the direction of less focus on quantitative inputs into production, and more on organisational and managerial issues. Such concerns necessarily implied greater selectivity of approach as the heterogeneity of British industry in respect of its capacity to manage resources effectively became apparent. One possible response to this complexity would have been to abandon the attempt to use government as an instrument of industrial modernisation in the name of restoring market forces, but there was little sign of this on the part of either government or others. It is notable, for example, that both the CBI and Conservative Party came to accept, if not love, the IRC after their initial hostility.

Interwoven with these pragmatic issues of policy was a more ideological debate within Labour circles on the relationship of the state to the private sector. By the late 1960s, the common perception in these circles was that Labour's efforts (and money spent) to increase efficiency had not yielded great dividends, and that a fundamental rethink was required. Partly this was 'oppositional' in tone, as disillusionment with Wilson within the party grew.[119] But this was by no means the whole story. As noted above, it was people on the right of the party who had first suggested public ownership of individual companies in a competitive environment as an alternative to 'old-fashioned' sectoral monopolies. Such ideas seemed increasingly relevant in the 1960s, as policy focused on manufacturing industries operating in an increasingly competitive international environment – and seemingly doing badly. This form of public ownership could then be seen not as an old shibboleth revived, but as a practical policy to address immediate policy issues, where other instruments seemed to have shown their frailty. The rise of the Bennite left around the issue of the National Enterprise Board in the early 1970s thus needs to be seen very much in the light of the approach to private industry tried and found wanting in the 1964–70 period.

Notes

The place of publication is London unless otherwise specified.

1 *The National Plan*, Cmnd 2764, BPP 1964/65, vol. 30, p. 55. While the Plan did not discuss the issue, Labour was also generally keen to augment investment by continuing to attract foreign companies into Britain (which also had favourable balance of payments consequences). See G. Jones, 'The British government and foreign multinationals before 1970', in M. Chick (ed.), *Governments, Industries and Markets* (Aldershot, 1990), pp. 194–214; for a contemporary example of this welcome, see PRO, BT 321/9, Booklet 'Get Ahead in Britain', April 1968, spelling out the advantages of Britain to potential American investors. But for a partial exception see note 101, below.
2 *National Plan*, pp. 56, and 15–16.
3 *Ibid.*, pp. 49–50.
4 *Ibid.*, pp. 8–9, also pp. 47–8.
5 Anthony Crosland noted this position in *The Future of Socialism* (1956), pp. 469–70, arguing 'Before the war, it was treated as axiomatic that ... large-scale production, especially when conducted in large-size firms, results in maximum efficiency', but he implied that doubts were now creeping in, doubts which were hardly evident until the very late 1960s.
6 J. Tomlinson, *Democratic Socialism and Economic Policy: The Attlee Years 1945–51* (Cambridge, 1997), pp. 81–4, 130–2.
7 *Ibid.*, pp. 275–6.
8 A. Shonfield, *British Economic Policy Since the War* (Harmondsworth, 1958), ch. 2; M. Shanks, *The Stagnant Society* (Harmondsworth, 1961), pp. 43–4; N. Tiratsoo and J. Tomlinson, *The Conservatives and Industrial Efficiency, 1951–64: Thirteen Wasted Years?* (1998), pp. 141–55.
9 *National Plan*, p. 64.
10 *Investment Incentives*, Cmnd 2874, BPP 1965/66, vol. 13.
11 Harold Wilson, in *LPACR* 1963, pp. 133–40.
12 *Investment Incentives*, paras 30, 34.
13 PRO, T 325/104, W. Armstrong to J. Anderson, 27 November 1964. A specific committee to look at industrial incentives was set up, called 'Fiscal Incentives', chaired by Austen Albu.
14 PRO, T 325/104, A. Johnston to I. Bancroft, 12 March 1965; R. Neild, 'Replacement policy', *National Institute Economic Review*, 30 (1964), pp. 30–43.

15 PRO, EW 25/215, 'Investment incentives: correspondence and briefs', 1965/66. In one respect, grants were less discriminatory than allowances – they did not benefit only those who made profits. But this was not an argument attractive to the CBI.

16 H. Pemberton, 'A taxing task: combating Britain's relative decline in the 1960s', *Twentieth Century British History*, 12 (2001), pp. 365–70; R. Whiting, *The Labour Party and Taxation* (Cambridge, 2000), pp. 159–68.

17 PRO, EW 25/215, 'First Secretary's meeting with CBI', 23 February 1966.

18 PRO, EW 25/124, 'Official Working Group on Investment Grants', 23 September 1965 and 6 October 1965.

19 PRO, EW 25/124, 'Ministerial meeting', 19 October 1965; PRO, T 325/105, Chancellor to Prime Minister, 9 December 1965. This scepticism was shared by the Board of Trade: T 325/105, D. Jay to Prime Minister, 10 December 1965.

20 PRO, EW 25/124, 'Investment Grants Committee meeting', 5 October 1965.

21 PRO, EW 25/215, 'National Joint Advisory Council minutes', 26 January 1966; see also, for example, *Sunday Times*, Business News, 'Not the right candy', 23 January 1966.

22 PRO, T 230/872, 'Help to investment', 17 October 1966.

23 PRO, T 230/872, A. Cairncross to F. Atkinson, 26 June 1967.

24 PRO, CAB 134/3199, 'Measures to stimulate industrial investment', 5 October 1967.

25 PRO, T 230/872, L. Pliatzky, 'Assistance to industry', 17 August 1967.

26 PRO, CAB 134/3196, 'Meeting of Economic Strategy Committee', 16 October 1967; PRO, T 230/987, G. Bell, 'Acceleration of payment of investment grants', 6 October 1967.

27 PRO, T 230/987, L. Pliatzky, 'Review of industrial policy following devaluation', 21 February 1968; T 230/987, A. Cairncross, 'Investment grants', 14 March 1968.

28 PRO, T 230/1051, DEA, 'Investment performance and prospects', 30 December 1968; T 230/1051, J. Carr to D. MacDougall, 'Investment', 21 January 1969; cf. Organisation for Economic Co-operation and Development, *Historical Statistics* (Paris, 1999), see table 10.6; T 230/987, J. Carr, 'Investment grants', 27 May 1968.

29 PRO, T 230/1051, J. Carr, 'Investment and economic growth', 16 May 1969.

30 PRO, T 230/1051, 'Review of measures to stimulate industrial investment', July 1968–November 1969; PRO, CAB 129/135, Chancellor, 'Public expenditure: post-devaluation measures', 3 January 1968.

31 PRO, T 230/1051, L. Pliatzky, 'Industrial investment: Treasury paper for NEDC', 3 January 1969; T 230/1051, J. Carr, 'Profits and investment', 7 February 1969.

32 PRO, T 331/151, M. Hawtin, 'Investment grants', 12 June 1968. On the hotels issue, see PRO, CAB 134/3202, 'Investment in hotels', 20 February 1968; PRO, CAB 128/43, 'Cabinet conclusions', 2 May 1968. Kaldor was opposed to this policy, arguing for more selectivity within the industrial sector: PRO, T 230/872, 'Committee on Industrial Incentives', 20 September 1967.

33 PRO, T 230/1051, 'Industrial innovation', 11 November 1969; T 230/987, M. Posner, 'Industrial policy, the balance of payments and devaluation', 20 February 1968, and 'Investment grants', 20 May 1968.

34 PRO, T 224/2136, 'Investment incentives review', 1970; PRO, FV 25/2, C. Thornley, 'Investment grant survey', 1969. This survey was organised

by Wilfred Beckerman, but its results were not available until after the government had fallen.

35 PRO, T 325/104, 'Fiscal Incentives Committee: note by Treasury', 25 May 1965. Again, Kaldor dissented: see PRO, T 325/105, 'Plan E and the nationalised industries', 3 December 1965.

36 *Investment Incentives*, and *Industrial Reorganisation Corporation*, Cmnd 2889, BPP 1965/66, vol. 13.

37 PRO, EW 25/124, 'Investment incentives', 15 September 1965.

38 Werskey, *The Visible College* (1979); D. Horner, 'The road to Scarborough: Wilson, Labour and the scientific revolution', in R. Coopey, S. Fielding and N. Tiratsoo (eds), *The Wilson Governments 1964–1970* (1993), pp. 49–71. On one of the key figures on this issue, see M. Kirby, 'Blackett in the "white heat" of the scientific revolution: industrial modernisation under the Labour governments, 1964–1970', *Journal of the Operational Research Society*, 50 (1999), pp. 985–93.

39 Tomlinson, *Democratic Socialism*, pp. 288–9; J. Tomlinson, *Government and the Enterprise Since 1900: The Changing Problem of Efficiency* (Oxford, 1994), pp. 176–8.

40 LPA, 'Research Department correspondence: automation' (1956), includes lots of American material, such as AFL/CIO, 'Labour looks at automation'.

41 Horner, 'Road to Scarborough'.

42 Labour Party, *Signposts for the Sixties* (1961), pp. 14–15.

43 LPA, RD 518, 'Labour and the scientific revolution' (1963).

44 Labour Party, *Let's Go with Labour for the New Britain* (1964), p. 48.

45 D. Edgerton, *England and the Aeroplane: An Essay on a Militant and Techno-logical Nation* (1991); *idem*, 'Liberal militarism and the British state', *New Left Review*, 185 (1991), pp. 138–169; *idem*, 'The "white heat" revisited: the British government and technology in the 1960s', *Twentieth Century British History*, 7 (1996), pp. 53–82; *idem*, *Science, Technology and the British Industrial 'Decline' 1870–1970* (Cambridge, 1996).

46 Edgerton, *Science, Technology*, pp. 61–3; this argument was being made in official circles by the mid-1960s – see Edgerton, 'White heat', pp. 73–5.

47 R. Coopey, 'Industrial policy in the white heat of the scientific revolution', in R. Coopey, S. Fielding and N. Tiratsoo (eds), *The Wilson Governments 1964–1970* (1993), p. 103; see also *idem*, 'The white heat of scientific revolution', *Contemporary Record*, 5 (1991), pp. 115–27.

48 Office of the Minister for Science, *Committee of Enquiry into the Organisation of Civil Science* (1963).

49 PRO, T 224/1292, F. Cousins, 'Address to the British automation conference', 8 November 1965.

50 PRO, T 224/1292, R. Clarke (Treasury) to M. Dean (MinTech), 11 November 1965; T 224/1268, 'Brief for Armstrong meeting with Sir Edward Playfair and Sir Gordon Ridley', 1 September 1965.

51 PRO, CAB 128/39, 'Cabinet conclusions', 3 June 1965; CAB 129/121, MinTech, 'Government procurement policy for computers', 31 May 1965.

52 PRO, CAB 128/39, 'Cabinet conclusions', 3 June 1965; CAB 129/121, Board of Trade, 'Computer purchases by the government', 1 June 1965.

53 PRO, CAB 128/39, 'Cabinet minutes', 3 August 1965; CAB 129/122, MinTech, 'Computers', 27 July 1965.

54 P. Mottershead, 'Industrial policy', in F. Blackaby (ed.), *British Economic Policy 1960–1974* (Cambridge, 1978), pp. 442–5.

55 *Guardian*, 15 June 1965; *Hansard* (Commons), vol. 714, 14 June 1965, cols 31–4.

56 PRO, T 224/1133, T. Marshall, 'The machine tool industry', 19 March 1965.
57 PRO, T 224/1133, MinTech, 'The machine tool industry', 10 March 1965.
58 Mottershead, 'Industrial policy', p. 443.
59 PRO, T 224/1401, 'Expenditure on civil R and D', 1966; PRO, CAB 134/3308–11, 'Ministerial Committee on Science and Technology'. This followed on from a working party chaired by Solly Zuckerman (the government's Chief Scientific Adviser), see CAB 134/3310, 'Technological innovation in Britain', 5 December 1968.
60 D. Burn, *Nuclear Power and the Energy Crisis* (1978), p. 10.
61 P. Henderson, 'Two British errors: their probable size and possible lessons', *Oxford Economic Papers*, 29 (1977), pp. 159–205.
62 L. Johnman and F. Lynch, 'The road to Concorde: Franco-British relations and the supersonic project', *Contemporary European History*, 11 (2002), pp. 229–52; E. Feldman, *Concorde and Dissent* (Cambridge, 1985).
63 G. Goodman, *The Awkward Warrior* (1979), pp. 421–3.
64 R. Clarke, *The Ministry of Technology and Industry* (1970), pp. 3–4; also, Ministry of Technology, *The Ministry of Technology 1964–69* (1969).
65 PRO, PREM 13/1550, H. Wilson to D. Healey, 'The future of the Ministry of Aviation', 11 November 1966; PRO, T 325/145, 'The Ministry of Technology', 11 November 1967.
66 Mottershead, 'Industrial policy', pp. 461–6.
67 PRO, T 334/138, C. France, 'Relations with the Ministry of Technology', 15 January 1969.
68 T. Benn, *Out of the Wilderness. Diaries 1963–67* (1987), pp. 459, 505.
69 T. Benn, *Office Without Power. Diaries 1968–72* (1988), pp. 15–16; PRO, T 334/12, I. Bancroft, 'The airframe industry', 11 December 1967; Benn, *Out of the Wilderness*, p. 450.
70 For example, PRO, CAB 134/3308, 'Expenditure on R and D in the UK', 28 October 1966, and CAB 134/3310, 'Technological innovation in Britain', 5 December 1968.
71 Benn, *Office Without Power*, p. 9.
72 PRO, T 334/138, 'PESC 1969; estimates for Ministry of Technology', May 1968–September 1969; T 224/1401, J. Hunt to P. Vinter, 30 November 1966; T 224/2639, 'Ministry of Aviation's research programmes', 18 February 1966; T 224/2109, F. Atkinson to S. Zuckerman, 6 August 1970.
73 PRO, CAB 134/3213, 'National priorities in science and technology', 23 April 1969; CAB 134/3212, MinTech, 'Research policy', 31 March 1969.
74 *Hansard* (Commons), vol. 764, 1 February 1968, cols 1578–9, 1584.
75 PRO, T 334/11, W. Armstrong, 'Industrial Expansion Bill', 24 November 1967.
76 PRO, T 334/64, Armstrong, 'Industrial Expansion Bill', 2 February 1968; T 334/151, K. Berrill, 'Industrial Expansion Bill: external economic factors', 6 May 1968; T 334/151, Armstrong to Chancellor, 'Industrial Expansion Bill', 22 May 1968.
77 PRO, CAB 134/3213, 'Industrial policy and the Monopolies Commission: future programme of work', 22 April 1969.
78 Coopey, 'Industrial policy', pp. 112–13; MinTech, *Ministry of Technology*, p. 3.
79 *Industrial Reorganisation Corporation*, Cmnd 2889, p. 2.
80 PRO, PREM 13/979, M. Stewart to Lord President, 19 September 1966. The royal assent was given in December 1966 after a second reading in October: see *Hansard* (Commons), vol. 734, 19 October 1966, cols 218–30.
81 Figures from Mottershead, 'Industrial policy', p. 436.

82 D. C. Hague and G. Wilkinson, *The IRC. An Experiment in Industrial Intervention* (1983); Mottershead, 'Industrial policy', pp. 431–9; S. Young and A. Lowe, *Intervention in the Mixed Economy* (1974), part II.

83 PRO, EW 25/124, 'Meeting on industrial incentives', 15 September 1965.

84 Hague and Wilkinson, *The IRC*, pp. 8–11.

85 PRO, EW 27/179, 5 June 1965.

86 PRO, EW 27/171, T. Balogh to PM, 8 September 1965.

87 Hague and Wilkinson, *The IRC*, pp. 12–13; M. Posner and R. Pryke, *New Public Enterprise* (1965). One inspiration for the IRC was the Italian Instituto per la Ricostruzione Industriale (IRI): see J. Tomlinson, 'Learning from Italy? The British public sector and the IRI', in W. Feldenkirchen and T. Gourvish (eds), *European Yearbook of Business History* (1999), pp. 109–24.

88 D. Jay, *Future Nationalisation Policy*, LPA Research Department, RD 161 (1948). Jay returned to the theme in *Socialism in the New Society* (1962), part 5. PRO, EW 27/171, R. Croft, 'The IRFC', 19 September 1966; PRO, CAB 134/2708, Board of Trade, 'IRFC', 6 January 1966; CAB 129/124, First Secretary of State, 'IRC White Paper', 24 January 1966.

89 Both the *Guardian* and *Financial Times*, 10 January 1966, suggested that Jay had 'constantly adopted the classical attitude of his Department to Government interference in industry'.

90 PRO, EW 27/170, 'The IRC: the views of the CBI', 31 March 1966.

91 PRO, EW 27/171, Draft Working Party report, 'IRFC', 18 November 1965.

92 Hague and Wilkinson, *The IRC*, pp. 231–2. Balogh had argued that putting a 'financial man' in charge of the IRC would be like putting 'a violent teetotaller in charge of a whiskey distillery or a boozer of a temperance hotel': PRO, PREM 13/979, Balogh to PM, 20 December 1965.

93 PRO, EW 27/171, R. McIntosh, 'The IRFC', 16 November 1965. On the eventual convergence of IRC and NRDC roles, see PRO, FV 3/37, 'Relations of ministers with IRC and NRDC', 5 June 1970.

94 PRO, T 224/1407, 'Notes of discussion of ministers with IRC', 7 November 1965.

95 Cited in Hague and Wilkinson, *The IRC*, pp. 231–2.

96 IRC, *Reports and Accounts 1969/70* (1970); Hague and Wilkinson, *The IRC*, pp. 240–2.

97 Hague and Wilkinson, *The IRC*, pp. 242–4.

98 W. McClelland, 'The IRC – an experimental prod', *Three Banks Review*, 94 (1972), pp. 23–42; PRO, FV 11/20, 'Brief for meeting with IRC', 20 November 1965, which points out that in the period December 1966 to March 1968 the IRC recorded ten out of fourteen interventions being in engineering, and nineteen out of twenty-four in the following financial year.

99 *Sunday Times*, 22 January 1967.

100 PRO, EW 27/239, F. Kearton, 'IRC views on the government memorandum on the proposed enabling legislation', 1 September 1967; PRO, FV 11/20, 'Brief for meeting with IRC', 20 November 1965, where it is reported that 'Sir Frank Kearton and the IRC regard the Act as too slow and cumbersome'. Mottershead, 'Industrial policy', p. 434.

101 PRO, PREM 13/1640, T. Benn to M. Stewart, 1 February 1967, concerning the conditions attached to allowing a takeover of the Rootes car company by Chrysler.

102 L. Hannah, *The Rise of the Corporate Economy* (2nd edn) (1983), appendix 1.

103 Mottershead, 'Industrial policy', p. 437.

104 S. Prais, *The Evolution of Giant Firms in Great Britain* (Cambridge, 1976), pp. 4, 51; Hague and Wilkinson, *The IRC*, pp. 244–6.

105 S. Wilks, *In the Public Interest: Competition Policy and the Monopolies and Mergers Commission* (Manchester, 1999), p. 338.

106 A. Crosland, *The Future of Socialism* (1956), pp. 89–91; PRO, BT 258/2657, H. Brown, 'Monopolies and restrictive practices policy and Mr. Crosland's *The Future of Socialism*', 10 October 1967.

107 Though note, as pointed out in Chapter 2, that Labour's decision to seek EEC membership was partly motivated by the belief that this would increase competition and thereby enhance efficiency.

108 PRO, EW 27/204, T. Balogh to P. Shore, 19 February 1968.

109 PRO, BT 258/2658, A. Crosland to H. Wilson, 24 September 1968; PRO, PREM 13/2795, R. McIntosh to H. Wilson, 'Industrial policy and the Monopolies Commission', 25 April 1969.

110 PRO, BT 258/2658, H. Wilson to A. Crosland, 20 September 1968; Wilks, *Public Interest*, p. 346.

111 PRO, PREM 13/1648, T. Balogh to H. Wilson, 22 February 1965, where Balogh, in opposing the Monopolies Bill, gives a classic statement of a powerful strand of Labour's doctrine in the 1960s: 'The Bill ... seems based on a simplistic philosophy of efficiency through greater competition, tout court. It is contrary to all modern economic theory. It is even more contrary to experience. Inefficiency typically is due to wrong size, to the consequential lack of R and D, to wrong (too short) runs in production due mainly to the multifariousness of products again due to the multifariousness of the firms'.

112 PRO, BT 258/1982, 'Monopolies and restrictive practices', 1964/65; PRO, PREM 13/1648, 'Monopolies 1965–1967'.

113 PRO, BT 258/2657, F. Glaves-Smith, 'Handling of mergers', 27 October 1967; Wilks, *Public Interest*, pp. 165–6.

114 PRO, BT 258/2657, 'Note of meeting D. Serpell with A. Roskill', 14 July 1967.

115 PRO, EW 27/204, D. Parmar, 'New references to the Monopolies Commission', 11 October 1965.

116 PRO, PREM 13/3233, A. Crosland to B. Castle, 17 December 1967; PRO, BT 258/2657, 'Note of meeting with B. Castle', 18 September 1968.

117 PRO, PREM 8/1183, H. Wilson, 'The state and private industry', 4 May 1950.

118 PRO, FV 25/4, 'Assistance to industry review', 26 August 1970. The report also calculated that the balance of tax paid over subsidies received by manufacturing fell from £1,360 to £863 million over the same period.

119 For example, LPA, Re 516, Statement by the NEC, 'Agenda for a generation', September 1969; M. Hatfield, *The House the Left Built* (1978).

6

The labour market and the trade unions

The National Plan focused a great deal on labour. The growth targets were predicated on increasing the supply of labour, improving skills and mobility, and increasing labour productivity. The general issue of productivity is central to Labour's whole approach and is taken up in detail in Chapter 8, but the quantity, quality and ease of movement of labour are sensibly dealt with together in this chapter. In addition to what may be called these supply-side aspects of labour, the National Plan highlighted the need for an effective incomes policy: in the characteristic terminology of the Plan, 'Planning for economic growth requires policies for price stability and for the orderly growth of money incomes'.[1] Incomes policy was to become a key issue for the Wilson government and is properly regarded as a central component of the attempt to 'modernise' the labour market. A third labour-related issue, of eventually huge importance in these years, was trade union law. In the later years of the 1960s, battles over the law in this area were to provoke enormous, almost fatal tensions within the Labour movement. But, unlike labour supply and incomes policy, industrial relations law did not figure in the National Plan. Rather, the attempts to change this framework must be seen as being in part the effect of the *failures* of policy in the government's early years, and as a major departure from the path foreseen in 1964/65.

Labour: supply, quality and mobility

The National Plan contrasted anticipated expansion in demand for labour, given its assumption of a 25 per cent growth in GDP for 1964–70 (see Chapter 4), with expected labour supply, and came up with a 'manpower gap' of 200,000, even after allowing for an extra 200,000 from reducing unemployment in the development areas to the national average and the consequent increase in activity rates in these areas.[2] By far the biggest reserve of labour identified was that of married women:

the forecasts embodied in the Plan assumed that the activity rate among married women aged over thirty-five would continue to increase, but 'they still assume that some 3 million married women between 45 and 65 will not be in the labour force in 1970'.[3]

There is a notable contrast in the Plan between this recognition of the quantitative significance of married women's labour and its lack of urgency in relation to the use of this resource. The checklist of actions in the Plan spoke only of government examining ways to help married women (and older workers) 'who wish to do so, to take or to remain in paid employment' and announced an enquiry 'into the present pattern of women's employment and of the conditions under which women not now working outside their homes would be ready to take such work'.[4] The sub-group which developed the labour supply forecasts in the Plan argued that schemes for encouraging married women into work 'may in fact be essential to the achievement of the forecast increase in the working population' but, beyond noting the key role of child care facilities, said that action would have to await the outcome of the enquiry.[5]

The results of that enquiry, carried out in 1965, were not published until 1968.[6] It showed a 'serious waste of women's talents', with most of them employed in low-wage, unskilled jobs with very little opportunity for training. It also showed how little formal child care was available – most was unpaid and was usually done by grandmothers.[7] Newspapers at the time accounted for the delay in publication of the report by the conditions it revealed: 'Shock Report on Women Censored' was the *Observer* headline.[8] But, in contrast to the 1940s, when the issue had led to serious policy disputes about the position of women in society, this time the idea that working was incompatible with women's 'proper' roles seems not to have figured in policy discussion. The Ministry of Health, which in the 1940s had opposed the Ministry of Labour's aim to increase the number of working women, this time seems to have contented itself with stressing the need not to allow labour supply issues to reduce the quality of nursery care, and for realism about how many women increased nursery provision would release into the labour force, given nurseries' own high staffing ratios.[9] Nevertheless, little was actively done to encourage more married women into the labour force, and the lack of serious policy consideration in this area is illustrated by the issue relating to women's employment that did excite considerable policy and political concern in this period – equal pay.[10]

Labour had long been committed in principle to such equality, but the issue came into prominence only when Barbara Castle became Secretary of State for Employment and Productivity in 1968. An inter-departmental working group had been set up in 1965, and consultations conducted with the CBI and TUC in 1966. This led to a further examination of the costs and further consultations with employers and unions at the end of 1967. Part of the slowness of the process was due to fundamental disagreements between the CBI and the TUC on whether the principle to be adopted should be that of the EEC, which talked of 'equal pay for the same work', or that of the International Labour Organisation, which favoured 'equal pay for work of equal value'.[11] Given the very high degree of gender-based job segregation, these definitions were likely to have major implications for the increase in costs, and cost was the key issue. Both the CBI and TUC favoured implementation largely or entirely by voluntary means, and neither regarded it as a high priority.

When Castle spoke on the issue in the Commons in June 1968, she addressed the cost issue by saying that movement to higher women's pay should be offset by lower settlements for men, thus keeping the total increase within the ceiling of 3.5 per cent stipulated by the incomes policy. However, this approach was strongly rejected by the TUC. Castle also argued that the government should act on the issue because equalisation was happening anyway, and it would be best if it were done in an orderly, planned fashion and would be cheaper than if it occurred as a result of industrial disputes. The Ford women workers' strike of July 1968 seemed to support the view that there was a groundswell of support for equal pay.[12]

Castle's desire to move to implementation of the policy met stiff opposition from the Treasury. It argued that, with the effects of devaluation still far from clear in 1968, 'our present economic circumstances were totally inappropriate to any fresh commitment to equal pay'. This hostility was enhanced by the prospect that equal pay for women might be coupled with movement to a national minimum wage (on which a working party had just been established) and the Chancellor linked an explicit opposition to any such national minimum to stressing that equal pay 'must be subject to economic circumstances'.[13] The best that Castle could achieve immediately was another working party to look in detail at the costs of equal pay in a sample of industries. The results of this became available in the summer of 1969, and the report revealed little that was not already known, for example that the cost of equal pay would vary greatly between industries – according to the report's calculations, occupying a range from 4 to 22 per cent of labour costs.[14]

Castle once again pressed for action. She argued for a phased introduction over five years, which would make the costs about 1 per cent per annum. There was considerable scepticism in Cabinet, focusing on the costs of the policy, the unlikelihood that male workers would moderate their wage demands in response, and the argument that equal pay was not a major method of reducing poverty because most poor households had no workers in them. On the other side of the argument was an important political calculation: 'while an announcement of early legislation on equal pay would not be particularly popular in the country generally it would be greeted with enthusiasm in the Parliamentary Labour Party and would do much to strengthen the hand of the moderates on the General Council of the TUC'. As a result, it was decided that the aim would be to announce a decision to legislate at the forthcoming party conference, but whether this would be possible would depend upon 'the implications for confidence in sterling'.[15] The CBI remained unhappy, and called not only for a nine-year phasing-in period, but also for the delaying of any commitment until the balance of payments was in £300 million surplus. But, after last-minute Treasury doubts, an announcement was made at the 1969 party conference and the legislation was passed in 1970.[16]

While it was an important issue in its own right, what is striking about the equal pay discussion in the context of economic 'modernisation' is the almost complete absence of linkage to the issues of labour supply as raised by the National Plan. The link is barely mentioned, and then only in passing by junior officials. It did not figure at all in the high-level policy debates about the costs and benefits of implementing the idea.[17] The basic point that women's labour supply might be linked to their wages was ignored. Here, indeed, was little evidence of 'joined up' government. This cannot be accounted for by the slackening in the general demand for labour, especially after July 1966, which was important in other labour market policy areas (see below). Although male unemployment had risen, as a Ministry of Labour official put it in early 1970, 'In many districts the current problems are a shortage of work for males and a shortage of girls and women for work'. Castle accepted that the economy was not making proper use of the abilities of women, but argued, at least in public, that this was linked to women's own attitudes, about which government policy could do little. Certainly, women hardly shared at all in the expansion of training of the late 1960s, despite public recognition of how poor this currently was. A telling statistic is that between 1965 and 1969 the number of female school-leavers taking jobs involving at least twelve months' training rose from 4.1 to just 5.0 per cent (see also Table 6.1, p. 130).[18]

Almost at the end of her period in office Castle did take up the issue of discrimination against women, including in the area of training. She argued that it would be very hard to get women to move from their traditional occupations, where there were plenty of jobs, into those where currently they lacked training. More generally, the line was repeated that 'the problem of under-utilisation of women's skills is largely one of changing the career attitudes of women themselves. Legislation would have little impact on the situation.'[19] In sum, despite the recognition of the potential, the government did little to encourage women to fill the 'manpower' gap.

If the only important action on women's work was the (eventual) passing of the Equal Pay Act, there was much more Whitehall activity on a much smaller group of workers, graduate qualified scientists and engineers. Concern with this group arose from the technology debate discussed in Chapter 5. The technological effort, it was believed, relied heavily on the numbers qualified to a high level and their deployment in areas deemed most effective in speeding up technological change.

A triennial survey of the supply of such workers began in 1956 under the Conservatives, but Labour had the ambition to go further down the route to 'manpower planning' in this area and established a range of committees to this end. A committee on 'Manpower Resources for Science and Technology' began work in 1965, concerning itself with both the supply and deployment of scientists and engineers. Its report focused on the need to bring a greater industrial influence on their training, but emphasised the need for much more investigation of the whole area. It spawned several other committees, including the Swann Committee, which focused on proposals for creating closer links between universities and industry, and the Jones Committee on the 'brain drain'.[20] The latter committee was perhaps typical of the general debate in this area in the 1960s, in that it picked up on a topic which, for a while, was politically very 'hot', but when it came to policy it was discovered that the 'problem' was much exaggerated, and in any event public policy could do little to change things.[21]

In 1966 the Campion Committee was established with a broader remit – to consider ways of 'establishing relationships between national needs and the output of all types of highly qualified manpower'. This suggested that policy should try to 'convert a forecast of a pattern of demand for goods and services into an industrial employment pattern, secondly into an occupational employment pattern and finally into a qualifications pattern'.[22] Unsurprisingly, such an ambitious prospectus led to the spawning of several more committees, so that by the end of 1967 the Treasury had identified 'a jungle of Whitehall bodies', consisting of twenty-nine separate committees, 'but none which links discussion closely to execution of policy'.[23]

One overarching committee, the Advisory Committee on Highly-Qualified Manpower, was notionally set up but seems to have been wholly inactive. Concern with the issues seems to have been reduced by the results of the triennial survey of 1968, which, unlike its predecessors, showed no prospective shortage of engineers and scientists.[24] Indeed, there was growing scepticism about the whole idea of a shortage of such people, an idea which in any case was often based on simply asking employers if they would like to employ more such people, without addressing the issue of salaries. Also, as academic sceptics pointed out, the idea that Britain was short of these workers created a climate in which lobbying by scientists and engineers generated pressures for policies which might not be of national benefit.[25]

The technocratic climate of the 1960s generated some policy changes of importance. For example, the turning of the eight colleges of advanced technology into universities such as Aston, Bath, Brunel and Salford expanded technological higher education. But much of the proliferation of committees and reports led to little action. Partly this was because the nature of the problem was difficult to pin down: Britain did not lack scientists and engineers, it was not losing huge numbers in the 'brain drain' and, despite the principle of allowing undergraduates to study subjects of their choice, the numbers going into science and technology were expanding.[26]

The question of the deployment of scientists and engineers was more complex with, for example, issues about the reallocation of those no longer employed when government research bodies shut down. But, overall, the Wilson government combined some useful but marginal policies in this area with the important discovery that the availability of trained graduate scientists and engineers was not in fact a major constraint on 'modernisation'.

The National Plan reflected the widespread view in the early 1960s that there was a broader problem of skills, with industrial expansion likely to be held back by shortages in a range of jobs. Ratios of vacancies to people registered unemployed suggested particular difficulties in engineering, construction, woodworking and vehicle building. Problems relating to jobs in computing and electronics were also identified.[27] The main mechanism for addressing these skill shortages were the industrial training boards (ITBs). These began to be set up after the Conservatives passed the Industrial Training Act in 1964, which allowed industries to establish ITBs with powers to impose a levy on all firms in an industry, in turn paying grants to firms that supplied approved training. A major impetus to this legislation had been the belief that under-training was widespread because of 'free-riding', whereby firms that trained workers saw them poached by firms that did not provide training. This was perceived as a classic case of market failure, which meant that the state had to step in to shift the incentives (in the form of grants) towards all firms engaging in training.[28]

Under Labour, the number and coverage of ITBs expanded, so that by 1969 there were twenty-seven, which covered approximately three-quarters of the total workforce, and around 90 per cent of those in eligible occupations.[29] In many ways, ITBs were classic creatures of the 1960s concern with growth: bipartisan in origin, state-sponsored, but tripartite in character, and with their activities resting on a fragile base of consent, especially among employers, who paid the levy. In 1967 the CBI restated its general support for the system, but articulated a number of concerns. These included the 'cost-shifting' of training from the education system on to industry, too much emphasis on 'off-the-job' training, and the burden of the levy and the administration of the system on small firms. By the following year these concerns seem to have increased, following a survey of members. In addition to those already noted, there was a general complaint that the ITBs were not doing enough to challenge the 'time-serving' aspect of apprenticeship: 'it seemed to the CBI that the time had now come for all the established boards to be grasping the nettles involved in tackling these fundamental issues, many of which had their roots in the industrial relations field'.[30]

The growing hostility of small firms to the ITBs was important in the setting up of the Bolton enquiry into small firms in 1969, and after 1970 to the major reform of the ITBs under the Conservatives. Concerns about apprenticeship were shared by Labour leaders. In 1966 Harold Wilson told the TUC that 'restrictions on out-dated apprenticeship and training requirements' threatened the productivity drive and were more likely to cause than to prevent unemployment.[31] The ITBs had some effects in eroding traditional forms of apprenticeship (which peaked in numbers in the mid-1960s), but the most direct action by the government in this area was the expansion of government training centres. These were aimed at adult industrial training. The numbers who passed through them approximately trebled under Labour, but this cannot hide the fact that the overall effect of the centres was marginal; by 1970 the annual 'throughput' was no more than 12,000 per annum, partly because of the difficulty of recruiting suitable trainers.[32] Even with these small numbers, the government complained about resistance to the proper deployment of these trainees, a complaint echoed by the Donovan Commission.[33]

The government accepted the doctrine of tripartism in industrial training, and the consequence that 'The bulk of the training for skill must be done in industry and this is the responsibility of the Training Boards'.[34] The ITBs could be nudged into action desired by government by grants and exhortation, but they retained a very large degree of autonomy. Their behaviour differed significantly, and the examples of the two most important are highly divergent. The engineering ITB was the biggest spender, with a levy of 2.5 per cent of labour costs, and had an ambitious agenda – which, however, met a great deal of resistance from engineering firms. In contrast, the construction ITB was much less ambitious but ran into financial difficulties, partly because of the domination of the industry by small firms, which were reluctant payers of the levy.[35] But the issue with the ITBs was not just their behaviour but their structure. By definition they were concerned with industrial rather than occupational (let alone national) concerns. The Industrial Training Act had led to the setting up of the Central Training Council, but while this was able to take a broader view of training requirements it was purely advisory, and this was how the majority of employers wanted it to stay.[36]

Alongside expanding the government training centres and trying to nudge the ITBs in certain directions, the government did try to address problems with training, and especially apprenticeship, by picking up recommendations from the numerous industry enquiries – Devlin on the docks, Cameron on printing, Pearson on shipping, Geddes on shipbuilding – which highlighted these issues. Also, one of Wilson's post-devaluation initiatives was to get the TUC and CBI to agree to a process whereby the CBI would report member firms' perceptions of restrictive behaviour by unions on training issues, and the TUC would take these up with the relevant union.[37] While one need not doubt the good faith of the TUC in this area, it seems clear that apprenticeship was an issue where its traditional respect for individual union autonomy was especially strong. It is notable, in particular, how little interest in this issue was shown by the TUC's Production Department, which in other respects was highly active in pursuing the productivity agenda.[38]

Overall, the period of Labour government saw slow rather than rapid reform of industrial training. With the beginnings of decline in the absolute number of apprenticeships, there was no compensating expansion in other forms of training (Table 6.1). By international standards Britain remained a poor trainer of its workforce, especially for those who left school at the statutory minimum age.[39] And, if the overall picture was poor, Table 6.1 shows that the picture for girls was nothing less than scandalous.

The third aspect of labour supply was its mobility. The Labour Party's motto here was 'easing the way to change', with the argument that, to

Table 6.1 Classes of employment entered by boys and girls, 1964 and 1970 (percentages)

	1964		1970	
	Boys	*Girls*	*Boys*	*Girls*
Apprenticeships	36	6	42	7
Professional	2	2	1	2
Clerical	11	39	8	40
With planned training:				
over 12 months	10	5	8	5
8 weeks to 12 months	5	8	6	10
Other	36	40	34	36

Source: R. Elliott, 'Industrial relations and manpower policy', in F. Blackaby (ed.), *British Economic Policy 1960–74* (Cambridge, 1978), p. 615.

achieve faster growth, 'large numbers of men and women will have to move out of firms and industries which can release labour and into other jobs'.[40] The assumption behind policy was that the economic insecurity associated with job movement generated restrictive attitudes and practices that could be addressed only if such movement was made much less financially painful. The major policies of 'easing' were the Redundancy Payments Act (RPA) and earnings-related unemployment benefit. Both had been discussed by the previous Conservative government, and were given significant weight by the NEDC in 1963, but it was not until 1965 and 1966, respectively, that the changes were introduced.[41]

While it would have been impossible to analyse the impact of the earnings-related unemployment benefit because of its integration into the rest of the benefits system, the RPA had a clear institutional identity, and its operations attracted a great deal of attention and study.[42] Like the ITBs, redundancy payments were funded overwhelmingly by employers, so were essentially a mechanism of redistribution towards those firms that cut back their labour force. Expenditure from the fund rose to average over £30 million per annum in Labour's period in office, a much higher level of expenditure than the government expected. Though precise figures are not available, the great bulk of these redundancies were in manufacturing industry. Payouts were related to length of service and, initially, were higher for those aged over forty-one.[43]

Nonetheless, assessment of the impact of the RPA is extremely difficult. Redundancies grew in number partly because of the weakening of the labour market from 1966, though this might also have functioned, other things being equal, to have increased resistance to movement. Estimates suggest that the number of redundancies may have doubled between 1962 and 1970. A survey of employers and trade union officers showed that both groups believed the RPA had affected attitudes to redundancy, with employers reporting that on average 85 per cent of those offered redundancy under the terms of the Act voluntarily accepted it. The criteria for payment provided an incentive for employers to break with 'first in, last out' policies, and age as well as sickness seem to have become more prominent in the redundancy process; this was logical from an employer's point of view, but hardly helpful to the government's stated aim of encouraging older workers to stay in the labour force.[44]

The Ministry of Labour's internal reporting system broadly supported this survey evidence, though it also made the point that, while the RPA may have encouraged occupational and industrial mobility, it may have discouraged geographical mobility; moreover, it may have promoted more efficiency in the labour market by financing longer periods of job search. Nonetheless, most redundancies (up to two-thirds of the total) were not compensated under the Act, mainly because of the two-year qualification period.[45]

While the RPA may have discouraged resistance to redundancy, it may not have helped the redeployment of workers to areas where they were most needed. Mackay's study of the 'shake-out' of labour in the Midlands following the July 1966 deflationary measures suggests that most of those who lost their jobs were semi-skilled rather than those whose skills were in short supply.[46] This shake-out was a deliberate policy of the government, designed to get the economy in better shape for when growth resumed.[47] But it marked a watershed in the labour market, with unemployment never again falling to the levels of 1965/66. This did not mean that the government changed its whole approach; after all, unemployment was still remarkably low by almost any standard. And the DEP, when founded in 1968, did try to reinvigorate policies on labour redeployment.[48] Nevertheless, the presumption of the RPA and other policies was that mobility could be encouraged by offering 'carrots' to workers to move, in the context of a very tight labour market. With deflation from the summer of 1966, this presumption was no longer so clearly justified.

While the RPA had been long in gestation, was bipartisan and had a straightforward (if arguable) rationale, Labour's other major initiative on labour mobility, the SET, was quite the opposite. Though its origi-nator, Nicholas Kaldor, says the idea was formulated in the autumn of 1965, it does not appear in the discussions in the archives until the following spring, only weeks before it became government policy.[49] It was treated with considerable scepticism by many in government and soon became unpopular outside Whitehall, especially among employers. Most importantly, the case for the tax was multiple, complex and con-troversial.[50]

At its most general, the tax derived from a particular analysis of Britain's relative decline. Kaldor had long argued that Britain's capacity to match the growth rates of other major Western European countries was constrained by the absence of a pool of under-employed labour in peasant agriculture and small-scale handicraft industries. Britain's structural shift to an urban, manufacturing country had been largely completed before the First World War, and the benefits of this were unrepeatable.[51] Kaldor argued that Britain could match the rate of growth in these countries, which he assumed was based on the dynamism of their manufacturing sectors, only by squeezing labour out of the service sector. Thus the core of the SET was that it would fall on the whole economy, but manufacturing would get a subsidy while services would be net payers. It was effectively a discriminatory employment tax. An employment tax had been much discussed in Whitehall in the early 1960s, but no one then had advocated that it should be discriminatory, its most controversial aspect.[52] Second, the tax was attractive to some who saw it as a way of restoring 'balance' to the indirect tax system, where manufactured goods were subject to purchase and excise taxes but services escaped.[53] Third, the tax could be used to favour exports, because its subsidies to manufacturing *de facto* favoured the sector of the economy from which most exports derived. Finally, these 'structural' arguments made the SET attractive to a Chancellor who was anxiously seeking a way of increasing taxes in the least politically unattractive way. The SET could be presented not as a short-term expedient but as part of a long-term strategy.[54]

The tax was announced in May 1966, but did not come into effect until September of that year. This delay meant that the deflationary aspect of the policy became more evident, and the net burden of the tax larger, as the subsidy to manufacturing was reduced to below what it would have been if it had operated for the full tax year. Employers in the service sector hated the tax, while in industry complex manoeuvres were pursued to get activity reclassified as 'manufacturing'. This discrimination undoubtedly threw up anomalies, even if one accepted the underlying logic of the tax. For example, the balance of payments rationale meant that, eventually, hotels serving tourists were given special concessions to compensate for SET payments.[55]

Whitehall accepted that the effects of the tax were complex, and as a result set up an enquiry by the Cambridge economist Brian Reddaway.[56] His final report, published in 1973, was not wholly conclusive, though it did suggest that the effects on productivity in the service sector might have been favourable. But such a conclusion had to be tentative because of the effects of other contemporary factors, such as the abolition of resale price maintenance. Also, Reddaway's argument that the SET's discriminatory benefits were evident in service sector productivity were challenged by those who detected a parallel acceleration in the manufacturing sector, which, even in the most optimistic view of the tax, came too quickly to be accounted for by its impact. There does seem clear evidence of a 'shake-out' in employment in services in the late 1960s, which may be partly accounted for by the tax,[57] but, as already noted, there was a parallel shake-out in manufacturing, so that many of those leaving service jobs may not have shifted across to Kaldor's favoured sector.[58]

Kaldor later published a robust defence of the logic of the tax, in which he suggested that, while it did fail in its objectives, this was not because it was misconceived but because of the context of deflation. This shortage of demand constrained manufacturing expansion and thus inhibited the transfer of labour. He had come to broadly the same conclusions by 1969, when it was apparent that manufacturing employment had fallen during the first year after the tax was introduced.[59] Other economists have challenged the underlying premise of the SET, that British manufacturing productivity was fundamentally constrained by slow output growth, and suggest that Kaldor's evidence for this was shaky.[60]

Kaldor's sophisticated case for the SET found an audience partly because of short-term macro-economic conditions, but also because its discriminatory aspect, which so appalled its opponents, appealed to some on the left who, with varying degrees of sophistication, viewed manufacturing as the key, dynamic sector of the economy. To some extent, the SET was only the most overt example of this attitude, which can be found clearly, if implicitly, in the National Plan, with its detailed discussions of industrial sectors, plus some analysis of agriculture, construction and energy, but with almost no attention to the service sector. Distribution, which, the Plan noted, employed one-seventh of the labour force, had just five paragraphs devoted to its problems. In this context, the SET is not anomalous, but rather starkly illustrates a characteristic mindset of the 1960s, which saw industry in general and manufacturing in particular as the key to growth and modernisation.[61]

Productivity, prices and incomes policy

By the time the National Plan was published in September 1965, Labour had already established its productivity, prices and incomes policy. According to the Plan, 'The Government believe that only as a long term and comprehensive strategy within the framework of the National Economic Plan, and with full agreement and co-operation of management and unions, can a policy for stable prices and planned growth of money incomes hope to succeed'.[62] The subsequent narrative of Labour's incomes policies has been told many times; this section concentrates on the strategic aspects of the policy and its links to 'modernisation'.[63]

Any commitment to a long-term policy on incomes was abandoned when Labour came to office and had to deal with the immediate economic crisis; the initial idea of a wage freeze was dropped in the face of TUC opposition, and instead broader ambitions, later summarised in the Plan, set the terms for the *Joint Statement of Intent on Productivity, Prices and Incomes*, agreed between the DEA, the TUC and CBI in December 1964.[64]

Incomes policy was a problem for the TUC because of the visceral union belief in free collective bargaining. A resolution passed at the 1964 TUC congress had reasserted that belief, but had simultaneously opened a route to incomes policy: 'Congress believes that if there is to be an acceptable incomes policy it must be based on social justice, taking into account all forms of incomes including rent, interest and dividends'.[65] In addition to this distributional point, the TUC agreed to Labour's proposals only as long as they were based on consultation, and were coupled with other appropriate policy actions, especially on the balance of payments. These conditions were to provoke recurrent difficulties in the TUC's attitude to the government's incomes policy.

Though George Brown at the DEA had early abandoned the idea of a wage freeze, the tensions between incomes policy as a short-term and long-term instrument were still evident in the negotiations leading up to the *Statement of Intent*. Brown was extremely anxious to get an agreement, at least in principle, as soon as possible because of his desire 'to persuade foreigners that Britain is a good risk', which could be done only with 'an irrevocable commitment by unions and employers'.[66] The CBI and TUC eventually agreed, mainly because of the way the policy was presented, as a part of the plans for growth and modernisation, which, as broad aims, they both were committed to. Of course, each side saw the new policy through its own lens: the employers believed it was essentially a wages policy, with prices tagged on to make it politically palatable within the Labour movement; conversely, the TUC wanted to emphasise the 'planned growth of incomes', while stressing that wage increases were not the centre of Britain's economic problems. Indeed, the TUC proposed the addition of the word 'productivity' to the statement precisely to contradict 'the fallacy that changes in prices are determined by changes in incomes'.[67]

The *Statement of Intent* was followed in early 1965 by the establishment of the NBPI and then by a further White Paper on the operation of the new policy.[68] The NBPI, chaired by the ex-Conservative minister Aubrey Jones, examined pay and price increases referred to it by the government. The White Paper set out the guidelines for policy, the centrepiece of which was a 3–3.5 per cent 'norm' for wage increases, tied to the growth rate envisioned in the National Plan. The assumption was that such a norm would be compatible with a stable price level, individual prices being raised only where there were cost increases which could not be absorbed, and in the expectation that some prices would be cut. On the other side, the wage norm was to be exceeded only where this could be justified by increased productivity, to secure a redistribution of labour, where pay was too low 'to maintain a reasonable standard of living', or where the pay of a particular group of workers had fallen seriously out of line with that of a comparable group.[69]

No one seems to have taken these norms too seriously. Even before they were published, Brown was stressing that he expected prices and wages to rise significantly faster than the norms in 1965, and that incomes policy was a gradual, educative policy for which not much could be expected in the short term. This view was certainly right. With productivity rising at less that 3 per cent per annum, wage settlements were running at 8.5 per cent by the third quarter of 1965.[70] By July 1965 the government was forced into deflationary measures to defend the exchange rate, and into a series of meetings with the TUC to try to find a more effective formula for incomes policy. A key argument from the government was that a failure on the incomes policy front would force a more serious deflation. The Chancellor told the TUC that 'it was his object to keep the incomes policy side going. If he was to follow the advice of the economists he would do a lot more disinflation or deflation. He could only hope that the incomes policy would in fact produce some results.'[71]

The government was especially anxious to secure a new agreement with the TUC because incomes policy was directly linked to the attempts to arrange renewed international support for the pound. By mid-August, Wilson was considering a ninety-day wage freeze (as implemented by US President John Kennedy in 1960) as a bargaining counter to gain help from the US Treasury, which, it was believed, would see such a measure as a sign of how determined the British government was to prevent wage inflation. The Chancellor supported this idea, 'in order to produce the element of drama', to drive home to the Americans the government's recognition of the seriousness of the situation. But Brown threatened resignation if such a policy was followed, despite Wilson's plea that he agree 'for the sake of getting support for sterling which would give the government a much freer hand in many directions'.[72]

After long discussions with the TUC and CBI, Brown headed off the threat of a freeze with an agreement establishing a voluntary system of notification ('early warning') and vetting of wage claims, coupled to much more limited notification on prices. The White Paper which eventually emerged from these discussions included statutory powers of government intervention, but these were to be held in reserve to see how the voluntary system worked. Neither the CBI nor the TUC was very happy with this agreement, both wanting to stress that they conceded only because of the economic emergency, but simultaneously arguing that the government was investing too much hope in incomes policy as a short-term instrument of economic management.[73]

Despite the mild deflationary measures of July 1965, the labour market remained tight, and both the government and the CBI saw this as meaning that wage pressure would continue to be strong. The early warning system did little to stem this pressure, and by the summer of 1966 it was evident that whatever 'educative' effects incomes policy might be delivering, it was not stemming inflation nor helping the balance of payments. By June the newly formed Ministerial Committee on Incomes Policy was discussing the option of a wage freeze. Brown was opposed. It would, he said, be limited in duration, bear most heavily on the public sector, be unfair and in breach of existing obligations, and be likely to be followed by a period of catch-up. In sum, he argued, 'the loss of goodwill generated by a standstill would be likely to prejudice the prospects of achieving a satisfactory longer-term policy'.[74] But despite these arguments a freeze was imposed. As in the previous summer, the clinching argument was that the existing policy was not delivering enough to prevent a foreign exchange crisis, this time exacerbated by the seamen's strike. As in the previous year, ministerial support for the policy was strengthened by the American belief that an effective incomes policy would make external support for the pound much more likely. Once again, the TUC and CBI were brought round to 'reluctant acquiescence' to the policy, only because the government could, with plausibility, play the national crisis card.[75]

In discussion with TUC officials in the summer of 1966, the Chancellor asked them 'to consider his feelings; he had tried for two years to run the economy at a high level, but he was about to put men out of work'.[76] Callaghan was referring to the sharp deflationary measures announced two days later. Their consequence was paradoxical for incomes policy. On the one hand, it made the prospect of some slowing in wage pressure more plausible as the labour market slackened. On the other hand, deflation made incomes policy even less palatable to the TUC; it would cause unemployment, and it made the government's claim that incomes policy was an *alternative* to deflation ring hollow. While both the TUC and CBI acquiesced in the new phase of policy, neither accepted the government's stated view that it was a response to being temporarily 'blown off course'. The CBI view was that this metaphor was misleading because 'our economic precariousness was due fundamentally to a level of government expenditure beyond our capacity, and tension in the labour market which allowed no real bargaining to take place'.[77] For its part, the TUC argued that the government had placed too many hopes on the short-run effects of incomes policy. It was also angry at the lack of consultation on the policy. One trade union leader said it was '1948 all over again', suggesting that rank-and-file pressures would soon grow against the policy even if the TUC leadership supported it.[78]

The freeze was announced in a White Paper in July, and the following month an Act was passed to give statutory backing to notification of price and wage increases, and to give the NBPI an enhanced role in investigating proposed increases. The six months of freeze were to be followed by six months of severe restraint, laid out in yet another government publication in November.[79] The immediate effects of this new policy were striking: for a year wage and price increases slowed down markedly. But the government recognised that this was not a sustainable long-term policy, and that it had to consider both the 're-entry' problem of the phase of policy to follow after the end of severe restraint, as well as the long-term shape of incomes policy. The economists Richard Kahn and Kenneth Berrill were asked to prepare a report on the prospects for a future incomes policy, a report which raised (even if it did not answer) all the strategic questions about incomes policy.

Kahn and Berrill argued that the 'freeze' had gained considerable acceptance, and provided the basis for a radical departure in policy. They criticised the characterisation of current policy set out in the July White Paper as providing a 'breathing space of twelve months in which productivity can catch up with excessive increases in incomes'. On the contrary, they argued, the deflation and freeze would slow down productivity growth, and incomes would tend to catch up with gains foregone. Thus the policy of wage restraint should become permanent, and incorporate a realistic level of price inflation of 2 per cent (rather than previous ideas of 'stable prices'); the report suggested that without an incomes policy the figure was likely to be around 4 per cent. To this figure for inflation could be added the prospective growth rate of productivity (estimated at 3.5 per cent) to give a total figure of 5.5 per cent as a possible ceiling on wage increases, but with a norm below this level, say 4 per cent, to allow for exceptional circumstances. This was their long-term 'steady state' position which they envisaged for the 1970s; in the immediate post-freeze/severe restraint years they suggested a lower target, of a 2 per cent norm. They called for the retention of back-up statutory powers, but envisaged the policy working primarily through the participation of the Ministry of Labour in *all* wage negotiations, with a right to 'speak up' before a settlement was reached and retaining a power of reference to the NBPI.[80]

These proposals and others emanating from the DEA were much discussed in the winter of 1966. Alec Cairncross welcomed them as at least having 'the great merit of providing the basis for discussion of general policy in a way that has been sadly lacking in the past'. The strongest objection to Kahn and Berrill's proposal was the idea of having the Ministry of Labour present at every wage negotiation, described by Cairncross as 'completely unrealistic'.[81] This proposal stemmed from Kahn and Berrill's recognition that the British wage bargaining system was highly fragmented, so that an effective policy would need to work at the local level, where many key decisions on wages were made. Policy before the freeze had responded to this situation partly by encouraging local bargaining on productivity, so that wage increases would, at least in principle, be financed out of productivity gains. But, as Kahn and Berrill pointed out, such bargains threatened to pre-empt all the national resources available for wage increases, leaving nothing for those in the wide range of industries where productivity bargaining was impossible. They argued that such localised productivity bargaining obscured the central idea of incomes policy as involving a *national* norm. In addition, they argued, productivity increases were often not the result of extra effort from workers, and should usually be reflected in price cuts rather than wage increases.[82] Such arguments struck at the heart of the development of productivity bargaining, which was such a notable feature of

Britain in these years, and is discussed in the broader context of productivity in Chapter 8.

A further crucial argument raised by Kahn and Berrill was the extent
to which incomes policy would be directed towards the pursuit of 'social
justice'. This, of course, had always been a key issue for the TUC, and
the low-pay condition in the pre-freeze policies had reflected this concern. But, again, Kahn and Berrrill identified a clash between the
political desirability of such a position and the economic dangers: any
attempt to squeeze differentials in the name of equality might accelerate
pay increases as the better-paid sought to restore those differentials.[83]

The proposal for the presence of the Ministry of Labour at all negotiations could readily be rejected as wholly unrealistic in administrative if
not political terms, but the other proposals were more difficult to decide
upon. Brown was worried that a 2 per cent inflation target would become
a minimum for price-setters and so increase inflation. This was linked
to the credibility of a 'nil norm' for wage increases; Kahn and Berrill
argued this would be widely seen as unfair and bring the policy into
disrepute.[84] As regards productivity bargains, these had now become
entrenched in the system, and their seeming 'fit' with the government's
rhetoric on the need for everyone to raise their productivity made it
impossible for the government to back off. Similarly with the distributional issue, some commitment on these lines was inescapable if the
TUC was to be kept on board.

The new policy announced in March 1967 embodied a 'nil norm'
with the same exceptions as before, including productivity and low pay.
The powers to prevent increases in wages under the 1966 Act were
allowed to lapse, and the sole legal power was now one to defer proposed price and wage increases for a maximum of seven months.[85] Despite
the concessions to union views in the new policy, the TUC majority now
shifted to outright opposition to it. The CBI was less hostile because it
feared a wage explosion, but the policy was becoming largely notional.
As Blackaby puts it, 'From mid-1967 to the end of the Labour Government's incomes policy there was less and less relationship between the
carefully worded criteria set out in the White Paper and actual events'.[86]
The dream in 1964 of a tripartite incomes policy to distribute equitably
the rewards of a growing economy was now effectively dead, and though
incomes policy was still much discussed, and White Papers published,
its role in economic strategy became increasingly marginal.

The deflationary measures of July 1966 increased unemployment
sharply, from 1.2 per cent at the time of the measures to 2.3 per cent by
the time of devaluation sixteen months later. Despite this slackening
pressure in the labour market, wage inflation rebounded from the previous restraint.[87] Incomes policy did nothing to prevent devaluation, but
after devaluation there was, for a period, increased interest in trying to

use this instrument to aid the shift in resources to exports (and shift out of consumption) that was now at the centre of economic policy, and simultaneously containing the wage–price spiral that devaluation threatened to unleash.[88] A new White Paper in April 1968 called for a ceiling on wage rises of 3.5 per cent per annum, but where all increases up to this figure would have to be justified by the existing four criteria. The only way to breach the ceiling would be for 'agreements which genuinely raise productivity and increase efficiency' in line with the NBPI guidelines on such agreements.[89] This formulation reinforced the worries set out by Kahn and Berrill that the emphasis on productivity deals would undermine the feasibility of a national norm; as a Treasury official put it: 'Thus a policy of the sky is the limit for wages based on productivity increases is a pretty dangerous development from the point of view of costs and our competitive position'.[90] Such anxieties led to an exchange of correspondence between the Chancellor (Jenkins) and Castle (now head of the newly formed DEP), which reveals a lack of meeting of minds between the macro-economic concerns of the former and the productivity mission of the latter.[91]

Castle's position was clear in the discussions aroused by Cabinet anxieties over the scale of settlements in the summer of 1968. She asserted the need for 'flexibility' in policy and strongly defended the stress on productivity:

> The current emphasis on productivity in the presentation of the incomes policy had been invaluable in creating a climate of opinion where wage increases were firmly associated with increased productivity ... but the Government could not be too perfectionist; they had simply to secure the best productivity deals they could.

Others were not convinced, the Chancellor noting that 'the policy was not making as large a contribution to economic strategy as many had hoped for a few months ago'.[92]

Later in 1968 Castle was asking whether incomes policy was still crucial to the government's economic policy. The fact that she could ask this question suggests a lack of conviction in her department that incomes policy could play the short-term macro-economic role the Chancellor hoped, rather than the long-term 'educative' role that the DEP emphasised. Unsurprisingly, in response Jenkins asserted its continuing importance, given that consumption was rising too fast and that the competitive advantage from devaluation was eroding. He again argued that the alternative to a more effective incomes policy was increased deflation.[93] The final incomes policy White Paper came in December 1969, and largely reflected the DEP's approach, combining a norm of 2.5–4.5 per cent with an emphasis on the educational and long-term nature of the policy and a defence of productivity bargaining.[94] Outside government, the TUC was trying to develop its own strategy for the economy, with its annual *Economic Review* from 1968, which reflected a complete rejection of a statutory policy, and tried to place wage increases in the context of the expansionary hopes of 1964/65. Unsurprisingly, this led to optimistic projections of economic growth and helped to license the acceleration of wage increases, which by 1970 was into double figures.

As well as productivity, the DEP was also keen on asserting the centrality of low pay to incomes policy. This, of course, fitted with the TUC's view that 'social justice' was a necessary part of such policies, but also found sympathy with some ministers who believed poverty reduction was central to Labour's purpose. Discussion of low pay in the context of incomes policy was complicated by its entanglement with wider issues about Labour's approach to poverty and inequality, including gender-based inequalities (see Chapter 9). There were periodic discussions about a national minimum wage throughout Labour's period in office. One major objection to this was cost, in part because it was taken for granted that if such a policy were introduced it would have to be based on equal pay for women.[95] The TUC did not want a legal national minimum wage but wanted to have low pay as a key criterion for exceptions to the norm in incomes policy. While this found sympathy in the DEP, the Treasury line was that unless others were willing to make sacrifices for the lower-paid, such a criterion would accelerate pay increases as the better-paid sought to restore differentials. In addition, it argued, poverty was best dealt with by the social security system rather than a minimum wage.[96] The paradox in respect of low pay was that while the TUC argued, rightly, that the government was not making low pay the core of incomes policy, and using this as a justification for its rejection of the policy, free collective bargaining was even less likely to reduce wage inequalities.[97]

The White Paper of December 1969 announced the government's intention to merge the NBPI with the Monopolies and Mergers Commission to form a Commission on Industry and Manpower (see also Chapter 5). The idea behind this was partly doubts about the role of the Monopolies and Mergers Commission, but more generally it stemmed from a desire to have a single body to link scrutiny of companies' pricing and efficiency, a role which the NBPI had increasingly taken on.[98] Unsurprisingly, this seemed to the CBI to threaten the kind of general 'interference' in industry it was committed to oppose, with the worst aspects of incomes policy and its concern with prices rather than wages. The Commission on Industry and Manpower could have taken incomes policy in a new, radical direction and combined it with the ambitious policies of government industrial intervention favoured especially by

MinTech. But there was no prospect of doing this on the consensual basis that the government had always said was a necessary underpinning of incomes policy, any more than such a policy had proved workable in the mid-1960s once the prospect of sustained rapid growth had receded.

Industrial relations and *In Place of Strife*

Where productivity, prices and incomes policy had been integral to Labour's 1964 vision of planned economic expansion and social justice, industrial relations merited hardly a mention. The key aim for Labour was to secure an agreement with the unions (and the CBI) on incomes policy, not in any way to enter into confrontation with the unions, as traditionally the party had accepted that government had little to do but maintain a legal framework that allowed the unions to pursue free collective bargaining.[99] But five years later the government and party were riven with a dispute about the proposal in the White Paper *In Place of Strife* (*IPOS*) to impose, in the last resort, financial penalties on unofficial strikers who refused to abide by a 'conciliation pause' or 'cooling-off period'. The high politics of this dramatic episode, which came close to toppling the government, are described in Peter Jenkins' book, and the archives do not suggest this picture needs substantial modification.[100] This section focuses on the strategic aspects of this episode.

Concern with industrial relations and their impact on economic performance was growing in the mid-1960s. The government had itself intervened strongly in the seamen's strike in the summer of 1966. But the issue which gained most political and public attention was not official strikes like that of the National Union of Seamen, but unofficial strikes, whose number grew sharply in the 1960s. The surge in unofficial strikes coincided with the deliberations of the Donovan Commission on Industrial Relations, set up by Wilson in 1965 and which reported in 1968. It discussed the upsurge in unofficial strikes, but came up with no short-term solutions. Its main focus was on repairing the damage brought about by what it diagnosed as the divergence between official, usually national, trade union industrial relations, and local, often unofficial, patterns of activity, though, as critics pointed out, this analysis was at best relevant to the private manufacturing sector, which covered only about a third of union members. The Commission's recommendations were predominantly procedural and long term, and it explicitly rejected such panaceas as strike ballots and cooling-off periods.[101]

The government began discussing the Donovan proposals with the TUC and CBI in the summer of 1968, but these two bodies also discussed procedural reforms between themselves. The CBI wanted stronger action on strikes than Donovan proposed, but there were other areas where some reforms could be agreed bilaterally with the TUC, and the TUC regarded this as *all* that was necessary.[102] However, key figures in the government were not content with this approach, and by December 1968 Castle had come up with the proposals which, after revision, became *IPOS*. These proposals offered much to the unions in terms of such issues as union recognition, but it was the proposals that included any legal penalties on the unions or workers that were to be the focus of attention. The initial proposal for strike ballots was dropped, partly because of the concern with unofficial strikes, where such ballots were irrelevant, but the proposed cooling-off period, backed by financial sanctions, in unofficial disputes was to form the centrepiece of the struggle over the next six months.[103]

When these proposals came to Cabinet at the end of December, their strongest supporters were Castle, Wilson and Jenkins. While the latter two put the legislation predominantly in the context of short-term economic management, Castle was keen to put them in the context of a longer-term policy of reshaping industrial relations by strengthening the unions while also adding a little to their responsibilities. But it was evident from the first Cabinet meetings that there was a sharp division of opinion, especially over the cooling-off period.[104] In these discussions Castle made it clear she regarded what came to be called the penalty clauses as a last resort, and that if the TUC came up with a workable alternative then the clauses would not be invoked.[105] The White Paper was published at the end of January 1969, but with the intention that legislation on its proposals would follow only after more discussion with the TUC.

No agreement had been reached by the time of the budget in April, and in the budget statement *IPOS* was presented as integral to the government's strategy. Following on from the discussions of incomes policy outlined above, Jenkins said in his speech that a 'rigorous compulsory' policy on wages and prices had been desirable only in the immediate aftermath of devaluation. Now the government could contemplate 'moving to a policy which can offer a long-term solution to the problem of moderating the rate of growth of prices and incomes without recourse to statutory powers'. This was directly relevant to industrial relations, because a continuation of stringent statutory powers on incomes would prejudice even further 'the present climate of industrial relations', which was already 'a serious obstacle to the attainment of our economic objectives'. Later in the budget debate Castle laid out her *IPOS* proposals, though again stressing she would like the penal powers to 'atrophy from disuse' if the TUC found a workable alternative.[106]

Just before the budget, the crisis in the government over *IPOS* had reached the state where Wilson called a special Cabinet meeting to denounce what he saw as the breakdown of collective responsibility on the issue, arising above all from Callaghan's support of a motion at the Labour Party National Executive Committee that suggested opposition to the penal clauses. Callaghan disputed the allegation that he had broken with collective responsibility, and argued that Castle was still holding out the prospects of amendment to the proposals; indeed, the Cabinet minutes record that the meeting reaffirmed its support for *IPOS* 'subject to further consideration in the light of any alternative proposals which might be put forward before the Cabinet had to approve the relevant legislation'.[107]

As well as tensions in the party, the TUC remained (at least in public) united in its hostility to the proposals. The strength of this opposition seems to have particularly borne in on Wilson and Castle after a dinner at Chequers at the beginning of June with Hugh Scanlon (head of the engineering union) and Jack Jones, new head of the Transport and General Workers' Union. Their unions covered the industries where unofficial disputes were most prevalent, and they made clear how far they were willing to go to prevent the government legislating on 'their' business. Wilson's own account of the meeting recorded that 'what had made the greatest impact on me was the clear intention of Jones and Scanlon not only, if they could, to prevent the legislation being introduced or going through, but thereafter to destroy it in operation'.[108] In resisting so strongly the government's mild proposals, the union leaders resisted compromises such as paying the financial penalties into a fund for union purposes. Frank Cousins, who had resigned his ministerial post over incomes policy, suggested the unions should call the government's bluff of a worse outcome if the proposals were defeated and a Conservative government came to power, in the belief that such a government would not legislate but simply allow the CBI to pursue its own policies.[109]

In the end, in the face of party divisions and union intransigence, Castle and Wilson did a deal with the TUC, under which they agreed to withdraw the penal clauses in return for a 'solemn and binding' agreement that the TUC would do everything in its power to reduce the incidence of unofficial strikes. The actual wording of this agreement, however, suggests how difficult it would be, regardless of how much goodwill existed in the TUC, for that undertaking to be effective where the union involved was not co-operative (let alone the unofficial strikers):

> If the General Council of the TUC find there should be no stoppage of work before procedure is exhausted, they will place an obligation on the organisation or organisations concerned to take energetic steps to obtain an immediate resumption of work, including action within their rules if necessary, so that negotiations proceed.[110]

The failure to go ahead with *IPOS* was a political humiliation for the government. It had all along argued that if the TUC came up with an acceptable alternative the penal clauses would be unnecessary, but the 'solemn and binding' agreement was difficult to see as a serious resolution of the problem of unofficial strikes. On the other hand, it was probably as much as the TUC could offer, given the claims for autonomy of the major constituent trade unions. The government was faced with the fact that the TUC simply did not have the power to impose policies on those constituents, so even where individual TUC leaders approved of government proposals, it could see that they would be inoperative given the balance of power within the union movement.[111] This was, of course, a long-standing institutional reality whose importance was to be shown even more dramatically in the 1970s and the problems of the Social Contract.

The more specific strategic question of the 1960s is the *economic* logic of *IPOS*. In January 1969 Andrew Graham, an economic adviser, had argued that *IPOS* would make any deal with the unions on incomes policy impossible, and in doing so would deliver a very bad deal for the government. He argued that unofficial strikes were economically almost irrelevant, costing at most 0.3 per cent of output each year, and that this was far less than the cumulative benefits of incomes policy. In summary, he said: 'While a policy to improve industrial relations may be complementary to an incomes policy it *cannot* be a *substitute* for it. Moreover, the incomes policy must remain the prime instrument for maintaining our competitiveness and making a success of devaluation.' Further, 'this legislation is *not* a substitute for incomes policy, and to push ahead with it *at the expense* of incomes policy would, in my view, spell disaster'.[112]

Such views seem to have little effect, but they do provide a useful perspective on the *IPOS* episode. If the government had gone ahead with the legislation, would that have been helpful from an economic strategy point of view? Arguably the unions were already so alienated over compulsory elements in incomes policy that penal clauses would have just compounded their discontent. Alternatively, if the threat of those clauses had been used to try to get a better agreement on incomes, something might have been salvaged from a desperate situation.

Notes

The place of publication is London unless otherwise specified.

1 *The National Plan*, Cmnd 2764, BPP 1964/65, vol. 30, p. 65.
2 *Ibid.*, pp. 34–5, 37–8. These sections of the Plan were based on PRO, LAB 8/3213, DEA, 'Labour supply situation in the Plan period', 10 May 1965.

Note that it was usual (but not universal) in the 1960s to refer to workers of both sexes under the heading of 'manpower'.

3 *National Plan*, p. 37. Declining activity rates among older men were also identified as a cause of slow labour supply growth, but little was made of this point. See also note 52.

4 *Ibid.*, pp. 19, 39.

5 PRO, LAB 8/3213, 'Labour supply situation', 10 May 1965. The general trends in women's participation were well established: see, for example, T. Chester, 'Growth, productivity and womanpower', *District Bank Review*, 143 (1962), pp. 18–35; W. Beckerman and J. Sutherland, 'Married women at work in 1972', *National Institute Economic Review*, 23 (1963), pp. 56–60.

6 A. Hunt, *A Survey of Women's Employment*, 2 vols (1968). See also PRO, RG 23/361, 362, Government social survey, 'A survey of women's employment', 1965.

7 Hunt, *Survey*, vol. I, pp. 13–15, and PRO, RG 40/283, 'Meeting of Ministry of Labour's Women's Consultative Committee', 18 July 1967.

8 *Observer*, 31 March 1968.

9 PRO, RG 40/283, 'Meeting of WCC', 18 July 1968; PRO, LAB 8/3215, Ministry of Health, 'Day nurseries', 20 May 1965. On the parallel issue in the 1940s, see J. Tomlinson, *Democratic Socialism and Economic Policy: The Attlee Years 1945–51* (Cambridge, 1996), ch. 9.

10 On the politics of equal pay, see Steven Fielding's companion volume, Chapter 5.

11 PRO, T 328/337, 'Brief for Secretary of State's meeting with CBI', 22 July 1968.

12 *Hansard* (Commons), vol. 767, 26 June 1968, cols 500–6; PRO, T 328/339, 'TUC meeting with Secretary of State', 9 September 1969; also, T 328/339, 'Wilson to TUC', 1 September 1969; *Times*, 2 July 1968.

13 PRO, T 328/337, R. Workman, 'Equal pay', 2 July 1968, and Jenkins to Castle, 13 September 1968.

14 PRO, T 328/338, DEP, 'Enquiry into costs of equal pay', July 1969.

15 *Ibid.*, H. Walsh, 'Equal pay: memo by the First Secretary', 25 July 1969; PRO, CAB 128/44, 'Cabinet minutes', 4 July and 25 July 1969.

16 PRO, T 328/339, 'Meeting with CBI', 17 September 1969.

17 PRO, T 328/339, B. Fensome, 'Equal pay for women', 2 September 1969.

18 PRO, LAB 43/568, 'Speech by B. Castle', 21 December 1969; LAB 43/568, 'Draft letter', H. Wilson to F. Lee, 24 March 1970. Lee had stressed the lack of training for women in the second reading debate, *Hansard* (Commons), vol. 797, cols 950–6. More generally, see N. Seear, 'The future employment of women', in B. Roberts and J. Smith (eds), *Manpower Policy and Employment Trends* (1966), pp. 98–110.

19 PRO, LAB 43/577, 'Sex discrimination in employment', 1970. In her first draft of what was to become *In Place of Strife*, Castle said that 'the Government has decided to set up a high-powered committee to review training opportunities for women', but I have found no trace of this committee's existence. PRO, PREM 13/2165, 'First draft of White Paper: parties in progress: a policy for industrial relations', December 1968.

20 *A Review of the Scope and Problems of Scientific and Technological Manpower Policy*, Cmnd 2800, BPP 1965/66, vol. 22 (October 1965); *The Flow into Employment of Scientists, Engineers and Technologists*, Cmnd 3760, BPP 1967/68, vol. 25 (September 1968); *The Brain Drain: Report of the Working Group on Migration*, Cmnd 3417, BPP 1966/67, vol. 39 (October 1967).

21 PRO, T 328/176, O. Simpson, 'Highly qualified manpower', 5 January

1970. The 'brain drain' issue was used to attack Labour's 'egalitarianism': see *Hansard* (Commons), vol. 741, 13 February 1967, cols 121–234.

22 PRO, LAB 8/3341, 'Establishment of a central unit for highly qualified manpower', November 1966.

23 PRO, T 227/2642, L. Pliatzky, 'Scientific and technological manpower', 12 December 1967; T 227/2642, L. Pliatzky, 'Manpower', 30 January 1968.

24 PRO, CAB 168/123, 'Arrangements for manpower planning', January 1970.

25 K. Gannicott and M. Blaug, 'Manpower forecasting since Robbins: a science lobby in action', *Higher Education Review*, 2 (1969), pp. 56–74.

26 D. Edgerton, *Science, Technology and the British Industrial 'Decline' 1870–1970* (Cambridge, 1996), pp. 22–4; M. Sanderson, *Education and Economic Decline in Britain, 1870 to the 1970s* (Cambridge, 1999), pp. 95–8.

27 *National Plan*, pp. 10, 40–2.

28 P. Perry, *The Evolution of British Manpower Policy* (1976); J. Sheldrake and S. Vickerstaff, *The History of Industrial Training in Britain* (1987), ch. 6. For an influential critique of ITBs, see D. Lees and B. Chiplin, 'The economics of industrial training', *Lloyds Bank Review*, 96 (1970), pp. 29–41; one of their most telling points was that half of all job changes in Britain involved shifts between occupations, thus crossing ITB boundaries.

29 Perry, *Evolution*, p. 177; R. Elliott, 'Industrial relations and manpower policy', in F. Blackaby (ed), *British Economic Policy 1960–74* (Cambridge, 1978), p. 606.

30 Modern Records Centre (MRC), University of Warwick, MSS 200/C/3/EDU/1/15, 'Statement by CBI to Sub-committee on Economic Affairs of House of Commons Estimates Committee', April 1967, and EDU/1/16, CBI survey, 'The operation of the Industrial Training Act', July 1968.

31 PRO, PREM 13/1242, 'Speech by PM to TUC', 5 September 1966.

32 Elliott, 'Industrial relations', p. 606.

33 PRO, LAB 8/3214, 'DEA: Plan Co-ordination Working Group', 1965; LAB 8/3221, 'Manpower research: Labour Market Policies Group', 1964–66; *In Place of Strife*, Cmnd 3888, BPP 1968/69, vol. 53, pp. 17–18; *Report of Royal Commission on Trade Unions and Employers' Associations*, Cmnd 3623, BPP 1967/68, vol. 32.

34 PRO, CAB 134/3198, Ministry of Labour, 'Industrial training facilities', 4 May 1967.

35 MRC, MSS 200/C/3/EDU/1/3, 'CBI Vocational Training Committee', July 1966; Perry, *Evolution*, pp. 195–6.

36 MRC, MSS 200/C/3/EDU/1/16, 'CBI survey'.

37 H. Wilson, *Hansard* (Commons), vol. 756, 18 January 1968, cols 1987–8; PRO, LAB 8/3479, 'Review of current problems and developments in the Ministry of Labour field', 19 January 1968.

38 MRC, MSS 292/B/552.48/4, TUC, 'Productivity 1960–70'.

39 Sanderson, *Education*, ch. 6; D. Aldcroft, *Education, Training and Economic Performance 1944 to 1990* (Manchester, 1992), pp. 58–60.

40 *National Plan*, p. 39.

41 NEDC, *Conditions Favourable to Faster Growth* (1963), pp. 10–13; P. Bridgen, 'The state, redundancy pay, and economic policy-making in the early 1960s', *Twentieth Century British History*, 11 (2000), pp. 233–58.

42 OECD, *Manpower Policy in the UK* (Paris, 1970), which generally gave a favourable account of Labour's policies, thought the earnings-related unemployment benefit had made unemployed workers more choosy about taking up new jobs, but 'Whether this also implies a better functioning of the labour market is as yet difficult to say' (p. 28).

43 S. Mukherjee, *Through No Fault of Their Own: Systems of Handling Redundancy in Britain, France and Germany* (1973), ch. 6.

44 Elliott, 'Industrial relations', pp. 601–2; S. Parker, C. Thomas, N. Elliott and W. McCarthy, *Effects of the Redundancy Payments Act* (1971), pp. 9–12.

45 PRO, LAB 8/3290, 'Research into the effects of the RPA', 1967; R. Fryer, 'The myths of the Redundancy Payments Act', *Industrial Law Journal*, 2 (1973), pp. 12–13. Quite separate schemes for redundancy were run in the coal industry, where the government sought to ease but not halt the outflow of labour: see PRO, CAB 134/1740, Ministry of Power, 'Colliery closures and special funds', 30 September 1965.

46 D. Mackay, 'After the shake-out', *Oxford Economic Papers*, 24 (1972), pp. 89–110.

47 PRO, CAB 134/3195, M. Stewart, 'Redeployment of labour', 20 October 1966.

48 PRO, LAB 8/3430, 'Redeployment: draft report to NEDC', 1968.

49 N. Kaldor, 'The economic effects of SET', in N. Kaldor, *Reports on Taxation. I. Papers Relating to the UK* (1980), pp. 200–29. R. Whiting, who has given a recent, archive-based discussion of the tax, cites a document of 5 April as the first mention of the tax. Whiting, 'Ideology and reform in Labour's tax strategy, 1964–1970', *Historical Journal*, 41 (1998), pp. 1135–8, and *idem*, *The Labour Party and Taxation* (Cambridge, 2000), pp. 198–205. The document is at PRO, T 171/813, Kaldor, 'The case for payroll tax and for a new incentive for exports'.

50 'Of all the taxes we have studied, SET was the most unpopular': A. Robinson and C. Sandford, *Tax Policy-Making* (1983), p. 127. For a contemporary critique, see *Economist*, 5 November 1966, pp. 547–8. For a discussion of both Kaldor's advisory role and the SET, see A. Blick, 'The origins and history of the government adviser with special reference to the 1964–70 Wilson administrations' (unpublished PhD dissertation, University of London, 2002), pp. 156–63, 201–14.

51 N. Kaldor, *Causes of the Slow Rate of Growth of the United Kingdom* (Cambridge, 1966). Such views, which suggested how hard it would be for Britain to emulate its Continental neighbours, were not popular at this time, though they were incisively stated by Phelps Brown in a paper to the NEDC. See MRC, MSS 200/C/3/EMP/1/10, 'Notes on the rise of productivity', 24 March 1966.

52 R. Price, 'Budgetary policy', in Blackaby, *British Economic Policy*, p. 151. Because it imposed a per capita tax, the SET unintentionally discriminated against part-time workers and hence women: PRO, LAB 43/456, 'Effect of SET on part-timers', 1966. Like the RPA, it may also have discouraged the employment of older workers. See PRO, T 328/397, N. Kaldor, 'Labour transfers between sectors, 1961–67', 25 July 1969: 'The main effect of SET appears to have been to cause a large increase in retirements, both male and female in the SET paying sectors and also in manufacturing'.

53 M. Stewart, *Politics and Economic Policy in the UK Since 1964: The Jekyll and Hyde Years* (1978), p. 65.

54 The long-termism and export subsidy aspect of the SET seem to explain Callaghan's willingness to override Treasury scepticism and implement the tax. Whiting, *Labour Party*, pp. 199–200; PRO, PREM 13/863, J. Callaghan to H. Wilson, 29 April 1966.

55 Stewart, *Politics*, pp. 66–7.

56 PRO, T 342/61, W. Armstrong, 'SET and prices', 8 September 1967; T 277/179, 'Activity rates and labour supply', March 1967.

57 W. B. Reddaway, *Effects of SET: Final Report* (Cambridge, 1973); Stewart, *Politics*, pp. 66–7.

58 J. Hutton and K. Hartley, 'The selective employment tax and the labour market', *British Journal of Industrial Relations*, 4 (1966), pp. 289–303.

59 Kaldor, 'Economic effects', pp. 226–7; PRO, T 328/397, Kaldor, 'Labour transfers', 25 July 1969.

60 R. Rowthorn, 'What remains of Kaldor's law?', *Economic Journal*, 85 (1975), pp. 10–19.

61 *National Plan*, pp. 158–9. One civil servant described Kaldor's use of the primary/secondary/tertiary industry distinction as akin to 'the medieval distinction between those who fight, those who work, and those who pray': PRO, EW 24/27, M. Powell, 'Professor Kaldor's Inaugural Lecture', 22 December 1966.

62 *National Plan*, p. 10; see also Chapter 4.

63 R. Taylor, *The Trade Union Question in British Politics: Government and Unions Since 1945* (1993), ch. 5; F. Blackaby, 'Incomes policy', in Blackaby, *British Economic Policy*, pp. 367–401; R. Jones, *Wages and Employment Policy 1936–1985* (1987), ch. 6; W. Fishbein, *Wage Restraint by Consensus: Britain's Search for an Incomes Policy Agreement 1965–79* (1984), ch. 2; R. Dorfman, *Wage Politics in Britain* (Iowa, 1973).

64 MRC, MSS 292B/560.1/9, 'TUC Economic Committee meeting', 20 November 1964.

65 *Ibid.* For the background to the *Statement of Intent*, see Taylor, *Trade Union Question*, pp. 126–34.

66 MRC, MSS 292B/560.1/9, 'Covering letter to draft statement', 17 November 1964.

67 MRC, MSS 200/C/3/EMP/1/10, 'Note by representatives of the TUC on NEDC prices and incomes policy', March 1966, and 'Productivity, prices and incomes: observations by management members of NEDC', March 1966; MSS 292B/560.1/9, 'TUC Economic Committee meeting', 20 November 1965.

68 *Machinery of Prices and Incomes Policy*, Cmnd 2577, BPP 1964/65, vol. 30 (February 1965); *Prices and Incomes Policy*, Cmnd 2639, BPP 1964/65, vol. 30 (April 1965). There is a very thorough history of the NBPI in A. Fels, *The British Prices and Incomes Board* (Cambridge, 1972).

69 PRO, EW 27/124, 'Government action on prices and incomes policy Feb. 1965–Feb. 1966'.

70 PRO, PREM 13/259, Burke Trend to PM, 4 February 1965; PRO, EW 27/124, 'First Secretary's meeting with TUC', 20 December 1965.

71 MRC, MSS 292B/560.1/10, 'TUC Economic Committee meeting', 28 July 1965.

72 PRO, PREM 13/259, 'Record of telephone conversation PM/Chancellor/First Secretary', 20 August 1965.

73 *Prices and Incomes Policy: An 'Early Warning' System*, Cmnd 2808, BPP 1965/66, vol. 13 (November 1965); MRC, MSS 200//C/3/EMP/1/10, 'M. Laing (President of CBI) to members', 10 November 1965.

74 PRO, CAB 134/3056, First Secretary, 'Further developments of the policy for productivity, prices and incomes', 9 June 1966, and 'Meeting of Committee on Productivity, Prices and Incomes', 13 June 1966.

75 Stewart, *Politics*, pp. 69–70; PRO, T 319/70, Brief for PM on visit to Washington, 'Prices and incomes standstill', 26 July 1966; PRO, CAB 134/3056, Draft White Paper, 'Prices and Incomes Standstill', 25 July 1966, and discussion, 26 July 1966.

76 MRC, MSS 292B/560.1/12, 'TUC meeting with Chancellor', 18 July 1966.
77 MRC, MSS 200/C/3/EMP/1/1, 'Director General of CBI to meeting of Labour and Social Affairs Committee', 27 July 1966.
78 MRC, MSS 292B/560.1/12, 'TUC meetings with ministers', 22 July–8 August 1966.
79 *Prices and Incomes Standstill*, Cmnd 3073, BPP 1966/67, vol. 59 (July 1966); Prices and Incomes Act, August 1966; *Prices and Incomes Standstill: Period of Severe Restraint*, Cmnd 3150, BPP 1966/67, vol. 59 (November 1966).
80 PRO, CAB 134/3059, R. Kahn and K. Berrill, 'Prices and incomes policy: an interim memo', December 1966.
81 PRO, T 328/52, A. Cairncross to W. Armstrong, 'Prices and incomes policy', 7 December 1966, and Cairncross to P. Baldwin, 'Prices and incomes policy', 11 January 1967.
82 Kahn and Berrill, 'Prices and incomes', pp. 23–6.
83 *Ibid.*, p. 9.
84 PRO, CAB 134/3059, First Secretary, 'Prices and incomes policy in the longer-term', 23 January 1967; PRO, T 328/52, R. Kahn and K. Berrill, 'The norm for July 1967–June 1968', 15 February 1967.
85 *Prices and Incomes Policy after 30th July 1967*, Cmnd 3235, BPP 1966/67, vol. 43 (March 1967).
86 MRC, MSS 200/C/3/EMP/1/1, 'CBI Economic Committee', 25 January 1967; Blackaby, 'Incomes policy', p. 375.
87 S. Henry and P. Ormerod, 'Incomes policy and wage inflation: empirical evidence for the UK 1961–1977', *National Institute Economic Review*, 85 (1978), pp. 31–9.
88 PRO, CAB 134/3058, 'Ministerial Committee on Prices and Incomes meeting', 8 December 1967.
89 *Productivity, Prices and Incomes Policy in 1968 and 1969*, Cmnd 3590, BPP 1967/68, vol. 39, pp. 8–9; NBPI report no. 36, *Productivity Agreements*, Cmnd 3311, BPP 1966/67, vol. 43.
90 PRO, T 328/208, R. Wakeman to K. Berrill, 'PM's personal minute of 3rd Apr: incomes policy', 2 May 1968; other senior advisers concurred – see T 328/208, A. Cairncross, 'Incomes policy', 6 May 1968, and N. Kaldor, 'Incomes policy and productivity agreements', 8 May 1968.
91 PRO, T 328/208, R. Jenkins to B. Castle, 13 June 1968, and Castle to Jenkins, 28 June 1968, followed up by PRO, CAB 134/3063, Jenkins to Castle, 'Future strategy on incomes policy', 23 July 1968.
92 PRO, CAB 134/3061, 'Meeting', 30 July 1968. In her memoirs Castle recalled her policy as being 'to switch the whole emphasis of prices and incomes policy from negative wage restraint. It must be seen as the way to a higher standard of living by making it possible to expand the economy without inflation by encouraging productivity': *Fighting all the Way* (1993), p. 398.
93 PRO, CAB 134/3061, 'Ministerial Committee on Prices and Incomes meeting', 13 November 1968; CAB 134/3063, B. Castle, 'Incomes policy – current problems', 12 November 1968.
94 *Productivity, Prices and Incomes Policy After 1969*, Cmnd 4237, BPP 1969/70, vol. 9 (December 1969). This argument was in line with that of the NBPI: A. Jones, 'Prices and incomes policy', *Economic Journal*, 78 (1968), p. 800. See also H. Clegg, *How to Run an Incomes Policy and Why We Made Such a Mess of the Last One* (1971), p. 35.
95 PRO, CAB 134/3057, Ministry of Labour, 'Implications and consequences of introducing legislation for a national minimum wage', 11 October 1966.

96 PRO, CAB 134/3058, 'Ministerial Committee on Prices and Incomes meet-
    ing', 26 January 1967; CAB 134/3059, Kahn and Berrill, 'Interim memo',
    p. 9; CAB 134/3061, 'Ministerial Committee on Prices and Incomes
    meeting', 30 July 1968. During the freeze some Labour local authorities
    were using low pay as a reason for increasing the pay of their employees
    above the norm: see PRO, T 319/71, 'Use of powers under Part IV of the
    Prices and Incomes Act', 10 October 1966. For the TUC's view, see MRC,
    MSS 292B/560.1/22, 'Economic Committee meeting', 11 February 1970.
97 B. Wootton, *Incomes Policy: An Inquest and a Proposal* (1970), pp. 107–8.
98 PRO, CAB 134/3213, 'Monopolies and Prices Reference Committee', 6 June
    1969; A. Jones, *Britain's Economy: The Roots of Stagnation* (Cambridge, 1985),
    pp. 112–13.
99 See L. Minkin, *The Contentious Alliance: Trade Unions and the Labour Party*
    (Edinburgh, 1991), p. 12, for the historical roots of this.
100 P. Jenkins, *The Battle of Downing Street* (1970); *In Place of Strife*, Cmnd 3888,
    BPP 1968/69, vol. 5 (January 1969); see also Taylor, *Trade Union Question*,
    pp. 157–72.
101 *Report of Royal Commission*; Taylor, *Trade Union Question*, pp. 151–7.
102 PRO, PREM 13/2725, 'Report of the Royal Commission: CBI/TUC action
    following the report', October 1968; PRO, CAB 128/44, 'Cabinet meeting',
    3 January 1969.
103 PRO, LAB 43/538, B. Castle, 'Meeting with GPC of TUC', 30 December
    1968; PRO, CAB 129/139, 'A policy for industrial relations: draft White
    Paper', 30 December 1968.
104 PRO, CAB 128/44, 'Cabinet conclusions', 3, 8–9, 14 January 1969.
105 PRO, CAB 128/44, 14 January 1969.
106 *Hansard* (Commons), vol. 781, 15 April 1969, cols 1003–6; *ibid.*, 16 April
    1969, cols 1180–9. See also PRO, T 171/854, D. Wass, 'Productivity, prices
    and incomes and industrial relations', 15 April 1969.
107 PRO, CAB 128/46, 'Confidential annex, Cabinet conclusions', 3 April 1969.
108 PRO, LAB 43/534, H. Wilson, 'Postscript on meeting of 1 June 1969'.
109 PRO, CAB 165/661, B. Castle to H. Wilson, 23 April 1969; PRO, PREM
    13/2725, B. Castle to H. Wilson, 'Industrial Relations Bill – financial
    penalties', 5 May 1969, and 'Meeting of Castle and Wilson with TUC', 11
    April 1969.
110 PRO, PREM 13/2728, 'Solemn and binding agreement', 18 June 1969.
111 M. Stewart, *Politics*, pp. 93–4. For an insightful view of the politics of the
    dispute, see Minkin, *Contentious*, pp. 114, 118.
112 PRO, PREM 13/2724, 'The White Paper on Industrial Relations: a bargain
    with the unions?', 14 January 1969. Original emphasis.

7

Modernising the public sector

From 1918 until the 1940s, expansion of the publicly owned sector of the economy was central to Labour's politics. After 1931, the party turned its 1918 constitutional commitment (in Clause 4) to the expansion of common ownership into a much more specific 'shopping list' of industries to be nationalised. After 1945 this list was largely followed, so that by 1951 approximately 20 per cent of the British economy (measured by output) was in public hands, overwhelmingly in the form of 'Morrisonian' public corporations, which secured considerable autonomy for their 'expert' boards. These nationalised industries dominated the transport, utility and energy sectors, but had little or no presence in manufacturing or finance. The most radical and controversial nationalisation was of iron and steel, which Labour eventually (and somewhat reluctantly) took into public ownership, in part because the Conservatives had turned it into a political symbol of where they believed the powers of the state should be excluded.[1]

Even before this process of nationalisation had been completed, debates were emerging in Labour circles about how far the model of sectoral monopolies was appropriate to industries beyond the programme of 1945. While few at this time doubted that the principle of common ownership needed to be retained by future Labour governments, many urged caution. Most radically, people like Douglas Jay urged the need to experiment with quite different forms of public ownership, such as state shareholding. More common was an emphasis on 'consolidation' – the need for the state to digest what had already been taken over before further bites were taken at the private sector.[2] Caution followed from the recognition that the state had embarked on a massive exercise in public management with few guiding principles. The commitment to the public corporation format had been fought over and then entrenched in Labour thinking in the 1930s, but it provided no more than a broad institutional arrangement, within which many key issues remained obscure.

The relationship between the Attlee government's commitment to national economic planning and the semi-autonomy of the public corporations was an emerging source of tension in the late 1940s, and behind this lay all sorts of questions about both the political and economic principles that should govern these corporations' behaviour. When Labour left office in 1951, no clear rules had been established about the degree of parliamentary and ministerial control over the nationalised industries, and there existed no accepted policies on pricing and investment for these industries to follow.[3] Under Clement Attlee, Labour had carried out its manifesto commitments on public ownership, but had barely begun to formulate policy on how these new corporations were to be controlled and managed in a mixed economy.

Policy in opposition

In opposition between 1951 and 1964, Labour was famously convulsed by arguments about the nature and extent of the party's commitment to future nationalisation.[4] In these arguments it was mainly the 'revisionists' who made the running, the most important extended statement being made by Tony Crosland in his *The Future of Socialism* (1956), whose central message was that, in the transformed capitalism of post-war Britain, public ownership was largely irrelevant to the pursuit of Labour's goals and should therefore be toppled from its pedestal in Labour thinking.[5] Crosland pushed this argument further than many revisionists wanted to go. The leader of the party during the controversy, Hugh Gaitskell, who had experienced some of the complexities of nationalised industry policy while Minister of Power, was willing to make the case for further nationalisation in some industries rather than abandon the policy entirely.[6] But he largely shared Crosland's view that the focus on nationalisation in Labour's constitution and rhetoric was damaging to its electoral prospects, and after the general election defeat of 1959 he attempted to change Labour's constitution to reflect this view. The attempt failed, not least because of the ideological conservatism of the trade unions.[7] But despite this failure, the 'revisionist' pre-eminence in Labour's thinking is evident from the late 1950s. The key party document *Industry and Society* (1957) accepted that large-scale industry in Britain was usually efficient, and that therefore arguments for nationalisation would have to be based on other grounds, especially those of democracy, redistribution or control of the economy. This was a huge concession to revisionist thinking because, while Labour's motives for nationalisation had always been multiple and complex, the idea of the fundamental inefficiency of private ownership had always been central. *Industry and Society* obscured this fundamental revisionism by talking of the desirability of further nationalisation where companies were 'failing the nation', but simultaneously made it clear that such firms were few in number.[8]

The left of the party in the 1950s remained committed to the idea that nationalisation was central to Labour's agenda and identity. They won a Pyrrhic victory in 1959 with the defeat of the proposal to alter Clause 4, but that outcome was highly misleading about who was winning the arguments and effectively controlling the policy agenda. In part the defeat of the left on this policy agenda beyond Clause 4 followed from its own weaknesses, especially evident in its economic analysis and policy-making, and their application to issues such as the control and management of nationalised industries. Aneurin Bevan, as leader of the left, was notably uninterested in policy, especially domestic policy, and there was nobody else on that wing of the party who had the intellectual and political weight to challenge the revisionists.[9]

The weakness of the left is evident in the much less public discussions that went on in Labour circles in the late 1950s leading up to the party's *Public Enterprise* (1957). This paper was drawn up by a study group chaired by Gaitskell on which the most prominent left-winger was Ian Mikardo. Judging by the papers and minutes of this group, the discussion was low key and rather meandering, with none of the participants showing much grasp of the issues beyond generalities. Much of the debate concerned accountability issues, with Mikardo focusing on workers' consultation, and others on consumer representation. The idea that the lack of awareness by consumers of the machinery of consumer representation 'is perhaps the greatest weakness of the nationalised industries' suggests an intriguing but surely bizarre perspective on the issue.[10] *Public Enterprise* offers a stout defence of the performance of the existing nationalised industries, but limits future proposals to the renationalisation of iron and steel and road haulage. Its perspective on the general issue of public ownership follows *Industry and Society*, and so it is not surprising that it could be seen as marking the abandonment by Labour of public enterprise as an important part of its future programme.[11]

Even if all the pressures were driving Labour away from emphasising new public ownership commitments in the years before it took office in 1964, the issue of how the existing nationalised industries were to be run still had to be faced. While Labour in opposition was focusing its attention on the principle of public ownership, the Conservatives in government were slowly evolving policies for the day-to-day management of the public corporations. They did little to 'roll back' the scope of Labour's nationalisations beyond denationalising iron and steel and road haulage. But they initiated a stream of investigations and reports into the industries, including the Herbert Committee on electricity, the Fleck Committee on the coal industry and the Beeching report on the railways. In addition, in 1956 they established a House of Commons Select Committee on Nationalised Industries, which itself published a series of reports. The Conservatives took some major policy decisions

on the nationalised industries, perhaps most importantly the break-up
of the British Transport Commission in 1962, in an attempt to inject
more competition into transport services, and the acceptance of the Beeching report's recommendation for a major slimming down of the railways.
Much of their concern was with the organisational aspects of the
industries, generally articulated as a desire for greater decentralisation

At an aggregate level, the Conservatives were increasingly concerned
about the losses incurred by the public corporations, especially coal and
the railways, but in the short term were caught between the unpalatable
alternatives of raising prices to try to eliminate the deficits (with doubtful likelihood of success because of competition from road freight and
oil), and the desire to limit expenditure on deficits in order to lower
taxes. In 1961 they published a White Paper, *The Financial and Economic
Obligations of the Nationalised Industries*, that marked a major turning
point and underpinned policy on the nationalised industries when Labour
came to power in 1964.[12]

The original nationalisation statutes called only for the corporations
to break even and conduct themselves efficiently, and provided no guidance on what was meant by efficiency; they stipulated only a minimum
standard of financial performance. The 1961 White Paper emphasised
the need for a commercial approach to the nationalised industries:
'although the industries have obligations of a national and non
commercial kind, they are not, and ought not, to be regarded as social
services absolved from economic and commercial justification'. The industries needed clearer financial responsibilities, to ensure that their
operations yielded an adequate return on investment and did not rely
so heavily on external (i.e. government) funding for their capital needs.
The White Paper pointed out that the rate of return in the industries
was well below that in private industry and that, while the quantity of
investment in the industries increased rapidly in the late 1950s, the
proportion financed from profits had fallen sharply. In the future, the
industries would have financial targets, requiring them to balance their
books over a five-year period, while fully covering replacement cost
depreciation and making a contribution to future capital development.
In imposing tighter controls on finances, the Conservatives did not lay
down any clear rules on the extent to which higher prices could be
used to increase the industries' revenues. They exhorted the industries
to improve their finances by lowering costs, and stressed the government's continuing interest in their prices, both because many of their
products 'are basic to the life of the community' and because of their
monopolistic powers.[13]

The emphasis in the 1961 White Paper was on improving the financial position of the nationalised industries and in particular restricting
their calls on Exchequer funding (Table 7.1). By the time Labour came

Table 7.1 Central government finance for nationalised industries,
1951–70 (£millions, current prices)

Year	Total borrowing	Of which subsidies
1951	154	–
1952	273	–
1953	259	–
1954	295	–
1955	489	–
1956	267	–
1957	560	–
1958	539	–
1959	590	–
1960	464	115
1961	530	137
1962	473	141
1963	402	136
1964	559	123
1965	624	142
1966	806	143
1967	1,003	174
1968	791	180
1969	487	125
1970	802	113

Source: K. Jones, 'Nationalised industries', in F. Blackaby (ed.), *British Economic Policy
1960–74* (Cambridge, 1978), p. 488.

to office, this new system was entrenched, though it was also evident
that the financial position of the major nationalised industries (especially
coal and the railways) remained very weak, and that resolving these
problems was not just matter of devising rules of conduct, but would
also involve extremely difficult political decisions about the speed of
reduction in employment which was acceptable. These two declining
industries had already shed 270,000 workers since nationalisation (and
in doing so helped to boost their labour productivity).[14] In this way
nationalisation had served an important purpose of greatly easing the
reallocation of labour out of low-productivity activities, while maintaining social peace (greatly aided by general full employment). But the
financial cost of this policy was high, and budgetary concerns were increasingly driving policy, as the 1961 White Paper showed.

Labour's agenda in 1964

In 1969 an internal party document looked back critically at Labour's
term in office and argued that 'Since 1964 it is to the private sector that

the government has looked as the main source of industrial expansion'
and called on the government to 'reassert the role of the public sector
in national planning and in the improvement in the efficiency of Britain's
economy'.[15] It was certainly true that, whatever the rhetoric, the substance of 'modernising' policy in the run-up to 1964 had been focused
on the private sector. Indeed, this is clear from the section on 'Public
ownership' in the 1964 manifesto, which begins by asserting that 'the
public sector will make a vital contribution to the national plan' but
which, beyond asserting that the government will have 'a co-ordinated
policy for the major fuel industries', shows little evidence of what that
vital contribution might be.[16] Indeed, what is striking with regard to
general ideological development in the Labour Party is the extent to
which the rhetoric of planning in the 1960s owed so little to the role of
the public sector, a very different position from the rhetoric of 1945. In
part this may have reflected the simple fact that the nationalised
industries had shrunk in relative importance since the 1940s. But it
may also be noted that, in practice, one of the many problems facing
Labour's attempts to plan after 1945 was the tensions with the autonomy of the nationalised industries, so in that sense Labour's lack of
ambitions to subordinate the nationalised industries to 'planning' was
more realistic than intentions had been in 1945.

In the National Plan of 1965, this limited ambition is also clearly
evident (see Chapter 4). The Plan set out highly tentative targets for
the expansion of investment in the nationalised industries (largely from
growth in gas, electricity and Post Office spending), but with the expectation that this growth would only broadly be in line with projected
growth of GDP. Beyond this, there was only a vague reference to the
hope that 'the purchasing power of the public authorities can be used
to promote efficiency in the supplying industries'.[17]

Labour had limited ambitions to use nationalised industries as
instruments of modernisation of the whole economy, and there is no
evidence of the development of a distinctive 'socialist' agenda in this
respect in the party before 1964. There was a very wide range of literature on the nationalised industries, much of it by Labour supporters
and sympathisers, but this had not led to a clear and agreed policy
position. There was an instinctive distaste for the extent to which the
Conservatives had emphasised their commercial nature, but no agreement on how Labour should change this, or with what it should be
replaced.[18] Therefore, as the account below suggests, most policy on
the nationalised industries under Labour tended to be closely linked
with short-term issues about managing the national economy, though
there were some important longer-term decisions concerning fuel and
transport. Labour inherited a largely Treasury-driven agenda to control
the finances of the industry more effectively, an agenda that assumed

that tighter financial controls over the public corporations would also encourage greater efficiency in their operations.

The Treasury agenda

The 1961 White Paper had its origins in the rising demand for Exchequer finance evident in the late 1950s (Table 7.1). The new financial targets may have had some effect in containing that demand in the early 1960s, but it is evident from the figures that this impact was short-lived, and so the Treasury was keen to strengthen this control. But the Treasury was well aware that financial targets were an important although limited weapon. In particular, it was obvious that, if the demand conditions for a particular industry were favourable, the financial targets could be met simply by raising prices, rather than by greater efficiency. As soon as the 1961 White Paper had been agreed, the Treasury was pursuing a parallel agenda of encouraging the public corporations to use more sophisticated investment appraisal techniques, especially discounted cash flow (DCF) methods, coupled to a test discount rate (TDR, a minimum rate of return that all investment projects should achieve).[19] These techniques were currently very fashionable, and were strongly pushed by economists, including those in the Economic Section of the Treasury.[20] The third issue was that of prices. Economists had long argued that the appropriate pricing policy for a nationalised industry was to charge long-run marginal costs, and the Treasury was broadly sympathetic to this as a way of forcing the industries to reduce cross-subsidies and price more rationally. However, there was a potential conflict here, because marginal cost pricing in an industry where long-run costs declined as output expanded would mean making a loss, as at given levels of demand marginal costs would be below average costs, and such losses were generally deemed incompatible with managerial responsibility in the nationalised corporations. This problem was well known, and lay behind the development of two-part tariffs in electricity, but it was nevertheless to be a cause of considerable controversy in the 1960s.[21]

When Labour came to power, the Treasury was eager to clarify the new government's policy in this area, especially given that 'the attitude of the Labour Party towards the [1961] White Paper has never been fully clarified'.[22] The Treasury was concerned with getting such a clarification partly because of immediate issues, such as the impending deficit in the coal industry, which needed to be resolved in the light of a general policy stance. The Treasury produced a draft paper in the autumn of 1964 which emphasised the importance of sustaining the financial position of the nationalised industries in order not to undermine overall public expenditure policy. However, it was recognised that nationalised industry pricing was bound to be a controversial issue because of the search for a viable prices and incomes policy, which was central to the government's agenda. As a senior Treasury official put it: 'We are here right on the frontier between the Chancellor's territory and the First Secretary's territory on any conceivable interpretation of the Concordat; which is another reason for caution'.[23] In the light of this tension, it was agreed not to press the government for a policy statement on the national-ised industries at this stage, but to deal with the issues case by case for the time being. However, in December 1964 the Chancellor publicly and specifically gave the government's support to 'retaining and developing' the system of public corporations' financial obligations.[24] On the other hand, and as a foretaste of arguments to come, George Brown told James Callaghan the same month that he was opposed to fully embracing the target policy, and stressed the 'political and psycho-logical' importance of prices within the nationalised industries in the context of the pursuit of a prices and incomes policy.[25]

The budgetary pressures that emerged in 1965 increased the Treasury's desire to contain the nationalised industries' calls on the public purse. This linkage was made explicit in the discussions with the IMF about credits for Britain: international financial confidence was linked to budgetary policy, including containing spending on public industries. But it was also recognised that pushing up the industries' prices would be inflationary, so to a degree policy was in a cleft stick.[26] This com-plexity was added to when Brown reiterated not only his worries about the impact of the nationalised industries' prices on the viability of prices and incomes policies, but added that 'through resistance to such increases we may sometimes be able to get special examinations of efficiency and organisation put in hand'.[27]

Accompanying these arguments at the highest political level were continuing debates within the Treasury about the focus on financial targets. In October 1965 two pro-Labour economists, Michael Posner and Richard Pryke, produced a paper entitled 'Economic and financial rules for public enterprise', which stated that the approach of the 1961 White Paper was 'a mistake, and should be abandoned' because financial targets were not the way to better management. They accepted the case for target rates of return for new investment (using DCF), but suggested that overall targets were too easily secured by price rises. As an alterna-tive they wanted efficiency audits and, generally, marginal cost pricing, though they argued such policies should be sensitive to whether the industry was contracting or expanding and to difficulties in allocating overhead costs. In a more political register, Posner and Pryke argued that 'there is nothing intrinsically socialist about arbitrary prices. Prices should reflect relative costs of different products.' Alongside this asser-tion they recognised that divergences could arise between private and social costs, but argued that these needed to be clearly identified (as, indeed, the 1961 White Paper had urged), and to this end favoured the extensive use of cost–benefit analysis (CBA), another technique with much academic support in the 1960s.[28]

Posner and Pryke in this paper summarised much of the centre-left thinking on nationalised industries in the 1960s, especially as argued by economists. In summary, they were suggesting more emphasis on economic issues as opposed to the purely financial. The obvious problem, however, was that financial targets had a simplicity which a combination of pricing rules, investment appraisal, efficiency audits and, possibly, CBA could never match. The Treasury response to Posner and Pryke was to accept that the 1961 White Paper was a 'blunt instrument', but to suggest that the Treasury had already moved on, especially by en- couraging widespread use of investment appraisal. Nevertheless, such critical arguments were one reason for a return to the idea of a new policy statement on the nationalised industries, and the first drafts of what eventually became the 1967 White Paper (see below) date from November 1965.[29]

Drafting a White Paper

The pressure for a public statement was a response not only to dis- cussions within the bureaucracy, but also the development of policy in the autumn of 1965. After deploying arguments about both inflation and its impact on the prices and incomes policy, Brown won agreement to freezing the prices of gas, electricity and coal.[30] The *Times* attacked this decision, saying 'Mr. George Brown destroyed the significance of the profit targets ... by his decision to keep their prices stable, at the expense of the taxpayer, in order to try and save his incomes policy.... The government are thus beginning to put the clock back in a particu- larly discouraging way.'[31] The linkage between nationalised industries and incomes policy formed the basis for the emergence of a new player in policy formation in this area, the NBPI. The NBPI, established in February 1965, was soon involved in assessing both price and wage issues in the nationalised industries, with references on electricity and gas tariffs, and on wages in the electricity supply industry, both in June 1965.[32]

This input into policy made the Treasury all the keener to have a statement of government policy to establish the parameters of decision- making. This was in addition to the need to agree new financial targets for the gas and electricity industries. In the Treasury view, it was the body which would have to push on this matter: 'for it is only here that *all* the issues, both long and short term, come together in relation to major decisions of government'.[33] The Treasury's desire to move on this issue was reinforced by the fact that the first new financial targets to be set by the Labour government were due in April 1967, and this led to a plan for the publication of a White Paper on the nationalised industries in the autumn of 1966. A draft went to the Chancellor in January 1966, who commented, somewhat opaquely, that he would 'pay especial atten-tion to the "feel" and language of the White Paper having regard to the Labour Party's interest in these industries'.[34]

But if the Treasury was taking the initiative, it had to negotiate with other powerful ministries. On the one hand were those that 'sponsored' the nationalised industries, such as the Ministry of Fuel and Power, and the Ministry of Transport, and on the other the DEA, with its broad interest in economic policy as well as its very specific concern with prices and incomes. In areas other than the purely financial, the Treasury was obliged to work closely with the sponsoring ministries, a process that, in the case of such issues as investment appraisal, could be prolonged and 'educative' rather than directive. The response of these ministries to the draft of the White Paper was said to be one of 'cautious welcome', but critical of the tone as 'too academic'.[35] But the view of the Ministry of Fuel and Power was altogether more hostile, partly because of the complex issues arising from the writing-off of existing investment in the fuel industries implied by the development of North Sea gas. It wanted to hang on to the 1961 position, and suggested that the new ideas were 'too sophisticated for the simple people in the gas and elec-tricity industry' and that such sophistication would lead to a weakening of financial discipline. The consensus among the ministries seems to have been that the only principle that should be enunciated by the new White Paper was marginal cost pricing (but on this see below).[36]

The DEA's view echoed this criticism, most specifically in its dis-cussion of marginal cost pricing:

> We are all still struggling with the basic difficulty that having enunci-ated long run marginal cost pricing (however interpreted) as the criterion towards which prices should trend, we are then forced to backtrack hastily to cover a number of particular situations when the principle cannot in fact apply. The result is anything but clear guidance.

This, it urged, needed sorting out, lest the public come to feel 'that the Government has been subverted by a lot of half-baked economists'. Along-side this complaint was a reiteration of the traditional DEA view that too much emphasis on rates of return would license big price increases.[37]

No White Paper was published in 1966, initially because of the March general election, for which Labour's manifesto promised that 'We shall further develop co-operation between nationalised industries to cut out waste: we shall set out more precise targets to guide their investment and price policy in the national interest'.[38] More significant than the delay imposed by the election was the impact of the 'July measures' that year. Already in 1965 the nationalised industries had been caught up in Labour's deflationary attempts to defend the pound, but in that year the impact was little more than the delay of some investment projects.[39] The July measures of 1966 were of a different order of significance. The prices and wages standstill threatened severely to dent the policy of restricting the nationalised industries' deficits. As Alec Cairncross emphasised, holding back on nationalised industry price increases would transfer purchasing power to the public, which would not only affect government finance but could 'also aggravate demand inflation at the same time as it may mitigate cost inflation'.[40] In this situation the Treasury had to fight hard to make its macro-economic arguments count. It pointed out, for example, that any delay in increasing electricity tariffs (due in April 1967) would involve £50–70 million in extra borrowing from the Exchequer.[41]

The difficulties caused by the July measures, while making the immediate position immensely more problematic, seems to have further emphasised to the Treasury the desirability of getting from the government a firming-up of policy on the nationalised industries. But in this endeavour it met stiff resistance from the industries themselves. The industries' boards generally liked financial targets, as they gave them lots of room for manoeuvre. They disliked marginal cost pricing, partly because they wanted to have autonomy to fix prices in relation to competition, but also they believed it a hard concept to operationalise. Typically, the transport holding company called long-run marginal cost 'an economist's abstraction from real life', only suitable for monopolies with uniform output and high indivisible fixed costs. Or, as the Post Office put it, 'No industry should be put in the position where it had to go into the red for the sake of a theoretical concept'.[42]

The Treasury was nevertheless determined to push on with a White Paper, though there was recognition that to try to bring in new pricing principles during a price freeze was probably not wise. In addition, even those sympathetic to the idea were worried about the consistency of Robert Neild's proposed three elements – long-run marginal cost pricing, targets rates of return on new investment, and *ex post* returns on assets. As he stressed, 'the objectives are consistent in certain ideal conditions and deviations are inevitable given sudden changes in technological progress or other factors which upset ex ante calculations'.[43]

The Treasury accepted both that Neild's trilogy covered the right elements to be emphasised in the White Paper and also that the qualifications should be explicitly recognised: 'this ought to satisfy the high priests of theory [and] make clear how Sinai should be interpreted among the children of the world'. At the same time the importance of the nationalised industries to the whole economy should be emphasised, as a 'corrective to those backwoodsmen from the nationalised industries who are unable to see beyond their statutory obligations'. Finally, for the politicians the White Paper could offer 'a charter for nationalised industries' in connection with steel nationalisation, and the need to get the nation's industrial image right in terms of productivity, industrial growth, innovation and so on.[44]

In late 1966 the Treasury hoped the White Paper would be published in the spring of 1967, after the end of the wage freeze reduced the political problems of higher prices within the nationalised industries. But it proved difficult to reconcile the economic principles with each other, to reconcile them with the diverse circumstances of the fourteen nationalised industries, and to express all this in politically congenial terms. One commentator on a draft gave it thirty-seven marks out a hundred for its economics, being 'full of platitudes and loose thinking', but ninety-five for the fact it 'should have great success politically'.[45] In addition to these problems in its formulation, external circumstances suggested delay, notably the prospect of a fuel price review and the prospect of steel nationalisation.[46] The DEA also continued to question what it saw as the Treasury's exaggerated emphasis on financial targets, though the Treasury accepted the view that, if investment were to be restricted for budgetary reasons, in the long run this should be done by changing the TDR rather that ad hoc adjustments to capital spending programmes.[47] Through the summer of 1967 redrafting continued, with the Treasury still determined on publication, for two reasons – first, 'The present government needs to state its own guidance for these industries: a six year old paper by its opponents is a feeble guide now'; and second, the immediate need to negotiate new targets for some of the industries.[48]

A further squall over the White Paper blew up in the summer of 1967 when Thomas Balogh described a draft as 'economic nonsense and political dynamite', telling Callaghan, 'I emphatically counsel against publishing the document as it represents a totally gratuitous gift to the Opposition of powerful ammunition to attack us with'. Balogh's alternative was social CBA as the core of decision-making in the public industries, with the emphasis on the *social* rate of return.[49] This seems to have been the main example of a challenge to the broad consensus among economists on the principles to be applied to running the nationalised industries. Balogh's arguments seem to have created political waves but had little effect on the policy debates, perhaps un-surprisingly given the technical and therefore political difficulties of calculating 'social' rates of return. The Treasury, in responding, accepted the case for some use of CBA, but stressed its relevance to only limited sections of nationalised activity (road and rail use), and the danger of permitting its inconsistent use to lead to the breaching of financial responsibility by the public corporations. In addition, the Treasury reiterated more strongly the budgetary issues: it noted that the price freeze had cut the proportion of self-funded investment in the national-ised industries from 55 to 45 per cent, which had raised Exchequer borrowing by £160–170 million, a fact noted by the IMF. In the light of the Balogh attack, the purpose of the White Paper was restated as: 'to show how social considerations can be taken into account without weakening good financial discipline within the industries or imposing an impossible burden on the Exchequer'.[50]

Balogh's doubts seem to have influenced the Prime Minister, who in July asked where the urgency for publication lay, especially in the light of the critical tone of the drafts towards the industries, and the forth-coming report of the Select Committee on Nationalised Industries. In response, the Treasury refuted that the White Paper was critical of nationalised industries, and stressed not only the need for economic criteria to go along with the financial concerns of 1961, but also, again, the politics: 'Here it is a pretty rum situation for the present Govern-ment, with its long-declared belief in nationalised industries, not to lay down some guidance of its own instead of using those which were pro-duced six years ago by the present Opposition'.[51]

In October the Cabinet Economic Policy Committee agreed to pub-lish the White Paper, but called for more consultation with the industries' chairmen. These consultations revealed continuing hostility to the White Paper, largely because the chairmen saw it as leading to greater govern-ment involvement in their affairs, under the banner of higher productivity and efficiency. In response, the Treasury argued that more emphasis on these issues was essential in the current political climate, and if the chairmen resisted the White Paper's general statements in this area, they would end up with something far worse – an external efficiency audit.[52]

While these discussions were going on, Wilson continued to question the merits and timing of the White Paper, partly on the grounds of waiting for Cabinet discussion of nationalised industries' pricing policies, but more broadly for ideological reasons. The government was in diffi-cult discussions with the private sector over the Industrial Expansion Bill, and Wilson argued that it would be difficult to bring out 'a paper which will be publicised as castigating publicly-owned industry, while we are still being blackmailed by industry in the private sector'. The Chancellor was becoming exasperated with this Prime Ministerial oppo-sition: 'I am becoming rather impatient with this stalling ... what is he up to?'[53]

In the event, agreement was reached to publish the White Paper, but with significant amendments, which reflected the deteriorating macro-economic circumstances and the government's response to those circumstances. In September 1967 it was announced that, as part of a tougher anti-inflation policy, in future all nationalised industries' price increases would go to the NBPI, and that it would be able to investigate whether such price increases could be reduced or avoided by increased efficiency or changes of practice. This decision had been taken in August, at the time of a considerable public storm over forthcoming electricity price increases. According to the published version of the White Paper, this role for the NBPI would involve strengthening its staff 'to make all necessary enquiries into the efficiency of the industries ... [as well as]) the industries' machinery for keeping down costs including the appropriate forecasting and decision-making techniques'.[54]

When the White Paper was published in November 1967, its contents reflected a combination of the long-term Treasury agenda and the immediate circumstances of the crisis-ridden autumn of 1967. The Treasury's central argument was that financial targets should be maintained, indeed toughened, but that these should 'be a reflection of sound investment and pricing policies rather than vice versa'.[55] Sound investment policies meant the application of DCF techniques, with a net TDR of 8 per cent. Social CBA could be used to justify projects with low rates of financial return, but to ensure consistency in the use of such techniques they would be deployed by the ministries rather than the industries themselves.[56] On prices, the White Paper endorsed the general principle of long-run marginal costs, though with a variety of caveats allowing deviation, such as cyclical changes in demand or major technological improvements.[57] The financial target system would continue, though in setting these the government 'will take into account the considerations – return on new investment, soundly based pricing policy, social obligations not covered by a subsidy, efficient operation, national prices and incomes policy – mentioned above'.[58]

The tone of the White Paper reflected the Treasury's growing concern with the impact of the financing of the nationalised industries. The figures given in the Paper itself showed total Exchequer financing in 1966–67 as £813 million (out of total fixed investment of £1,492 million).[59] This figure had risen sharply, partly reflecting higher investment, but also the effects of the July 1966 measures, and the consequent slow-down in the economy, such slow-downs having disproportionate effects on the demand for the output of the public sector.[60] The contribution of the nationalised industries to the general problems of public finance was highlighted in the crisis of autumn 1967, and this aspect played an important part in the final ministerial decision-making on the White Paper.[61] It was no coincidence that the White Paper appeared as the government was making its last-gasp attempt to defend the value of the pound.

After the White Paper

The immediate institutional innovation accompanying the White Paper was the new role for the NBPI. From a Treasury perspective this involved significant dangers. One was the difficulty of making this role meaningful 'without detracting from constitutional responsibilities of Departments, making life intolerable for the management of the industries'. Another was the ambition of the NBPI, or at least its chairman (Aubrey Jones), who 'seems to have been mainly concerned with trying to use the nationalised industries to build up the Board's job in relation to the economy as a whole'. In the light of these dangers the Treasury line was to try to limit NBPI investigations into efficiency to the context of a price reference, and to focus its attention on techniques such as management information systems and investment appraisal, rather than substantive issues such as new technologies. The Treasury seems to have reached agreement with the NBPI on these lines, and it was agreed to drop the term 'efficiency audit' in favour of the less provocative notion of 'strengthening the NBPI to enable it to investigate cost containment and management information systems more thoroughly'.[62]

Despite this agreement, the Treasury continued to try to 'educate' Aubrey Jones in macro-economic realities, especially the inflationary effects of holding down prices within the nationalised industries in terms of both increasing consumer demand and boosting the government deficit. There was a clear concern that, especially in the aftermath of devaluation, the desire to limit inflation would lead to politically appealing short-term policies with damaging medium-term consequences.[63] Alongside trying to constrain the role of the NBPI, the Treasury wanted to apply pressure for the application of the principles of the White Paper. On investment appraisal, the principle seemed to be accepted by the industries, but implementation was slow and, where used, often very crude. On marginal cost pricing there seems to have been more stubborn resistance outside the electricity and gas industries.[64]

One institutional innovation successfully resisted by the Treasury was that for a Ministry of Nationalised Industries. This was put forward by Ian Mikardo as chairman of the Select Committee on Nationalised Industries, which enquired into the relationship between the Treasury and nationalised industries in the winter of 1967–68. Mikardo's proposal was based on the belief that there was a fundamental conflict between the requirements of national economic policy and the autonomy of the public corporations, and the way to resolve this was to create a new ministry to impose those national priorities. This was, of course, quite at odds with prevalent Treasury and governmental doctrine, which held that considerable autonomy for the corporations was the only way to secure responsible and effective management. In responding to

Mikardo's ideas, the Treasury argued that nationalised industries should be seen primarily *as* industries and only secondarily as part of the public sector. This doctrine, it suggested, explained why the 1967 White Paper was 'so thin', because it dealt with only the limited number of things that the industries had in common. By contrast, the White Papers on fuel and transport were much more substantial because they dealt with specific features of these industries.[65]

This doctrine ran into difficulties when it was suggested that it was desirable to put nationalised industries' investment expenditure into the public expenditure review process, alongside other public expenditure. This idea was much disliked by the sponsoring ministries because of the time lags it would introduce into the investment approval process. But the Treasury took the view that, despite the differences between the nationalised industries and the rest of the public sector, it would be a useful discipline to have all expenditure decisions taken together. From 1969 the annual nationalised industries' investment review was integrated with the overall public expenditure review.[66]

This move reflected the continuing concerns with the scale of investment in the nationalised industries and its financial consequences. At the time of the 1967 White Paper, it had been argued that this investment was close to the peak of a hump and so would soon decline. In fact this did happen, with fixed investment rising from £1,024 million in 1963/64 to a peak of £1,668 million in 1967/68, then falling to £1,448 million the following year, and to £1,366 million in 1969/70, while, as Table 7.1 shows, government finance fell even more sharply.[67] This followed the unprecedented tough budgetary policies followed in the wake of devaluation (see Chapter 3).

Modernising?

When elected in 1964, Labour had limited ambitions for the nationalised sector and limited ideas on what to do about these industries. Only the steel industry was brought into public ownership in the next six years, though a Bill to nationalise the docks was lost only because of the 1970 general election.[68] At the highest level of government there was continuing interest in the issue of public ownership, but most of this was focused on 'new kinds' of ownership, such as equity stakes in individual companies rather than Morrisonian sectoral nationalisation. Indeed, as suggested in Chapter 5, by the end of the 1960s this 'new kind' of role for the state was gaining support on the left of the Labour Party as well as on the right, where it had originated.

At the level of the experts, there was more interest in the management issues posed by the existing nationalised industries, and here there

developed a broad consensus between most of Labour's advisers and
the views of the Treasury. Balogh, because he had the ear of the Prime
Minister, could create waves, but, as in so many other areas, he had
little to offer as a constructive alternative to the dominant view. The
nearest to a socialist alternative was the idea of running the nationalised
corporations on a non-commercial basis, using generalised CBA. This
was never plausible given the impossibility of running such a large part
of the economy without substantial autonomy for the corporations.

While these explicitly ideological issues occasionally surfaced, the
driver for policy in these years was finance, and this was especially clear
after devaluation. This did not mean that issues of efficiency and
resource allocation were ignored in policy-making. The Treasury strongly
hoped that the imposition of a tougher financial regime would be
accompanied by a range of efficiency-enhancing measures, especially
marginal cost pricing and DCF-based investment appraisal. But the
autonomy of the corporations meant the levers of government – other
than the financial – were largely indirect. The focus on finance underpinned movement towards commercialisation, but faced opposition not
so much from socialist concerns with non-commercial issues, but from
those who wanted to use the nationalised industries in other ways to
manage the economy. In particular, wages and prices policy suggested
a quite different way of viewing the role of the industries – as *instruments*
of policy rather than simply as objects of policy. This view had some
successes initially but, of course, the effect of holding down their prices
was to magnify their financial problems, and so increase the incentive
to subject them to greater financial discipline. After the White Paper,
but especially after devaluation, and with the growing concern with
government finances, this alternative view was pushed aside, and the
integration of nationalised industries' spending into the public spending process effectively symbolises this policy outcome.

One insider's verdict on this period is that 'Labour's success in 1964–70
was in bringing the public sector up to date, in a way which reasonably
respected fairness and justice, but was mainly aimed at a sort of Whitehall
rationality'.[69] This 'rationality' progressed slowly; investment appraisal
was slowly and unevenly deployed, marginal cost pricing less so.[70]

Despite the limits on price increases, especially in the mid-1960s,
the financial position of the industries did generally improve in that
decade.[71] While Labour did increase subsidies to the railways and provided extra money to cushion redundancies in the coal industry, it did
not generally inhibit the rundown of these industries' workforces, which
continued apace. Numbers employed in coal fell from 556,000 in 1964
to 387,000 in 1968, railway workers from 439,000 to 327,000 over the
same period.[72] This was in line with the government's overall policy of
encouraging labour mobility out of declining sectors in order, it was

hoped, to expand the supply of labour to manufacturing. Paradoxically, labour-shedding turned out to be the nationalised industries' main contribution to national planning.

Notes

The place of publication is London unless otherwise specified.

1 R. Millward and J. Singleton (eds), *The Political Economy of Nationalisation in Britain, 1920–50* (Cambridge, 1995); J. Tomlinson, *Democratic Socialism and Economic Policy: The Attlee Years 1945–51* (Cambridge, 1997), ch. 5; M. Chick, *Industrial Policy in Britain 1945–51* (Cambridge, 1998); M. Francis, *Ideas and Policy Under Labour 1945–1951: Building a New Britain* (Manchester 1997), ch. 4.
2 LPA, RD 161, D. Jay, 'Future nationalisation policy', 1948; for example, TUC, *Public Ownership: An Interim Report* (1953).
3 Chick, *Industrial Policy*, chs 5, 6.
4 For the debates on public ownership, see D. Howell, *British Social Democracy* (1980), ch. 7; N. Thompson, *Political Economy and the Labour Party* (1996), ch. 13.
5 M. Francis, 'Mr. Crosland's Ganymede? Re-assessing Crosland's *The Future of Socialism*', *Contemporary British History*, 11 (1997), pp. 50–64.
6 H. Gaitskell, *Socialism and Nationalisation* (1956); Chick, *Industrial Policy*, pp. 118–19, 201–3.
7 T. Jones, *Remaking the Labour Party: From Gaitskell to Blair* (1996), ch. 4; S. Haseler, *The Gaitskellites: Revisionism in the Labour Party* (1969), ch. 5.
8 Labour Party, *Industry and Society* (1957), especially p. 49.
9 J. Campbell, *Nye Bevan: A Biography* (1994), pp. 327–9. Powerful critiques from the left did exist, such as C. Jenkins, *Power at the Top* (1959).
10 LPA, 'Study Group on the Publicly Owned Industries', 1956–7; the quotation is from Re 107, '2nd Paper for the Study Group on Publicly Owned Industries', November 1956.
11 Labour Party, *Public Enterprise* (1957); W. A. Robson, *Nationalized Industry and Public Ownership* (2nd edn) (1962), pp. 479–80.
12 *The Financial and Economic Obligations of the Nationalised Industries*, Cmnd 1337, BPP 1960/61, vol. 27 (April 1961). On the political pressures on this issue, see L. Pliatzky, *Getting and Spending: Public Expenditure, Employment and Inflation* (Oxford, 1982), pp. 22–3.
13 *Financial and Economic Obligations of the Nationalised Industries*, paras 2, 10–13, 30.
14 R. Pryke, *Public Enterprise in Practice* (1971), pp. 19–77.
15 LPA, Re 468, 'Labour's economic strategy: a draft report'.
16 Labour Party, *Let's Go with Labour for the New Britain* (1964), p. 7.
17 *National Plan*, Cmnd 2764, BPP 1964/65, vol. 30, pp. 56–8, 51.
18 Robson, *Nationalized Industry*; M. Shanks (ed.), *The Lessons of Public Enterprise* (1963).
19 PRO, T 319/871, 'History of Command 3437', 8 December 1967.
20 PRO, T 319/943, P. Middleton to L. Airey, 8 November 1967; T 230/874–6, 'Public sector investment: government policy', 1966–7.
21 Chick, *Industrial Policy*, ch. 5.

22 PRO, T 319/42, P. Vinter, 'Nationalised industry policy', 6 October 1964.

23 PRO, T 319/42, O. Clarke to W. Armstrong, 'Price increases in nationalised industry', 5 November 1964. The Concordat was the agreement on the division of responsibility on economic policies between the Chancellor (Callaghan) and the First Secretary and Head of the DEA (Brown).

24 PRO, T 319/43, O. Clarke to D. Proctor, 16 November 1964; *Hansard* (Commons), vol. 704, 22 December 1964, cols 213–14.

25 PRO, T 319/43, Brown to Callaghan, 4 December 1964. Such comments glossed over arguments about the *relative* prices for nationalised industries' outputs.

26 PRO, T 319/44, J. Callaghan, 'Role of the nationalised industries', 28 May 1965.

27 PRO, T 319/44, G. Brown to H. Wilson, 'Role of the nationalised industries', 2 June 1965.

28 PRO, T 319/45, M. Posner and R. Pryke, 'Economic and financial rules for public enterprise' (n.d., but October 1965). For a public attack on the 1961 White Paper, see M. Posner, 'Fuel crisis: whose fault?', *New Statesman*, 20 January 1966. Posner was the author of the chapter on 'Policy towards nationalised industries', in W. Beckerman (ed.), *The Labour Government's Economic Record 1964–1970* (1972).

29 PRO, T 319/45, P. Middleton, 'Comments' (on Posner and Pryke), 15 October 1965, and P. Dixon, 'The nationalised industries – a new White Paper', 22 October 1965.

30 PRO, CAB 128/39, 'Cabinet conclusions', 4 November 1965.

31 *Times*, 22 November 1965.

32 On the NBPI, see A. Fels, *The British Prices and Incomes Board* (Cambridge, 1972), which gives a list of references to the NBPI in appendix C. See also Chapter 6.

33 PRO, T 319/46, P. Vinter to O. Clarke, 10 January 1966.

34 PRO, T 319/47, R. Lavelle, 'Review of economic objectives for nationalised industries', 31 January 1966; T 319/617, J. Hunt to P. Vinter, 'Nationalised industries White Paper', 18 October 1966.

35 PRO, T 319/617, J. Hunt to O. Clarke, 'White Paper on targets', 25 January 1966.

36 R. Toye, 'The new commanding height: Labour Party policy on North Sea oil and gas, 1964–74', *Contemporary British History*, 16 (2002), pp. 89–118; PRO, T 319/48, J. Hunt, 'White Paper on nationalised industries', 5 May 1966.

37 PRO, T 319/48, D. Henley to J. Hunt, 'Nationalised industries draft White Paper', 11 March 1966.

38 Labour Party, *Time for Decision* (1966), p. 6.

39 PRO, T 319/60–2, 'Measures to deal with economic situation 1965: deferment of capital projects by the nationalised industries'.

40 PRO, T 319/70, A. Cairncross to W. Armstrong, 'A prices and incomes standstill', 18 July 1966.

41 *Ibid.*, P. Vinter to I. Bancroft, 'Nationalised industry prices', 22 July 1966.

42 PRO, T 319/617, L. Airey, 'Draft White Paper on nationalised industries', 27 September 1966, and P. Middleton, 'Nationalised industries White Paper: comments from boards', 2 August 1966.

43 PRO, T 319/617, J. Hunt to P. Vinter, 'Nationalised industries White Paper', 18 October 1966, and R. Neild to P. Vinter, 19 October 1966.

44 PRO, T 319/617, P. Vinter to J. Hunt, 'Nationalised industries White Paper', 26 October 1966.

45 PRO, T 319/618, R. Tuvey to L. Airey, 24 January 1967. A note on Turvey's memo says of its critical tone: 'Not untypical. It wasn't written by him'.
46 PRO, T 319/618, D. Grafton to J. Hunt, 14 February 1967.
47 PRO, T 319/619, J. Hunt to P. Vinter, 'Nationalised industries White Paper', 18 April 1967, and Vinter to Hunt, 2 May 1967.
48 PRO, T 319/619, P. Vinter to W. Armstrong, 'Nationalised industries White Paper', 31 May 1967.
49 PRO, T 319/620, T. Balogh to J. Callaghan, 27 June 1967. On Balogh's arguments, see also T 319/622, A. Graham to J. Hunt, 'Nationalised industries White Paper', 14 September 1967.
50 PRO, T 319/620, J. Hunt to P. Baldwin, 30 June 1967.
51 PRO, T 319/620, P. Vinter to P. Baldwin, 'Nationalised industries White Paper', 6 July 1967, and J. Hunt to R. Lavelle, 7 July 1967.
52 PRO, CAB 134/3196, 'Economic Policy Committee', 10 October and 18 October 1967; PRO, T 319/621, Lord Melchett to D. Pitblado, 26 July 1967. The CBI and TUC were also consulted: see J. Davis (CBI) to J. Callaghan, 19 October 1967, and L. Murray (TUC) to P. Baldwin, 19 October 1967.
53 PRO, T 319/621, P. Le Chenivant to P. Baldwin, 4 August 1967, and Callaghan note on P. Baldwin to J. Callaghan, 'Nationalised industries White Paper', 10 August 1967.
54 *Nationalised Industries: A Review of Economic and Financial Objectives*, Cmnd 3437, BPP 1967/68, vol. 39, paras 1, 32; PRO, T319/943, 'Preparation of a historical note on the White Paper on nationalised industries'. This storm also led to a confidential agreement to review nationalised industries' investment and financing to try to reduce unpopular future price increases. The September announcement on the NBPI came unexpectedly: see D. Coombes, *State Enterprise: Business or Politics?* (1971), p. 120.
55 PRO, T 319/626, 'Draft questions and answers for press conference on White Paper', 30 October 1967.
56 *Nationalised Industries*, paras 6–16.
57 *Ibid.*, paras 18–24.
58 *Ibid.*, para. 34.
59 *Ibid.*, Table 2.
60 PRO, T 319/627, J. Hunt to P. Vinter, 'Nationalised industries prices', 27 January 1967.
61 PRO, CAB 134/1399, 'Public sector prices', 1 September 1967.
62 PRO, T 319/801, J. Hunt to L. Airey, 'Nationalised industries efficiency', 6 November and 7 November 1967. An Efficiency Audit Unit had been suggested by William Robson to the Select Committee on Nationalised Industries, though it was an idea that went back to the 1940s: see PRO, T 319/871, P. Mountfield to L. Airey, 'Select Committee: efficiency audit: steel', 23 January 1968. The subsequent role of the NBPI in relation to nationalised industries was wider than this 'agreement' with the Treasury suggested: see Coombes, *State Enterprise*, pp. 128–45.
63 PRO, T 319/801, P. Mountfield to L. Airey, 'Mr Aubrey Jones and nationalised industries prices', 13 December 1967.
64 PRO, T 319/802, L. Airey to J. Hunt, 'CMND 3437 – next steps', 29 November 1967.
65 PRO, T 319/871, I. Mikardo, 'The control of nationalised industries', December 1967, and P. Mountfield, 'Select Committee: proposal for a Ministry of Industries'. If this suggestion of the Select Committee was easily resisted, others, more in line with Treasury ideas, were taken up. For example, the Committee had suggested the Treasury organise a conference

on investment appraisal techniques. This conference, held in 1969, led to a revision of the previous (1966) memo on investment appraisal, which also embodied as shift upwards in the TDR from 8 to 10 per cent. PRO, T 319/1040, 'Sunningdale conference 1969'.

66 PRO, T 319/1057, D. Crofton to D. McKean, 6 December 1968, and P. Mountfield to L. Kelley, 'PERC(N) follow-up', 14 December 1968.
67 K. Jones, 'Nationalised industries', in F. Blackaby (ed.), *British Economic Policy 1960–74* (Cambridge, 1978), p. 507.
68 K. Ovenden, *The Politics of Steel* (1978). The Post Office was converted from a government department to a public corporation.
69 Posner, 'Policy towards nationalised industries', p. 261.
70 Jones, 'Nationalised industries', pp. 495, 498–501.
71 J. Foreman-Peck and R. Milward, *Public and Private Ownership of British Industry 1820–1990* (1994), pp. 304–6.
72 Pryke, *Public Enterprise*, p. 22.

8

The productivity issue

If 'planning' was the key term in Labour's modernisation rhetoric in the run-up to the 1964 election and through to 1965, it quickly lost its lustre in the deflationary period that followed. No other word would ever have quite the same resonance for such a wide spectrum of Labour opinion, but in important respects 'productivity' served a similar over-arching role in the policy debate of the following years. Like 'planning', the term 'productivity' usually lacked precise definition, and indeed because of this imprecision could bring together a diversity of concerns without ever denoting a single-minded, coherent 'project'. Like plan-ning, productivity had a long if less overt and more controversial history in Labour thinking about the economy, but a variety of circumstances meant that, for a period in the late 1960s, increasing productivity became what, in many policy-makers' eyes, 'modernisation' was largely about.

The productivity 'problem' up to the mid-1960s

The term 'productivity' first came into widespread use in policy-making circles under the Labour government of 1945–51, having previously been largely confined to academic discussions. The context of that use was a fully employed economy with powerful pressures of excess demand. The capital stock and labour supply could not be readily expanded, yet the government was desperate to expand output, especially to ease the post-war balance of payments situation. In these circumstances, much of the concern with productivity was effectively about maximising out-put from a highly constrained volume of resources. The point at issue at that time was not primarily the desire to raise either living standards or competitiveness. Governments had not yet come to regard economic growth and higher mass consumption as an explicit goal of policy, and competitiveness was not a key issue, certainly not in the early post-war years, when, at least outside dollar markets, anything that could be made in Britain could be exported.[1]

The debate on productivity in the 1940s focused on *labour* productivity. This stemmed in part from the apparent ease of measurement of labour inputs in comparison with capital.[2] It also reflected the belief that labour *effort* was an important issue in an economy where consumer goods were in short supply and therefore had a limited ability to provide an incentive to work, taxes especially on working-class consumer items were high, and governments feared a post-war relaxation of worker enthusiasm for production and productivity.[3] On the other hand, the post-war Labour government was keen to qualify this emphasis on the labour input in three ways: first, by stressing that, in principle, it recognised the contribution of other factors to productivity, especially capital equipment, but that there was little it could do in the short run to increase inputs on this front; second, by recognising the importance of technical change to productivity, though in practice the substantial efforts which were put into encouraging such change in the Labour years were usually disconnected from the issue of productivity, both analytically and in terms of the policy instruments deployed; and third, while accepting the focus on labour productivity, through its concern not only to avoid blaming labour for low productivity, but, more positively, to emphasise that inducements to higher productivity should take the form of 'carrots' rather than 'sticks'. There emerged from this last direction of policy what may be called a social democratic strategy of trying to improve labour productivity through better 'human relations' in the factory, which generic term could embrace everything from joint consultation at plant level to the appointment of personnel managers, through to better 'tea and toilets'.[4] This 'human relations' agenda also facilitated the acceptance by the TUC and union leaderships of productivity-raising policies, an acceptance which was also attractive in the context of the overall bargaining relationship between the unions and the Labour government. From a union point of view, enthusiasm for productivity was seen as a price willingly paid to sustain the government's full-employment and welfare policies.

The productivity 'problem' of the 1940s clearly emerged from highly specific circumstances and had a particular set of meanings and consequences. As suggested above, there was a distinctly social democratic tinge to the Labour government's approach to the issue. In addition, British enthusiasm for making productivity a high-profile issue was encouraged by contemporary US enthusiasm for exporting 'the American model' of production and higher productivity to Western Europe and Japan. This model, whose precise meaning was and is contested, could be construed as compatible with the contemporary social democratic approach, the latter being marked by its enthusiasm for large-scale industry and 'advanced' technology alongside its concern with the interests of labour.[5]

The context of the 'problem' of the 1960s was significantly different from that of the 1940s. In understanding the differences, it first needs to be stressed that there is a discontinuity here. The replacement of the Labour government in 1951 by Conservative administrations did not mean that concern with productivity suddenly disappeared. As Booth shows, most trade unions leaderships and the TUC still regarded it as a live subject at the beginning of the 1950s.[6] But with Conservative governments, the possibility of 'selling' such an approach to the mass of workers was weakened, as it was less clear what, if anything, could be expected from such governments in return. Moreover, it seems clear that, partly because the macro-economic circumstances were less critical, and partly because the Conservatives were much more sceptical about the role of government in actively pursuing this matter than their Labour predecessors, the issue tended to fade from public debate. This accorded with the attitude of employers' organisations, which had resisted many of the Labour government's overtures on this front in the name of resisting state interference outside its 'proper' sphere.[7]

Productivity concerns therefore did not disappear entirely from debates in the early and mid-1950s, but they no longer occupied the significant role in high politics that they had achieved in the 1940s. Some trade unions continued to focus attention on productivity, as did some firms, but public policy undoubtedly backed away from the issue. Especially in the early 1950s, the Conservatives' 'softly softly' approach to the unions tended to reinforce a focus on rather herbivore, mini-malist notions of 'human relations' from the Ministry of Labour, while other ministries lost any enthusiasm they might have had for pursuing other productivity ideas.[8]

Disputes about productivity and its place in Labour's agenda were not central to the party's great internal debates of the 1950s, though for modernisers of different hues it could be deployed in their polemics. In *The Future of Socialism* Tony Crosland saw a concern with productivity as part of the new complexity of socialist politics: 'But now the certainty and simplicity are gone; and everything has become complicated and ambiguous. Instead of glaring and conspicuous evils, squalor and injustice and distressed areas, we have to fuss about the balance of payments, and incentives and higher productivity'.[9] It was not debates in the Labour Party but events in the wider society, beginning in the late 1950s under the Conservatives, which worked to put productivity back on the policy agenda.

Three particular elements seem to have caused its re-emergence. One was the issue of incomes policy, especially national norms for pay increases. In the 1950s, the debate about how to combine full employ-ment with low inflation eventually led to attempts to revive this policy instrument, which had been successfully used for the first time in the

late 1940s.[10] In 1957 the Conservatives created the Council on Productivity, Prices and Incomes, which at least in its title established the
link between changes in wages and productivity, though the reports of
the Council had little to say on productivity, and were mostly concerned
with the competing merits of deflation and incomes policies in the anti-
inflationary battle.[11] In 1962 the government produced a White Paper
that explicitly linked wage issues with productivity, though again this
was more of a straw in the wind than in itself a sign of a major shift in
policy. However, the Labour government's attempts at incomes policy
were to make this much more than a juxtaposition of words. The *Joint
Statement of Intent on Productivity, Prices and Incomes* of December 1964,
trumpeted as central to the new government's strategy, made the connection very publicly.[12]

Paragraph 7 of the *Statement* began: 'much greater emphasis will be
given to increasing productivity', a clause inserted at the behest of the
TUC, which wanted to avoid the idea of a direct link between wage and
price increases. At this stage productivity, while not disregarded, does
not seem to have been central to the government's agenda; while the
message that enhanced productivity was the non-inflationary route to
higher incomes was, of course, welcome in government circles, there
were also worries about making it a focus of concern. For example, it
was recognised that 'productivity' was much more difficult to calculate
in service rather than manufacturing industries, and that profits might
provide a better guide to 'affordable' levels of wage increases.[13] The
NBPI, established in 1965, had an explicit remit to look at productivity
issues in its assessment of pay bargains – but as yet the government
maintained only voluntary controls on such bargains. It was the clause
making enhanced productivity the key means of avoiding the constraints on wage increases in the *statutory* incomes policy of 1966 that
gave the issue a much higher status.[14]

The second element in the re-emergence of the productivity issue
was that it gained greatly in importance from the forging of another
connection between wage bargaining and productivity, largely separate
from the framing of incomes policy. Quite independently of government, the Esso petroleum company had, in the early 1960s, negotiated
a productivity deal with unions at its Fawley refinery that was soon to
achieve fame as a major new departure in collective bargaining and
productivity improvement. The Fawley case received extensive publicity,
and was written up in a widely noted book by Allan Flanders, an
industrial relations academic. He presented the case as not just about
the improved management of industrial relations, but about workers
and unions moving towards power sharing in the enterprise, so that
productivity bargaining could be regarded as a key part of a social
democratic notion of enhancing the workers' status at the workplace.[15]

Third, the tremendous interest in this experiment was underpinned by its coincidence with the outbreak of the 'what's wrong with Britain' panic of the early 1960s. This panic saw a massive wave of publications on the theme of Britain's decline and possible remedies, and concern with productivity fed directly on this. A key player in the Fawley deal, William Allen, wrote an article in the *Sunday Times* in March 1964 entitled 'Is Britain a half-time country getting half-pay for half-work under half-hearted management?', a title that effectively summarises the nature of much of the contemporary declinist debate, with its sweeping generalisations.[16]

This declinist flurry drew upon, among other statistics, data on Britain's comparative productivity performance. Whereas up to the mid-1950s such comparisons were overwhelmingly with the USA, from the late 1950s especially Western European figures on rates of increase in productivity were commonly quoted to try to show how Britain was lagging behind its near neighbours.[17] Typically, for example, a Political and Economic Planning book on growth published in 1960 argued that: 'It is likely that the really significant lessons for economic policy came not from the US, but from countries in Western Europe whose economic problems are much nearer to our own'. This shift in the focus of comparison was, in turn, an important underpinning for Britain's application for membership of the EEC in 1961, the hope being that through membership Britain would acquire the economic dynamism and productivity growth of that group of countries. This focus on Europe also meant that, unlike in the 1940s, the US desire to export the 'American model' of high-productivity industry, and the British desire to import that model, were far less evident in government rhetoric two decades later. However, the enthusiasm for encouraging US multinationals to locate plants in Britain was partly driven by a perception that they would bring with them high-productivity techniques, which might in turn stimulate British firms into emulation.[18]

Declinism and productivity

Declinism at this time was never associated with any single view on the roots of Britain's alleged weaknesses; indeed, it would be truer to say that it provided an opportunity for practically every conceivable nostrum to be paraded as a 'solution'. However, two key books did set out declinist agendas that were to receive widespread backing. On the one hand there was Andrew Shonfield's *British Economic Policy Since the War*, which focused on the linked issues of Britain's global pretensions, the desire to maintain a world role, defence of the international use of the pound and the propensity to export large amounts of capital as crucial problems, on the basis that in combination they led to restrictive macro-economic policies in Britain, which in turn inhibited investment and growth. On the other hand, the main alternative narrative, deployed by Michael Shanks in his *Stagnant Society*, emphasised both the deleterious effects of class attitudes and the 'them and us' society on relationships at work – which were claimed to lead to negativism on the part of unions – and the productivity problem as the key to increasing economic growth.[19] Variants of these two general approaches dominated declinism in the 1960s. Both fed into the Labour government's agenda. Labour scaled back Britain's overseas commitments, constrained capital outflow and ultimately devalued the pound in 1967. But it also took up the second approach, which located the problems of the economy primarily at the workplace, above all in the *attitudes* of workers and the unions.

Here there is another link with Labour, especially revisionist, thinking, which was to affect how productivity was linked to the bigger 'modernisation' project. In *The Future of Socialism* Crosland famously argued that the pursuit of equality should be the centrepiece of Labour's agenda. In supporting this argument he emphasised 'subjective' feelings about social and class inequality. For him, such feelings were often at the root of collective discontents, which he believed to be widespread in Britain, and in industry a major source of 'unofficial strikes, lack of co-operation and a general atmosphere of suspicious antagonism'.[20]

The constraints on productivity growth imposed by ineffectual management were not ignored by the Labour government. In formal policy statements such as the National Plan it was argued that 'the most important factor in improving industrial efficiency is the quality of industrial management'. From this argument there followed a series of initiatives in such areas as management education and encouragement of the use of management consultants.[21] But the management side of the productivity issue never achieved the *political* salience of the labour and union role. The focus on labour connected directly with the linkage made in other domains of policy between wage bargaining and productivity. Both had a similar concentration on labour as the key element in the production process. This focus is very evident in the work of one of the key institutional products of declinism, the NEDC's 'Orange Book', entitled *Conditions Favourable to Faster Growth*, which put issues of training, education and labour mobility at the centre of its story of what needed to be done to improve economic performance. The opening sentence read: 'Economic growth is dependent upon a high and advancing level of education because of the improvements that education brings in human skills and the greater spread of knowledge'.[22]

In the National Plan of 1965, productivity is also largely discussed in terms of labour, though in this case in more macro-economic format. As described in Chapter 4, the Plan's central concern was to explore the implications of raising British GDP by 25 per cent between 1964 and 1970. It calculated the likely expansion of the labour force over this period, and then estimated the 'gap' that would exist which would have to be filled by accelerated increases in output per head to deal with the anticipated 'manpower' shortage.[23] Thus the Plan did not see productivity increase as the key to efficiency or solving the balance of payments problem; rather, it saw what it called 'the efficient use of labour' as the answer to the problem of how increased output was to be reconciled with a slow-growing workforce. Nevertheless, the Plan articulated many ideas about the problems of that efficiency that were eventually to become an important element in the productivity debate. Carefully balancing any suggestions about where the fault lay, the Plan suggested that:

> Under-employment arises in many ways, but chiefly through the, often unconscious, acceptance by managements and workers of traditional job structures and methods of labour deployment. Insistence on over-rigid demarcation and unrealistic manning scales also keep productivity down, although formal restrictive practices are only one among many sources of under-employment.[24]

To contemporaries, then, the productivity problem of the 1960s was predominantly a 'labour' problem. While the term was sometimes used in this period as a synonym for general economic efficiency, and thus linked with many other economic concerns, such as investment and technical change, there is no doubt that, for most political and policy discussion, it was the 'labour' aspect that really mattered.

In this respect, as in others, the productivity debate in the 1960s paralleled that of the 1940s. In the 1940s the emphasis on labour can perhaps partly be explained by the crudity of the economic statistics then available, for example the absence of any decent statistics on the capital stock, which would have been necessary to calculate capital productivity. Despite advances in the statistics available, this remained a constraint into the 1960s. In 1966, K. Lomax, at that time the leading British authority on productivity measurement, wrote: 'though capital stock figures are now available, we cannot really be said to have started to measure capital productivity'.[25] But while the statistical position was of some significance in the 1960s as in the 1940s, we must look elsewhere for much of the explanation for the continuing focus on labour as the key to productivity. At least part of the answer is obvious, as the link between wage bargains and productivity implied that labour was the key input into productivity change. This idea was, in the late 1960s, to pose problems for the framers of incomes policy, who wanted to differentiate 'justified' wage increases (i.e. those arising from changes in work patterns and effort levels) from those which arose directly from technological change (see Chapter 6). But such sophistications are rarely the stuff of public debate.

The idea that the key to higher productivity lay in 'labour' also stemmed from the rather different source of Conservative discussions, going well back into the 1950s, about the need to make the labour market more 'flexible'. This word has now become used so promiscuously that it has almost lost any specific meaning, but in the late 1950s and early 1960s it usually referred to two issues. First was the perceived need to encourage more mobility between occupations and regions, so that sectors and areas of increasing output and efficiency would not be starved of labour in a fully employed economy. Interestingly, the approach to this problem most commonly suggested was to focus on reducing the pain of mobility by redundancy payments and higher short-term unemployment pay. These issues, as shown in Chapter 6, were pursued with enthusiasm by Labour after 1964.

The other 'flexibility' issue was that of alleged restrictive practices. After the 1955 election victory the Conservatives appeared to have the room for political manoeuvre to start questioning what they saw as entrenched practices that inhibited productivity improvement. However, while backbench opinion came off the leash on this issue, the government moved only slowly, partly because of the desire to maintain union goodwill in other areas, notably wage inflation, but also perhaps because of the great difficulty of actually pinning down these practices, which, though the stuff of countless saloon bar and boardroom conversations, were actually rather hard to verify empirically, especially in the mainstream of British manufacturing.[26]

More overt emphasis on obstructionism on the part of workers and the unions as a key issue for economic 'modernisation' began to emerge before the Conservatives lost office in 1964, but it was only under Labour that it really came to the fore. In part this stemmed from the macro-economic context, especially the concern with the balance of payments, as the commitment to a fixed exchange rate meant that labour costs and productivity became the factors that determined international competitiveness. Labour sought a non-confrontational way to address this problem, and in its 1966 election manifesto the party promised to tackle the issue by establishing 'pay and productivity' committees in factories. But this attempt to approach 'labour problems' through a revival of 1940s-style joint consultation amalgamated with plant bargaining (arguably a version of the Fawley arrangements) foundered in the face of opposition from the main employers' organisation, the CBI, and some ministerial opposition to such a radical challenge to the collective bargaining status quo.[27] The CBI and TUC were, very reluctantly, persuaded to pursue pilot projects in this area. These were eventually established in nine private sector firms and two Royal Ordnance factories, but the evidence available suggests that the CBI, TUC and the Ministry of Labour, which became the agency overseeing the idea, were happy to use the ongoing Donovan Commission (1965–68) enquiry into trade unions to delay drawing any policy conclusions from the pilots.[28]

The archives suggest that while the DEA (which had drawn up the National Plan) was insistent that a 'single channel' should combine the discussion of pay and productivity, the Ministry of Labour was, at best, neutral about any change. The Ministry's stance reflected shifting views in trade union circles. In the 1940s, unions had been insistent that normal wage bargaining channels be kept quite separate from joint consultation, and this view had carried the day. But such consultation suffered a long-term erosion from its peak at the time of the Attlee government's revival of the wartime pattern of factory and pit consultative committees. In the 1950s many of these joint production committees had closed down, often being replaced by shop steward committees. But the concerns of these were mainly confined to wages and conditions. By the early 1960s the idea of a 'single channel' of bargaining, in which pay and productivity matters would be combined, found favour in some union circles. But this change in opinion was by no means universal, and the TUC was wary of pursuing any policy that would divide its membership. The TUC and CBI launched their own, rather anodyne productivity initiative in October 1967 (without telling ministers beforehand), and this gave them an alibi for resisting government pressure on the joint consultation front.[29]

The failure of the government's initiative in this area, plus the worsening of political relations between the government and unions brought about by deflation and statutory incomes policy, opened the ears of ministers and their advisers to the claims that unions and their practices were key problems for economic performance, and that government should be more active in trying to address these problems. As always, such a view could draw on assertions by 'authorities' on the issue, even if hard evidence was much more difficult to find. Both facets are evident in the research done for the Donovan Commission, itself a monument to the growing obsession with industrial relations in 1960s Britain.[30]

The Labour government did not shy away from public attacks on restrictive labour practices. At the 1966 TUC annual congress, Wilson told the delegates: 'But the biggest challenge facing the trade union movement in the productivity drive is the elimination of every avoidable restrictive practice, whether at national or workshop level. And the biggest problem here is over-manning, deliberately employing more men than are needed on the job.' It was intended that such practices would be reformed by pay and production committees and by the expansion of productivity bargaining (discussed below). The government also encouraged the 'Little Neddies' (the EDCs) to address 'manpower utilisation' issues, though concerns about commercial confidentiality hindered inter-firm collaboration in this area. Nevertheless, the car-making EDC, for example, set up a human resources working group to address the issue.[31] In addition, the government put pressure on the unions when enquiries into specific industries (e.g. that of Geddes into shipbuilding) suggested that restrictive labour practices were a source of significant problems.

Attacking such practices was undoubtedly a political problem for Labour because of its close ties with the unions. It was easier to do so where changes in working practices could be seen as a *quid pro quo* for government financial assistance, as in shipbuilding. Also, it was deemed easier to attack the labour practices if there were parallel moves against employers' restrictionism.[32] But there was a deeper problem. Restrictive labour practices were widely alleged in the 1960s, but evidence of their scale or nature was very thin.[33] First, the cases that were reasonably well attested, as in shipbuilding, were easily exaggerated. Thus the key issue here was demarcation, but a contemporary empirical enquiry suggested the cost of this practice was about 2 per cent per ship – 'not an in-significant amount ... but only a stepping stone to bridging the 7.5 to 20 per cent gap between UK and Japanese prices which is at the root of the industry's competitive problems'.[34] Second, other relatively clear cases, such as docks, railways and printing, all fell outside the main-stream of manufacturing, on which the government's attention was very much concentrated, above all because of the perception that this was the sector that mattered for the balance of payments. Third, and most intractable, was the problem of definition. As Allan Flanders pointed out in opposing the terminology of 'restrictive practices' in this area: 'all rules are to some extent restrictive, what one party regards as restrictive is just protective to another'.[35]

One answer to the last problem is to use international comparisons as a benchmark. But such comparisons were in their infancy in the 1960s, and are in any event fraught with difficulties. Standardising out-puts across counties is immensely difficult and, as was well understood in the 1960s, using such comparisons as levers to try to change behaviour is fraught with difficulties because such differences as may be estab-lished can easily but quite erroneously be presented as the result of international differences in effort levels.[36]

The rise and fall of productivity

The high tide of political concern with productivity began in 1966. In the context of the July deflationary measures, a set of papers on the topic went to Cabinet. Ministers agreed that productivity was the key policy issue, because of its links with the balance of payments: 'There must be no doubt that the essential longer term objective must be to improve productivity, exports and import substitution'. While recognising the need for reform of management, the Cabinet went on to agree that: 'another essential factor was to relate earnings and productivity in wage-bargaining between the two sides of industry. Both management and unions had proved reluctant to link pay, productivity and consultation; and the last of these factors was an essential element in wage settlements.'[37] The main follow-up to this discussion was the staging of a 'productivity conference' in September the same year.

Wilson intended that 'the conference should be seen not as an isolated occasion, but as the beginning of a continuing campaign'. Even more grandiosely, he argued that: 'it might well be that from this conference there could grow something in the nature of a Parliament of industry'. But far from such ambitious hopes, the occasion was most notable for its use by employers to berate the government's deflationary July measures, especially as undermining the incentive to invest in order to raise productivity. What was seen by government advisers as a key objective of the conference, to get the CBI and TUC to sign up for at least some experimental pay and production committees, was relegated to a minor place. Wilson's keynote address became a defensive argument that, despite deflation, productivity could be enhanced by companies determined to do so.[38]

A further government-sponsored productivity conference was held in June 1967, based on papers from the NEDC on the topics of marketing, economic planning and the application of technology. The second of these topics was included at the behest of the CBI, because it wanted this time to berate the government for its failure to deliver the sustained expansion that the National Plan envisaged. The TUC was highly sceptical regarding these very public and political discussions about productivity, and wanted them replaced by negotiations in the confines of the NEDC. In such an atmosphere of distrust, it is unsurprising that the conference seemed to achieve little.[39]

While the government's concern with productivity was never one dimensional, the central focus on labour issues is nicely illustrated by the renaming of the Ministry of Labour as the Department of Employment and Productivity in April 1968. This marked an attempt to give a new impetus to the productivity drive in the wake of devaluation. There was a proliferation of discussion of productivity matters in government publications at this time, though most of this was in the *Board of Trade Journal*, not in the *Department of Employment and Productivity Gazette*. The creation of the DEP did represent an attempt to 'rationalise' government activity in the productivity area. On its creation the DEP, as well as taking over the functions of the Ministry of Labour, also took over responsibility for incomes policy and the NBPI from the DEA, and later for agencies such as the British Productivity Council (BPC) and the British Institute of Management from the Board of Trade. This rational-isation was certainly needed, as responsibility for productivity seems to have been scattered haphazardly across Whitehall. On the other hand, the fact that it was the DEP which took on the key role serves to empha-sise the focus on 'labour' in the productivity debate.[40]

Under its minister, Barbara Castle, the DEP created the Manpower and Productivity Service. This clearly articulated the conception of the productivity problem held at the time, the remit of the Service being to encourage 'increased productivity through the more effective use of manpower and will facilitate the redeployment that flows from this and from other technological and industrial change'.[41] Castle was keen on promoting the productivity issue, but largely in the context of indust-rial relations. As seen in Chapter 6, she believed that the carrot of productivity-related wage increases was a much better approach to the unions than what she saw as the stick of incomes policy. This led her in particular into a willingness to ignore the macro-economic problems of productivity deals that other ministers, notably the Chancellor, saw as 'a real threat to incomes policy'.[42]

Castle received occasional nudges on the issue from the Prime Minister, who came closest to playing the prominent role of Stafford Cripps in the productivity campaign in the 1940s. Wilson in that decade had been a pioneer in the development of productivity statistics and he continued to press on this issue in the 1960s. He pressed for monthly data on productivity, but was persuaded by the Treasury that such short-term figures would be misleading. Quarterly figures were calculated and eventually published in *Economic Trends*.[43] But his capacity to generate policy action seems to have been limited by departmental powers. This was especially so where Prime Ministerial enthusiasm for pay and pro-duction committees was seen as disruptive to the traditional Ministry of Labour agenda of encouragement of voluntary pay bargaining, while broadly accepting managerial prerogatives in running companies.[44] As strikes and wage inflation moved sharply up the party and public agenda, Castle at the DEP placed most of her attention on the reform of the legal framework of collective bargaining rather than specifically productivity issues. At a meeting with Castle in 1968 Frank Cousins, a leader of the Transport and General Workers' Union (but previously a minister in the government), suggested that the government was 'too pre-occupied with wage levels' and that 'it was more important to raise productivity'.[45]

The lack of focus for the productivity campaign was not helped by the continuing weakness of the BPC. It was variously described as a 'problem child', as 'not a dynamic body' and as lacking an 'active leader-ship'. It was given significantly more money in the early 1960s, mainly to be spent at local level, and this may have had favourable effects. But it was not the body to lead a high-profile national campaign as some ministers thought the situation needed. Its major national initiative in this period was Quality and Reliability Year (1966/67), which was not regarded in Whitehall as an overwhelming success.[46]

It was not only in government circles that productivity enjoyed a vogue from 1966. In September of that year, *New Society*, the key journal at that time for the popular presentation of social science ideas, had a special issue on productivity, said to be 'the crux of the crisis'.[47] The various contributions from prominent academics showed how every-body's favourite nostrum could be trotted out as a solution to 'the crisis', though 'labour' issues played a prominent part in *New Society*'s overall approach to the question. But, as in politics, a week is a long time in the social sciences, and productivity did not long remain topical in such public forums.

After the initial high-profile activity of 1966/67, especially around the two productivity conferences, the issue faded somewhat from public concern. In late 1967 and early 1968, policy attention was, of course, on devaluation and then the hoped for improvement in the balance of payments. However, once it became clear that devaluation, while prob-ably necessary, was not a sufficient condition for that improvement, attention once again shifted to 'the efficient use of labour'. Wilson tried to revive the idea of pay and production committees, even talking of making them compulsory. This drew in part on the Donovan report, which had shown support for this idea.[48]

However, the government's relationship with the unions was now much more difficult than it had been when the idea was originally floated. The deterioration in this relationship was sparked initially by the July measures of 1966 and culminated in the government's proposed *IPOS* legislation in 1969. This made any kind of agreement to make productivity a key issue, evident to a degree in the early years of the Labour government, increasingly difficult to sustain. In 1966 Jack Jones, a leader of the Transport and General Workers' Union, was able to appear at a Ministry of Labour-sponsored conference on 'the efficient use of manpower' and to argue that Britain suffered from 'considerable underemployment of labour', and that this could be addressed by greater job flexibility, the only basis for 'real security'. He endorsed Fawley-style deals (though noting that they were not suitable in all workplaces) and went on to criticise the 'foolish' separation of consultation over work and negotiation over pay: 'I think the time has now come to look at Pay and Production Committees, with shop-stewards as members, and at the idea of having shop-stewards on Management Boards, together with technical representatives'. But the climate for such ideas soon deteri-orated. By 1969 Jones was a key opponent of the government's proposals for the reform of industrial relations, and union enthusiasm for linking pay and productivity bargaining seems to have sharply declined after its peak in the initial stages of the 1966 incomes policy.[49] Wilson's hope that the post-Donovan atmosphere would be conducive to such ideas proved optimistic.

On the employer's side, the willingness to deal with the government declined as Labour's fortunes seemed to fall away during the economic crises of 1966 and 1967. In any case, the CBI's enthusiasm for pay and production committees or productivity bargaining was always weak. Both of these ideas, it seemed to most employers, threatened the framework of national bargaining that they saw as crucial to their interests. The NBPI, it should be noted, was also sceptical, fearing that such committees would become a source of wage drift and undermine incomes policy.[50]

The government, as we have noted, while making a strong political pitch for pay and production committees in 1966, never pursued them beyond a few pilot projects. Equally, productivity bargaining soon came to be widely regarded as often fraudulent, with spurious gains in output being allegedly the excuse for excessive wage increases.[51]

The complex high politics of the productivity debate are important but are not the whole story; productivity was important in the 1960s not only because it engaged such high-level attention, but also because it seeped into policy discussion at many points and with many connotations. While the discussion here has stressed the episodic attention of high policy to the issue, at lower levels the focus was more sustained. For example, alongside the activity of bodies like the BPC, the British Institute of Management and the Industrial Society, as well as literally dozens of other bodies, it was a continuing concern of some of the Little Neddies. The agenda pursued was equally diverse, ranging across work study, inter-firm comparison, standardisation, management education and, indeed, almost any topic that might be deemed relevant. Much of this was oriented towards labour issues – the BPC, for example, seems to have been extremely focused on work study – but it would be wrong to suggest that there was any over-arching strategy to this endeavour. It is also notable that, while much of the productivity effort was focused on the private sector, especially private manufacturing, it was also an important issue in some nationalised industries, where some important productivity bargains were struck.[52]

Conclusions

With the advantage of hindsight, a number of conclusions may be drawn from this account of the 'career' of productivity as a term of debate and policy formulation in the 1960s.

First, while the term was used widely, not to say promiscuously, in policy debates in this decade, its main significance was in the discussion of 'labour' issues. Second, and unsurprisingly, productivity had different significance for different actors. For most employers it was a term that they were happy to deploy in making their well established economic arguments to the government and to the public, for example the CBI's use of the first productivity conference to argue for more favourable treatment of profits, or the second to try to embarrass the government over the failure of the National Plan. But, more specifically, they could deploy the term in long-standing arguments against trade unions and their alleged restrictive practices. On the other hand, they were un-happy when the government seemed to be using the need to increase productivity to propose institutional changes that would cut across exist-ing collective bargaining procedures and, even more threateningly, to undermine management prerogatives.

On the union side, many of the leaders had long pursued the logic of the link between higher wages and higher productivity by setting up productivity committees and departments within their organisations. In that sense they were happy to embrace at least the rhetoric of the govern-ment's productivity agenda, especially as they believed they could hope for a *quid pro quo* from a Labour government. But they, like the employers, were wary of radical institutional change, especially perceived threats to free collective bargaining. Around 1966 there are some signs that they might have been persuaded by a sympathetic government to weaken their resistance to such changes, but the economic and political climate shifted rapidly from the end of that year. In particular, the 'shake-out' of labour and consequent unemployment evident after the July measures were bound to make support for 'labour-saving' more problematic. For example, when the DEA agreed with Hugh Cudlipp, owner of the *Daily Mirror*, that the paper's 'Boom City' supplements should have discussion of the productivity drive, a DEA official from Newcastle noted: 'the timing of the supplement is not a particularly happy one. Not everyone would regard Newcastle as "booming"' at the moment, with unemploy-ment on Tyneside at 3.6 per cent, and considerable redundancies due to rationalization in the marine engineering industry.[53]

The government (as always?) sought for a panacea for economic difficulties in the productivity idea and failed to find one.[54] Wilson's argument in 1966 that deflation should not inhibit measures to increase productivity was not absurd. Even if the macro-economy was slowing down, many sectors were still experiencing increased output and profits. But that process of deflation was *politically* fatal to any major tripartite agreement on the issue: it allowed the employers to take up a much more hostile stance to the government, and drove the unions into a much more conservative frame of mind.

In a declinist framework, this episode could be written off as one more wasted opportunity to effect a major progressive, productivity-enhancing reform of workplace relations. Against this, it is essential to emphasise that the concentration on these relations within the debate on productivity was both contingent and highly problematic. Much of the 1960s debate can be seen as just another version of the long-running saga of blaming the workers for Britain's economic weaknesses.[55] But even if we accept the terms of debate as they existed in the 1960s, the outcome of the focus on productivity remains unclear. There is good evidence that the Fawley deal was much less successful than popular accounts at the time suggested. It was not a model for 'sharing power' in the workplace; nor did it generate huge gains in productivity.[56] More generally, the focus on productivity in wage bargaining as a result of incomes policy undoubtedly led to some spurious deals, though whether these were as widespread as is commonly alleged is not easy to judge. As Robinson points out, both unions and managers had good motives for claiming that they had found ways to evade the government's incomes policy, so those claims cannot be taken at face value.[57]

As to the effects on productivity growth of all this activity, again the evidence is unclear (a problem returned to in the concluding chapter). Labour productivity does seem to have been on a rising trend in this period, but how much this owes to the policy emphasis on the issue remains indeterminate. It is notable, however, that even if productivity bargaining was a contributory factor to this acceleration, it was also accompanied by faster wage inflation, so that higher productivity was accompanied by *declining* competitiveness up until the time the pound was devalued. Increasing productivity *per se* could not be the sovereign solution to Britain's balance of payments problems.[58]

Overall, the revival of public policy concern with productivity in the 1960s can be linked to rising perceptions of 'decline', exacerbated by the short-term problems of the balance of payments from 1964. To treat this problem as one of productivity (and largely one of *labour* pro-ductivity) linked the macro-economic issue to pre-existing debates about wage inflation, the role of the unions, and questions of labour mobility and training. But while making the productivity problem one of the workforce fitted with a number of well established discourses about British economic life, politically it also created a fragile strategy in which labour, as represented by the trade unions, would have to accept a sig-nificant degree of responsibility for correcting the problem, a role it was willing to play only in highly contingent circumstances. By the late 1960s, after wage freezes and *IPOS*, these circumstances no longer existed.

Notes

The place of publication is London unless otherwise specified.

1 A. Cairncross, *Years of Recovery: British Economic Policy 1945–51* (1985), pp. 35–6.
2 J. Tomlinson, 'Productivity policy', in H. Mercer, N. Rollings and J. Tomlinson (eds), *Labour Governments and Private Enterprise: The Experience of 1945–51* (Edinburgh, 1992), pp. 37–54; *idem*, 'The politics of economic measurement: the rise of the "productivity problem" in the 1940s', in A. Hopwood and P. Miller (eds), *Accounting in Its Social Context* (Cambridge, 1994), pp. 168–89. This alleged ease of measurement is an illusion, as it is not at all clear how labour inputs are to be measured – the convention of using units of labour time begs all the questions about the relation between time and effort expended. The focus on labour productivity is surveyed in International Labor Organization, *Measuring Labour Productivity* (Geneva, 1969).
3 I. Zweiniger-Bargielowska, 'Rationing, austerity, and the Conservative Party recovery after 1945', *Historical Journal*, 37 (1994), pp. 173–97.
4 N. Tiratsoo and J. Tomlinson, *Industrial Efficiency and State Intervention: Labour 1939–51* (1994), ch. 5.
5 C. Maier, 'The politics of productivity: foundations of American international economic policy after World War II', in *In Search of Stability: Explorations in Historical Political Economy* (Cambridge, 1987), pp. 121–52; J. Zeitlin and G. Herrigel, *Americanization and Its Limits: Reworking US Technology in Post-war Europe and Japan* (Oxford, 2000).
6 A. Booth, 'Corporate politics and the quest for productivity: the British TUC and the politics of productivity growth, 1947–1960', in J. Melling and A. McKinlay (eds), *Management, Labour and Industrial Politics in Europe* (1996), pp. 44–65. The academic debate on productivity in the 1950s evinced more faith in direct economic incentives than had been common in the 1940s. J. P. Davison, P. Sargant Florence, B. Gray and N. Ross, *Productivity and Economic Incentives* (1958); this appears to be the only study directly focused on productivity paid for by Counterpart Funds derived from US economic aid.
7 Tiratsoo and Tomlinson, *Industrial Efficiency*, ch. 8.
8 N. Tiratsoo and J. Tomlinson, *The Conservatives and Industrial Efficiency, 1951–64: Thirteen Wasted Years?* (1998), chs 2, 10.
9 A. Crosland, *The Future of Socialism* (1956), p. 99.
10 R. Jones, *Wages and Employment Policy 1936–85* (1986), ch. 5. Productivity had been mentioned in the incomes policy agreement of the 1940s, but it did not play the same role it was to assume in the policies of the 1960s – see pp. 36–7.
11 Discussion at and about the Council on Productivity, Prices and Incomes focused overwhelmingly on inflation. The official record is in PRO, T 234/730–3. For a summary of its approach, see S. R. Denison and J. R. Presley, *Robertson on Economic Policy* (1992), ch. 7.
12 DEA, *Joint Statement of Intent on Productivity, Prices and Incomes* (1964).
13 MRC, MSS 292/B/M560.1/9, 'TUC Economic Committee meeting', 20 November 1964; PRO, EW 8/6, J. Sargent' 'A policy for incomes', 26 October 1964.
14 PRO, EW 8/1, DEA, 'Discussions leading up to the Statement on Productivity, Prices and Incomes', 1964; EW 8/7, DEA, 'Papers relating to Joint Statement'; R. McKersie and L. Hunter, *Pay, Productivity and Collective Bargaining* (1973).

190   *Tomlinson*

15 A. Flanders, *The Fawley Productivity Agreements. A Case Study of Management and Collective Bargaining* (1964). Flanders' assessment of the case for Fawley-like agreements was notably cautious. Compare E. Owen Smith, *Productivity Bargaining: A Case Study in the Steel Industry* (1971), which is much less temperate in its advocacy. For a more political case for productivity bargaining, see K. Jones and J. Golding, *Productivity Bargaining*, Fabian Research Series 257 (1966).
16 William Allen, quoted in McKersie and Hunter, *Pay*, pp. 10–11.
17 Pioneering serious comparative (labour) productivity data were produced by both official bodies and academics in the 1960s: see International Labor Organization, *Comparative Labour Productivity* (Geneva, 1969); J. Dunlop and V. Diatchenko (eds), *Labour Productivity* (New York, 1964); A. Silberston, 'The motor industry', *Bulletin of the Oxford University Institute of Statistics*, 27 (1965), pp. 253–86.
18 Political and Economic Planning, *British Economic Growth* (1960), p. 198; G. Jones, 'The British government and foreign multinationals before 1970', in M. Chick (ed.), *Governments, Industries and Markets* (Aldershot, 1990), pp. 194–5.
19 A. Shonfield, *British Economic Policy Since the War* (Harmondsworth, 1958); M. Shanks, *The Stagnant Society* (Harmondsworth, 1961).
20 Crosland, *Future of Socialism*, pp. 183–4, 193–5.
21 *The National Plan*, Cmnd 2764, BPP 1964/65, vol. 30, p. 53. For such initiatives, see PRO, CAB 134/2744, NEDC, 'Management education, training and development', 27 April 1967; PRO, LAB 10/2759, 'Encouraging small firms to make use of management consultants', 1965/66.
22 NEDC, *Conditions Favourable to Faster Growth* (1963), p. 1.
23 *National Plan*, ch. 2.
24 *Ibid.*, p. 52.
25 K. Lomax, 'Measurement of industrial productivity in the UK', in OECD, *Productivity Measurement. Vol. 3, Global Measurement of Productivity* (Paris, 1966), p. 386. There is evidence of the beginnings of 'growth accounting' of a modern form in PRO, CAB 130/308, 'Role of technology in productivity', 15 May 1967.
26 N. Tiratsoo and J. Tomlinson, 'Restrictive practices on the shopfloor in Britain, 1945–60: myth and reality', *Business History*, 36 (1994), pp. 65–84.
27 Labour Party, *Time for Decision* (1966), p. 5; PRO, EW 8/453, 'Productivity: proposal to seek management/trade union discussions at factory level', 1965–7.
28 PRO, LAB 10/2924, 'National productivity conference: plant bargaining pilot scheme', 1967; PRO, PREM 13/2723, P. Shore to B. Castle, 30 May 1968, and DEA, 'JPCs: background note', May 1968.
29 PRO, EW 8/453, I. F. Hudson, 'Briefing for PM and Secretary of State', 29 June 1967; W. E. J. McCarthy, *The Role of Shop Stewards in British Industrial Relations*, Royal Commission on Trade Unions and Employers Associations, Research Paper no. 1 (1967).
30 H. Clegg, *Productivity Bargaining and Restrictive Labour Practices*, Royal Commission on Trades Unions and Employers Associations, Research Paper no. 4 (1968), p. 56: 'Under-employment of labour is one of the major scandals of the British Economy'. The same document cites Flanders' estimate, in *Fawley*, that productivity at Fawley grew by 50 per cent in two years after the agreement, a figure that is extremely doubtful – see B. Ahlstrand, *The Quest for Productivity. A Case Study of Fawley After Flanders* (Cambridge, 1990).
31 PRO, PREM 13/1242, 'Speech by H. Wilson to TUC conference', 5

September 1966; PRO, LAB 8/3480, DEA, 'Manpower utilisation', 4 April 1968.
32 PRO, PREM 13/1648, G. Brown to H. Wilson, 5 August 1965. On Geddes, see L. Johnman and H. Murphy, *British Shipbuilding and the State Since 1918* (Exeter, 2002), ch. 6.
33 For example, William Allen attacked the National Plan for suggesting that Britain had a labour shortage when, if only labour was used efficiently, there would be a surplus of 'several million'. He went on to suggest that the growth rate could be increased to 8–10 per cent if the government pursued a tough enough redundancy policy: 'Britain in blinkers', *Sunday Times*, 12 June 1966.
34 G. Roberts, *The Cost of Demarcation* (Cambridge, 1967), pp. 35–6.
35 PRO, LAB 10/2390, 'Talk by A. Flanders', March 1965. The peculiar problems of the docks are discussed by J. Wilson, *The Dockers: The Impact of Industrial Change* (1972), who notes that there 'modernisation became synonymous with post-Devlin reforms in the field of labour', p. 10.
36 K. Williams, C. Haslam, J. Williams and S. Johal, *Cars: Analysis, History, Ideas* (Providence, RI, 1994), ch. 10; PRO, EW 24/27, R. Ainscow to B. Brown, 'International productivity comparisons', 4 November 1965.
37 PRO, CAB 128/41, 'Cabinet conclusions', 12 July 1966.
38 PRO, CAB 130/296, 'National productivity conference meeting', 23 September 1966.
39 PRO, LAB 10/2564, 'National productivity conference', 1966; PRO, LAB 43/449, 'Conference on productivity', 1966. See also P. Jenkins, *Harold Wilson's Productivity Conference* (1967). There are official accounts in the *Board of Trade Journal*, 7 October 1966, pp. 852–3, and 23 June 1967, pp. 1602–3. For the CBI's role, see MRC, MSS 200/C/3/DG1/16, 'National Productivity Council and related matters', 1967, and MSS 200/C/3/DG1/41, 'CBI/TUC joint committee'.
40 The number of references to productivity in the *Board of Trade Journal* rose from zero in the first half of 1966 to ten in the second half of 1967, with a further peak of eleven in the second half of 1968, before declining to three in the first half of 1970. For ministerial positions on the general issue of productivity at this time, see PRO, CAB 129/125, DEA, 'The growth rate and productivity', 8 July 1966, Board of Trade, 'Survey of current work on productivity', 8 July 1966, and MinTech, 'Productivity', 8 July 1966. On the diversity of agencies involved in the issue, see PRO, LAB 8/3495, 'Official Steering Committee on Economic Policy: Sub-committee on Manpower Productivity, minutes and papers', 1968.
41 B. Castle, *The Castle Diaries 1964–70* (1984), p. 43; PRO, LAB 12/1648, 'Setting-up of Manpower and Productivity Division', 1968/69; LAB 8/3493, 'Manpower and Productivity Service – general', 1968. On the limits of the Manpower and Productivity Service, see PRO, EW 8/949, 'Draft report on the development of productivity, prices and incomes policy', November 1968, which refers to this body 'which by reason of its relatively small resources and manpower restrictions cannot amount to much more than a series of pinpricks in the balloon of inertia'. The Service was headed by George Cattell, previously Personnel Director at the Rootes car company.
42 PRO, EW 8/948, R. Jenkins to B. Castle, 23 July 1968, and B. Castle to R. Jenkins, 'Future of incomes policy', 26 July 1968.
43 PRO, PREM 13/2040, 'Treasury to PM's Office', 2 December 1968. Tony Benn noted in his diary that, in 1976, 'Wilson said he had invented the concept of output per man-shift and even the concept of productivity which

had been a theoretical concept before but he had got it extended over all industry. A terrible thing to have on his conscience', *Against the Tide. Diaries 1973–76* (1989), p. 506. 'Statistics on output per hour and labour costs in the UK', *Economic Trends*, 180 (1968), pp. 46–54.

44 PRO, PREM 13/2723, B. Castle to H. Wilson, 7 November 1969.

45 PRO, LAB 43/493, 'Meeting with TUC Economic Committee', 20 May 1968.

46 PRO, BT 258/2174, G. Parker, 'Note', 2 December 1964; BT 258/1677, 'Brief on BPC', 1 December 1964; PRO, LAB 10/2825, E. Roll to R. Powell, 12 August 1966; PRO, BT 258/2341, H. Heinemann, 'BPC', 28 October 1965; PRO EW 4/105, BPC, 'Review of aims, activities and organisation', 1970.

47 *New Society*, 208, 22 September 1966, p. 434.

48 PRO, LAB 8/3479, 'Review of current problems in the Ministry of Labour field', 19 January 1968; LAB 8/3493, 'Manpower and Productivity Service', June 1968.

49 McKersie and Hunter, *Pay*, p. 64. Union views are surveyed in MRC, MSS 292/B/552.48/4, 'Productivity 1960–1970', and MSS 292B/557.84/1, 'Productivity bargaining 1965–70'.

50 PRO, EW 8/453, 'Meeting of officials with Secretary of State', 24 March 1967, where it is recorded that the CBI opposition to combining pay and productivity issues in a single forum is based on the fear that the establishment of plant bargaining would be likely to cause difficulties for poorly-managed firms. CBI, *Productivity Bargaining* (1968); Transport and General Workers' Union, *Productivity Bargaining* (1970).

51 H. Clegg, *How to Run an Incomes Policy and Why We Made Such a Mess of the Last One* (1971).

52 PRO, LAB 10/2999, NEDO, 'Report of the Advisory Group on Productivity Advisory Services', 1966; PRO, FG 2/499, 'BPC', 1966/67; R. Pryke, *Public Enterprise in Practice* (1971), ch. 5.

53 PRO, EW 4/105, R. Robertson to J. Groves, 8 March 1967. There were persistent worries in official circles that the term 'productivity' had been 'oversold' and that 'efficiency' would be a better slogan: 'Efficiency is much more emotive and by appealing to emotions it might be more successful in improving industrial attitudes. No one likes to be accused of being inefficient, whereas the word "productivity" is cold, is not easily understood, and, of course, always applies to someone else. Equally, the national press is tired of productivity years, drives, and promotions, and the word gives rise to suspicions of do-gooding and exhortation': PRO, FG 2/919, R. Kelsall to J. Groves, 26 October 1967.

54 A. Cairncross, *The Wilson Years: A Treasury Diary, 1964–66* (1997), p. 146.

55 T. Nichols, *The British Worker Question: A New Look at Workers and Productivity in Manufacturing* (1986).

56 Ahlstrand, *Quest for Productivity*, pp. 107–9.

57 D. Robinson, 'The pay board, incomes policy and productivity bargaining', in P. Seglow (ed.), *Productivity Bargaining in Perspective* (Uxbridge, 1973), pp. 51–3.

58 McKersie and Hunter, *Pay*, p. 102; F. Blackaby, 'General appraisal', in F. Blackaby (ed.), *British Economic Policy 1960–74* (Cambridge, 1978), p. 647.

9

Social justice and economic efficiency

Social justice and economic efficiency summarise the key aims of the Labour Party for most of its existence.[1] After a brief discussion of the relevant background, this chapter looks at the meaning given to 'social justice' under the Wilson government, and how its pursuit interacted with the aims of efficiency and modernisation.

Labour and 'social justice'

The achievement of social justice is set out as an explicit objective of the National Plan. But the term is not defined and, indeed, it is a term whose very elasticity of meaning adds to its political attractiveness even as it detracts from its analytical usefulness. In the decades preceding the 1960s, much of Labour's ideological debate about the nature of socialism linked social justice to notions of equality. These two terms were often treated as synonymous, as when, in 1953, Hugh Gaitskell referred to Labour's goal as 'social justice, equality, the classless society – call it what you will'.[2]

Equality was placed at the centre of Labour's ideological agenda by R. H. Tawney's influential work of that name, first published in 1931.[3] Twenty-five years later Tony Crosland's *Future of Socialism* sought to make pursuit of equality the centrepiece of modern 'revisionist' socialism. Yet, for all its currency, equality had no simple meaning in Labour discourse, nor did its pursuit have any uncontroversial policy implications. Tawney made a powerful rhetorical case against inequality and linked this to a 'strategy of equality' which, in summary, involved 'social policies to extend collective provision and equalise opportunities in education, health and housing, of taxation policies to strengthen the position of the worker, and of economic policies to bring the power of private capital under public direction'.[4] By contrast, Crosland placed much more emphasis on the 'subjective' aspects of inequality and explicitly rejected the view that the power of private capital was a major obstacle to furthering equality.[5] Plainly, however, there was common ground between these two in their advocacy of extending collective social provision and this, crudely put, was the unifying feature of much of Labour's advocacy of equality and social justice in the middle decades of the twentieth century. From the late 1950s the phrase 'private affluence and public squalor' was commonly used by Labour's theorists and publicists to attack the current state of affairs, and to suggest that 'government and local authority expenditure has always been too low: it is too low today and ought to be increased'. As the Labour minister Joel Barnett put it in 1969: 'our purpose in political life [is] to expand the social wage through large increases in public expenditure on education, health, housing and the social services'.[6]

The extension of such collective social provision was, of course, at the heart of the policies of the Attlee administration. Yet it would be wrong to see these measures as characterised by an over-riding priority being given to equality. Rather, they are better seen as carrying out Labour's historic purpose of creating a secure 'national minimum' of income, education and health care. This approach was, in fact, in line with Crosland's argument that:

> social equality cannot be held to be the ultimate purpose of the social services. This must surely be the relief of social distress and hardship, and the correction of social need; though naturally measures directed to this end will often also enhance social equality, which in any case remains an important subsidiary objective.[7]

The contents of Labour's 1964 manifesto suggest that the contemporary understanding of social justice broadly conformed to Crosland's 'relief of social distress and hardship, and the correction of social need'. The manifesto made a number of promises on social security, including: increasing national insurance benefits in line with earnings, financed by graduated contributions; an income guarantee system for pensioners and widows; earnings-related payments for the retired, sick and unemployed; and a national severance pay scheme. On health, the manifesto focused on the abolition of prescription charges, expanded hospital building and, especially, an increase in local authority health and welfare services. Education was discussed in terms of 'investment in people' and here the manifesto prioritised the reduction of class sizes, financial aid for those staying on beyond the minimum school-leaving age and a 'massive expansion' of higher, further and university education.[8]

The route to achieving these aims lay through spending more money, but it was clear, to most Labour policy-makers, that this money could be spent only as the economy expanded. Social justice was to be paid for out of the fruits of faster growth and greater efficiency. The National

Plan presented the prospect of a 25 per cent increase in GDP being distributed between correcting the balance of payments, increasing investment, more personal consumption and rising collective provision, but with personal consumption growing more slowly than GDP and public provision faster, because 'a substantial part of the increase in the standard of living to be expected in an advanced modern community comes about through rising standards in the public sector…. It also reflects the increasing proportion during the next few years of children and old people'.[9] This approach led the government to plan for a real-terms 4.25 per cent annual average increase in public spending (excluding nationalised industry investment) over the period encompassed by the Plan. This was, in fact, slower than the increase envisaged in the late 1960s by the Conservatives in their last expenditure plan, but faster than the projected rise in GDP. It was also slower than had actually been achieved in the last five years of the Conservative government. As a critic pointed out, 'Labour's plan gives more relative weight to personal consumption compared with public services and housing than the Tories during the last six years of their administration'.[10]

Most of the contemporary and subsequent debate about Labour's achievements in the field of 'social justice' has revolved around the pattern of public spending and the accompanying changes in taxation. Spending had to be paid for out of taxation, as any substantial increase in borrowing aroused fears about the monetary effects of budget deficits and the impact on international confidence, especially when borrowing from the IMF brought explicit scrutiny of Britain's level of borrowing and credit expansion (see Chapter 3). Borrowing did increase in the middle years of Labour's period in office, though as in the rest of the 'golden age' the government obeyed the 'rule' that borrowing should be only for investment, not for current spending.[11] In later years borrowing was cut back, so that, overall, the quantitative link between spending and taxing was a close one. Other issues, notably the treatment of low pay (discussed in Chapter 6), a national minimum wage and industrial democracy (both discussed in the last part of this chapter), are relevant to the broad theme of social justice, but the bulk of the discussion is appropriately focused on 'spend and tax'; each of these is discussed in turn before a section which draws broad conclusions on the development and impact of Labour's overall policies in this field.

Public spending

The detailed development of Labour's social welfare policies is dealt with by a number of authors, and is not described here, where the focus is on the links between such spending, 'social justice' and issues of growth and efficiency. This entails most attention being paid to social security, where the tensions between social justice and other governmental objectives were generally most acute.[12]

Within a month of taking office, Labour fulfilled some major manifesto commitments by substantially increasing spending in the fields of pensions, benefits for widows and by abolition of the 'sacred cow' of prescription charges.[13] But the high priority given in the manifesto to the income guarantee for widows and pensioners was not reflected in action. Part of the problem was the nature of the income guarantee and how it was to be administered to achieve the aim of ending 'means testing', which was central to Labour's concerns.[14] But alongside this was the unfavourable market response to the initial spending announcements, and their link to the rise in interest rates in November 1964. Indeed, already in October James Callaghan was promising a 'stern review' of public spending to try to reassure the markets. That review eventually led to a 4.25 per cent expansion limit, announced in February 1965, which put a tight limit on what could be spent on social security. However, Labour soon announced that earnings-related unemployment pay would be introduced, along with similar supplements for sickness, industrial injury and widows' benefits.

Douglas Houghton, the minister in overall charge of social welfare spending, argued that these early policies, in the context of expenditure constraints, had set Labour off in the wrong direction. He emphasised that 'nothing can be more fundamental to socialist policy than the abolition of poverty', and that the income guarantee had been presented by Labour before coming into office as the key measure for that purpose. Unfortunately, he suggested, Labour's 'priorities appear now to give a higher place to the link between pensions and earnings than to bringing low incomes to a reasonable minimum'. He also argued against the priority given to earnings-related supplements, as these had originally been proposed for economic reasons, to speed the mobility of labour, but had been expensively expanded into a much broader social programme.[15] However, a majority of ministers argued that a change on the scale of a shift to an income guarantee would take so long that immediate measures should be taken to raise benefits, and this view prevailed. In fact, the idea of an income guarantee was soon dropped because of its administrative complexity and cost, and replaced by a reformed system of national assistance, now called supplementary benefit.[16]

The first period of Labour government had demonstrated the dilemmas arising from the limited resources available for social security spending, given the range of pressures on the government. These pressures were greatly reinforced by the publication in December 1965 of the book *The Poor and the Poorest*, by Brian Abel-Smith and Peter Townsend, followed by the creation of the Child Poverty Action Group. The book was a key moment in the 'rediscovery of poverty', as it suggested that, under the post-war welfare state, poverty had increased rather than decreased, and it put especial emphasis on the number of children in families living in poverty, and the fact that over 40 per cent of those families contained a wage earner.[17] This new pressure undoubtedly had an effect on the government, and in particular led to an important debate about what was termed at the time 'family endowment'.[18]

The debate about family endowment concerned how aid was to be given to families with children, but in posing this question it raised much broader questions for Labour's social spending. The prominence given to the income guarantee in the run-up to the 1964 election arose from recognition of the need to concentrate resources on the poorest, but without a means test. Opposition to the means test remained extremely powerful and so, when attention focused on child poverty, the solution advocated by some ministers was to raise family allowances, but to concentrate the effects on the poor, by reducing tax allowances for children rather than by means testing. This would mean that most of the increased expenditure would be 'clawed back' by the tax system, albeit by lowering tax thresholds.[19]

Callaghan rejected these proposals as incompatible with the need to keep a tight rein on public spending,[20] but Margaret Herbison, the Minister for Pensions and National Insurance (retitled Minister for Social Security in 1966), continued to make the case, broadening the issue as she did so. She pointed out the attractions of such a scheme in gaining support for incomes policy. She also argued that it was inappropriate to treat such a proposal as on a par with other proposed increases in public spending. First, social security was different because it did not involve any use of real resources, unlike government provision of goods and services. Second, because about 40 per cent of social security generally was paid for by national insurance contributions, it could not, she suggested, be regarded as reducing the taxable capacity available for other areas by the full amount of any increased spending.[21]

While the first point could readily be responded to by stressing the need nevertheless to finance transfer payments, the second point was much more radical in its challenge to customary policy assumptions. The general argument about relying on national insurance contributions was responded to by stressing the regressive character of such contributions, a Treasury official opining that it would be 'extremely odd for the present government to rely upon the proceeds of the most regressive form of taxation in our system'.[22] But the more specific argument about the logic of looking at the net cost of an increase in family allowances after deduction of the effects of cutting child tax allowances was not so easily resisted. Alex Johnston, head of the Inland Revenue, argued for a complete separation of tax and spending issues, but this was not regarded as realistic by the Treasury, partly because the two had been clearly integrated in the discussion of the replacement of tax allowances for investment by cash grants, as was recognised in the expenditure White Paper of February 1966.[23]

When the issue went to Cabinet early in 1967, the Chancellor continued to resist the proposal. He did not argue about the logic of focusing on the gross cost, but simply asserted that this was the figure that mattered to both taxpayers and 'foreign gnomes'. He also attacked the proposal for increased family allowances as unpopular among wage earners and ineffective as a means of reducing poverty. The first point was linked to the perception that the policy involved switching money from men's wallets to women's purses, which would be unpopular with Labour's core, male working-class, constituency. Callaghan's alternative was an increase in family allowances financed by a means test, but the majority of the Cabinet were opposed to this.[24] The Chancellor had any decision on the matter postponed and when discussion was resumed in July 1967 Callaghan proposed the alternative of means-tested housing allowances. When this was rejected he eventually agreed to an interim seven-shilling increase in family allowance, but without committing himself to paying for this by matching reductions in tax allowances. Wilson recognised Treasury sensitivities on this matter by summarising that the Cabinet would 'need to preserve the Chancellor's freedom to determine how expenditure should be financed'. On the other hand, this debate provided one reason for the reform of the presentation of public spending announced in a Green Paper in 1969, allowing a somewhat more coherent judgement on spending decisions.[25]

A few days after the above decision, the Cabinet also agreed to the Chancellor's arguments that the linking of pensions to earnings could not be afforded, and that the rise should fall somewhere between those in prices and earnings.[26] The Chancellor's intransigence on these matters was, of course, the consequence of continuing balance of payments and 'confidence' problems, and the centrality of public spending and borrowing to judgements of the economy's strength. Periodically since the publication of the 4.25 per cent target in February 1965, the government had been forced into public spending cuts to appease adverse judgements. But it is important to note that, before devaluation, all these 'cuts' were reductions in rates of growth and that, in fact, despite these 'cuts', expenditure continued to grow above planned rates. While there are definitional problems in the precise quantification of the increases, the broad pattern seems clear: compared with the planned rate of 4.25 per cent, real expenditure grew at 3.8, 5.9, 5.7 and 13.1 per cent, respectively, in the years from 1964/65 to 1967/68.[27] However, it would be wrong to presume that the only motor for this increase was welfare expenditure; to a significant degree, the Chancellor's tough-ness was effective. The figures suggest that social security, health, welfare and education all grew at approximately the same rate as total spend-ing. Housing spending rose at a fast rate, but this is ambiguous as a measure of the government's commitment to welfare and social justice. As Price notes, housing investment was considered by Labour to be 'crucial to faster growth' because of the impact on labour mobility, which, as noted in Chapter 6, was regarded as crucial to industrial modern-isation. In addition, in characteristic 1960s fashion, housing was linked to productivity: 'The incentive to buy or rent a decent house of one's own is one of the driving forces behind the worker's will to earn higher wages through increased productivity'. Defence spending was again cut, while programmes involving assistance to industry showed the fastest rate of growth.[28]

The pre-devaluation 'cuts' were therefore very limited, and their impact was felt (apart from in defence) mainly in investment in roads and environmental services, and electricity, where the huge expansion of recent years was slowing down. Even so, total public investment down to 1967/68 grew faster than the estimates set out in the National Plan, while the still faster growth in current expenditure was hardly even notionally restricted.[29] The overall picture on welfare spending in the first three years of the Labour government was one of big political battles, particularly on social security, with spending ministries finding that even the growth of spending above the Plan targets left many mani-festo commitments unfulfilled, because unaffordable. Yet these years were to be a period of consensus and expansion compared with the period after devaluation.

The government's grand strategy after devaluation was to restrain the growth in public expenditure, in order to make resources available for exports without restricting private consumption growth to an in-tolerable extent, while also trying to gain support from the trade union movement for a reduction in wage growth. This restraint was severe, and for the years 1968/69 to 1970/71 the rates of increase fell to –1.1, –0.1 and –2.7 per cent, respectively. These cutbacks came in stages. At the time of devaluation, alongside cuts in 'east of Suez' spending, reduc-tions included a postponement in the raising of social security benefits, the reintroduction of prescription charges and the postponement of the raising of the school-leaving age (RoSLA).[30] The first of these was offset, to a degree, by a pledge soon given to protect the poorest against the price-increasing effects of devaluation; the decision on RoSLA was to provoke considerable dispute, but nothing on the scale of that over prescription charges.[31] But these were only the first instalment of a pro-cess of attrition which was to stretch over the next fifteen months, down to the 1969 budget.

The period between devaluation and the January announcement of back-up measures saw intensive discussions about the scale of cuts in public spending. Partly this was a macro-economic debate about the size and speed with which demand needed to be switched into exports, with divisions between 'hawks' and 'doves' on the scale of the reductions, and between those who believed all the cuts should be made in one go and those who wanted to take more than one bite at the cherry as the situation unfolded.[32] This budgetary debate focused on the taxation side, while a parallel debate took place up to Cabinet level about where spending cuts were to fall.

Initially Roy Jenkins argued for cuts in civil expenditure of about £325 million (out of total spending of around £15,000 million), saying that any less would require such large tax increases that personal consumption would have to fall, and that the actual outcome would be accelerating wage demands, as this squeeze would be unacceptable to wage earners. While in dispute over the prescription and RoSLA issues, the Cabinet agreed without recorded dissent to the tying of benefit increases to prices rather than wages, but once again the issue of family allowances proved much more contentious.[33] Eventually a further three shillings increase in the allowance was accepted, but the principle of 'claw-back' was also agreed, after much debate and against the wishes of both Callaghan and Jenkins.[34]

The politically most dramatic consequences of the post-devaluation cuts were the retreat from the east of Suez and the rejection of Jenkins' initial suggestion that the 'independent' nuclear deterrent be abandoned. On the civil side, prescription charges and the postponement of RoSLA provoked most internal party problems, though the first of these in particular involved quite small amounts of money when all the exemptions are allowed for. But the overall thrust of the cuts reflected Jenkins' argument that: 'The over-riding priority was to restore our economic health; it was this rather than the pursuit of social objectives which must govern the action to be taken in the present crisis'.[35] The White Paper of January 1968 showed planned cuts of about £300 million, with the annual rate of increase in public expenditure reduced to 4.8 per cent in 1968/69 and 2.6 per cent in 1969/70, and this did not include the foregoing of up-rating of benefits – because up-rating was not at the time an automatic process, such expenditure was not built into the baseline figures.[36] But the actual falls were larger than anticipated, largely because of a decline in housing investment, though this was partially offset by faster than expected rises in investment grants, with ministers coming ruefully to emphasise that grants, unlike allowances, figured in the public expenditure total.[37]

In December 1968, the Ministerial Committee on Economic Policy was presented with a series of papers summarising Labour's achievements in social welfare. The overall tone was one of disappointment when measured against the 1964 manifesto promises, though it was noted that, in aggregate, spending had grown more rapidly than under the last five years of the Conservatives (6.7 per cent per annum as against 4.8 per cent). But by this time not only was the rate of expansion slowing, but also the Chancellor was looking for further cuts for 1969/70.[38] These were announced in February 1969. Again, the rhetoric favoured limiting cuts in the economic areas at the expense of social welfare, though nationalised industry investment, which was now included in the total, was planned to show a substantial fall.[39]

The Labour government's final public expenditure White Paper, issued in December 1969, summarised the pattern of growth over the government's tenure. After noting the fall in defence spending, it went on:

> In the civil sector regional development policy was combined with measures to modernise and restructure industry, and with expenditure on other items under this heading, including scientific and technological research and other measures in support of industry and employment, this became the fastest growing group of programmes – 9.0 per cent per annum. Priority was also given to the social services on which expenditure was increased by an annual average rate overall of 6 per cent, including 4.9 per cent on education, 3.9 per cent on health and welfare and 8.3 per cent on social security.[40]

The White Paper announced some modest increases in expenditure for 1969/70, but these, of course, were largely to take effect under the next government.

For the Labour period as a whole, Table 9.1 shows the pattern of expenditure growth, and though the basis of these figures differs from that used in the 1969 White Paper, the table bears out the priority given to spending on 'industrial modernisation' as against 'social justice'. Some other brief conclusions on Labour's public spending policies may be suggested.

First, spending on 'social services' (the generic term for social welfare most commonly used in the 1960s) was defined in a purely conventional way under Labour. For example, even roads were sometimes included under this category and, despite the belief in its impact on growth, often so was housing. Second, spending under this overall heading was not subject to an overarching strategy; attempts were made to give the Ministerial Social Services Committee such a role, but this did not happen, partly because the ministers concerned did not want such co-ordination. It was also suggested that a minister be appointed to oversee the redistributive effects of government policy, but this again did not happen. As we have seen, some attempt was made to differentiate transfer payments (mainly social security) from direct expenditure on goods and services,

Table 9.1 Public expenditure growth, 1963/64 to 1969/70
(in 1971/72 prices)

Expenditure category	Annual average increase (%)
Defence	–0.8
Overseas aid	–0.7
Agriculture, fisheries and food	–3.3
Trade, industry and employment	14.5
Research councils	12.5
Nationalised industries	0.7
Surface transport	1.4
Roads	6.1
Education and libraries	5.5
Social security	5.5
Health and personal social services	5.1
Housing	4.6
Miscellaneous local services	5.3
Total public spending	3.8

Source: S. Goldman, *The Developing System of Public Expenditure Management and Control* (1973), table B.

such as the health service and education, but this had limited impact, though ministers were sensitive to the consequences on labour supply of the latter compared with the former.[41]

It is appropriate to focus here on social security, as this, then as now, was undoubtedly the form of social expenditure most closely associated with notions of social justice, and which also had the most redistributive effects. Paradoxically, one of the reasons for this redistributive effect was that, despite its long-standing hostility to the concept, Labour did expand the scope of means testing, especially in rent and rate rebates.[42]

In other respects too, Labour did not deliver the hopes of 1964. No income guarantee was introduced, though the new supplementary benefit system was an advance on national assistance, and had substantially greater take-up. Second, benefits had not been tied to earnings after 1967, though because of taxes on earnings the disposable income of those on benefit did match the rise in take-home pay.[43] Third, Labour had failed to introduce the long-mooted superannuation scheme – this fell with the general election.[44] Despite these failures, social security spending had undoubtedly been given priority within social spending, allowing for the 'modernisation' aspect of education, even allowing that a considerable part of the growth was the automatic response to demographic shifts. This priority over other forms of social spending was the usual pattern for Labour governments.[45]

The growth in health spending reflected a big expansion in hospital building, perhaps the area of most striking need of modernisation in the infrastructure of the welfare state, but this was partly offset in the slow growth of current expenditure, despite some notable improvements, especially in general practitioner services.[46] Education spending grew surprisingly slowly, especially given that it was seen not just as 'welfare' but also as an important part of industrial modernisation. On the other hand, within the overall total, it is noticeable that areas which might be seen as more egalitarian (e.g. RoSLA, day release for training) were sacrificed to the highly inegalitarian sectors such as university expansion. Within the education budget, 'social justice' clearly lost out to Labour's view of 'economic modernisation'.[47]

Taxation

One of the reasons Labour fell short of its promises on social welfare spending was that these were in addition to the plans for rapid expansion bequeathed by the Conservatives. In similar fashion, Labour inherited 'a sort of tax prison' from the Conservatives.[48] This confinement arose from the range of pressures the tax system was under by the 1960s. First, and most obvious, was the need to find more revenue to pay for higher levels of expenditure. The ability to do so was constrained by a number of factors, as crisply summarised by a Treasury official specifically in relation to spending on social services, and which is worth quoting at length:

> It is true that the current level of taxation and of expenditure on social services is not high in the UK in comparison with many other advanced countries, excluding the USA. But it will be difficult to educate the public to accept this fact and to accept the changes in taxation that would be required to bring a larger proportion of the National Income into the Exchequer. The scope for enlarging the tax take is limited in a number of directions. Increasing graduated direct taxation may prove inimical to growth; higher social security contributions placed on employers will raise costs; extending indirect taxation in the main field not now covered would be regressive in effect and repugnant to the present administration at least. It may be that more money could be raised for social services from those who benefit if the contributions were more closely related to the benefits, but hypothecation has some serious disadvantages mainly in potential distortion in the right balance of use of resources.[49]

Almost all the pressures mentioned here had become more intense during the 1960s. Not only were taxes supposed not to be 'inimical to growth' (a very traditional measure of a good tax) but the search now was for taxes that would positively encourage efficiency and modern-isation.[50] The classic example from the Wilson period was, of course, the SET, discussed in Chapter 6, which conveniently seemed to offer both a new source of revenue while delivering higher productivity – but only at the cost of great hostility from employers and others, and with all sorts of arbitrary effects which had to be resolved in ad hoc fashion. The incentive aspects of tax were also prominent in the 1960s, partly because of the recognition that marginal direct tax rates at the top end of the range were probably the highest in the world. Few people paid these rates, and in consequence their effects on behaviour may have been often exaggerated, but they appeared anomalous at a time when international comparisons of tax patterns were becoming increasingly popular.[51] Probably more practically significant, and ideologically more problematic, was the fall in income tax thresholds, as a result of the decision not to index these during a period of rising prices. In the 1940s Labour had probably unnecessarily worried about the small number of highly paid manual workers being drawn into the income tax net, but by the 1960s this was happening on a significant scale. Policy-makers in the 1960s were well aware of this trend and it provided an important reason for the Treasury's resistance to family allowances paid for by 'claw-back', as outlined in the previous section.[52]

Efficiency and distributional issues were combined in Labour's approach to company taxation. The 1965 budget introduced corporation tax, which represented a huge change in the way company tax was calculated.[53] While this was seen as having the incidental advantage of discouraging foreign investment, the main motive was to discourage the distribution of company earnings, both to reduce the incomes of the wealthy and to encourage investment. This, in fact, was not a new idea: Labour had introduced a similar scheme in 1948, which had been abandoned by the Conservatives in 1958.[54] In the 1960s Labour was, of course, still persuaded that higher investment was the key to faster growth, while the egalitarian aspect of this and other tax issues was enhanced by the attempt to get incomes policy to 'stick'.

Increasing reliance on employee national insurance contributions was advocated in the 1960s, based on the argument that this would not reduce taxable capacity, as it was alleged that contributors regarded these payments as different in kind to other forms of tax. This view was treated with scepticism by the Treasury, which was losing faith in Keynes's famously cynical view that national insurance contributions were a 'useful fiction'. In any event, contributions were highly regressive, as they had only a limited element of earnings linkage, which had been introduced by the Conservatives in 1959. This was an area where little was actually known about public opinion, but a proposed survey seems never to have got off the ground.[55]

It was also well recognised in the 1960s that Britain's tax structure differed notably from that of most Continental European countries in its limited reliance on employers' social insurance contributions. Wilson suggested that increases in these might be a way out of the 'tax prison', but his advisers firmly pointed out that any increase would be swiftly passed on in prices, with serious damage to competitiveness.[56]

An extension to indirect taxation faced powerful obstacles from different directions. Another well recognised peculiarity of the British tax system was the narrow base of such tax, with a purchase tax falling on a restricted range of goods and excise duties on motoring, tobacco and alcohol. One of the reasons for the acceptance of the SET in 1966 was the belief that it would broaden this tax base by levying higher taxes on services, which were under-taxed in comparison with manufactured goods. But this still left a large question about a more general broadening of that base. A further impetus in this direction came from the decision to apply for EEC membership and the expectation that this would require movement to a value added tax (VAT). By judicious use of rebates, VAT also had the potential to act as a way of indirectly promoting exports, always a concern in the 1960s. The potential for this tax was investigated in detail under Labour, but the committee came out against its introduction, partly because of the administrative complexity, partly because of the implications for redistribution. The left had long been hostile to indirect taxes in principle as regressive, and this was why purchase tax was not levied on items like food, where the distributive issues were obviously pronounced. Opposition to distributive taxation remained pronounced in the 1960s, and Conservative advocacy of VAT added to the suspicion that it was a reactionary way of funding expenditure.[57]

Labour opinion generally had a strong but perhaps naïve faith in the redistributive capacity of direct taxation. Expert opinion, on the other hand, clearly recognised its limits. Nicholas Kaldor, Labour's most important tax expert, had based his advocacy of an expenditure tax from the 1950s on the recognition of the limits of direct tax. Partly this was a problem at the top end of the income distribution, where evasion and particularly expenditure out of capital were seen as 'leakages' from the system. The 1965 budget at least partly addressed both of these issues, by tightening rules on business expenses and, much more radically, by introducing corporation tax and extending capital gains tax. But the taxation of wealth remained an important issue throughout Labour's tenure and is returned to below.

Even more of a problem for a simple advocacy of direct taxation as a route to equality was the fall in the income tax threshold. Kaldor highlighted the impact of this trend when he showed how it had rendered income tax decreasingly progressive as the number of payers expanded, from 67 per cent of the working population in 1955/66 to 78 per cent in 1966/67. By this time direct taxation had become broadly proportional in its impact, rather than the progressive instrument it had been in the early post-war years, when a large proportion of the working class was exempted.[58]

In sum, Labour in the 1960s was faced with some extremely difficult tax policy choices. It came to power with a reform agenda, which was largely implemented in 1965, with corporation and capital gains tax. In this early period it also raised income tax and national insurance contributions. In 1966 a new tax was imposed, the SET, which at least offered a fresh source of revenue, if at a considerable administrative and political cost, and much controversy as to its economic effects. These imposts contained the pressures from the rapid growth of expenditure for the moment. But from the time of devaluation, the pressures became much greater and macro-economic policy demanded a combination of deflation and reductions in borrowing, which meant huge tax increases, even if the rise in expenditure was being curtailed. At the same time, criticism of the government's commitment to social justice made redistributive issues more prominent, especially as the government was fighting an uphill battle to make an incomes policy palatable to workers and unions. Furthermore, the slow-down in growth was enhancing political sensitivity to the argument that penal taxation was inhibiting investment and enterprise. These pressures came together around the key budget of 1968, easily the most dramatic since the war.

The 1968 budget, following the January White Paper, imposed the first significant cuts in Labour's expenditure plans. But it also involved a huge rise in taxation, and determining how this was to be distributed required a difficult balancing act. From the beginning of the budget discussions, Jenkins was clear that he wanted a 'simple' budget, because both the Inland Revenue and the City were complaining about the complexity of and the frequent changes to the tax system. He also wanted to make some concessions to high earners, 'preferably at the expense of those with high incomes from capital'. However, while Treasury advice accepted the principle of such concessions, it argued that 1968 would not be a good year in which to make them, because of the generality of tax increases that would be required.[59] Attention therefore focused on trying to get more from those with high incomes from capital. Labour's traditional view of this had been to combine a capital gains tax and higher tax on distributed profits (as legislated for in 1965) with a wealth tax. In 1968 a wealth tax was not ruled out in principle, but it was regarded as both politically inopportune and too complex to introduce without much further work, especially on the tricky issue of the valuation of assets.[60] Instead, a one-off 'special charge' was devised to fall on investment income, again the brainchild of Kaldor, although it was similar to Stafford Cripps' 'special contribution' of 1948. The Inland Revenue was predictably antagonistic, arguing that it would arouse 'great hostility' and be a form of double taxation in addition to that paid under corporation tax. But support came from those like the Chief Secretary to the Treasury, Jack Diamond, who argued that the budget would be 'severely regressive' and that the government needed something 'to induce an acceptance of a very tough budget by demonstrating that the burden is shared'. This demonstration was particularly important given the weight attached by the Chancellor to trying to have an effective incomes policy, and the tax was imposed. However, in voicing his opposition, the Governor of the Bank of England made a powerful point about the likely effectiveness of this attempt to use tax to affect attitudes to wages: 'The problem is not one of striking a single bargain with a central negotiating body for labour, but of carrying through a policy in the face of opposition from some trade unions and of far more widespread resistance at a number of local bargaining points'.[61]

At the other end of the range for direct tax, the Treasury favoured doing something about the income tax threshold. The main proposal on the table was Kaldor's minimum earned income relief, which followed on from his account of the loss of progressiveness in the system as the threshold fell. Under this proposal there would be a fixed-sum allowance (£143) for single people, added to by a relief of two-sevenths of additional personal allowances on account of a wife and child. This would take 900,000 people out of the tax net, but, by being coupled with a small cut in personal allowances, would still yield extra revenue of £136 million. Kaldor's case for this change ran as follows:

> In consequence of devaluation there will have to be a considerable cut in the standard of living of everybody (through the rise in prices or increase in taxation or both) and in the circumstances this is not an unreasonable thing to ask … it would make one important form of welfare payment selective instead of universal, and do it in a way that fully protects the most vulnerable members of the community.

Effectively what Kaldor proposed would have followed up on the 'clawback' process by taking back the whole benefit of family allowances from all families except the poor.[62] As was usual, the Inland Revenue attacked this attempt to use the tax system for a 'social measure', but made the perhaps more telling point that Kaldor's proposal would be administratively complex and hard to understand. As a Treasury paper put it: 'One must not forget that in the real world, a tax clerk in her teens has to be able to explain the tax system to a navvy'. But the fundamental objections to Kaldor's proposal were political. It would hit hardest at the skilled manual and lower-middle-class groups, which was especially dangerous politically as 'the mother would receive the family allowance;

the father would pay for it by an increase in tax on his pay packet'. This
line of argument was supported by the Minister of Social Security, who
highlighted the fact that Kaldor's proposal would favour the poor family
at the expense of better-off families *with children*; politically it would be
acceptable to deny better-off groups any increase in family allowances,
but not to take away what they already received.[63]

Opposition to Kaldor won the day, and in the budget there was no
significant change in income tax. However, one by-product of the discussion was the decision to set up a high-level working group to look at
the prospects for a negative income tax. In proposing this committee,
Jenkins said:

> It seems to me very important that we should devise ways of helping
> those with low incomes selectively but, so far as possible, without
> having to use individual means testing. We are still a long way from
> finding an effective long-term solution to the problems of relative
> poverty.[64]

A negative income tax would, at least in principle, get round all the
problems of overlapping tax and social security systems by going over
to a single assessment of income, and with cash payments to those below
the threshold coming through the tax system. However, the working
group found that this Holy Grail of tax reform was not within reach.
There were insurmountable problems, such as the incompatibility of
the yearly assessments of the income tax system with the weekly pattern
in social security, the difficulties of calculating the income of those outside the tax net without an intrusive means of investigation and, above
all, the fact that 'providing a workable incentive, while guaranteeing a
basic minimum, necessarily involved payments to people already above
that minimum, and was therefore very expensive'.[65]

The 1968 budget put up taxes more than any budget since the war –
by an estimated £923 million. This revenue was raised by: a 50 per cent
increase in the SET (which current advice suggested was indeed improving productivity in the service industries); the special charge; and big
increases in almost all indirect taxes, barring that on beer, which Jenkins
felt had too big an impact on the cost of living.[66] For what seems to
have been the first time, preparation of the budget was informed by a
relatively sophisticated judgement about its effects on the distribution
of income, employing Gini coefficients.[67] The changes to indirect taxation were regressive in effect, and the special charge was progressive,
while the impact of the changes to the SET depended on difficult assessments of who would ultimately pay the extra impost. The progressivity
of the budget as a whole depended primarily on the increased spending
on family allowances (partly offset by prescription charges). But on a

broader front, the overall impact of policy was likely to be mildly regress-ive, given that devaluation would have this effect by shifting income from wages to profits.[68] The evidence suggests that these considerations weighed on the budget judgement, but that the focus on indirect tax, despite its regressive effects, meant priority was being given to raising revenue and avoiding increased income tax. The Chancellor would have liked to have gained greater consent for incomes policy but, as one adviser put it, 'A successful incomes policy was of great importance in demand management, but no substitute for taxation'.[69]

The budget of March 1968 was followed by an emergency budget in November the same year, and then the ordinary budget of 1969. All three followed a deflationary pattern, though the first was by far the most severe. The general pattern of tax changes was similar in each, with indirect axes bearing the main brunt, with some help for those on low incomes from benefit increases. Jenkins expressed a belief in incomes policy as an alternative mechanism to taxation for reducing consumption, but his budgetary measures were not significantly affected by any idea of gaining support for that policy by redistributive measures. Though on a smaller scale, the 1969 increases in tax were probably more regressive than those of 1968, because there was no repeat of the special charge to offset the increases in indirect tax. Again, however, for the budget as a whole this was offset by the increases in benefits.[70]

In defending his policies against TUC criticism, Jenkins argued strongly that the old adage of 'direct taxes good, indirect taxes bad' no longer applied, reviving arguments made by Labour Chancellors in the last years of the Attlee government. Income tax was now paid by most wage earners and indirect taxes were much broader in impact than previously. He pointed out that because many indirect taxes were fixed sum rather than proportional, they tended to fall as a proportion of tax revenue over time, and therefore had to be raised just to keep that share con-stant. He also argued against emphasising capital taxes, because the main aim of current budgetary policy was to restrain consumption, and capital taxes were not very effective for this purpose.[71]

Labour's policies on spending and tax

After the 1970 defeat the impact of Labour's spending and tax policies on the income distribution were hotly disputed. Whiting provides an insightful summary of these arguments, focused on the contributors to Beckerman's *The Labour Government's Economic Record* and the Fabian book *Labour and Inequality*.[72] The first of these encapsulated what was to become the conventional judgement on this government's modernis-ation strategy – that its prime error was to fail to devalue, which had

prevented growth and hence made redistribution much more difficult –
but added that, nevertheless, Labour had done 'better than might be
expected' on redistribution. Allied to this argument was the view that
redistribution was very difficult for Labour because 'the trade union
elements are concerned mainly with the maintenance of income differentials at the lower end of the income range'.[73] However, this judgement
was not based on any evidence as to either the positions taken or the
impact of trade unions on Labour's policies, and that evidence would
seem to support neither the view that all trade unions were keen on
emphasising differentials, or that in doing so they had a big impact on
government policy. Undoubtedly some unions were unambiguously anti-
egalitarian, like Clive Jenkins' Association of Scientific, Technical and
Managerial Staff, but the general stance of the unions was much more
equivocal, and the (voluntary) incomes policy they advocated in 1968
and 1969 was a flat-rate and therefore equalising policy.[74] In any event,
it is far from clear that the trade unions were that powerful in policy
formation; more typical, certainly in the later 1960s, and as suggested
by the 1969 budget, was the government doing what it wanted to do
and then trying to persuade the TUC that this was the right course.[75]

The chapter in the Beckerman collection on the income distribution
shows that Labour's policies did have equalising effects. The incomes
and other policies did not have significant effects on the initial distribution of income, but both tax and spending changes were progressive.
Despite the budgets of 1968 and 1969, the overall pattern between 1964
and 1970 was a shift from indirect to direct taxes, though, as noted
above, while remaining, the progressivity of income taxation was falling
as the threshold fell. Within indirect taxation, the most regressive taxes
(those on tobacco and alcohol) tended to rise more slowly than the more
progressive taxes (on motoring). Tending in the opposite direction was
national insurance, where flat-rate contributions rose only in line with
earnings, but these fell more heavily on low-paid workers.[76] On benefits,
the pattern is also of a growth in equalising effects, in both cash benefits
and benefits in kind. In particular, because it was so much a cause of
contention, it should be noted that while benefit levels did not fully
keep pace with average wages, they rose faster than disposable wages,
that is, after increases in taxes are taken into account.[77] Such figures put
paid to any notion that 'the poor got poorer under Labour', but not, of
course, to the argument that Labour should have done better. Undoubtedly there is force in the argument made by the critics that it was difficult
to discern a 'strategy for equality' under Labour, certainly once it became
clear that the hoped for growth was not going to happen.[78] This disquiet
about the trend in Labour's policies is understandable given the undoubted
ideological retreat in budgetary policy evident, for example, in the 1968
budgetary statement. This included the argument that incentives mattered

not because there was any evidence of their effects, but because people thought they mattered.[79]

No definitive judgement is possible on the outcome of Labour's tax and spending policies for social justice, because there is no agreement on the appropriate benchmark, a point returned to in the broader context of the government's overall performance in the concluding chapter. But a little may be said about the processes of policy-making in this area – how far were they 'modernised'?

First, there was a clear failure to integrate the spending and taxing decisions. While the 1969 Green paper heralded an improvement in the treatment of decision-making on spending, this was still separated from taxation, which remained the closely guarded realm of the budget committee. Jenkins suggested amalgamating the two in 1969, but was resisted.[80] His concern was with the macro-economic aspect, but such joint consideration would have made even more sense in relation to distributional issues, where, as we have seen, the disjuncture made rational decisions hard to take. Part of the obvious overlap here was in the field of tax allowances, but while those for children were avidly discussed, others with major distributional consequences, such as mortgage interest relief, seem to have been wholly unconsidered. This compartmentalisation may in part have reflected the expertise available to the Labour Party. On the one hand were the social welfare experts, who focused attention on encouraging spending, while on the other hand (and better represented in Labour's high policy-making) were the economists, who focused more attention on the effects of taxation and consequential limits on spending.

Second, it may be argued that while the discussion of so many tax and spending issues in the 1960s depended on notions of what the public wanted or would accept, very little attempt was made to look at this issue at all systematically.[81] Policy could thus easily descend into rival unsubstantiated views as to, for example, whether the population really did differentiate between paying national insurance contributions and the generality of tax.

Plainly, taxation and spending in this period were dominated by short-term economic management, which, especially after 1966, made it hard to pursue longer-term policies on either side of the accounts. However, it would be wrong to say that Labour's thinking was entirely 'short-termist': considerable effort went into the investigation of long-term issues such as VAT and a negative income tax, and Labour had a great deal of politically sympathetic tax expertise at its disposal. The problem was that the political mood by the late 1960s made it very hard to initiate further major tax reforms after so much had been changed in 1965 (corporation tax and capital gains tax) and 1966 (the SET).[82] Reform was also not helped by the attitude of the Inland Revenue, which, more than the Treasury, seems to have been a consistent opponent of radical thinking. While, plainly, the Revenue had a legitimate role in highlighting the administrative problems likely to accompany radical changes, it often seems to have played an overtly political role in suggesting what was 'tolerable'.[83] The overall consequence was that the system for dealing with spending and taxing was only slightly 'modernised' by Labour, and that the relation between economic efficiency and social justice was not as well explored as might have been the case, even allowing for the inescapable attention given to pressing macro-economic concerns.

Social justice by other means

Most discussion of social justice in the 1960s focused on spending and tax. But these did not exhaust the agenda. There was considerable interest in a national minimum wage as a method of combating poverty. A working party to look at this issue had been set up by the Conservatives just before Labour came to power. This arose from the same concern with family poverty as the parallel interest in family allowances. The working party issued a report in February 1965, which argued there was 'not a strong case for a national minimum wage' on the grounds that poverty among wage earners was not that prevalent, was most common among large families, and was best dealt with by family allowances.[84]

The issue was revived in 1967, partly because of continuing concerns with poverty, not least because of the evidence in *The Poor and the Poorest* that a significant proportion of poverty was among families that contained a wage earner. This was also at the time when increased family allowances were being fought over as the alternative route to relieving family poverty. Some argued that a national minimum wage would be a necessary *complement* to better family allowances, otherwise there would be a danger of a 'Speenhamland' system of state-subsidised low wages.[85]

A completely different impetus arose from the concerns of the DEA, which saw a minimum wage as a way of reducing the significance of the low-pay criteria in incomes policy while responding to the view that something should be done about low pay. The DEA also suggested that a minimum wage might stimulate higher productivity, but although this argument had a respectable pedigree in the 'efficiency wage' arguments of Alfred Marshall, it figured little in the debates of the 1960s.[86] That debate was dominated by questions of cost. The Treasury summarised its view as follows: 'a national minimum wage would be a clumsy way of trying to relieve poverty and would, on any realistic view as to an acceptable level and as to repercussions on pay above the minimum, represent a serious erosion of our competitive position'. The Treasury was especially concerned because the issue of a minimum wage was entangled with that of equal pay for women. Given the government's commitment, in principle at least, to equality, it was deemed impossible not to have, at least eventually, a common minimum for men and women, but plainly this would add enormously to the cost. After some high-level negotiations the Chancellor successfully fought off Barbara Castle giving any commitment on the minimum wage exactly as he had fought against any promise to implement equal pay.[87]

Most discussion of social justice in the 1960s was about money – about public spending, taxation and wages. But historically in Labour circles the term had wider implications, not least the distribution of power. While never a prominent issue, this concern did surface a little in the 1960s, in the guise of a debate about industrial democracy. Industrial democracy is an ambiguous term, and in particular can be deployed in a managerialist context in pursuit of efficiency goals (normally in the form of the extension of consultative procedures – see Chapter 8), as well as in pursuit of notions of social justice and greater equality within the enterprise. Within the latter perspective, there is, in turn, a divide between those who see it as requiring new democratic structures within the enterprise ('workers on the board') and those who see it as an extension of existing collective bargaining arrangements. By and large, it was this second version which found some favour with the government in the 1960s.

A Labour Party working group on the issue led to a statement by the National Executive Committee at the 1968 conference, which called for action 'to extend democracy in industry, not by evolving new and complex (and perhaps alien) structures, but by gradually increasing involvement in a development of existing machinery – which is already known and used because it deals with fundamental questions like pay and conditions'.[88] This was the classic 'single channel of representation' argument, which had been decisive in the discussion of joint production committees, promoted in the name of increased productivity. There were signs that the TUC was moving away from this towards a greater willingness to consider West German-style co-determination (undoubtedly the 'alien' structure of the National Executive Committee's statement). The TUC's evidence to the Donovan Commission had called for permissive legislation on worker representatives on boards of directors of private companies. This sympathy with co-determination was not shared by the government (though it was willing to discuss possible representation on the boards of nationalised industries), and its ideas were firmly of the 'extension of collective bargaining' kind.[89] But even on this, the Industrial Relations Bill did not go so far as conceding a key union demand for a right to specific information about company policies and intentions, but included only a general obligation on companies to provide information. The unions were particularly concerned about being consulted on intended mergers, but this was not seriously considered.[90] Overall, while the government strengthened the unions' position in some respects, for example over unfair dismissal, there was never any likelihood that the existing structure of power in the corporations would be challenged in the name of 'social justice'.

Notes

The place of publication is London unless otherwise specified.

1 J. Tomlinson, 'Economic policy', in D. Tanner, P. Thane and N. Tiratsoo (eds), *Labour's First Century* (Cambridge, 2000), pp. 46–79. Gaitskell, for example, argued that the party's aims were 'full employment, high productivity and social justice': H. Gaitskell, 'The economic aims of the Labour Party', *Political Quarterly*, 24 (1953), p. 6.

2 *The National Plan*, Cmnd 2764, BPP 1964/65, vol. 30, p. 1; Gaitskell, 'Economic aims', p. 6.

3 A. W. Wright, *R. H. Tawney* (Manchester, 1987), ch. 5.

4 *Ibid.*, p. 67; R. H. Tawney, *Equality* (5th edn) (1964), part iv, 'The strategy of equality'.

5 A. Crosland, *The Future of Socialism* (1956), ch. 9; B. Hindess, *Freedom, Equality and the Market* (1987), chs 1, 6; Labour Party, *Signposts for the Sixties* (1961), p. 8.

6 D. Jay, *Socialism in the New Society* (1962), p. 22; J. Barnett, 'The budget and after', *Socialist Commentary*, May 1969, cited in R. Whiting, *The Labour Party and Taxation* (Cambridge, 2000), p. 210.

7 J. Tomlinson, *Democratic Socialism and Economic Policy: The Attlee Years, 1945–51* (Cambridge, 1997), pp. 265–8; R. Lowe, *The Welfare State in Britain Since 1945* (1993), pp. 11–12, 292; Crosland, *Future*, p. 148.

8 Labour Party, *Let Us Face the Future* (1945), pp. 9–12.

9 *National Plan*, pp. 15–16.

10 Conservative policies would have involved a growth rate of 4.4 per cent down to 1968/69 – see PRO, T 320/93, 'Public Expenditure Survey Committee: preparation of revised report', October 1964; B. Abel-Smith, *Labour's Social Plans*, Fabian Tract 369 (1966), p. 6.

11 J. Tomlinson, 'The "economics of politics" and public expenditure', *Economy and Society*, 10 (1981), pp. 383–402.

12 P. Townsend and N. Bosanquet (eds), *Labour and Inequality* (1972); N. Timmins, *The Five Giants: A Biography of the Welfare State* (1996), chs 12, 13; K. Banting, *Poverty, Politics and Policy: Britain in the 1960s* (1979).

13 T. Bale, *Sacred Cows and Common Sense: The Symbolic Statecraft and Political Culture of the British Labour Party* (Aldershot, 1999). In the light of subsequent events, it may be noted that the limited size and slow speed of implementation of these benefit improvements was attacked in the House of Commons by M. Thatcher and K. Joseph: see *Hansard* (Commons), vol. 702, 20 November 1964, cols 679–85.

14 PRO, CAB 134/2534, Ministerial Committee on Social Services, 'Notes on income guarantee scheme', 4 December 1964.

15 PRO, PREM 13/1209, 'A reappraisal of social policy', 22 December 1965; PREM 13/1835, D. Houghton to H. Wilson, 'Social security benefits and income guarantee', 23 July 1965.

16 Lowe, *Welfare State*, pp. 143–5.
17 *Ibid.*, pp. 135–41.
18 For example, PRO, T 227/2227, P. Herbison to J. Callaghan, 8 February 1966, and D. Houghton to J. Callaghan, 16 March 1966.
19 PRO, T 227/2227, P. Herbison to J. Callaghan, 8 February 1966.
20 PRO, T 227/2227, J. Callaghan to P. Herbison, 25 February 1966.
21 PRO, T 227/2454, P. Herbison, 'Social services development to 1970', 14 June 1966.
22 PRO, T 227/2454, J. Marshall, 'Social services development to 1970', 21 June 1966.
23 PRO, T 227/2227, A. Johnston to T. Balogh, 15 March 1966, and J. Rampton, 'Reappraisal of social policy', 21 March 1966; PRO, PREM 13/2396, T. Balogh to H. Wilson, 2 March 1967; *Public Expenditure: Planning and Control*, Cmnd 2915, BPP 1965/66, vol. 13 (February 1966), para. 54.
24 PRO, CAB 128/42, 'Cabinet conclusions', 23 February 1967; PRO, PREM 13/2396, B. Trend to H. Wilson, 'Family endowment', 13 March 1967.
25 PRO, CAB 128/42, 'Cabinet conclusions', 13 and 17 July 1967. Herbison resigned in protest at the scale of the family allowance increase. CAB 129/31, Chancellor of the Exchequer, 'The economic implications of public expenditure', 19 June 1967; *Public Expenditure: A New Presentation*, Cmnd 4017, BPP 1968/69, vol. 53 (April 1969).
26 PRO, CAB 128/42, 'Cabinet conclusions', 20 July 1967.
27 L. Pliatzky, *Getting and Spending: Public Expenditure, Employment and Inflation* (Oxford, 1982), p. 80.
28 PRO, CAB 134/3208, 'Public expenditure and health and social security policy', December 1968; R. Price, 'Public expenditure', in F. Blackaby (ed.), *British Economic Policy 1960–74* (Cambridge, 1978), p. 112; PRO, CAB 134/3208, 'Housing performance and public expenditure', 4 December 1968.
29 Price, 'Public expenditure', pp. 113–15.
30 Pliatzky, *Getting and Spending*, p. 85; *Public Expenditure: 1968/9 and 1969/70*, Cmnd 3515, BPP 1967/68, vol. 39 (January 1968).
31 PRO, CAB 129/135, First Secretary to Treasury, 'Public expenditure: post-devaluation social security consequences', 3 January 1968, and 'Public expenditure post-devaluation: postponement of RoSLA', 3 January 1968; Bale, *Sacred Cows*.
32 PRO, T 171/829, Budget papers, 1968: for example, compare A. Cairncross to W. Armstrong, 'The size of the package', 18 January 1968, with K. Berrill to W. Armstrong, 'Scale of possible tax changes', 23 January 1968.
33 PRO, CAB 129/135, Chancellor of the Exchequer, 'Public expenditure: post-devaluation measures', 3 January 1967; CAB 128/43, 'Cabinet conclusions', 4–15 January 1968.
34 PRO, CAB 128/43, 'Cabinet conclusions', 23 February 1968; Banting, *Poverty*, p. 103.
35 PRO, CAB 128/43, 'Cabinet conclusions', 15 January 1968; budget debate in *Hansard* (Commons), vol. 761, 19 March 1968, cols 266–9.
36 *Public Expenditure*.
37 Price, 'Public expenditure', p. 116; S. Goldman, *The Developing System of Public Expenditure Management and Control* (1973); Pliatzky, *Getting and Spending*, notes that MinTech, faced with pressures on its budget, tried to get investment grants categorised as 'negative expenditure'.
38 PRO, CAB 134/3208, 'Education expenditure', 5 December 1968, 'Public expenditure and health and social security policy', 5 December 1968, and 'Housing performance and public expenditure', 4 December 1968; CAB

134/3204, for example, Chancellor of the Exchequer, 'Public expenditure: 1968/69', 24 June 1968.

39 *Public Expenditure: 1968/9 to 1970/1*, Cmnd 3936, BPP 1968/69, vol. 53 (February 1968).

40 *Public Expenditure 1968/9–1973/4*, Cmnd 4234, BPP 1969/70, vol. 21, p. 9.

41 PRO, T 227/2636, 'Review to co-ordinate the government's policies and priorities for the social services', 1967/68; T 230/948, 'Ministerial Committee on Social Services: briefs and correspondence 1968'. For roads as social welfare, see PRO, CAB 134/3048, Chancellor, 'Public expenditure to 1970', 4 January 1967; PRO, T 230/948, J. Carr, 'Financing of social security', 2 April 1968.

42 A study in the late 1960s identified at least fourteen separate means tests currently in use. PRO, T 328/318, 'Working Group on Negative Income Tax meeting', 14 June 1968.

43 A paradox of the failure to introduce an income guarantee was that this was the only social programme that the 1964 manifesto had *not* made conditional on economic performance; M. Stewart, 'The distribution of income', in W. Beckerman (ed.), *The Labour Government's Economic Record 1964–1970* (1972), pp. 99–101.

44 The proposal on superannuation which was eventually agreed in 1969 would have given an inflation-proofed pension of at least half average wages.

45 PRO, T 331/540, A. Wiggins, '1969 PESC Survey: performance indicators', 30 May 1969; R. Middleton, *Government Versus the Market* (Cheltenham, 1996), pp. 118, 506.

46 PRO, T 331/540, A. Langdon, 'Health and welfare: NHS', 30 May 1969; Timmins, *Five Giants*, pp. 217–25.

47 One argument against implementation of RoSLA was its effects in reducing the labour supply – PRO, CAB 129/135, First Secretary to Treasury, 'Postponement of RoSLA', 3 January 1968. The distributional aspects of expenditure on education is explored by H. Glennerster, 'Education and inequality', in Townsend and Bosanquet, *Inequality*, pp. 83–197. Labour had discussed introducing student grants to replace loans, which would have at least partly changed this effect, but this had not been implemented: see PRO, T 230/948, J. Carr, 'Financing of social services', 2 April 1968.

48 M. Daunton, 'A sort of tax prison', in M. Francis and I. Zweiniger-Bargielowska (eds), *The Conservatives and British Society 1880–1990* (Cardiff, 1996). There is a detailed account of the Labour Party's approach to taxation in this period in R. Whiting, *Labour Party*, chs 3, 4.

49 PRO, T 230/948, R. Workman, 'Social Services Committee', 14 March 1968.

50 H. Pemberton, 'A taxing task: combating Britain's relative decline in the 1960s', *Twentieth Century British History*, 12 (2001), pp. 354–75.

51 As noted in Chapter 6 in the context of discussions of the 'brain drain', enquiries found no evidence that tax was an important element in explaining this phenomenon. Application for entry to the EEC made comparisons with Western Europe more pertinent.

52 Whiting, *Labour Party*, p. 186.

53 *Ibid.*, pp. 159–68.

54 *Ibid.*, ch. 3; Tomlinson, *Democratic Socialism*, p. 276.

55 PRO, T 227/2592, 'Social survey on attitudes to national insurance contributions', June–August 1968.

56 PRO, PREM 13/1835, H. Wilson, comments on 'Report of Committee on Social Security', December 1965, and T. Balogh to H. Wilson, 13 December 1965; PREM 13/1033, N. Kaldor, 'Employers' national insurance contributions',

18 November 1966; PRO, T 171/832, 'Report of the Chief Secretary's Committee on value-added tax questions', 1967.
57 PRO, T 171/832, 'Chief Secretary's report'; Whiting, *Labour Party*, pp. 201–5.
58 PRO, T 171/831, N. Kaldor, 'Minimum earnings income relief', 26 January 1968. It is interesting to note that the discussions of the 1960s do not seem to have taken on board Richard Titmuss's argument in his *Income Distribution and Social Change* (1962) about the regressive effects of tax allowances, these allowances being little discussed except in the context of the switch from allowances to grants in the attempt to encourage investment.
59 PRO, T 171/829, Chancellor of the Exchequer, 'Meeting with A. Johnston and P. Baldwin', 1 December 1967, 'Meeting with Chief Secretary and Financial Secretary', 19 December 1967, and Treasury, 'Direct taxation: main possibilities', 19 January 1968.
60 Whiting, *Labour Party*, pp. 189–95; PRO, T 171/832, H. Lever to R. Jenkins, 5 March 1968.
61 PRO, T 171/832, A. Johnston, 'Dividend surcharge', 26 February 1968, J. Diamond, 'Investment income: surtax charge', 26 February 1968, and L. O'Brien, 'Special contribution', 5 March 1968.
62 PRO, T 171/831, N. Kaldor to Chancellor of the Exchequer, 'Minimum earnings income relief', 26 January 1968, and N. Kaldor, 'Family allowances', 17 November 1967.
63 PRO, T 171/829, 'Chancellor's meeting with Johnston and Baldwin', 1 December 1967, and Treasury, 'Direct taxation: main proposals', 19 January 1968; T 171/832, Inland Revenue, 'Family allowances', 20 December 1967.
64 *Hansard* (Commons), vol. 761, 19 March 1968, col. 278; PRO, PREM 13/2027, R. Jenkins to H. Wilson, 8 January 1968; PRO, T 328/318, 'Working Group on Negative Income Tax', 1968.
65 PRO, T 328/318, 'Working Group meeting', 21 June 1968.
66 Budget statement, *Hansard* (Commons), vol. 761, 19 March 1968, cols 251–301. The view of the SET was affected by evidence from the Ministry of Labour that labour shedding in the service sector was faster than could be explained by anything other than the tax: PRO, T 171/832, A. Cairncross, 'SET and changes in employment 1966/7', 14 February 1968 – he argued that the onus of proof on the effects of the tax had now shifted to the sceptics.
67 A Gini coefficient measures how far the income distribution is from absolute equality (equal to zero) and complete inequality (i.e., where all income is received by one unit) (equal to 100 per cent). The data for such calculations were derived from the Family Expenditure Survey, and a summary of the distributional effects of government policy was published in *Economic Trends*. (The 1968 results were published as 'The incidence of taxes and social service benefits in 1968', *Economic Trends*, 196 (1970), pp. 16–46.) PRO, T 171/829, J. Nicholson, 'The redistributive effects of the budget', 15 March 1968.
68 PRO, T 171/829, J. Nicholson, 'The redistributive effects of the budget', 25 March 1968.
69 PRO, T 171/829, D. Hubback to S. Goldman, 11 March 1968.
70 Whiting, *Labour Party*, p. 210; PRO, T 171/839, F. Butler, 'Effects of possible budget decisions on Gini coefficient of income inequality', 7 March 1969, and F. Butler, 'Briefing for the budget debate: effects of the budget on income distribution', 2 April 1969.
71 PRO, T 171/848, 'Chancellor of the Exchequer's meeting with the TUC', 16 December 1968.
72 Whiting, *Labour Party*, pp. 179–90; Beckerman, *Labour Government's Economic Record*; Townsend and Bosanquet, *Labour and Inequality*.

73 W. Beckerman, 'Objectives and performance', in Beckerman, *Labour Government's Economic Record*, p. 41.

74 Clive Jenkins of the Association of Scientific, Technical and Managerial Staff campaigned vociferously against incomes policy on the grounds that it would reduce differentials: see C. Wrigley, 'From ASSET to ASTMS: an example of white-collar union growth in the 1960s', *Historical Studies in Industrial Relations*, 7 (1999), pp. 55–74; TUC, *Economic Review 1968* (1968) and *Economic Review 1969* (1969).

75 TUC, *Economic Review 1969*, p. 6.

76 Stewart, 'Distribution of income', pp. 86–98.

77 *Ibid.*, pp. 98–106.

78 Whiting, *Labour Party*, p. 183.

79 *Hansard* (Commons), vol. 761, 19 March 1968, cols 276–7. Jenkins was strong in telling his colleagues that 'Government policy in recent years has resulted in a shift of resources from the private sector to social purposes at a rate faster than the growth of the economy could sustain': PRO, CAB 134/2201, 'Economic Policy Committee meeting', 12 June 1968.

80 R. Jenkins, *A Life at the Centre* (1991), p. 230; Goldman, *Developing System*, pp. 32–3.

81 PRO, T 227/2592, 'Social survey on attitude to NI contributions', 1968. The general lack of empirical knowledge was clear to policy-makers at the time, though there had been small-scale surveys, such as that in Glasgow in 1967 into marginal rates of tax, from which the conclusion was that 'If this sample was typical it points to a nation which substantially over-estimates its tax burden and consequently underestimates the rewards of working harder': PRO, T 171/839, W. Pattinson, 'Personal taxation and incentives', 8 April 1969.

82 *Hansard* (Commons), vol. 761, 19 March 1968, cols 273–4.

83 PRO, T 171/831, N. Kaldor, 'Family allowances', 2 January 1968. Kaldor argued that 'The Revenue's objections to restricting any reduction in the personal allowances only to families who benefit from the family allowances are entirely political and ideological, not administrative or technical'. The legitimacy of tax bureaucrats resisting innovation is as old as the story of modern tax systems – see M. Daunton, *Trusting Leviathan: The Politics of Taxation in Britain, 1799–1914* (Cambridge, 2001), pp. 16–18.

84 PRO, T 227/2092, 'Inter-Departmental Working Party on National Minimum Wage', 1964/65.

85 PRO, T 328/327, R. Workman, 'A national minimum wage', 10 September 1968. The Speenhamland system, introduced in 1794, provided for 'outdoor relief' (i.e. subsidies) to those on low wages.

86 PRO, T 227/2719, 'Second Inter-Departmental Working Party on a National Minimum Wage', 1967/68.

87 PRO, T 328/327, R. Workman, 'A national minimum wage', 10 September 1968, and R. Jenkins to B. Castle, 13 September 1968. For an appreciation of the interplay of the policy concerns surrounding a national minimum wage, see PRO, PREM 13/2031, A. Graham, 'A national minimum wage', 18 September 1968.

88 LPA, 'Industrial Democracy Working Party', 1966/67, especially 'Draft report' Re 98, February 1967; LPA, Re 314, 'Industrial democracy – a statement by the NEC', July 1968. On this issue see Steve Fielding's companion volume.

89 TUC, 'Evidence to Royal Commission', June 1967, included in PRO, LAB 43/538, 'Discussions with TUC on Donovan', 1968/69; LAB 43/558, 'Industrial democracy', B. Castle to P. Shore, 15 January 1970.

90 PRO, LAB 43/558, 'Industrial democracy'.

10
Conclusions:
outcomes and constraints

Harold Wilson famously said that 'a week is a long time in politics', but six years is a short time in the history of economic policy. In a small open economy like that of Britain in the 1960s, faced with a range of both external and domestic constraints on its actions, the capacity of any government to change much in such a short period of time is small. Any judgements made about Labour's policies must have these constraints very firmly in mind. This chapter provides a summary of the outcomes of Labour's economic policies, and this is followed by a discussion of the constraints on those policies. The conclusions offered are necessarily tentative.

Outcomes and assessments

The summary statistics of macro-economic performance are given in Table 10.1. Isolating Labour's years in government from long-run trends can be highly misleading, especially as these figure obscure the cyclical behaviour of the economy (see Table 10.5). Nevertheless, such numbers give us a starting point for looking at each of these outcomes.

Historically Labour has, of course, given a high priority to low unemployment, and for many the clear upward shift in this figure in 1967 was a major disappointment. The precise causes of this cannot be stated, but the answer must be part macro- and part micro-economic. On the macro side (see Chapter 3) there was the deflationary package of July 1966, though however important this was politically, in economic terms it was relatively mild.[1] On the micro side (see Chapter 6) there was the 'shake-out' of labour that was the deliberate purpose of both the RPA and the SET. Also perhaps important was the government-encouraged merger boom and drive for increased productivity, both of which promoted 'rationalisation' of the labour force. Insofar as the increase in unemployment was limited to short-term idleness, and cushioned by earnings-related unemployment benefit, then the welfare consequences

Table 10.1 Macro-economic outcomes, 1964–70

	Unemployment (%) (claimant count)	Inflation (%) (RPI)	Balance of payments (current account/ GDP)[a]	Growth (%) (GDP)
1964	2.6	3.2	(1.1)[b]	5.4
1965	1.5	4.8	(0.2)	2.3
1966	1.6	4.0	0.3	2.0
1967	2.5	2.5	(0.7)	2.3
1968	2.5	4.7	(0.6)	4.1
1969	2.5	5.5	1.0	1.8
1970	2.7	6.4	1.6	2.3

[a] Note that these figures cannot be easily reconciled with those in Table 1.1, which are based on 1971 data, since amended.
[b] Figures in parentheses indicate a deficit.
RPI, retail price index; GDP, gross domestic product.
Source: *Economic Trends Annual Supplement* (various years).

Table 10.2 The character of unemployment, 1964–70

	Total number unemployed (1,000s) Male & female	Number unemployed for over 6 months (1,000s) Male & female	Male	Percentage unemployed for over 6 months Male & female
1964	308	107	89	35
1965	272	85	72	31
1966	256	76	64	30
1967	469	137	118	29
1968	502	159	142	32
1969	501	158	143	32
1970	549	168	152	31

Source: J. Baxter, 'Long-term unemployment in Great Britain 1953–71', *Bulletin of the Oxford University Institute of Economics and Statistics*, 34 (1972), pp. 330–2.

for those involved might be thought small – and the possible benefits in terms of structural changes and lower inflationary pressure 'a price worth paying'. Table 10.2 gives some sense of the character of the unemployment. Long-term unemployment did increase, chiefly among men, especially older men, but not as a proportion of total unemployment. This bias against older workers, as noted in Chapter 6, was one of the unintended consequences of the RPA.

Table 10.3 Decline in employment in 'traditional industries',
1964–69

Industry	Decline in employment
Coalmining	208,000
Agriculture, forestry and fishing	134,000
Railways	128,000
Textiles and clothing	123,000
Metal manufacturing	43,000
Ports and waterways	21,000
Shipbuilding	20,000
Total	677,000
Total for same industries 1959–64	466,000

Source: *Hansard* (Commons), vol. 801, 6 May 1970, col. 432.

It would seem to be clear that the structural change that was occurring
was hitting particularly hard at male manual employment in traditional
occupations, while being relatively favourable to sectors such as education, health and welfare, where women were more strongly represented.[2]
What seems to have occurred in the mid-1960s is a coincidence of a
short-term 'shake-out' with the accentuation of a long-term trend towards
fewer people being employed in 'basic' industry, so that in retrospect it
is clear that Labour presided over a historic turning point in the labour
market, with industrial employment never to reach the same level again.[3]
Table 10.3 gives the figures for the decline in 'traditional industries'
between 1964 and 1969, and shows how rapid structural change was in
these years.

The figures show that the Labour government was allowing an accelerated rundown of the workforce in the big nationalised corporations,
but was also facing a decline in sectors such as metal manufacturing,
which was much more at odds with its intention of giving priority to
manufacturing. Finally, it should be emphasised that Labour was successful in constraining the rise in unemployment in 'the regions'. The northern
region lost 45 per cent of its coalmining jobs over 1964–69 and 39 per
cent of its railway jobs, and Wales 40 and 43 per cent respectively, but
the regional differential in unemployment rates declined.

While not figuring in the traditional lists of macro-economic objectives, Labour was, in the qualified way discussed in Chapter 9, concerned
with equality. After the mid-1970s, the rise in unemployment was to be
a major cause of the reversal of the long-run post-war trend to greater
equality. But the unemployment increase of the 1960s was too small in
its impact on the labour market to have any such radical effects on the

distribution of income, and Labour cushioned the effects directly on the unemployed by the earnings-related supplement. Overall, as suggested in Chapter 9, equality increased a little under Labour, particularly as benefits rose faster than post-tax wages.[4]

To critics of the government like Hugh Scanlon, its policies had failed to embody the 'simple, straightforward socialist belief of ensuring that less of the gross national product goes in rent, interest and profits and more goes in wages and salaries'. Of course, for the government the problem was to combine such a distributional goal with the desire to see investment increase; such a combination had been one purpose of the corporation tax, with its aim of increasing the proportion of profits reinvested. The evidence suggests that Labour did deliver such a redistribution, though any calculation is complicated by the rise in self-employment, which seems to have been another unintended consequence of the SET.[5]

Inflation rose under Labour, 1967 being the first year of an upward trend that was to last until 1975. The simultaneous rise in unemployment and inflation suggests the breakdown of the traditional Phillips curve relationship, in which, at the margin, higher inflation could be traded off against lower unemployment. The causes of this may have been partly the devaluation, with its impact on import prices (which rose by 11 per cent in 1968) and the failure of Labour to find an effective incomes policy to prevent these higher prices passing on into wages. But purely national explanations seem inadequate to explain this upward movement in inflation, because it was found not only in Britain but across Western Europe. Part of the explanation may lie in the international consequences of US inflationary policies, which, under the system of fixed exchange rates, tended to impact on all other countries. In Britain, as on the Continent, the late 1960s saw an upsurge of industrial militancy that has been linked by some to a generational change in workers' expectations, as the experience of full employment eroded worries about the employment consequences of wage pressure. With governments, including Labour in Britain, unwilling to respond to wage pressure with even sharper deflationary policies, this upsurge, too, had an inflationary effect.[6]

On the balance of payments the figures show that the current account improved markedly after 1964, with a surplus in 1966. This improvement, it should be noted, occurred in the period before the 'big' deflation of July 1966, helped by the import surcharge of November 1964. However, this improvement was reversed in 1967 and a further loss of confidence in that year culminated in devaluation. A paradox of the period is that Labour was stimulated into tough action on the balance of payments only *after* devaluation, with further military cutbacks, the withdrawal from east of Suez and the imposition of a tight ceiling on aid. Likewise, it was only after devaluation that effective steps were taken to stabilise the sterling balances held overseas, by entering into the Basle agreements. This sequence at least raises the question of whether, had these measures been taken earlier, the devaluation could have been avoided. It is impossible to answer this definitively, not least because so much would have depended on the impact of such policy decisions on international confidence; but such measures would have suggested a commitment to cutting the coat to suit the cloth, which international opinion seems to have regarded as crucial to the pound's position. This question seems more interesting than the one that is usually posed, as to whether an earlier devaluation (in 1964, or perhaps 1966 or 1967) would have allowed the much faster growth rate that Labour so much desired. The issue of the feasible growth rate is returned to below, but this traditional question about the timing of devaluation needs first to be addressed.

The belief that an earlier devaluation would have made all the difference to Labour's success is evident in a variety of commentators. A. Mitchell and D. Wienir reiterate a traditional 'leftish' position that sees the unwillingness to devalue as evidence of Labour's inability to give the 'real' economy priority over finance, one of the standard themes of writing on this government, whose wider ramifications is returned to in the discussion of 'constraints' below.[7] From a different ideological perspective comes the all-knowing work of Edmund Dell, who argues that a better-performing Treasury should have fought for devaluation against ministerial obstinacy.[8] A more interesting view comes from the 'insider' authors of the introduction to the Beckerman collection, who argue that 'Those who assert that the pound should have been devalued in 1964 know their economics but not their politics'.[9]

Taking this last perspective, we can ask whether the economic arguments were so clear-cut? First, plainly, the current account deficit of 1964 was substantial (though exaggerated by contemporary data) but not necessarily evidence of that 'fundamental disequilibrium' that the IMF believed was necessary to justify devaluation. The Tories' pre-election boom had plainly over-heated the economy, but the mild deflationary measures taken by Labour in 1964 and 1965, plus the import surcharge, led to a marked improvement by early 1966. Second, the data show no clear, strong trend in the deterioration of British trade competitiveness that would require devaluation.[10] Third, as emphasised in Chapter 1, while the current account was part of the problem, a large part of the overall balance of payments difficulty (and what made the pound so open to speculative pressure) was the non-commercial side, plus capital exports, where actions other than devaluation would have been appropriate.[11] The complexity of this economic evidence suggests the reasons why the government's economic advisers were split over the issue.

Table 10.4 The National Plan: targets and out-turn (percentage growth, 1964–70, constant prices)

	Plan	Out-turn	Ratio (Plan/out-turn)[a]
Personal consumption	21	12	0.59
Public consumption	19	11	0.61
Gross fixed investment	38	20	0.53
Exports	36	42	1.17
Imports	26	29	1.12
Gross national product (market prices)	25	14	0.55

[a] Note that small arithmetical errors seem to have crept into some of the calculations.
Source: M. Surrey, 'The National Plan in retrospect', *Bulletin of the Oxford University Institute of Economics and Statistics*, 34 (1972), pp. 249–68.

On the political side, the predominant reasons why devaluation was rejected in 1964 have already been noted in Chapter 3. Perhaps the most compelling was that it would require deflation to shift resources into export industries, and this would have been an extraordinarily hard policy for a new Labour government to pursue. But also very important was the desire to sustain the stability of the international financial system, a goal obviously pressed on the British by the Americans, but hardly an issue that the managers of such an open economy could be indifferent to in their own interests.

One reason that so much emphasis has been put on the perceived constraining effects of devaluation is, of course, the failure of Labour to accelerate the growth rate.[12] Nothing has encouraged the 'what went wrong' approach to this government more than the falling short of the targets set out in the National Plan. The scale of this shortfall is indicated in Table 10.4.

There is no gainsaying this failure, but it must be noted that these figures are complicated by the fact that they ignore the cyclical behaviour of the economy. Table 10.5 shows growth rates between cyclical peaks. Taking first GDP growth, we can see how this slowed in Labour's early years as the Tory boom was reined back, but held on a steady course after devaluation as the increase in exports provided an expansionary force. Growth was clearly slower than under the Conservatives' last years, but the expansion of 1960–64 was clearly at an unsustainable rate, given its balance of payments consequences. The figures for GDP per person-year suggest an acceleration in productivity in the mid-1960s, diverging from the GDP figures because of the 'shake-out' of labour that occurred after 1966. The productivity trends are particularly

Table 10.5 Annual percentage growth in gross domestic product
(GDP) between cyclical peaks, 1951–73

Period	GDP	GDP per person-year
1951–55	2.8	2.0
1955–60	2.5	2.1
1960–64	3.4	2.7
1964–68	2.6	2.8
1968–73	2.6	2.5

Source: R. Matthews, C. Feinstein and J. Odling-Smee, *British Economic Growth 1856–1973* (Oxford, 1982), p. 25.

difficult to assess. Partly this is because of the cyclical aspect, with productivity normally tending to rise fastest when output is growing quickly, but the figures for the 1960s suggest that this relationship was breaking down. Short-term productivity figures are therefore especially unreliable.[13]

As the National Plan suggested, an upward trend in the productivity level was evident from the mid-1950s. But the Plan seems to have exaggerated the speed of this acceleration, so that its starting point was over-optimistic, and its hope about what could be achieved in the Plan period even more so. Surrey estimates that the actual rate of increase in productivity was about 2.75 per cent per annum at the beginning of the Plan period, rising on *trend* to about 2.9 per cent by 1970. But, he suggests, once the beneficial effects of the shake-out of 1966/67 had been absorbed, the low pressure of demand depressed the actual rate for the Plan period to 2.5 per cent.[14] Because of the SET, there was a particular contemporary focus on productivity behaviour in the 1960s. These debates showed the difficulty of determining the precise effects of the SET, but did support the idea of some acceleration in the increase in the mid-1960s, especially in manufacturing. Of course, this improvement was not unambiguously favourable, given that fewer people were actually working in manufacturing. Higher productivity regardless of output and employment levels is not a sensible measure of economic success. Equally, productivity needs to be linked to trends in working hours, which saw a sharp cut in the 1960s, as a result of both a reduction in the length of the working week and longer holidays – obviously an important way in which the populace wanted to benefit from higher productivity.[15]

Finally on the productivity data, it is worth noting the consequence of the labour-shedding summarised in Table 10.3. Two of the biggest drops in employment were in the nationalised industries, coalmining and railways, continuing trends from the 1950s. The government did little to slow this process, but focused its attention on trying to cushion its effects by finding alternative employment for redundant workers. This suggests that any general condemnation of 1950s and 1960s 'supply-side' policies for propping up declining industries, as voiced by Crafts, needs to be qualified.[16] The main case of such propping up under Labour was shipbuilding, which was a relatively small industry compared with the shrinking giants of coal and railways, and also a case where decline was not so obviously irreversible. The rapid shedding of labour in the nationalised industries as a whole, without proportional reductions in output, boosted the (labour) productivity record of the nationalised sector, so that its productivity record was superior to that of manufacturing in the period.[17]

Constraints

It would be perverse to claim that economic performance could not have been better under the Wilson governments of 1964–70. But in much of the literature the declinist tradition in general British historiography has been combined with politically hostile accounts of the Labour administration to suggest that policy-makers, if only they had applied the right nostrums, could have done very much better. No precise quantitative assessment of what was possible can be given, but a useful perspective can be obtained by looking at the constraints on policy.

Because so much of the negative assessment of British performance (especially on growth) derives from unfavourable comparisons with what was happening in Continental Europe, it is useful to begin with the convergence literature. This notes that Britain started the 1950s as the richest large economy in Western Europe, and that the rapid growth rates of France, Italy and West Germany over the next two decades meant that they were catching up with Britain. There is, in fact, a very good inverse relationship between the absolute level of income per head attained by a country in 1950 and its subsequent growth rate.[18] This does not, of course, mean that Britain could not have grown faster, but it does suggest that there were quite tight limits on growth, and that there was a limited amount that any kind of government policy could achieve.

Part of a plausible explanation for this convergence process would be the capacity of Continental Europe to contract its low-productivity agriculture and thereby to provide low-cost labour to industry, boosting average productivity, keeping wage pressure low and investment high. This explanation was known in the 1960s, and indeed was central to Nicholas Kaldor's ideas that lay behind the SET.[19] It is, however, a controversial argument. It may be that the switch from agriculture simply yields benefits from the reallocation of labour from low- to high-productivity sectors, whereas Kaldor's argument went much beyond this, in suggesting that manufacturing is the key dynamic sector, where economies of scale yield sustained improvements in efficiency. Sceptics suggest that this analysis conflates the particularities of Continental European 'super-growth' in the 1950s and 1960s with universal truths about what fuels economic expansion.[20] Whatever the truth of these arguments, it may be doubted whether any device, however ingenious, could substitute for this unique historical process of urbanisation. No government could conjure up the benefits of this process a second time, Britain having enjoyed them previously with the great contraction in agricultural employment of the late nineteenth century.

In most discussions of this government's growth and productivity record, the assumption is made that an earlier devaluation would have enabled more expansionary policies, and hence faster growth. As already noted, an initial problem with this hypothesis is that devaluation and defla-tion were not alternatives but complements: as events after November 1967 showed, if devaluation is to work it needs accompanying 'expenditure-switching' policies for a considerable period. But there is a bigger issue here: was growth really constrained by the balance of payments problem in the 1960s, or does the chain of causation run the other way, with better growth performance the cause of balance of payments improve-ment? One piece of evidence is the geographical and commodity pattern of Britain's trade, analysis of which suggests that British exports were not especially ill-favoured by being focused on slow-growing markets or commodities. In particular, there is no compelling evidence that Britain was locked into 'fragmented' imperial markets, to its competitive detri-ment.[21] In other words, Britain was losing export share because of relatively slow growth at home, not vice versa.

The hypothesis that an early devaluation would have aided growth is part of a broader argument that 'stop–go' policies were the major inhi-bition on Britain's growth in the 1950s and 1960s, above all by inhibiting investment. Aside from any scepticism about the significance of 'stop–go', the investment figures sound a note of caution about this argument. As suggested in Chapter 5, the adverse comparisons made with Euro-pean levels of investment need disaggregation. Table 10.6 suggests that Britain's deficiencies in comparative investment levels were not in the 'machinery and equipment' sector, which is what is suggested by both contemporary and retrospective accounts of Britain's industrial failings. Of course, the machinery and equipment data do not relate solely to manufacturing, where most attention has been focused, but include such areas as electricity generating capacity, which was certainly important in the 1960s. Nevertheless, the picture of a manufacturing sector starved of investment is also challenged by Panic's comparison of British and West German manufacturing investment, which also found little sig-nificant difference.[22]

Table 10.6 Investment (as a percentage of GDP) in Britain and all
member states of the Organisation for Economic Co-operation and
Development (OECD), 1960–73

	Britain	*OECD*
Gross fixed-capital formation	18.3	22.3
Residential construction	3.7	5.8
Non-residential construction	6.0	7.8
Machinery and equipment	8.6	8.7

Source: OECD, *Historical Statistics* (Paris, 1999).

These investment figures shed some light on the plausibility of other
arguments about the constraints on economic policy in the 1960s. First
is the issue of the Treasury, a popular object of hostility in Labour circles
(and beyond) for its alleged obsession with 'financial' issues at the expense of the 'real' economy.[23] This hostility was, of course, the rationale
for the DEA. But on the central 'financial' issue of devaluation we have
seen that the Treasury was divided, and in any event almost powerless
in the face of initial ministerial support for maintaining the value of
the pound. While the Treasury paper prepared for the new government
on this topic was very poor, it is doubtful whether, at this stage, ministers
could have been shifted on the issue.[24]

Leaving aside the devaluation issue, the papers prepared in October
1964 give a clear picture of the Treasury's preferred policies. These
included: reduced expenditure on defence and prestige projects such
as Concord; 'measures to release for more productive employment manpower where it is not fully or efficiently employed e.g. mines and railways';
and an incomes policy. Though it did not favour immediate deflationary measures, as it believed the expansionary period was already going
into reverse, the Treasury did advocate running the economy at a higher
rate of unemployment. Its favoured rate was 1.8 per cent: 'Anything
much higher than this, quite apart from being socially and humanly
intolerable, would imply a waste of resources and a disincentive to new
investment and industrial innovation out of proportion to any gains
from greater flexibility in industrial redeployment and mobility'.[25] Thus,
any idea that the Treasury acted as a reactionary restraint on Labour's
agenda should be treated with scepticism. Many of its policy positions
echoed those of Labour, and it is more to be criticised for not suggesting
an earlier restraint on demand than for advocacy of highly deflationary
policies. Certainly, the Treasury was sceptical of the National Plan, but
while this was partly ideological preference, it was also based on the not
unreasonable position that a plan which did not deal with the balance
of payments issue was undeserving of such a title.

All this is not to suggest that important criticisms cannot be made of the Treasury. One key area was the management of public expenditure. First, and relating to investment, Table 10.6 suggests that Britain lagged a great deal behind in non-residential construction, or infrastructure, which was, of course, publicly financed but which was given low priority. One example would be road building. We may now believe that road building is no answer to infrastructural problems, but in the 1960s it clearly should have had high economic priority – and this the Treasury failed to give it.[26] This may be seen as part of a wider lack of clarity about the economic role of the public sector, perhaps especially of social welfare spending, which was such large part of the total. The Plowden reforms of the early 1960s provided a mechanism that gave some greater control over priorities, but the Treasury failed to evolve a positive doctrine for guiding this huge expenditure.[27] In addition, as suggested in Chapter 9, the reluctance to consider tax and spending together in discussions of welfare provision was a huge obstacle to rational debate on many issues.

Alongside the Treasury, the City ranks as a leading 'usual suspect' in accounts of the obstacles faced by the Labour government. There is no doubt about the hostility in City circles to the Labour government. These hostilities were pursued across a broad swathe of policy issues. Perhaps most anger was roused by Labour's external economic policies, where the City saw major errors of both commission and omission. As part of the effort to improve the balance of payments, controls over foreign investment were greatly intensified under Labour and were 'informally' extended to the sterling area, which had previously been exempt. In 1965 the Bank of England accepted extremely reluctantly that, given the payments position, some temporary constraint on foreign investment might be inescapable, but fought very hard against any proposals that implied that such investment should be permanently curtailed. This was, of course, to hit at many in the City, who saw it as a supplier of capital to the world.[28] Particular hostility was evinced to proposals that suggested that any depth of crisis could justify government requisition of privately held foreign assets.[29] While the City was broadly unsuccessful in its general resistance to tightening controls on British investment outside the sterling area, and investment there did fall quite sharply,[30] it successfully fought against formal controls on flows within the area. Instead, informal 'guidance' was instituted, especially relating to developed members of the area.[31] Success in this respect was probably helped by Labour's continuing attachment to the idea of the (largely political) benefits of the sterling area, an attachment only slowly eroded after 1964.[32]

The City was also highly critical of Labour's slowness in cutting overseas public expenditure, where it contrasted the profligacy of government with the earning power of the City.[33] This was part of a more general set of criticisms of the failure of the government to pursue the City's own preferred strategy of public spending cuts, lower direct taxes and emphasis on constraining the public rather than the private sector. As Governor in the years 1964–66, Cromer evinced little reluctance in pressing this agenda on the Labour government, showing little concern with the argument that this involved a direct conflict with Labour's democratic mandate for its own policies. Bitter clashes between Wilson and the Governor occurred in November 1964 and again in March 1966.[34] In the latter case, Cromer used a classic ploy when he said that, though he did not himself agree, foreign bankers believed that Labour's intention to nationalise steel and its failure to bring in an effective incomes policy were fundamental mistakes in policy. The argument then became even more heated, as Cromer wanted to raise the bank rate, while Wilson said that for the Bank to do so in the run-up to an election and against the will of the government 'would constitute deliberate interference with politics'.[35] On this occasion Cromer's bluff was called, but plainly he was willing to try to pursue his own agenda to an extent that was bound to antagonise the government. Yet, in following this line, there is evidence that he was doing no more than expressing the generality of City views, which were often absurdly paranoid at this time.[36] Labour was happy to see the back of Cromer later in 1966. His successor, O'Brien, had less of Cromer's patrician arrogance and was more sensitive to constitutional and political realities, but nevertheless continued to urge the same deflationary, anti-public sector policies on the government.[37]

An area of particular contention between City and government in the 1960s was taxation. The City combined a general distaste for higher direct taxation with particular venom for corporation tax and the extension of capital gains tax. A prize for silliness must go the financial journalist Harold Wincott, who wrote (in 1965) of Labour's proposals for these taxes: 'There really hasn't been anything like it since Hitler wrote Mein Kampf'.[38] Hostility to the capital gains tax was linked to the foreign investment issue, as Labour's aim was to use the tax to equalise the treatment of home and foreign investment to the disadvantage of the latter. The Bank commissioned an opinion survey on this tax, which, unsurprisingly, revealed enormous hostility among City institutions. Aware of such hostility, Wilson arranged a dinner to make more personal contact with senior financiers, only to be met with a barrage of generalised hostile questions about taxation.[39] Another of Labour's initiatives, the SET, was a red rag to the City bull, because it quite explicitly rested on the assumption that service industries, including finance, should be squeezed for the benefit of the manufacturing sector.[40]

This battle between widely differing ideologies and policies threatened occasionally to get out of hand, especially under Cromer, but it never did so. Partly this was because both sides were constrained by over-arching considerations which prevented them going too far in pursuit of particular policy goals. On the government's part the central concern was, of course, to find a 'third way' between deflation and devaluation, to reconcile its ambitions of having both a faster-growing economy and a sounder balance of payments. To prevent either a devaluation or (major) deflation required the maintenance of financial confidence, and this in turn meant that substantial regard had to be had to financial opinion, however unwelcome the prejudices underlying that opinion. For this reason the government could never disregard what it was being told by Cromer or O'Brien, however much it was suspicious of the way 'confidence' could be manipulated by the Bank.

Undoubtedly the Bank did use its recognition of the government's weakness to advance its own policy agenda. Thus, for example, a common ploy was to suggest that concerns of the government about the perceived volatility of the sterling balances, or the diversification of reserves out of sterling, were not really important, as they could be readily prevented by more deflationary domestic policies.[41] Equally, the Bank was active in trying to shape foreign financial opinion about what acceptable policies on the part of the Labour government would look like. For example, and with an echo of the manoeuvring of 1931, Cromer in June 1966 wrote to Bill Martin of the US Federal Reserve urging that, if the British government made enquiries about the possibility of further borrowing, beyond that already agreed, it would be desirable if it could be told that no such facilities were available, in order to persuade the government that the only real way forward was 'a display of resolute policy', that is, deflation.[42]

The government was, of course, aware of the extent to which the need to maintain confidence constrained its freedom of action.[43] Part of the government's response was to behave, as Barbara Castle put it, like the parson who preaches against sin on Sunday and then fornicates the rest of the week.[44] This behaviour understandably infuriated the Bank, because it saw the government as telling one story to its domestic supporters and another to those whose confidence it wanted to retain.[45] Undoubtedly, this meant that the government was involved in what would now be called a complex process of 'spin', which involved putting the most confidence-boosting varnish on the least level of policy concessions, an approach which ultimately failed in 1967, but which might be said to have worked with a degree of success until that time.

Finally, there is the constraint imposed on Britain by the USA. For a country with a weak balance of payments position (however derived), the need to borrow money meant that some amount of dancing to the US tune was inescapable. Of course, there were all sorts of other reasons why the British hung on to their fantasy of a 'special relationship', but the simple logic of a borrower–lender relationship was crucial. The British do seem to have realised that, in this relationship, they were not without bargaining power: the US concern that the whole edifice of the international financial system was at risk if the pound fell gave Britain some leverage. Nevertheless, British economic policy did have to take account of American views, as Ponting and others have stressed.[46] Yet it is hard to point to a decision which was largely the consequence of US pressures. If the Americans were keen on incomes policy, so were most Labour ministers. If the Americans encouraged policies to stimulate higher productivity, they found ready allies in the Cabinet. Couple these convergent ideas with the divisions of opinion in the US administration over issues such as 'east of Suez' policy, and it is plain that a story of Britain simply following US wishes is not an adequate account of these years.

Summing up

The Labour government came to power at a time when belief in the effectiveness of government was high. On the back of this, coupled with a desire to dish the Tories, it made big promises about what better economic policy could achieve. These promises were not delivered, though a view taken after the end of the twentieth century would want to place what *was* achieved in the context of the much worse decades that were to follow – especially the 1980s. By 1970 unemployment had risen, but only to 2.7 per cent, and from incredibly low levels, and income inequalities had been reduced, albeit marginally; the balance of payments and public finances were (eventually) put in good order. By the late 1960s inflation was rising, but mainly as part of a largely international process. Growth, on which so much effort was expended, remained stubbornly lower than that in much of Western Europe, but respectable by any other benchmark. The government had lots of sensible policies on growth, many of them articulated in the National Plan. Some of these were delivered, for example the transfer of technology resources from military to civilian use, or the politically much more difficult rundown of employment in coal and the railways. Others were not, perhaps the biggest failing being in training. Mergers were successfully supported, but here the outcomes were disappointing; what probably mattered most for efficiency were *plant level* economies of scale, which company mergers could not guarantee and often did not bring about.[47] This was only one area in which Labour learnt how difficult it was to change the behaviour of the private sector – perhaps, in retrospect, one of its greatest areas of naïvety.

The conduct of macro-economic policy has prompted much hostile comment, and certainly the lurching from excessively high demand to persistent deflation was quite at odds with the promise of an end to 'stop–go'.[48] But the importance of macro-economic policy to growth was probably exaggerated in the 1960s, and it was on growth that the government most fatally both raised and disappointed expectations. The evidence in this book suggests that there were no feasible policies which, within six years, could have delivered outcomes to satisfy those exaggerated expectations.

Notes

The place of publication is London unless otherwise specified.

1 N. Woodward, 'Labour's economic performance', in R. Coopey, S. Fielding and N. Tiratsoo (eds), *The Wilson Governments 1964–1970* (1993), p. 81.
2 J. Baxter, 'Long-term unemployment in Great Britain 1953–71', *Bulletin of the Oxford University Institute of Economics and Statistics*, 34 (1972), p. 333.
3 Within industrial employment, mining and quarrying were on a long downward trend, whereas manufacturing peaked in 1966 and construction in 1965. See 'Employment in public and private sectors', *Economic Trends*, 180 (1968), pp. 42–5. Longer-term patterns are discussed by R. Millward, 'Industrial and commercial performance since 1945', in R. Floud and D. McCloskey (eds), *The Economic History of Britain Since 1700. Vol. 3, 1939–1992* (2nd edn) (Cambridge, 1994), pp. 124–9.
4 D. Robinson, 'Labour market policies', in W. Beckerman (ed.), *The Labour Government's Economic Record 1964–1970* (1972), pp. 314–15, suggests that despite the 'low pay' clause in incomes policies in the 1960s, there was no significant narrowing of wage differentials.
5 H. Scanlon at the 1968 Labour Party conference, cited by R. Taylor, *The Trade Union Question in British Politics: Government and Unions Since 1945* (1993), p. 146. On the redistribution of factor income, see Robinson, 'Labour market policies', pp. 313–14.
6 Woodward, 'Labour's economic performance', pp. 93–8.
7 A. Mitchell and D. Wienir, *Last Time: Labour's Lessons from the Sixties* (1997), ch. 6.
8 E. Dell, *The Chancellors: A History of the Chancellors of the Exchequer, 1945–90* (1997), ch. 11.
9 A. Graham and W. Beckerman, 'Introduction', in Beckerman, *Labour Government's Economic Record*, p. 11.
10 B. Tew, 'Policies aimed at improving the balance of payments', in F. Blackaby (ed.), *British Economic Policy 1960–74* (Cambridge, 1978), pp. 344–7, suggests that the surcharge saved around £250 million over two years.
11 Woodward, 'Labour's economic performance', p. 77.
12 For one contemporary assessment, see A. Maddison. 'How fast can Britain grow?', *Lloyds Bank Review*, 79 (1966), pp. 8–11.
13 Graham, 'Industrial policy', in Beckerman, *Labour Government's Economic Record*, pp. 200–4. On the severe problems of productivity data, see PRO, T 230/999, A. Cairncross to P. Baldwin, 'Measuring productivity in manufacturing', 20 September 1966.
14 *The National Plan*, Cmnd 2764, BPP 1964/65, vol. 30, pp. 24–5; M. Surrey, 'The National Plan in retrospect', *Bulletin of the Oxford University Institute of Economics and Statistics*, 34 (1972), p. 259.
15 PRO, T 267/22, 'The control of demand 1964–1970', January 1975, p. 2.

16 N. Crafts, 'Economic growth', in N. Crafts and N. Woodward (eds), *The British Economy Since 1945* (Oxford, 1991), p. 279.

17 R. Pryke, *Public Enterprise in Practice* (1971), chs 7, 8, argues that labour shedding is only part of the story and that the British nationalised industries performed better than the same industries elsewhere.

18 N. Crafts, 'The golden age of economic growth in Western Europe, 1950–1973', *Economic History Review*, 48 (1995), pp. 429–47.

19 N. Kaldor, *Causes of the Slow Rate of Growth of the United Kingdom* (Cambridge, 1966); C. Feinstein, 'Structural change in the developed countries during the twentieth century', *Oxford Review of Economic Policy*, 15 (1999), pp. 35–55.

20 Crafts, 'Economic growth', pp. 270–1; R. Rowthorn, 'What remains of Kaldor's law?', *Economic Journal*, 85 (1975), pp. 10–19.

21 R. Major, 'Notes on Britain's share in world trade in manufactures, 1954–1966', *National Institute Economic Review*, 44 (1968), pp. 50–6; J. McCombie and A. Thirlwall, *Economic Growth and the Balance of Payments Constraint* (1994), pp. 515–34; G. Worswick, 'Trade and payments', in A. Cairncross (ed.), *Britain's Economic Prospects Reconsidered* (1971), pp. 72–80.

22 M. Panic (ed.), *UK and West German Manufacturing Industry, 1954–1972: A Comparison of Performance and Structure* (1976).

23 For a discussion of anti-Treasury views, see C. Thain, 'The Treasury and Britain's decline', *Political Studies*, 32 (1984), pp. 581–95.

24 PRO, PREM 13/758, Treasury, 'Devaluation', 15 October 1964.

25 PRO, PREM 13/758, 'General briefing for new administration', 15 October 1964, and 'Economic policy and the balance of payments', 15 October 1964.

26 PRO, T 230/1049, Treasury historical memorandum, 'Reduction in public expenditure 1968–71', 1969, pp. 22–3.

27 R. Lowe and N. Rollings, 'Modernising Britain 1957–64: a classic case of centralisation and fragmentation?', in R. Rhodes (ed.), *Transforming British Government* (2000), pp. 114–16; N. Deakin and R. Parry, *The Treasury and Social Policy* (Basingstoke, 2000), pp. 30–6.

28 Bank of England (hereafter BoE), G 1/260, Lord Cromer to W. Armstrong, 17 March 1965; PRO, T 171/801, Cromer to Armstrong, 5 March 1965. Eventually, scepticism on the impact of foreign investment led to W. Reddaway, *Effects of UK Direct Investment Overseas* (Cambridge, 1968).

29 BoE, G 1/260, Cromer to J. Callaghan, 23 March 1965.

30 PRO, T 171/809, 'Draft budget statement', 3 April 1965.

31 BoE, G 1/260, Cromer to Callaghan, 11 February 1966, 6 April 1966

32 The economic consequences of the sterling area came to greater prominence as attention focused more on the capital account of the balance of payments. See, for example, PRO, T 171/811, D. Mitchell to I. Bancroft, 'Economic forecasts', 17 November 1965.

33 There was, of course, counter pressure from the USA (not to cut overseas expenditure). See, for example, PRO, T 312/1206, 'Briefs for Chancellor's visit to the USA and Canada', June 1965.

34 PRO, PREM 13/261, 'Meeting of H. Wilson, J. Callaghan and Governor', 24 November 1964; PREM 13/851, 'Meeting of 9 Mar 1966'; D. Kynaston, *The City of London. Vol. 4, A Club No More 1945–2000* (2001), pp. 304–5.

35 PRO, PREM 13/851, 'Meeting of 9 Mar 1966'; also BoE, G/260, Cromer to Callaghan, 24 July 1965.

36 Kynaston, *A Club No More*, pp. 306–7.

37 BoE, OV 44/124, Cromer to Callaghan, 12 July 1966; PRO, PREM 13/1447, O'Brien to Callaghan, 17 November 1967; PRO, T 171/829, 'Governor's tax proposals', 8 February 1968.

38 *Times*, 15 December 1965.
39 BoE, G 1/260, Cromer to Armstrong, 2 December 1964, and 26 January 1965; G 1/182, 'Dinner for PM and Chancellor', 14 July 1965.
40 Kynaston, *A Club No More*, p. 319.
41 PRO, T 312/1701, 'Bank of England comments on Treasury Paper on OSA diversification', 1 March 1967.
42 BoE, OV 44/123, 15 June 1966.
43 PRO, PREM 13/852, 'Economic strategy', 15 April 1966.
44 B. Castle, *The Castle Diaries, 1964–70* (1984), p. 281, cited by R. Stones, 'Government–finance relations in Britain 1964–7: a tale of three cities', *Economy and Society*, 19 (1990), pp. 41–2.
45 BoE, G 1/260, Cromer to Wilson, 21 December 1964.
46 C. Ponting, *Breach of Promise. Labour in Power 1964–1970* (1989); R. Roy, 'The battle of the pound: the political economy of Anglo-American relations 1964–1968' (unpublished PhD dissertation, University of London, 2001).
47 S. Prais, *The Evolution of Giant Firms in Britain* (Cambridge, 1976), chs 3, 4.
48 For example, A. Cairncross, *Managing the British Economy in the 1960s: A Treasury Perspective* (1996), pp. 262–75.

Bibliography

Archives

Public Record Office, Kew

BT 177   Board of Trade, Distribution of Industry
BT 241   Board of Trade, Commercial Relations and Exports
BT 258   Board of Trade, Industry and Manufactures
BT 321   Board of Trade, Investment and Regional Development Grants
CAB 128 Cabinet Conclusions
CAB 129 Cabinet Papers
CAB 130 Miscellaneous Cabinet Committees
CAB 134 Cabinet Committees
CAB 147 Balogh Papers
CAB 168 Sir Solly Zuckerman Collection
DO 162   Commonwealth, Commercial Policy
DO 215   Commonwealth, Economic Aid
DSIR 17 Department of Scientific and Industrial Resources, General Series
EW 4   Department of Economic Affairs, Information
EW 8   Department of Economic Affairs, Growth, Incomes and Prices Policy
EW 24   Department of Economic Affairs, Economic Planning
EW 25   Department of Economic Affairs, Public Expenditure
EW 27   Department of Economic Affairs, Industrial Policy
EW 28   Department of Economic Affairs, George Brown Correspondence
FCO 20   Commonwealth Relations, Common Market Department
FG 1   National Economic Development Council, Minutes and Memoranda
FG 2   National Economic Development Office
FV 3   Ministry of Technology, Finance and Machine Tools
FV 11   Ministry of Technology, Industrial Policy
FV 25   Ministry of Technology, Finance and Economic Appraisal
HF 7   Ministry of Technology, Economics
HF 9   Ministry of Technology, Industrial Reorganisation Corporation
HF 19   Ministry of Technology, Ministerial Meetings
LAB 8   Ministry of Labour, Employment Policy
LAB 10   Ministry of Labour, Industrial Relations
LAB 12   Ministry of Labour, Establishment
LAB 43   Ministry of Labour, Private Office Papers
PREM 13 Prime Minister's Papers
RG 23   Social Survey

236

T 171	Treasury, Budget Papers
T 224	Treasury, Agriculture, Trade and Transport
T 227	Treasury, Social Services
T 230	Treasury, Economic Advisory Section
T 234	Treasury, Home and Overseas Planning Staff
T 267	Treasury, Historical Memoranda
T 312	Treasury, Finance, Overseas and Co-ordination
T 319	Treasury, Nationalised Industries
T 320	Treasury, Public Expenditure Survey Committee
T 325	Treasury, Otto Clarke Papers
T 328	Treasury, Fiscal and Incomes Policy
T 331	Treasury, General Expenditure
T 334	Treasury, Establishment and Supply
T 338	Treasury, Economic Assessment
T 342	Treasury, Industrial and Incomes Policy

Conservative Party Archives, Bodleian Library, Oxford

CRD 2	Policy Committee on Science and Industry

Labour Party Archives, Manchester

Policy Committees and Study Groups of the National Executive Committee Research Department

Modern Records Centre, Warwick University, Coventry

MSS 200	Federation/Confederation of British Industry
MSS 292	Trades Union Congress

Bank of England, London

G 1	Governor's Files
OV 44	Sterling and Sterling Area Policy

US National Records and Archives Administration, Washington, DC

RG 59	Department of State, Central Foreign Policy Files

Lyndon Baines Johnson Library, Austin, Texas

NSF Country Files
NSF Name Files
G. Ball Papers
F. Bator Papers
H. Fowler Papers

Parliamentary Papers

Cmd 9703   *Technical Education*, BPP 1955/56, vol. 34.
Cmnd 124   *Defence: Outline of a Future Policy*, BPP 1956/57, vol. 23.
Cmnd 827   Committee on the Working of the Monetary System (Radcliffe),
            Report, BPP 1958/59, vol. 17.
Cmnd 1337   *The Financial and Economic Obligations of the Nationalised Industries*,
            BPP 1960/61, vol. 27.
Cmnd 2577   *Machinery of Prices and Incomes Policy*, BPP 1964/65, vol. 30.
Cmnd 2639   *Prices and Incomes Policy*, BPP 1964/65, vol. 30.
Cmnd 2764   *The National Plan*, BPP 1964/65, vol. 30.
Cmnd 2800   *A Review of the Scope and Problems of Scientific and Technological
            Manpower Policy*, BPP 1965/66, vol. 22.
Cmnd 2808   *Prices and Incomes Policy: An 'Early Warning' System*, BPP 1965/66,
            vol. 13.
Cmnd 2874   *Investment Incentives*, BPP 1965/66, vol. 13.
Cmnd 2889   *Industrial Reorganisation Corporation*, BPP 1965/66, vol. 13.
Cmnd 2915   *Public Expenditure: Planning and Control*, BPP 1965/66, vol. 13.
Cmnd 3073   *Prices and Incomes Standstill*, BPP 1966/67, vol. 59.
Cmnd 3150   *Prices and Incomes Standstill: Period of Severe Restraint*, BPP 1966/
            67, vol. 59.
Cmnd 3235   *Prices and Incomes Policy after 30th July 1967*, BPP 1966/67, vol. 43.
Cmnd 3311   NBPI report no. 36, *Productivity Agreements*, BPP 1966/67, vol. 43.
Cmnd 3417   *The Brain Drain: Report of the Working Group on Migration*, BPP
            1966/67, vol. 39.
Cmnd 3437   *Nationalised Industries: A Review of Economic and Financial Objectives*,
            BPP 1967/68, vol. 39.
Cmnd 3515   *Public Expenditure: 1968/9 and 1969/70*, BPP 1967/68, vol. 39.
Cmnd 3590   *Productivity, Prices and Incomes Policy in 1968 and 1969*, BPP 1967/
            68, vol. 39.
Cmnd 3623   *Report of Royal Commission on Trade Unions and Employer's Associ-
            ations*, BPP 1967/68, vol. 32.
Cmnd 3760   *The Flow into Employment of Scientists, Engineers and Technologists*,
            BPP 1967/68, vol. 25.
Cmnd 3888   *In Place of Strife*, BPP 1968/69, vol. 5.
Cmnd 3936   *Public Expenditure: 1968/9 to 1970/1*, BPP 1968/69, vol. 53.
Cmnd 3998   *Report of Hunt Committee on Intermediate Areas*, BPP 1968/69,
            vol. 35.
Cmnd 4017   *Public Expenditure: A New Presentation*, BPP 1968/69, vol. 53.
Cmnd 4234   *Public Expenditure 1968/9–1973/4*, BPP 1969/70, vol. 21.
Cmnd 4237   *Productivity, Prices and Incomes Policy After 1969*, BPP 1969/70,
            vol. 9.

Other official publications

DEA, *The Task Ahead* (1969).
DEA, *Joint Statement of Intent on Productivity, Prices and Incomes* (1964).
Estimates Committee, *Government Statistical Services* (4th report), appendix A,
    DEA, 'Preparation of the National Plan', HCP 246, BPP 1966/67, vol. 12.
Office of the Minister for Science, *Committee of Enquiry into the Organisation of
    Civil Science* (1963).

Books

The place of publication London unless otherwise specified.

Abel-Smith, B. *Labour's Social Plans*, Fabian Tract 369 (1966).
Acland, R., *et al. Keeping Left* (1950).
Ahlstrand, B. *The Quest for Productivity: A Case Study of Fawley after Flanders* (Cambridge, 1990).
Aldcroft, D. *Education, Training and Economic Performance 1944 to 1990* (Manchester, 1992).
Ashworth, W. *The History of the British Coal Industry. Vol. 5, 1946–1982: The Nationalised Industry* (Oxford, 1986).
Bale, T. *Sacred Cows and Commonsense: The Symbolic Statecraft and Political Culture of the British Labour Party* (Aldershot, 1999).
Ball, G. *The Past Has Another Pattern* (New York, 1982).
Balogh, T. *Planning for Progress*, Fabian Tract 346 (1963).
Balogh, T. *Unequal Partners. Vol. 2* (Oxford, 1963).
Banting, K. *Poverty, Politics and Policy: Britain in the 1960s* (1979).
Barker T. and Lecomber, J. *Economic Planning for 1972: An Appraisal of 'The Task Ahead'* (1969).
Barnett, C. *The Lost Victory* (1995).
Beckerman, W. (ed.) *The Labour Government's Economic Record 1964–1970* (1972).
Benn, T. *Arguments for Socialism* (1979).
Benn, T. *Out of the Wilderness. Diaries 1963–67* (1987).
Benn, T. *Office Without Power. Diaries 1968–72* (1988).
Benn, T. *Against the Tide. Diaries 1973–76* (1989).
Bevan, A. *In Place of Fear* (1952).
Biagini, E. F. and Reid, A. (eds) *Currents of Radicalism. Popular Radicalism, Organised Labour and Party Politics in Britain, 1850–1914* (Cambridge, 1991).
Blackaby, F. (ed.) *British Economic Policy 1960–74* (Cambridge, 1978).
Blackburn, R. and Anderson, P. (eds) *Towards Socialism* (1965).
Booth, A. and Pack, M. *Employment, Capital and Economic Policy: Great Britain 1918–1939* (Oxford, 1985).
Boyce, R. *British Capitalism at the Crossroads 1919–32* (Cambridge, 1987).
Brennan, G. and Milward, A. *Britain's Place in the World: A Historical Enquiry into Import Controls 1945–60* (1996).
Brittan, S. *Inquest on Planning* (1967).
Brittan, S. *Steering the Economy: The Role of the Treasury* (1971).
Brivati, B. and Heffernan, L. (eds) *The Labour Party: A Centenary History* (2000).
Broad, R. *Labour's European Dilemma: From Bevin to Blair* (2001).
Brooke, S. *Labour's War* (Oxford, 1992).
Brown, G. *In My Way* (1971).
Budd, A. *The Politics of Economic Planning* (1978).
Bullock, A. *Ernest Bevin, Foreign Secretary* (Oxford, 1985).
Burn, D. *Nuclear Power and the Energy Crisis* (1978).
Cairncross, A. (ed.) *Britain's Economic Prospects Reconsidered* (1971).
Cairncross, A. *Years of Recovery: British Economic Policy 1945–51* (1985).
Cairncross, A. *The British Economy Since 1945* (1992).
Cairncross, A. *Managing the British Economy in the 1960s: A Treasury Perspective* (1996).
Cairncross, A. *The Wilson Years: A Treasury Diary, 1964–1969* (1997).
Cairncross, A. and Eichengreen, B. *Sterling in Decline* (Oxford, 1983).

Callaghan, J. *Time and Chance* (1987).
Campbell, J. *Nye Bevan: A Biography* (1994).
Camps, M. *Britain and the European Community 1955–1963* (1964).
Castle, B. *The Castle Diaries, 1964–70* (1984).
Castle, B. *Fighting All the Way* (1993).
Caves, R. (ed.) *Britain's Economic Prospects* (Washington, DC, 1968).
CBI. *Productivity Bargaining* (1968).
Chick, M. (ed.) *Governments, Industries and Markets* (Aldershot, 1990).
Chick, M. *Industrial Policy in Britain 1945–1951* (Cambridge, 1998).
Clarke, R. *The Ministry of Technology and Industry* (1970).
Clarke, W. *The City in the World Economy* (Harmondsworth, 1967).
Clegg, H. *Productivity Bargaining and Restrictive Labour Practices*, Royal
  Commission on Trades Unions and Employers Associations, Research Paper
  no. 4 (1968).
Clegg, H. *How to Run an Incomes Policy and Why We Made Such a Mess of the Last
  One* (1971).
Cohen, C. *British Economic Policy 1960–69* (1971).
Coombes, D. *State Enterprise: Business or Politics?* (1971).
Coopey, R., Fielding, S. and Tiratsoo, N. (eds) *The Wilson Governments 1964–
  1970* (1993).
Crafts, N. and Woodward, N. (eds) *The British Economy Since 1945* (Oxford,
  1991).
Croome, D. and Johnson, H. (eds) *Money in Britain 1959–69* (1970).
Crosland, A. *Britain's Economic Problem* (1953).
Crosland, A. *The Future of Socialism* (1956).
Crossman, R. H. S. (ed.) *New Fabian Essays* (1952).
Crossman, R. H. S. *The Diaries of a Cabinet Minister*, 3 vols (1975–7).
Cutajor, M. Z. (ed.) *UNCTAD and the South North Dialogue* (Oxford, 1985).
Daddow, O. (ed.) *Wilson and Europe 1964–67* (2002).
Daunton, M. *Trusting Leviathan: The Politics of Taxation in Britain, 1799–1914*
  (Cambridge, 2001).
Davison, J. P., Sargant Florence, P., Gray, B. and Ross, N. *Productivity and
  Economic Incentives* (1958).
Day, A. C. L. *The Future of Sterling* (Oxford, 1954).
Deakin, N. and Parry, R. *The Treasury and Social Policy* (Basingstoke, 2000).
Dell, E. *The Schuman Plan and the British Abdication of Leadership in Europe*
  (Oxford, 1995).
Dell, E. *The Chancellors: A History of the Chancellors of the Exchequer, 1945–90*
  (1997).
Denison, S. R. and Presley, J. R. *Robertson on Economic Policy* (1992).
Denman, R. *Missed Chances: Britain and Europe in the Twentieth Century* (1996).
Dorfman, R. *Wage Politics in Britain* (Ames, Iowa, 1973).
Dunlop, J. and Diatchenko, V. (eds) *Labour Productivity* (New York, 1964).
Durbin, E. *The Politics of Democratic Socialism* (1940).
Edgerton, D. *England and the Aeroplane: An Essay on a Militant and Technological
  Nation* (1991).
Edgerton, D. *Science, Technology and the British Industrial 'Decline' 1870–1970*
  (Cambridge, 1996).
Ellison, N. *Egalitarian Thought and Labour Politics: Retreating Visions* (1994).
Feldenkirchen, W. and Gourvish, T. (eds) *European Yearbook of Business History*
  (1999).
Feldman, E. *Concorde and Dissent* (Cambridge, 1985).
Fels, A. *The British Prices and Incomes Board* (Cambridge, 1972).

Fishbein, W. *Wage Restraint by Consensus: Britain's Search for an Incomes Policy Agreement 1965–79* (1984).

Flanders, A. *The Fawley Productivity Agreements. A Case Study of Management and Collective Bargaining* (1964).

Floud, R. and McCloskey, D. (eds) *The Economic History of Britain Since 1700. Vol. 3, 1939–1992* (2nd edn) (Cambridge, 1994).

Foreman-Peck, J. and Milward, R. *Public and Private Ownership of British Industry 1820–1990* (1994).

Francis, M. *Ideas and Policies Under Labour 1945–1951: Building a New Britain* (Manchester, 1997).

Francis, M. and Zweiniger-Bargielowska, I. (eds) *The Conservatives and British Society, 1880–1990* (Cardiff, 1996).

Freeden, M. *Liberalism Divided* (Oxford, 1996).

Friedberg, A. *The Weary Titan: Britain and the Experience of Relative Decline 1895–1905* (Princeton, 1988).

Gaitskell, H. *Socialism and Nationalisation* (1956).

Gamble, A. *Britain in Decline* (4th edn) (1994).

Garside, W. *British Unemployment 1919–39* (Cambridge, 1990).

George, S. *Britain and European Integration* (1991).

Goldman, S. *The Developing System of Public Expenditure Management and Control* (1973).

Goodman, G. *The Awkward Warrior* (1979).

Gourvish, T. *British Railways 1948–73* (Cambridge, 1986).

Green, E. H. H. (ed.) *An Age of Transition: British Politics 1880–1914* (Edinburgh, 1997).

Gummett, P. *Scientists in Whitehall* (Manchester, 1980).

Gupta, P. S. *Imperialism and the British Labour Movement 1914–1964* (1975).

Hague, D. C. and Wilkinson, G. *The IRC. An Experiment in Industrial Intervention* (1983).

Hannah, L. *The Rise of the Corporate Economy* (2nd edn) (1983).

Haseler, S. *The Gaitskellites: Revisionism in the Labour Party* (1969).

Hatfield, M. *The House the Left Built* (1978).

Hennessy, P. *The Prime Ministers: The Office and Its Holders Since 1945* (2000).

Hindess, B. *Freedom, Equality and the Market* (1987).

Hirsch, F. *The Pound Sterling: A Polemic* (1965).

Hopwood, A. and Miller, P. (eds) *Accounting in Its Social Context* (Cambridge, 1994).

Howell, D. *British Social Democracy* (1980).

Hunt, A. *A Survey of Women's Employment*, 2 vols (1968).

International Labor Organization. *Measuring Labour Productivity* (Geneva, 1969).

IRC. *Reports and Accounts 1969/70* (1970).

James, H. *International Monetary Co-operation Since Bretton Woods* (Washington, DC, 1996).

Jay, D. *Socialism in the New Society* (1962).

Jay, D. *Change and Fortune: A Political Record* (1980).

Jay, D. and Jenkins, R. *The Common Market Debate* (1962).

Jenkins, C. *Power at the Top* (1959).

Jenkins, P. *Harold Wilson's Productivity Conference* (1967).

Jenkins, P. *The Battle of Downing Street* (1970).

Jenkins, R. *The Labour Case* (1959).

Jenkins, R. *Essays and Speeches* (1967).

Jenkins, R. *A Life at the Centre* (1991).

Johnman, L. and Murphy, H. *British Shipbuilding and the State Since 1918* (Exeter, 2002).

Jones, A. *Britain's Economy: The Roots of Stagnation* (Cambridge, 1985).

Jones, K. and Golding, J. *Productivity Bargaining*, Fabian Research Series 257 (1966).

Jones, R. *Wages and Employment Policy 1936–1985* (1987).

Jones, T. *Remaking the Labour Party: From Gaitskell to Blair* (1996).

Kaldor, N. *Causes of the Slow Rate of Growth of the United Kingdom* (Cambridge, 1966).

Kaldor, N. *Reports on Taxation. I, Papers Relating to the UK* (1980).

Kent, J. *British Imperial Strategy and the Origins of the Cold War* (Leicester, 1993).

Kirby, M. W. *The British Coalmining Industry 1870–1946* (1977).

Kitzinger, U. *The Second Try: Labour and the EEC* (Oxford, 1968).

Kynaston, D. *The City of London. Vol. 4, A Club No More 1945–2000* (2001).

Labour Party. *Labour and the New Social Order* (1918).

Labour Party. *Labour and the Nation* (1928).

Labour Party. *For Socialism and Peace* (1934).

Labour Party. *Let Us Face the Future* (1945).

Labour Party. *Industry and Society* (1957).

Labour Party. *Public Enterprise* (1957).

Labour Party. *Plan for Progress* (1958).

Labour Party. *Signposts for the Sixties* (1961).

Labour Party. *Labour and the Common Market* (1962).

Labour Party. *Let's Go with Labour for the New Britain* (1964).

Labour Party. *Time for Decision* (1966).

Lee, D. *Middle Powers and Commercial Diplomacy: British Influences at the Kennedy Trade Round* (New York, 1999).

Leruez, J. *Economic Planning and Politics in Britain* (1975).

Lowe, R. *The Welfare State in Britain Since 1945* (1993).

Luckin, B. *Questions of Power* (Manchester, 1990).

MacDougall, D. *Don and Mandarin: Memoirs of an Economist* (1987).

MacKenzie, N. and MacKenzie, J. (eds) *The Diaries of Beatrice Webb. Vol. 4, 1923–1943* (1985).

Maier, C. *In Search of Stability: Explorations in Historical Political Economy* (Cambridge, 1987).

Manser, A. *Britain in Balance: The Myth of Failure* (1971).

Matthews, R., Feinstein, C. and Odling-Smee, J. *British Economic Growth 1856–1973* (Oxford, 1982).

May, A. (ed.) *Britain, the Commonwealth and Europe. The Commonwealth and Britain's Application to Join the European Communities* (2001).

McCarthy, W. E. J. *The Role of Shop Stewards in British Industrial Relations*, Royal Commission on Trade Unions and Employers Associations, Research Paper no. 1 (1967).

McCombie, J. and Thirlwall, A. *Economic Growth and the Balance of Payments Constraint* (1994).

McKersie, R. and Hunter, L. *Pay, Productivity and Collective Bargaining* (1973).

Melling, J. and McKinlay, A. (eds) *Management, Labour and Industrial Politics in Europe* (1996).

Mercer, H. *Constructing a Competitive Order: The Hidden History of British Anti-trust Policies* (Cambridge, 1995).

Mercer, H., Rollings, N. and Tomlinson, J. (eds) *Labour Governments and Private Industry: The Experience of 1945–51* (Edinburgh, 1992).

Middleton, R. *Government Versus the Market* (Cheltenham, 1996).

Middleton, R. *Charlatans or Saviours? Economists and the British Economy from Marshall to Meade* (Cheltenham, 1998).

Miller, J. B. D. *Survey of Commonwealth Affairs* (Oxford, 1974).

Millward, R. and Singleton, J. (eds) *The Political Economy of Nationalisation in Britain, 1920–50* (Cambridge, 1995).

Ministry of Technology, *The Ministry of Technology 1964–69* (1969).

Minkin, L. *The Contentious Alliance: Trade Unions and the Labour Party* (Edinburgh, 1991).

Mitchell, A. and Wienir, D. *Last Time: Labour's Lessons from the Sixties* (1997).

Morgan, K. *Callaghan: A Life* (Oxford, 1997).

Mosley, P. *The Making of Economic Policy: Theory and Evidence from Britain and the US Since 1945* (Brighton, 1985).

Mukherjee, S. *Through No Fault of Their Own: Systems of Handling Redundancy in Britain, France and Germany* (1973).

NEDC. *Conditions Favourable to Faster Growth* (1963).

NEDC. *Growth of the British Economy to 1966* (1963).

Newton, C. and Porter, D. *Modernization Frustrated* (1988).

Nichols, T. *The British Worker Question: A New Look at Workers and Productivity in Manufacturing* (1986).

O'Day, A. and Gourvish, T. (eds) *Britain Since 1945* (1992).

Organisation for Economic Co-operation and Development. *Productivity Measurement. Vol. 3, Global Measurement of Productivity* (Paris, 1966).

Organisation for Economic Co-operation and Development. *Manpower Policy in the UK* (Paris, 1970).

Organisation for Economic Co-operation and Development. *Policy Perspectives for International Trade and Economic Relations* (Paris, 1972).

Organisation for Economic Co-operation and Development. *Historical Statistics* (Paris, 1999).

Organisation for European Economic Co-operation. *4th Report on Europe: The Way Ahead* (Paris, 1952).

Ovenden, K. *The Politics of Steel* (1978).

Owen Smith, E. *Productivity Bargaining: A Case Study in the Steel Industry* (1971).

Panic, M. (ed.) *UK and West German Manufacturing Industry, 1954–1972: A Comparison of Performance and Structure* (1976).

Parker, S., Thomas, C., Elliott, N. and McCarthy, W. *Effects of the Redundancy Payments Act* (1971).

Parsons, W. A. *The Political Economy of British Regional Policy* (1986).

Peden, G. *The Treasury and British Public Policy 1906–1959* (Oxford, 2000).

Perry, P. *The Evolution of British Manpower Policy* (1976).

Pimlott, B. *Harold Wilson* (1992).

Pliatzky, L. *Getting and Spending: Public Expenditure, Employment and Inflation* (Oxford, 1982).

Political and Economic Planning. *Growth in the British Economy* (1960).

Ponting, C. *Breach of Promise. Labour in Power 1964–1970* (1989).

Posner, M. and Pryke, R. *New Public Enterprise* (1965).

Prais, S. *The Evolution of Giant Firms in Great Britain* (Cambridge, 1976).

Preeg, E. H. *Traders and Diplomats: An Analysis of the Kennedy Round Under the GATT* (New York, 1970).

Prest, A. R. and Coppock, C. *The UK Economy: A Manual of Applied Economics* (1972).

Pryke, R. *Public Enterprise in Practice* (1971).

Reddaway, W. *Effects of UK Direct Investment Overseas* (Cambridge, 1968).

Reddaway, W. *Effects of SET: Final Report* (Cambridge, 1973).

Rhodes, R. (ed.) *Transforming British Government* (2000).

Ritschel, D. *The Politics of Planning* (Oxford, 1997).

Roberts, A. and Smith, J. (eds) *Manpower Policy and Employment Trends* (1966).
Roberts, G. *The Cost of Demarcation* (Cambridge, 1967).
Robins, L. J. *Labour and the European Community* (Ormskirk, 1979).
Robinson, A. and Sandford, C. *Tax Policy-Making* (1983).
Robson, W. A. *Nationalized Industry and Public Ownership* (2nd edn) (1962).
Rowthorn, R. and Wells, J. *De-industrialization and Foreign Trade* (Cambridge, 1987).
Sanderson, M. *Education and Economic Decline in Britain, 1870 to the 1970s* (Cambridge, 1999).
Sassoon, D. *One Hundred Years of Socialism: The West European Left in the Twentieth Century* (1996).
Schenk, C. *Britain and the Sterling Area: From Devaluation to Convertibility in the 1950s* (1994).
Seglow, P. (ed.) *Productivity Bargaining in Perspective* (Uxbridge, 1973).
Shanks, M. *The Stagnant Society* (Harmondsworth, 1961).
Shanks, M. (ed.) *The Lessons of Public Enterprise* (1963).
Sheldrake, J. and Vickerstaff, S. *The History of Industrial Training in Britain* (1987).
Shepherd, R. *Iain Macleod* (1994).
Shonfield, A. *British Economic Policy Since the War* (Harmondsworth, 1958).
Stewart, M. *Politics and Economic Policy in the UK Since 1964: The Jekyll and Hyde Years* (1978).
Strange, S. *The Sterling Problem and the Six* (1967).
Strange, S. *Sterling and British Policy* (Oxford, 1971).
Streeten, P. (ed.) *Unfashionable Economics: Essays in Honour of Lord Balogh* (1970).
Streeten, P. and Corbet, H. (eds) *Commonwealth Policy in a Global Context* (1973).
Tanner, D., Thane, P. and Tiratsoo, N. (eds) *Labour's First Century* (Cambridge, 2000).
Tawney, R. H. *The Acquisitive Society* (1921).
Tawney, R. H. *Equality* (5th edn) (1964).
Taylor, R. *The Trade Union Question in British Politics: Government and Unions Since 1945* (1993).
Thompson, N. *Political Economy and the Labour Party* (1996).
Thorpe, A. *A History of the British Labour Party* (1997).
Timmins, N. *The Five Giants: A Biography of the Welfare State* (1996).
Tiratsoo, N. *Reconstruction, Affluence and Labour Party Politics: Coventry 1945–60* (1990).
Tiratsoo, N. (ed.) *The Attlee Years* (1991).
Tiratsoo, N. and Tomlinson, J. *Industrial Efficiency and State Intervention: Labour 1939–51* (1994).
Tiratsoo, N. and Tomlinson, J. *The Conservatives and Industrial Efficiency, 1951–64: Thirteen Wasted Years?* (1998).
Titmuss, R. *Income Distribution and Social Change* (1962).
Tomlinson, J. *Government and the Enterprise Since 1900: The Changing Problem of Efficiency* (Oxford, 1994).
Tomlinson, J. *Democratic Socialism and Economic Policy: The Attlee Years 1945–51* (Cambridge, 1997).
Townsend, P. and Bosanquet, N. (eds) *Labour and Inequality* (1972).
Transport and General Workers' Union. *Productivity Bargaining* (1970).
TUC. *Public Ownership: An Interim Report* (1953).
TUC. *Economic Review 1968* (1968).
TUC. *Economic Review 1969* (1969).
United Nations. *Macro-economic Models for Planning and Policy-Making* (Geneva, 1967).

Webb, S. and Webb, B. *Problems of Modern Industry* (1902).
Webb, S. and Webb, B. *Constitution for a Socialist Commonwealth of Great Britain* (Cambridge, 1920).
Werskey, P. *The Visible College* (1979).
Whiting, A. (ed.) *The Economics of Industrial Subsidies* (1976).
Whiting, R. *The Labour Party and Taxation* (Cambridge, 2000).
Wilks, S. *In the Public Interest: Competition Policy and the Monopolies and Mergers Commission* (Manchester, 1999).
Williams, K., Haslam, C., Williams, J. and Johal, S. *Cars: Analysis, History, Ideas* (Providence, RI, 1994).
Williams, P. *Hugh Gaitskell* (Oxford, 1982).
Wilson, H. *In Place of Dollars* (1953).
Wilson, H. *Post-war Economic Policies in Britain*, Fabian Tract 309 (1957).
Wilson, H. *The New Britain: Selected Speeches 1964* (1964).
Wilson, H. *The Labour Government 1964–70: A Personal Record* (1974).
Wilson, J. *The Dockers: The Impact of Industrial Change* (1972).
Wootton, B. *Incomes Policy: An Inquest and a Proposal* (1970).
Wright, A. W. *G. D. H. Cole and Socialist Democracy* (Oxford, 1979).
Wright, A. W. *R. H. Tawney* (Manchester, 1987).
Young, J. *Britain, France and the Unity of Europe* (Leicester, 1984).
Young, S. and Lowe, A. *Intervention in the Mixed Economy* (1974).
Zeitlin, J. and Herrigel, G. *Americanization and Its Limits: Reworking US Technology in Post-war Europe and Japan* (Oxford, 2000).
Ziegler, P. *Wilson: The Authorised Life* (1993).
Zweiniger-Bargielowska, I. *Austerity in Britain: Rationing, Controls, and Consumption 1939–1955* (Oxford, 2000).

Articles, chapters and theses

'Employment in public and private sectors', *Economic Trends*, 180 (1968), pp. 42–5.
'Statistics on output per hour and labour costs in the UK', *Economic Trends*, 180 (1968), pp. 46–54.
'The economic situation and the home economy', *National Institute Economic Review*, 45 (1968), pp. 10–11.
'The incidence of taxes and social service benefits in 1968', *Economic Trends*, 196 (1970), pp. 16–46.
'UK: use of an input–output model in the preparation of the National Plan', in United Nations, *Macro-economic Models for Planning and Policy-Making* (Geneva, 1967), pp. 85–90.

Albu, A. 'The organisation of industry', in Crossman, R. H. S. (ed.), *New Fabian Essays* (1952), pp. 121–42.
Alexander, P. 'The Labour government, Commonwealth policy and the second application to join the EEC, 1964–67', in May, A. (ed.), *Britain, the Commonwealth and Europe. The Commonwealth and Britain's Application to Join the European Communities* (2001), pp. 132–55.
Bale, T. 'South African arms and the statecraft of British social democracy', *Labour History Review*, 62 (1997), pp. 22–40.
Bale, T. 'Dynamics of a non-decision: the "failure" to devalue the pound, 1964–7', *Twentieth Century British History*, 10 (1999), pp. 192–217.

Balogh, T. 'The weakness of Neddy', *New Statesman*, 11 May 1962.

Balogh, T. 'The drift towards economic planning', in Blackburn, R. and Anderson, P. (eds), *Towards Socialism* (1965), pp. 53–76.

Baston, L. 'The age of Wilson', in Brivati, B. and Heffernan, L. (eds), *The Labour Party: A Centenary History* (2000), pp. 86–102.

Baxter, J. 'Long-term unemployment in Great Britain 1953–71', *Bulletin of the Oxford University Institute of Economics and Statistics*, 34 (1972), pp. 329–44.

Beckerman, W. and Sutherland, J. 'Married women at work in 1972', *National Institute Economic Review*, 23 (1963), pp. 56–60.

Bevir, M. 'Fabianism and the theory of rent', *History of Political Theory*, 10 (1989), pp. 313–27.

Bevir, M. 'The Marxism of George Bernard Shaw', *History of Political Theory*, 13 (1992), pp. 299–318.

Blaazer, D. '"Devalued and dejected Britons": the pound in public discourse in the mid-1960s', *History Workshop Journal*, 47 (1999), pp. 121–40.

Blackaby, F. 'Narrative', in Blackaby, F. (ed.), *Economic Policy 1960–74* (Cambridge, 1978), pp. 11–76.

Blick, A. 'The origins and history of the government adviser with special reference to the 1964–70 Wilson administrations' (unpublished PhD dissertation, University of London, 2002).

Booth, A. 'The Labour Party and economics between the wars', *Bulletin of the Society for the Study of Labour History*, 47 (1983), pp. 36–42.

Booth, A. 'Corporate politics and the quest for productivity: the British TUC and the politics of productivity growth, 1947–1960', in Melling, J. and McKinlay, A. (eds), *Management, Labour and Industrial Politics in Europe* (1996), pp. 44–65.

Booth, A. 'Inflation, expectations, and the political economy of Conservative Britain, 1951–1964', *Historical Journal*, 43 (2000), pp. 827–47.

Bridgen, P. 'The state, redundancy pay, and economic policy-making in the early 1960s', *Twentieth Century British History*, 11 (2000), pp. 233–58.

Broadberry, S. and Crafts, N. 'British economic policy and industrial performance in the early post-war period', *Business History*, 38 (1996), pp. 65–91.

Catherwood, F. 'The dialogue', *National Westminster Bank Quarterly Review*, May 1969, pp. 2–9.

Catherwood, F. 'Witness seminar: the NEDC 1962–67', *Contemporary British History*, 12 (1998), pp. 99–130.

Chester, T. 'Growth, productivity and womanpower', *District Bank Review*, 143 (1962), pp. 18–35.

Clifford, C. 'The rise and fall of the DEA 1964–69: British government and indicative planning', *Contemporary British History*, 11 (1997), pp. 94–116.

Coopey, R. 'The white heat of scientific revolution', *Contemporary Record*, 5 (1991), pp. 115–27.

Coopey, R. 'Industrial policy in the white heat of the scientific revolution', in Coopey, R., Fielding, S. and Tiratsoo, N. (eds), *The Wilson Governments 1964–1970* (1993), pp. 102–22.

Crafts, N. 'Economic growth', in Crafts, N. and Woodward, N. (eds), *The British Economy Since 1945* (Oxford, 1991), pp. 261–90.

Crafts, N. 'The golden age of economic growth in Western Europe, 1950–1973', *Economic History Review*, 48 (1995), pp. 429–47.

Crosland, A. 'On economic growth', *Encounter*, 91 (1961), pp. 65–8.

Daunton, M. 'A sort of tax prison', in Francis, M. and Zweiniger-Bargielowska, I. (eds), *The Conservatives and British Society 1880–1990* (Cardiff, 1996), pp. 289–315.

Day, A. C. L. 'What price the sterling area?', *Listener*, 21 November 1957.

Day, A. C. L. 'The myth of four per cent growth', *Westminster Bank Review*, November 1964, pp. 2–13.

Dell, S. 'The origins of UNCTAD', in Cutajar M, Z, (ed.), *UNCTAD and the South North Dialogue* (Oxford, 1985), pp. 10–32.

Dumbrell, J. 'The Johnson administration and the British Labour government: Vietnam, the pound and east of Suez', *Journal of American Studies*, 30 (1996), pp. 211–31.

Edgerton, E. 'Liberal militarism and the British state', *New Left Review*, 185 (1991), pp. 138–69.

Edgerton, E. 'The "white heat" revisited: The British government and technology in the 1960s', *Twentieth Century British History*, 7 (1996), pp. 53–82.

Elliott, R. 'Industrial relations and manpower policy', in Blackaby, F. (ed.), *British Economic Policy 1960–74* (Cambridge, 1978), pp. 564–618.

Favretto, I. '"Wilsonism" reconsidered: Labour Party revisionism, 1952–64', *Contemporary British History*, 14 (2000), pp. 54–80.

Feinstein, C. 'Structural change in the developed countries during the twentieth century', *Oxford Review of Economic Policy*, 15 (1999), pp. 35–55.

Finlayson, A. 'Tony Blair and the jargon of modernisation', *Soundings*, 10 (1998), pp. 11–27.

Francis, M. 'Mr. Crosland's Ganymede? Re-assessing Crosland's *The Future of Socialism*', *Contemporary British History*, 11 (1997), pp. 50–64.

Fryer, R. 'The myths of the Redundancy Payments Act', *Industrial Law Journal*, 2 (1973), pp. 1–16.

Gaitskell, H. 'The economic aims of the Labour Party', *Political Quarterly*, 24 (1953), pp. 5–18.

Gannicott, K. and Blaug, M. 'Manpower forecasting since Robbins: a science lobby in action', *Higher Education Review*, 2 (1969), pp. 56–74.

Godley, W. and Shepherd, J. 'Long-term growth and short-term policy', *National Institute Economic Review*, 29 (1964), pp. 26–38.

Graham, A. 'Industrial policy', in Beckerman, W. (ed.), *The Labour Government's Economic Record 1964–70* (1972), pp. 178–217.

Graham, A. and Beckerman, W. 'Introduction: economic performance and the foreign balance', in Beckerman, W. (ed.), *The Labour Government's Economic Record 1964–70* (1972), pp. 11–27.

Hardie, J. 'Regional policy', in Beckerman, W. (ed.), *The Labour Government's Economic Record* (1972), pp. 218–46.

Harris, J. 'Enterprise and the welfare state: a comparative perspective', in O'Day, A. and Gourvish, T. (eds), *Britain Since 1945* (1992), pp. 39–58.

Henderson, P. 'Two British errors: their probable size and possible lessons', *Oxford Economic Papers*, 29 (1977), pp. 159–205.

Henry, S. and Ormerod, P. 'Incomes policy and wage inflation: empirical evidence for the UK 1961–1977', *National Institute Economic Review*, 85 (1978), pp. 31–9.

Horner, D. 'The road to Scarborough: Wilson, Labour and the scientific revolution', in Coopey, R., Fielding, S. and Tiratsoo, N. (eds), *The Wilson Governments 1964–1970* (1993), pp. 49–71.

Howell, D. 'Expanding prosperity', in L. Beaton (ed.), *Principles into Practice* (1961), pp. 22–32.

Hutton, J. and Hartley, K. 'The selective employment tax and the labour market', *British Journal of Industrial Relations*, 4 (1966), pp. 289–303.

Johnman, L. 'The Labour Party and industrial policy, 1940–45', in Tiratsoo, N. (ed.), *The Attlee Years* (1991), pp. 29–53.

Johnman, L. and Lynch, F. 'The road to Concorde: Franco-British relations and the supersonic project', *Contemporary European History*, 11 (2002), pp. 229–52.

Jones, A. 'Prices and incomes policy', *Economic Journal*, 78 (1968), pp. 800–6.

Jones, G. 'The British government and foreign multinationals before 1970', in Chick, M. (ed.), *Governments, Industries and Markets* (Aldershot, 1990), pp. 194–214.

Jones, H. 'The Cold War and the Santa Claus syndrome: dilemmas in Conservative social policy-making, 1945–1957', in Francis, M. and Zweiniger-Bargielowska, I. (eds), *The Conservatives and British Society, 1880–1990* (Cardiff, 1996), pp. 240–54.

Jones, K. 'Nationalised industries', in F. Blackaby (ed.), *British Economic Policy 1960–74* (Cambridge, 1978), pp. 484–514.

Jones, M. 'A decision delayed: Britain's withdrawal from S.E. Asia re-assessed, 1961–68', *English Historical Review*, 117 (2002), pp. 569–95.

King, M. 'The profits crisis: myth or reality?', *Economic Journal*, 85 (1975), pp. 33–54.

Kirby, M. 'Blackett in the "white heat" of the scientific revolution: industrial modernisation under the Labour governments, 1964–70', *Journal of the Operational Research Society*, 50 (1999), pp. 985–93.

Lees, D. and Chiplin, B. 'The economics of industrial training', *Lloyds Bank Review*, 96 (1970), pp. 29–41.

Lomax, K. 'Measurement of industrial productivity in the UK', in OECD, *Productivity Measurement. Vol. 3, Global Measurement of Productivity* (Paris, 1966), pp. 385–99.

Lowe, R. 'Millstone or milestone? The 1961 Plowden Committee and its impact on British welfare policy', *Historical Journal*, 40 (1997), pp. 463–93.

Lowe, R. 'Plumbing new depths: contemporary historians and the Public Record Office', *Twentieth Century British History*, 8 (1997), pp. 239–65.

Lowe, R. and Rollings, N. 'Modernising Britain 1957–64: a classic case of centralisation and fragmentation?', in Rhodes, R. (ed.), *Transforming British Government* (2000), pp. 99–118.

Mackay, D. 'After the shake-out', *Oxford Economic Papers*, 24 (1972), pp. 89–110.

Maddison, A. 'How fast can Britain grow?', *Lloyds Bank Review*, 79 (1966), pp. 8–11.

Major, R. 'Notes on Britain's share in world trade in manufactures, 1954–1966', *National Institute Economic Review*, 44 (1968), pp. 50–6.

McClelland, W. 'The IRC – an experimental prod', *Three Banks Review*, 94 (1972), pp. 23–42.

Mellis, B. and Richardson, P. 'Value of incentives for manufacturing industry 1946 to 1974', in Whiting, A. (ed.), *The Economics of Industrial Subsidies* (1976), pp. 23–43.

Middleton, R. 'Struggling with the impossible: sterling, the balance of payments and British economic policy, 1949–72', in Young, W. and Arnon, A. (eds), *The Open Economy Macro Model: Past, Present and Future* (Amsterdam, 2002), pp. 202–31.

Millward, R. 'Industrial and commercial performance since 1945', in Floud, R. and McCloskey, D. (eds), *The Economic History of Britain Since 1700. Vol. 3, 1939–1992* (2nd edn) (Cambridge, 1994), pp. 123–67.

Morgan, A. D. 'Commercial policy', in Blackaby, F. T. (ed.), *British Economic Policy 1960–74* (Cambridge, 1978), pp. 515–63.

Mottershead, P. 'Industrial policy', in Blackaby, F. (ed.), *British Economic Policy 1960–1974* (Cambridge, 1978), pp. 418–83.

Neild, R. 'Capital movements and the problem of sterling', *District Bank Review*, 124 (1957), pp. 3–20.

Neild, R. 'Replacement policy', *National Institute Economic Review*, 30 (1964), pp. 30–43.

Neild, R., 'Symposium: 1967 devaluation', in Brittan, S. (ed.), *Contemporary Record*, 1 (1988), pp. 46–8.

O'Hara, G. 'British economic and social planning, 1959–70' (unpublished PhD dissertation, University of London, 2002).

Oldfield, A. 'The Labour Party and planning – 1934 or 1918?', *Bulletin of the Society for the Study of Labour History*, 25 (1972), pp. 41–55.

Opie, R. 'Economic planning and growth', in Beckerman, W. (ed.), *The Labour Government's Economic Record* (1972), pp. 157–77.

Parr, H. '"Gone native": the Foreign Office and the second application', in Daddow, O. (ed.), *Wilson and Europe 1964–67* (2002), pp. 75–94.

Parr, H. 'Harold Wilson, Whitehall and Britain's policy towards the EEC, 1964–1967' (unpublished PhD dissertation, University of London, 2002).

Pemberton, H. 'A taxing task: combating Britain's relative decline in the 1960s', *Twentieth Century British History*, 12 (2001), pp. 345–75.

Posner, M. 'Fuel crisis: whose fault?', *New Statesman*, 20 January 1966.

Posner, M. 'Policy towards nationalised industries', in Beckerman, W. (ed.), *The Labour Government's Economic Record 1964–1970* (1972), pp. 247–61.

Price, R. 'Budgetary policy', in Blackaby, F. (ed.), *British Economic Policy 1960–74* (Cambridge, 1978), pp. 135–217.

Price, R. 'Public expenditure', in F. Blackaby (ed.), *British Economic Policy 1960–74* (Cambridge, 1978), pp. 77–134.

Ringe, A. 'Background to Neddy: economic planning in the 1960s', *Contemporary British History*, 12 (1998), pp. 82–98.

Robinson, D. 'Labour market policies', in W. Beckerman (ed.), *The Labour Government's Economic Record 1964–1970* (1972), pp. 300–34.

Robinson, D. 'The pay board, incomes policy and productivity bargaining', in Seglow, P. (ed.), *Productivity Bargaining in Perspective* (Uxbridge, 1973), pp. 51–8.

Rollings, N. '"The Reichstag method of governing"? The Attlee government and permanent economic controls', in Mercer, H., Rollings, N. and Tomlinson, J. (eds), *Labour Governments and Private Industry: The Experience of 1945–51* (Edinburgh, 1992), pp. 15–36.

Rollings, N. 'British industry and European integration, 1961–1973', *Business and Economic History*, 27 (1998), pp. 444–54.

Rollings, N. and Ringe, A. 'Responding to relative decline: the creation of the NEDC', *Economic History Review*, 53 (2000), pp. 331–53.

Rowthorn, R. 'What remains of Kaldor's law?', *Economic Journal*, 85 (1975), pp. 10–19.

Roy, R. 'The battle of the pound: the political economy of Anglo-American relations 1964–1968' (unpublished PhD dissertation, University of London, 2001).

Roy, R. 'The battle for Bretton Woods: America, Britain and the financial crisis of October 1967–November 1968', *Cold War History*, 2 (2002), pp. 33–60.

Schenk, C. 'The sterling area and British policy alternatives in the 1950s', *Contemporary Record*, 6 (1992), pp. 271–4.

Schenk, C. 'Sterling, international monetary reform and Britain's application to join the European Economic Community in the 1960s', *Contemporary European History*, 11 (2002), pp. 345–69.

Seear, N. 'The future employment of women', in Roberts, B. and Smith, J. (eds), *Manpower Policy and Employment Trends* (1966), pp. 98–110.

Seers, D. and Streeten, P. 'Overseas development policies', in Beckerman, W. (ed.), *The Labour Government's Economic Record 1964–1970* (1972), pp. 118–56.

Shanks, M. 'The "irregular" in Whitehall', in P. Streeten (ed.), *Unfashionable Economics: Essays in Honour of Lord Balogh* (1970), pp. 244–62.

Silberston, A. 'The motor industry', *Bulletin of the Oxford University Institute of Statistics*, 27 (1965), pp. 253–86.

Stewart, M. 'The distribution of income', in Beckerman, W. (ed.), *The Labour Government's Economic Record 1964–1970* (1972), pp. 75–117.

Stones, R. 'Government–finance relations in Britain 1964–7: a tale of three cities', *Economy and Society*, 19 (1990), pp. 32–55.

Surrey, M. 'The National Plan in retrospect', *Bulletin of the Oxford University Institute of Economics and Statistics*, 34 (1972), pp. 249–68.

Tanner, D. 'Ideological debate in Edwardian Labour politics: radicalism, revisionism and socialism', in Biagini, E. F. and Reid, A. (eds), *Currents of Radicalism. Popular Radicalism, Organised Labour and Party Politics in Britain, 1850–1914* (Cambridge, 1991), pp. 271–93.

Tanner, D. 'The development of British socialism, 1900–1918', in Green, E. H. H. (ed.), *An Age of Transition: British Politics 1880–1914* (Edinburgh, 1997), pp. 48–66.

Tew, B. 'Policies aimed at improving the balance of payments', in Blackaby, F. (ed.), *British Economic Policy 1960–74* (Cambridge, 1978), pp. 304–59.

Thain, C. 'The Treasury and Britain's decline', *Political Studies*, 32 (1984), pp. 581–95.

Thorpe, A. 'The industrial meaning of "gradualism": the Labour Party and industry, 1918–1931', *Journal of British Studies*, 35 (1996), pp. 84–113.

Tiratsoo, N. and Tomlinson, J. 'Restrictive practices on the shopfloor in Britain, 1945–60: myth and reality', *Business History*, 36 (1994), pp. 65–84.

Tomlinson, J. 'The "economics of politics" and public expenditure', *Economy and Society*, 10 (1981), pp. 383–402.

Tomlinson, J. 'Productivity policy', in Mercer, H., Rollings, N. and Tomlinson, J. (eds), *Labour Governments and Private Enterprise: The Experience of 1945–51* (Edinburgh, 1992), pp. 37–54.

Tomlinson, J. 'The politics of economic measurement: the rise of the "productivity problem" in the 1940s', in Hopwood, A. and Miller, P. (eds), *Accounting in Its Social Context* (Cambridge, 1994), pp. 168–90.

Tomlinson, J. 'Inventing "decline": the falling behind of the British economy in the post-war years', *Economic History Review*, 49 (1996), pp. 731–57.

Tomlinson, J. 'Conservative modernisation, 1960–64: too little, too late?', *Contemporary British History*, 11 (1997), pp. 18–38.

Tomlinson, J. 'Learning from Italy? The British public sector and the IRI', in Feldenkirchen, W. and Gourvish, T. (eds), *European Yearbook of Business History* (1999), pp. 109–24.

Tomlinson, J. 'Economic policy', in Tanner, D., Thane, P. and Tiratsoo, N. (eds), *Labour's First Century* (Cambridge, 2000), pp. 46–79.

Tomlinson, J. 'Marshall aid and the "shortage economy" in Britain in the 1940s', *Contemporary European History*, 9 (2000), pp. 137–55.

Townsend, P. 'Social planning and the control of priorities', in Townsend, P. and Bosanquet, N. (eds), *Labour and Inequality* (1972), pp. 274–300.

Toye, R. 'Gosplanners versus thermostatters: Whitehall planning debates and their political consequences, 1945–49', *Contemporary British History*, 14 (2000), pp. 81–106.

Toye, R. 'The Labour Party's external economic policy in the 1940s', *Historical Journal*, 43 (2000), pp. 189–215.

Toye, R. 'The new commanding height: Labour Party policy on North Sea oil and gas, 1964–74', *Contemporary British History*, 16 (2002), pp. 89–118.

Whiting, R. 'Ideology and reform in Labour's tax strategy, 1964–1970', *Historical Journal*, 41 (1998), pp. 1121–40.

Wilson, H. 'A four-year plan for Britain', *New Statesman*, 24 March 1961.

Wilson, H. 'Planning in a vacuum', *New Statesman*, 26 October 1962.

Woodward, N. 'Labour's economic performance', in Coopey, R., Fielding, S. and Tiratsoo, N. (eds), *The Wilson Governments 1964–1970* (1993), pp. 72–101.

Worswick, G. 'Trade and payments', in Cairncross, A. (ed.), *Britain's Economic Prospects Reconsidered* (1971), pp. 61–100.

Wrigley, C. 'From ASSET to ASTMS: an example of white-collar union growth in the 1960s', *Historical Studies in Industrial Relations*, 7 (1999), pp. 55–74.

Young, J. 'Britain and LBJ's war', *Cold War History*, 2 (2002), pp. 63–92.

Zweiniger-Bargielowska, I. 'Rationing, austerity, and the Conservative Party recovery after 1945', *Historical Journal*, 37 (1994), pp. 173–97.

Index

Lightning Source UK Ltd.
Milton Keynes UK
13 October 2009

144921UK00001B/15/P